THE GREAT DRAGON FANTASY

A Lacanian Analysis of Contemporary Chinese Thought

THE GREAT DRAGON FANTASY

A Lacanian Analysis of Contemporary Chinese Thought

Guanjun Wu

East China Normal University, China

World Scientific

NEW JERSEY • LONDON • SINGAPORE • BEIJING • SHANGHAI • HONG KONG • TAIPEI • CHENNAI

Published by

World Scientific Publishing Co. Pte. Ltd.
5 Toh Tuck Link, Singapore 596224
USA office: 27 Warren Street, Suite 401-402, Hackensack, NJ 07601
UK office: 57 Shelton Street, Covent Garden, London WC2H 9HE

Library of Congress Cataloging-in-Publication Data
Wu, Guanjun.
The great dragon fantasy : a Lacanian analysis of contemporary Chinese thought / Guanjun Wu.
pages cm
ISBN 978-9814417914
1. Economic development--China--History--21st century. 2. Economic development--Psychological aspects--China. 3. China--Economic conditions--2000– 4. China--Economic policy. 5. China--Foreign economic relations. I. Title.
HC427.95.W8224 2014
338.951--dc23

2013051170

British Library Cataloguing-in-Publication Data
A catalogue record for this book is available from the British Library.

In-house Editor: Dong Lixi

Typeset by Stallion Press
Email: enquiries@stallionpress.com

Contents

For Gloria Davies,
to whom I owe so much

About the Author

Guanjun Wu is Professor of Political Theory in the Department of Politics at East China Normal University. He also serves as Vice President of Department's Academic Board and Executive Editor-in-Chief of *ECNU Review*. He is the author of a number of books published in China, including *The Eleventh Thesis (2014)*, *The Philosophy of Living Together* (2011), *The Hauntology of Love and Death* (2008), *The Perverse Core of Reality* (2006), and *Multiple Modernities* (2002).

Introduction

The Fantasmatic Narrative of Contemporary Chinese Thought

China has undergone a unique path of development in its post-Maoist incarnation. The decades since 1978 witnessed China's rapid rise to economic wealth and superpower status. The 2000s have seen China's national prosperity being frequently contrasted with the severe recessions that have troubled the West. Chinese thought or critical inquiry (*pipanxing de sixiang*) in the last three decades has also developed new outlooks: indeed, there is even a radical break between the intellectuality of the Maoist time (1949–1978) and that of the post-Maoist era (1978–present). One major difference between the two periods is that the latter saw the rise of intellectuals as a leading group in mainland society. Whereas it was the Party leadership that had previously set the tone of cultural and intellectual life, academics and independent scholars now guided the production of Chinese social and political thought. Another key feature of the post-Maoist era is the development of critical independence that enabled intellectual discourse to flourish once more after the strict ideological control of the Maoist era.

The intellectual activities of post-Maoist China have been observed and studied in diverse ways in both mainland Chinese and Western scholarship (for example, Gloria Davies 2007; Xu Jilin *et al.* 2007; Deng Zhenglai and Hao Yufan eds. 2008). The post-Maoist intellectuality as it has developed since the 1980s forms the object of critical examination of this study. What differentiates this study from those existing works is that it adopts the Lacanian account of the operations of fantasy to explore the assumptions and expectations of contemporary Sinophone intellectual discourse. I argue that attention needs to be paid to the *psychological* dimension of Chinese thought today and that discursive analysis alone is insufficient for understanding the *underlying forces* that have been fundamentally shaping the (changing) contours of post-Maoist intellectuality. With the aim of tracing and interrogating these underlying forces, this study seeks to show how the fervor for discussing "Chinese problems" (*Zhongguo wenti*), "China's modernization," "Chinese modernity," the "China model," and so on, reveals a hidden psychical mechanism. Although it is futile to attempt to "master" discursive production that is as rich and voluminous as post-Maoist Sinophone intellectual inquiry, we can nonetheless still productively explore distinctive features of the discourse for what they reveal of underlying mechanisms that shape and propel its production. Hence, this study places contemporary Chinese intellectual inquiry under critical scrutiny, with the primary aim of examining the hidden *psychical mechanism* that gives its ever-expanding textuality a recognizable pattern.

In terms of its methodology, this study relies heavily on Slavoj Žižek's uses of Jacques Lacan's psychoanalytic theory to examine the intellectual *psyche* of post-Maoist China. The works of several other Lacanian scholars have also been utilized. The common knowledge regarding psychoanalysis is that it is an analytic theory and therapeutic practice revolving around the psyche of the individual. The assumption is that this makes it inappropriate for the analysis of social change and debates over social change. Against this type of objection, Yannis Stavrakakis argues that one of the main features of Lacanian psychoanalysis is that it utterly rejects the dominant bipolarities individual/collective and subjective/objective. For Lacan, the analysand is not a "solitary wanderer." The individual and the collective are one and the same level (Stavrakakis 1999: 40–41). The basic Lacanian thesis is that what constitutes both the social (in Lacanian jargon, the big Other) and the subject is *lack* (often termed by Lacanian theorists as "the fundamental Lack"), which prevents them from acquiring real fullness, and in turn, spurs the desire — not only the desire of the subject, but also the Other's desire — for fullness.[1] It is this *constitutive impossibility* that

[1] I will discuss what the "fundamental Lack" means in Lacanian theory later. The best I can do at this stage is to quote Stavrakakis's succinct yet precise explanation of the notion, which is introduced in Lacanian psychoanalysis "at the intersection of the real with the symbolic": "Entering into language entails a loss of immediacy, the loss of a direct unmediated fulfillment of need. It entails symbolic castration." Thus: "It is the symbolic that entails lack. Lack emerges in and through the symbolization of the real." (Stavrakakis 1999: 44, 52–53)

marks both the domain of the individual and that of the social: it is *impossible* not only for the subject to acquire a full identity, but also for the Other to be fully constructed in a given socio-symbolic order. In this sense, Lacanian psychoanalysis opens a new path to the understanding of subjectivity and objectivity: a proper *psycho*-analysis moves within what Žižek phrases as a "bizarre category of the objectively subjective" (Žižek 2000: 83; also 2005a: 113, 115).

Since desire is split into the desire of the subject and that of the Other, what, then, is the relationship between these two kinds? Desire seems by definition related to persons, hence the question: where can we locate the desire of the Other? The Lacanian argument apropos of such questions — which I will further illustrate in this study by analyzing writings of contemporary Chinese intellectuals — is that what we experience in our everyday life as our own "desire" is indeed not our own at all, but precisely the desire of the Other, because such desire is fundamentally framed and sustained by our fantasies. Fantasy, in Lacanian psychoanalysis, is the very device staging and regulating the relationship between the individual and the social. It is, to quote Žižek, "an answer to the question, 'What am I for the Other? What does the Other want from me?'" By offering us such answer with specific motifs and coordinates, fantasy literally "teaches us how to desire" (Žižek 1999b: 100). In order to encounter truly our own desire (frequently termed as "drive"), and further "to name, to articulate, to bring this desire into existence," we have to *traverse the fundamental fantasy of ours*. For Lacan one must *not* give in his/her *own desire*, concede it to the Other's desire. The aim of psychoanalytic treatment is thus to lead the analysand to recognize "the truth about his desire." The radical traversing of the fantasy constitutes the "closing moment" of the treatment.[2]

In this study, by adopting Lacanian theory, I will tackle critically what I view as the *generative force* of contemporary Sinophone critical inquiry — the desire of contemporary Chinese intellectuals for *an imaginary fullness of China* (Chinese civilization, Chinese nation, etc.). Such desire is essentially the desire of the Other — its desire to be full. The question is: if, following the Lacanian argument, Chinese intellectuals are indeed *taught* to

---

[2]One can find detailed discussions on this line of Lacanian argument in Žižek 2005a: 48–50, 57; Fink 1997: 206; Evans 1996: 37, 54.

desire in such a way, then what is responsible for the "teaching"? For the purpose of tackling this question, in this study I coin the term "the Great Dragon fantasy," which also serves as the title of the book. By tracing the movement of their shared desire, and further uncovering the device manufacturing and sustaining it, we are able to acquire a deeper understanding of the specific ways in which contemporary Chinese intellectuals link themselves to national-civilizational construction (such as, in the form of moral responsibilities). The findings of this study will also reveal *shared assumptions* in rival Chinese arguments and how these assumptions shape Chinese understandings of present-day mainland society and China's relations with the world.

Assuming Personal Responsibility for Social Change

A brief overview of the socio-political background as well as the cultural background from which the post-Maoist critical inquiry emerged will be helpful here. It can be said that the post-Maoist intellectual discourse was enabled by the sudden shift from the revolutionary doctrine of the Maoist era to Deng Xiaoping's post-Maoist paradigm of "modernization construction" — following Deng's seizure of power in 1978 from Mao's chosen successor, Hua Guofeng.[3] Deng's slogan that "practice is the sole criterion for evaluating truth" (*shijian shi jianyan zhenli de weiyi biaozhun*), along with his pragmatic, utilitarian approach towards socialism, provided intellectuals with the political legitimacy to create new spaces for intellectual activities in the early to mid-1980s. To distinguish this new post-Maoist era from the Cultural Revolution (*wenhua da geming*, 1966–1976), the 1980s came to be widely known in the state-owned media as the "new era" (*xin shiqi*).

Deng Xiaoping regarded science and education as the key to national development and Chinese intellectuals were keen to reflect this new direction in their discourse. The most important institutional change that

[3]In the Third Plenum of the Central Committee of the Eleventh Party Congress in November 1978, Deng Xiaoping and his allies gained control of the party and started to lead the country by practical pursuits of economic development instead of Mao's idealistic pursuit of communism.

occurred in 1977 was the reintroduction of nationwide college and university entrance examinations, after these examinations had been halted for almost a decade. In 1978, graduate schools were reopened. Most participants in the post-Maoist intellectual movement known as the "New Enlightenment movement" (*xin qimeng yundong*, which was also called *wenhua re*, the "cultural fever") in the mid- to late 1980s were beneficiaries of this policy of revitalizing high education. The discussions over "postmodernism" in the mid-1990s, the debate between "liberalism" and the "New Left" in the late 1990s, and so on, were further developments out of the New Enlightenment movement. However, although intellectual independence was a key goal of the 1980s, the Chinese government maintained a careful ideological control. The Anti-Spiritual Pollution Campaign that lasted for three months between November 1983 and January 1984 reflected the effectiveness of state censorship over intellectual activities. Nonetheless, economic development also expanded the space for cultural expression and the development of a cultural marketplace in the 1980s resulted in the production of a large variety of journals, books, films, TV series as well as fee-paying courses of study conducted by independent groups of intellectuals.

In this sense, the Shanghai-based historian Xu Jilin is right when he observed that the intellectual movements of post-Maoist China were initiated *from the top downwards by the Party's reformist ideology*. It is "in keeping and in tandem with this complex process of transformations," wrote Xu, that "the intellectual world of China experienced constant splits and realignments." The topics of contemporary debates and discussions among Chinese scholars and intellectuals are intertwined with the ongoing socio-political changes of post-Maoist China. According to Xu, China's intellectual world (re)emerged formally in 1984, for during that year "[a] number of things occurred in the academic and publishing world that, although not particularly sensational in and of themselves, proved to be of profound significance," including the initiation of a new publishing project called the *Towards the Future* (*Zouxiang weilai*) books series, and the establishment of the Academy of Chinese Culture (*Zhongguo wenhua shuyuan*); around the same time, a group of young scholars became the core contributors to the monthly journal *Reading* (*Dushu*), a publication that had been a forum for cautious intellectual debates since it was founded in 1979. These occurrences, for Xu, indicate that a new public intellectual sphere had emerged to provide intellectuals in the post-Maoist "new era," with unprecedented space for independent criticism (Xu Jilin 2000: 169, 173–174).

The (re)emergence of an intellectual sphere and the normalization of intellectual life in China in the mid-1980s was indeed a product of the "complex process of transformations" China has undergone since Deng took power. However, Xu's observation, which is primarily focused on external socio-political factors, does not fully reveal the cause of such "cultural fever" in the post-Maoist era. It is important to note that the new space for intellectual activities flourished in the 1980s was made possible *not merely* by the Party's reformist ideology. A vigorous intellectual world (re)emerged in the 1980s also *because Chinese intellectuals were able once again to regard themselves as playing an important role in the work of government and in society*. The exploration of the new relationship between Chinese intellectuals and the state should include this crucial subjective (psychical) factor. Contemporary Chinese intellectuals,[4] primarily the new generation of scholars who resumed their education in the late 1970s and entered graduate school, do not see themselves anymore as the humble, useless "stinking ninth" (*chou laojiu*), who need to learn from workers and peasants in order to become "socialist new men." The rapid withering of the Maoist ideology in the new era (many intellectuals persecuted during the Anti-Rightist Movement of the late 1950s and the Cultural Revolution were "rehabilitated" (*pingfan*) by the Party-state in the late 1970s and early 1980s), allowed them to regain confidence about the importance and significance of their work. In other words, they were able once again to assume that "intellectual praxis itself has the power to guide and transform society" (Davies 2007: 18). Though often employing various translated scholarly jargons from the discourses of Western humanities and social sciences in their writings, contemporary Chinese

---

[4]Gloria Davies mentions that "Chinese intellectuals" can be a useful category simply because it is a category "which has remained significant in Sinophone writings from the 1920s on, produced by authors who, in fact, call themselves 'Chinese intellectuals'" (Davies 2007: 14). For the same reason, I will be referring to "Chinese intellectuals" throughout this study.

intellectuals do not confine themselves to the academic realm. They also see themselves as *leaders of social change* who are engaged in producing a social blueprint for China's transformation. In this sense, with the resumption of higher education, the establishment of a cultural market, some freedom of expression in post-Maoist China, many prominent intellectuals regard themselves as agents of social change. They portray their writings as works that are carrying out the task of solving the "problem of China" (*Zhongguo wenti*) and guiding China's transformation.

As Gloria Davies points out, although there is an evident diversity in the intellectual discourse of post-Maoist China, with many intellectuals disagreeing with each other about what changes are needed, nonetheless the arguments on offer all "share one thing in common":

> They all point to the strength of the belief held by many Chinese intellectuals in the power of intellectual labor to shape and change social life. More specifically, this belief is informed by a certain assumption that the individual intellectual laborer is — within a post-Maoist idiom — the *zhe* (the "one") or *fenzi* (element) who can remake society by harvesting from the *jie* (fields) that he or she oversees the appropriate knowledge items to produce a social blueprint. (Davies 2001: 3)

Davies is right to indicate that although it is produced largely by academics and graduate students, contemporary Chinese intellectual inquiry is nonetheless not purely academic discourse. Shaping and changing the social life of the Chinese people is deemed as the ultimate goal of any serious intellectual work. Intellectual debates are, by the same token, much more than just an exchange of ideas. The ambition of producing a social blueprint is the larger task that Chinese intellectual discourse assumes. For instance, the influential book series *Towards the Future* that appeared in the 1980s states this goal explicitly in the title of the series. In general Chinese intellectuals believe that adopting the correct path is the key issue in social reform and in the 1980s, many imagined their ideas as playing a part in changing China. This is why the "cultural fever" of the 1980s was also often called a "fever for intellectuals" (*zhishifenzi re*): in the post-Maoist new era the intellectuals as the producer of *sixiang* (thought, inquiry) and *xueshu* (knowledge, scholarship), assumed themselves — and to a large extent, were socially recognized as — "fit to judge how the quality of Chinese culture and 'the people' should be improved" (Davies 2007: 17). It is exactly with reference to this shared belief and assumption held by many Chinese intellectuals that one can locate, to put in psychoanalytic terms, the desire of contemporary Chinese intellectuality, with improving and perfecting China being its object.

At this juncture, it is crucial to note that in contemporary Chinese language there are two common understandings of the term *zhishifenzi* (intellectuals): the broader understanding of *zhishifenzi* tends to include all educated people who are well-educated professionals, whereas the narrower understanding links *zhishifenzi* to the *shi* (or scholar) and the Confucian moral mandate of "assuming personal responsibility for all under Heaven" (*yi tianxia wei jiren*). The literal translation of *zhishifenzi* is "knowledgeable elements" but it is in terms of the Confucian *shi* that post-Maoist intellectuals regard as its ideal model. Thus, it is appropriate to consider the modern Chinese term "intellectual" as having a strong moral-political connotation. Davies notes that in Chinese-language scholarship, *zhishifenzi* are often represented qualitatively as the somewhat marginalized contemporary counterpart of the traditional *shi*, and quantitatively as "those who meet the cultural standard of the university-educated." She further comments that such understanding is still not entirely adequate to the task of exploring contemporary Chinese intellectuality since, firstly, many members of this community had little involvement or interest in the intellectual discourses that have emerged in the Chinese-speaking world since the 1980s, and secondly, it fails to indicate the symbolically privileged status of *zhishifenzi* in the Chinese language (Davies 2001: 18).

The symbolically privileged status of *zhishifenzi* in contemporary China is a cultural legacy of the Confucian privileging of *shi* (scholars, intellectuals): in traditional China, the social status of *shi* was much higher than those of farmers (*nong*), workers (*gong*), and merchants (*shang*). Confucian *shi* were privileged and highly respected in society not only as imperial officials or *shi dafu* (often translated as "scholar-official"), but also due to their commitment to assure the welfare for "all under Heaven" (*Tianxia*). Tu Wei-ming characterizes the pursuits of Confucian scholars and intellectuals into these three categories — *Dao* (the ontological Truth, the literal translation of which is "way"), *xue* (learning), and *zheng* (politics). As Tu argues, Confucian intellectuals are indeed political activists, and the primary goal of their endeavors is to shape the existing political order from the inside out (Tu Wei-ming 1993: 10–11). In the system of orthodox Confucian doctrine, intellectual "learning" (*xue*) was structured around a moral-political purpose (*zheng*), that is, to rectify the existing order in accordance to *Dao* (or *Tian-Dao*, the Way of Heaven). In this sense, Confucianism can be said to privilege *an instrumentalist approach towards knowledge*: intellectual ideas are perused in the services of grasping the truth and establishing an ideal order.[5] "Politics" in classical Confucian understanding refers to an act of "rectifying" (*zheng*) the existing order in accordance with *Dao*; thus, in pursuit of revealing *Dao* via their scholarship ("learning"), Confucian *shi* endeavored to find the correct way through which an ideal political order can be established.

Hence, Confucian scholars were, as Tu Wei-ming argues, also *political activists*. It is not only because they endeavor to present the Confucian classics of past sages as aimed at unveiling the ontological structure of *Dao*, but, and more importantly, because they do so in an attempt to shape social life and establish an ideal political order — and in thoroughly proper Confucian terms, that is, to *ping Tianxia* (establish peaceful and harmonious order everywhere under Heaven).[6] In traditional China the socially privileged status of the *shi* was based on the authority invested in persons who had acquired the "learning" or "thought" needed for planning a peaceful and

[5]Suffice it to recall the famous four-sentence motto written by Song-dynasty Confucian scholar Zhang Zai (1020–1077), which very well summarizes the Confucian-dominated intellectual tradition of China: (To be a Confucian scholar proper is) to reveal the core essence of nature for Heaven and Earth (*wei tiandi li xin*), to ascertain the mandate of life for the people (*wei shengmin li ming*), to continue the lost learnings of past sages (*wei wangsheng ji juexue*), and to establish universal peace and harmony for ten thousand generations to come (*wei wanshi kai taiping*).

[6]It is important to note that in the Confucian system of moral imperatives for a Confucian scholar to follow in his lifetime practices, the highest one is *ping Tianxia* (to establish order everywhere under Heaven). The others, from the lowest, are *xiu shen* (to cultivate oneself), *qi jia* (to regulate properly one's family), *zhi guo* (to improve state governing). This is the primary teaching of the *Great Learning* (*Da xue*), one of the most essential texts of Confucianism.

harmonious order (i.e. an order in accordance with *Dao*). The Chinese Communist Party (CCP) also presents its history as organized around the system of thought (*sixiang*) of Party leaders. From Mao Zedong to Xi Jinping, persons who occupy the highest position (as the Party's General Secretary) are implicitly accorded the role of not only political but intellectual leadership. Theoretically at least, their "thought" (or "theory," "doctrine," etc.) is presented as the blueprint for the nation's development. This unique contemporary phenomenon of Chinese intellectual life — the persistent representation of the Party's top leaders as intellectual leaders — can also be read as a Confucian heritage of sorts. This emphasis on intellectual leadership, viewed as an integral part of Chinese political culture, has led both officials and scholars to be preoccupied with gaining authority for their ideas. In their desire to play a leading role in social reform, Chinese intellectuals of the 1980s reflected the depth of Confucian cultural influence in twentieth-century China: by adopting ideas presumed to have the power to change social reality, contemporary Chinese intellectuals, just like the Confucian *shi* before them, assume their *personal* responsibility for China's transformations (or "all under Heaven"). Of course, the explicit difference between the two is that for the latter the learning (or thought, theory: *sixiang*) they adopt is no longer from past sages, but from the modern West. In this sense, it is in terms of the *form* rather than the *content* that this contemporary Confucian inheritance can be spoken of.

Regarding the intellectual fever of the 1980s, Xu Jilin observes that

> In the discursive context of the 1980s, the core of the "fever for intellectuals" was in fact the issue of "returning to the centre" (*chongfan zhongxin*). From 1949 onwards, intellectuals have been excluded from the centre of [the nation's] socio-political life. It was not until the 1980s when China's modernization was re-initiated that intellectuals regained such life. Intellectuals regard themselves as the elite who lead the social reform and thus carry the great mission of guiding the development of modernization. They think in the Confucian vein — this mission of theirs is bestowed by Heaven. Therefore, at that time the heated topics were "Chinese intellectuals' sense of mission (*shiming gan*)," "the function intellectuals play in the modernization transformation," etc. (Xu Jilin 1999: ix)

In the Maoist era, intellectuals were radically marginalized and officially defamed as the "stinking ninth" — the lowest group of society, which was in stark contrast with the tradition of China where intellectuals were regarded and revered as the top elite. As the thesis of "returning to the center" in the 1980s "intellectual fever" presupposes that intellectuals *once again* occupy the central spot of the political stage, this call implies an attempt to bring about a contemporary revivification of the old Confucian privileging of the *shi*. By such an attempt to return to the center of the nation's "socio-political life," post-Maoist intellectuals once again aimed at establishing an ideal order in accordance with the Way of Heaven (*Tian-Dao*) in China. Through their new, Western-inspired learning, intellectuals of the 1980s viewed the project of modernization as the correct "Way" for China's transformation. It is in this sense that they regarded advancing China's modernization as their moral-political mission. Through their socio-political engagement in leading China's transformation, intellectuals in turn re-identified themselves as a "social elite" or "cultural heroes" (*wenhua yingxiong*). Thus, they commanded social respect. One of the typical statements of contemporary Chinese intellectuals' demand for social respect can be found in Xu Jilin's — who was also an active participant of the 1980s intellectual movement — famous account of "the third kind of dignity" (*disanzhong zunyan*) which refers to "dignity of thought" (*zhizhe de zunyan*) possessed only by intellectuals (the other two kinds of dignity being "dignity of money" and "dignity of power") (See Xu Jilin 1991; 1996). The U.S.-based scholar Jing Wang commented in her study of Chinese intellectual discourse of the 1980s that:

> The 1980s dawned on China with the promise that *zhishi* (knowledge) and *rencai* (talent) would reemerge as the primary capital that drove China's modernization program. Throughout the decade, the popularity of the slogan, "Respect knowledge, respect talent" signaled the exit of Maoism and the re-entry of intellectuals as the harbingers of modernity. One cannot tell whether it was Culture Fever that set loose the "fever for 'knowledgeable elements'" [Wang's translation of *zhishifenzi re*] or if it was the dramatic ascendance of intellectuals that triggered the outbreak of Culture Fever. (Jing Wang 1996: 113)

When translating *zhishifenzi re* of the 1980s as the "fever for 'knowledgeable elements'," Wang was being slightly ironic in that "knowledgeable elements" reduces the role of the intellectual to something more modest. It is thus important to differentiate two sources of this Chinese respect for intellectuals — their *knowledge* as well as their *moral-political engagement*. It is based on precisely the latter rather than the former that intellectuals of the 1980s commanded proudly social respect. Modernization and re-traditionalization are actually *intertwined structurally* in the intellectuality of the 1980s: although "China's modernization" constituted the primary focus of the intellectual discourse of the 1980s, the desire of Chinese intellectuals for social recognition reflected a Confucian assumption of moral and intellectual leadership.

This Confucian hinge can in fact already be detected in the "Chinese Enlightenment movement" of the May Fourth (*wusi*) era of the 1910s and 1920s, even as that intellectual movement claimed to be radically anti-traditional and thoroughly modern: despite the many differences of view among May Fourth thinkers, they shared a common desire for producing a social blueprint for China. Furthermore, as discussed above, one consequence of such Confucian idea of "assuming personal responsibility for all under Heaven" is an *instrumentalist* approach toward knowledge. Echoing this Confucian characteristic, May Fourth discourse strongly emphasized the need for useful and effective knowledge. The call for "appropriatism" (*nalaizhuyi*) by Lu Xun (1881–1936), one of the best known May Fourth thinkers, is a case in point.[7] In such respects, May Fourth intellectuality can also be viewed as a modern version of the Confucian idea that the purpose of learning is to discover the correct path. But unlike the Confucian emphasis on "continuing the lost teachings of past sages," May Fourth intellectuals aimed at importing and adopting new ideas from the West in order to enlighten the Chinese people and save the nation. Thus, in the broadest terms, the practical emphasis of Confucian learning since the Song era (or Neo-Confucianism) on finding solutions to social, economic and political problems has persisted

[7] I am using Gloria Davies' translation of Lu Xun's term which has also been translated as "grabism" and, the English translation of Lu Xun's *Selected Works*, as "the take-over policy" (Davies 2007: 250).

throughout the twentieth century and since. What is in common between May Fourth Enlightenment thinkers of the 1910s and 1920s and New Enlightenment intellectuals of the 1980s is (1) the shared belief on the necessity of learning from the West, as well as (2) such an attitude towards knowledge — it is regarded as an instrument for strengthening and perfecting the nation. Clearly, the latter is in accordance with the Confucian motto that "Everyone has a share of responsibility for achieving the welfare for *Tianxia*" (*Tianxia xingwang, pifu youze*).[8]

Hence, contemporary Chinese intellectuals commonly work under the unspoken presupposition that their writings can *make a difference* to social transformations of post-Maoist China. They regard their intellectual works as carrying the great mission of providing an enlightened vision via which they are able to change the national status quo, and improve the quality of Chinese culture and the welfare of "the people." Davies employs the phrases "worrying about China" and "voicing concerns" (in the titles of her books) to highlight this feature of contemporary Chinese intellectual engagement. As a direct, salient result of such features, the usual procedure that resonates powerfully in the writings of many contemporary Chinese intellectuals contains the following two steps: (1) to identify "Chinese problems" (whether social, political, cultural, historical, or economic), and (2) to solve perceived problems in accordance with a stated argument serving as a blueprint for change and reform. This type of intellectual inquiry is indeed at odds with its EuroAmerican counterpart.

Davies' *Worrying about China* offers us an excellent comparison between contemporary Sinophone and Anglophone critical inquiries: although "critical inquiry is always an act of worrying about some or other aspect of received knowledge or the status quo (no matter the language or culture in which it finds expression)," Sinophone and Anglophone critical discourses are nonetheless radically different in that the object of the former's worrying is essentially "the nation's well-being" whereas the latter

[8]When the Party-state in the 1950s started to preach the concept of the "great Self" (*da wo*) as a reference to the Chinese nation, and encouraged people to devote themselves (the lower self) into the service of improving the great Self, it also invoked the traditional moral teaching of "assuming personal responsibility for all under Heaven."

is "generally focused on refining existing knowledge paradigms, interrogating their limitations or probing relations between the academy and politics." Davies terms this characteristic worrying of Chinese intellectuals (i.e. worrying about China) as "patriotic worrying" (Davies 2007: 16–18). In tackling this feature of Chinese intellectuality that is significantly and strikingly discordant with the "decidedly non-nationalistic tenor of self-reflexive EuroAmerican critical inquiry," Davies further comments that Chinese intellectual discourse reflects a tone of *certitude* that is the result of taking language to be an unproblematic tool or instrument for articulating plans and blueprints. Resulting from their patriotic worrying, Chinese intellectuals often write in "diagnostic and prescriptive terms," "as if the words that one enlists for the description of things and feeling, or indeed 'reality,' carry *an inherent truth* that must be restored against the adverse influence of the 'wrong' kinds of ideas." According to Davies' observation, Chinese intellectual discourse tends to presume that "language represents 'what is *really* happening out there,' as opposed to the self-reflexive notion that language constructs powerful but multiple narratives of 'what is really happening out there' through its effects of figuration." This Sinophone characteristic "linguistic certitude" enables many contemporary Chinese authors to write about China as "a powerful *metaphysical presence* [...] which is then tacitly assigned the status of a transcendental signified (like History, Being, Truth, or God)," "a presence imagined as the eventual return to civilizational grandeur." Through analyzing texts written by prominent Chinese intellectuals such as Wang Hui, Zheng Min, Yang Fan, Jin Guantao and Liu Qingfeng, Davies remarks that despite these intellectuals' own critical stance, they nonetheless write about China "as if it were a sign for a self-evident entity that, once endowed with the proper set of meanings, would 'glow finally in the luminosity of its presence,' to borrow Derrida's words." (Davies 2007: 7, 11, 18, 20–23, emphases mine)

Davies' analysis of this Sinophone "linguistic certitude" paved the preliminary path for this study. By dealing with the metaphysical assumptions of Sinophone discourse that have remained largely unseen ("unconscious"), Davies' work represents a significant difference from positivistic approaches in China Studies that are confined only to identifying forms of knowledge. The following crucial observation of hers would be precisely my starting point: Sinophone preference for "linguistic certitude" is clearly at odds with a widespread contemporary Anglophone privileging of the opacity of writing and "linguistic contingency" (Davies 2007: 11, 26–27, 34). Davies elaborates "linguistic contingency" as the "ways in which statements relate to other statements rather than to meanings, truth or a reality 'out there'" (Davies 2007: 26). Such "linguistic certitude" versus "linguistic contingency" analysis, needless to say, moves primarily within a Derridean deconstructive terrain, enabling a critique of the "metaphysics of presence" by detecting in the linguistic certitude the traces of inconsistencies, predicaments, contradictions, emotional/rhetorical expressions (disguised as logical arguments).[9] In this study I would like to supplement the path opened up by Davies' seminal works by adding a *psycho*-analysis of Chinese intellectuality, with the purpose of tracing the *desire* of contemporary Chinese intellectuals to solve the "problem of China" and guide China's transformation. To replace "worrying (about China)" with "desire (to improve China)" is not just a play of words. To investigate desire, one has to move beyond the horizon of deconstruction and discourse-analysis to tackle these questions: What generated this shared desire, and kept it alive (from the May Fourth generation down to post-Maoist intellectuals)? What sustains its everyday operation? How does it run and operate? Would such desire be fully satisfied (i.e. the desiring object achieved, obtained) and thus subside? From a psychoanalytic perspective, historical analyses of contemporary Chinese intellectuals' patriotic worrying (e.g. tracing it back to its Confucian origin) are indeed not sufficient. An analyst has to further probe what makes it *still* so strong *today*. Deconstructive textual analyses (detecting rhetorical deployments and discursive strategies, dissolving metaphysical certitude amidst a bundle of inconsistencies, deferrals and traces) are also not really up for this job. Understanding such patriotic worrying as desire, thus opens up a unique way for the further investigation: it allows us to explore the *psychological mechanism* that is responsible for generating such desire and has been sustaining its running.

[9]Davies (2007: 21–23, 28–29) openly admits her Derridean approach, setting Jacques Derrida as "an example of a highly reflexive *style* whose influence remains negligible in Sinophone critical discourse."

Slavoj Žižek has suggested two *complementary* ways to engage in "ideology critique":

> [O]ne is *discursive*, the "symptomal reading" of the ideological text bringing about the "deconstruction" of the spontaneous experience of its meaning — that is, demonstrating how a given ideological field is a result of a montage of heterogeneous "floating signifiers," of their totalization through the intervention of certain "nodal points." [T]he other aims at extracting the kernel of *enjoyment*, at articulating the way in which — beyond the field of meaning but at the same time internal to it — an ideology implies, manipulates, produces a pre-ideological enjoyment structured in *fantasy*. (Žižek 1989: 125, last emphasis mine)

It is suitable to apply this methodological distinction to Davies' and my analyses of contemporary Sinophone critical inquiry: while Davies has primarily adopted the first approach, this study will make use of many of her findings and move further in the new direction of a psychoanalytic reading of Chinese intellectuality. Davies' deconstructive approach focuses "on *how* the language of analysis and interpretation produces the 'picture,' tracing the clarity of any 'picture' to the performative powers of language rather than to any prior extralinguistic truth that could be assumed or invoked" (Davies 2001: 5). Instead of focusing only on such *symbolic* dimension of language, a psychoanalytic reading will include the (often neglected) *imaginary* dimension of language, and deal further with the question: *What mechanism* ensures and guarantees that the language of Sinophone critical inquiry smoothly and effectively produces — and keeps producing — blueprint pictures (of Chinese problems, of China's transformation), *as if* they are grounded in extralinguistic truth? If statements are, as Davies noted, only "relate[d] to other statements rather than to meanings, truth or a reality 'out there'," what then makes Chinese intellectuals collectively write in the way *as if* their statements are related "to meanings, truth or a reality 'out there'"? Such questions draw us to the examination of the crucial "missing link" embedded in Sinophone discourse between the practices of language and the promise of (extralinguistic) truth.

Rather than immediately "tracing the clarity of any 'picture' to the performative powers of language," Lacanian psychoanalysis notices that there is something operating — as a "vanishing mediator" — in a "spectral" space *between* the *ontic* field of signifying and performative practices and the *ontological* assumption of extralinguistic truth, efficiently covering up the traces of the impotence (inexistence) of the latter. The psychoanalytic name for that which guarantees the smooth running of mundane symbolic practices by producing the illusory assumption of ontological grounds, is *fantasy*. This study tackles critically the "plague of fantasy" permeating contemporary Chinese intellectual world, tracing and analyzing *those specific scenarios staged in the "fantasmatic"*[10] *space* which have nonetheless orchestrated and sustained those unique features of Sinophone discursive production, such as "linguistic certitude" to which Davies has drawn our attention.

Thus, the initial question posed by this study is simple and clear: is there any hidden *generative mechanism* that has been structuring and supervising the production of various post-Maoist intellectual discourses, and making the production the way it has appeared (drastically at odds with its EuroAmerican counterpart)? Again, one should bear in mind that when contemporary Chinese intellectuals engage in intellectual discussions and debates, in which various terms and jargons imported from Anglophone critical inquiry are employed, they are also competing with each other for intellectual authority in determining the correct path ahead for China's perfection. They see their intellectual work carrying the task of guiding China's transformation and improving its well-being. Such moral responsibility for the well-being of the nation (or *Tianxia*[11]) can be seen in psychoanalytic terms serving as the *ego-ideal* of contemporary Chinese intellectuals, the ideal that they set for themselves and against which they measure their own (always inadequate) performance. Freud equates such ego-ideal with the superego (see Fink 1997: 62; Evans 1996:

[10]To avoid messing up with everyday usage of the word "fantastic," I follow Žižek and other Lacanian theorists such as Yannis Stavrakakis, etc. to use the word "fantasmatic" to denote not only something "of fantasm," but more essentially "of fantasy." In fact, being primarily a matter of translation, "fantasm" and "fantasy," when discussed with regard to Lacanian psychoanalysis, can be used interchangeably. See Evans 1996: 59.

[11]As Davies notes, "because *tianxia* refers to the geopolitical sphere of China, writings in aid of this sphere since the early 1900s have invariably been couched in the modern sense of 'the national interest'" (Davies 2007: 19).

200), the moral agency which judges and censures the subject, and by doing that, fundamentally governs the subject's position in the symbolic world. It is, to paraphrase Žižek, "the very place *from where* we are being observed, *from where* we look at ourselves so that we appear to ourselves likeable, worthy of love" (Žižek 1989: 105).[12] Where, then, is this superego-place? The Lacanian answer is: in a spectral space called fantasy. It is through my fantasmatic vision that my ego-ideal exerts its regulative power on me in the form of an impossible gaze.[13]

Fantasy not only offers the space for the superego agency to operate, but also — more crucially — generates and organizes our desire, and by so doing, controls and supervises the very way we *enjoy* our life (work, lover, etc.). Superego can be precisely viewed from this angle as the agency that ensures — and indeed, enjoins — us to enjoy: it not only measures the gap between the subject's actual ego and the ego-ideal (s)he is supposed to emulate, and finds him/her guilty of failure in the endeavor, but also, as Žižek stresses, more fundamentally, makes the subject feel guilty if (s)he fails to *enjoy* the endeavor. It exhorts us to derive enjoyment — a specific type of enjoyment termed frequently by Lacan and Žižek as phallic *jouissance* or symbolic *jouissance*[14] — from following the Law of desire. Hence, a psychoanalytic reading of contemporary Sinophone critical inquiry will aim at extracting "the kernel of *enjoyment*" from the authors' patriotic worrying: whereas their worrying about China is sym-

[12]That is also why Žižek sees superego as "the annoying 'ghost,' the shadowy double that always accompanies the public law" (Žižek 1994a: 194).

[13]This analysis indeed quite coincides with Davies' following point made in a Derridean vein: "In the prose of Chinese intellectuals, little if any attention is given to interrogating how the rhetorical power of 'assuming personal responsibility for all under Heaven' has shaped critical inquiry. Rather, this phrase is discussed as if it were a second skin that Confucian scholars traditionally wore and a 'spirit' or 'presence' that continues to demand of contemporary intellectuals that they focus their sights on perfecting China and Chinese thought." (Davies 2007: 24)

[14]I will discuss this phallic *jouissance* in Chapter 1. Here let me just quote a good theoretical summary of Lacan's point: "The *jouissance* of man is produced by the structure of the signifier, and is known as phallic *jouissance*. The structure of phallic *jouissance* is the structure of the signifier. Lacan proposes a precise definition of man as being subject to castration and lacking a part of *jouissance*, that which is required in order to use speech. All of man is subjected to the signifier." (Levy-Stokes 2001: 105)

bolically expressed in their written texts (ready for historical and textual analysis), the hidden enjoyment brought by their act of worrying is however entirely structured and sustained in fantasy — a spectral space.

"China's Reality" and the Fantasmatic Space

As discussed in the preceding section, the proximity of intellectual work to the practical guidance of nation-building and social change is a unique characteristic of Chinese intellectuality. It affects fundamentally the ways in which contemporary Chinese thinkers write and debate with each other. In contrast to its EuroAmerican counterpart, contemporary Chinese intellectual inquiry features a lot of passionate and emotional statements. Very often, these statements are violent attacks on the writings of rival intellectuals and they often trigger fierce debates. Once a debate among intellectuals is launched, it can quickly turn into something nasty. It is not an exaggeration to say that, in mainland China, intellectual discussions and debates often have a tendency of dividing their participants into hostile ideological camps. Published moral accusations and attacks on the character of one's opponent were and remain very common in mainland intellectual circles. For example, during the controversy over the Beijing-based historian Wang Hui's nomination for and subsequent acceptance of the Cheung Kong-*Reading* Awards in 2000, Wang Hui called all criticisms of him malicious "slanders" and "calumnies" and claimed that "those people who believe they can use filth and calumnies to prevent our intellectual search will not be successful" (Wang Hui 2000c: 13–19). Evaluated by the academic standards of contemporary Anglophone scholarship, this style of writing can hardly be seen as academic critique but rather as arbitrary accusation. Nonetheless, it is highly prevalent in contemporary Chinese intellectual discourse. In this sense, Sinophone critical inquiry, as Gloria Davies notes, drastically "differs from its EuroAmerican counterpart of an institutionally sanctioned and funded inquiry quite removed from the very idea of a battlefield."[15] Davies further insightfully comments that it is the shared "diagnostic and prescriptive approach to intellectual inquiry [that]

[15]Davies further emphasizes that from the May Fourth era Chinese critical inquiry "was and remains a battlefield."

encourages the production of polemics insofar as it tends to exclude or negate outright those formulations that do not agree with the particular solution or way an author proposes, or the set of worries he (and it is generally a man) has identified" (Davies 2007: 2–3, 18). I fully agree with Davies' analysis on the genesis of polemics in contemporary Sinophone intellectual world. However, this analysis leaves the striking degree of intensity unexplained. To better appreciate the language of Sinophone critical inquiry and avoid simply dismissing it as unprofessional or primitive, we then need to deal properly with the frequently ferocious, nasty — I am indeed tempted to use the word "violent" — writing style embedded in contemporary Chinese intellectual polemics.

In tackling this issue, I find Žižek's use of the Lacanian psychoanalytic concept of fantasy very useful. It is necessary now to approach the notion in a more theoretic manner. Instead of the everyday understanding of fantasy as wild and unrealistic imagination, in Lacanian psychoanalysis, fantasy plays a crucial role in our perception of what we experience as "reality." Žižek figuratively describes it as "the little piece of imagination by which we gain access to reality." Indeed, this little piece of imagination is precisely what grounds our "sense of reality," and "when our fundamental fantasy is shattered, we experience the 'loss of reality'" (Žižek 1999b: 122). Fantasy is in this sense not an imaginary scene functioning as an "exit" for people to "escape" from the "raw reality" of life. On the contrary, it projects an imaginary scenario through which we can relate ourselves to (what we experience as) "reality."

This psychoanalytic notion of fantasy, however, depends on the proposition that "reality" can only ever be seen or experienced from a subjective *perspective*, that it always already presupposes a *specific point of view*, entailing *transcendentally* an act of "looking awry" (to borrow one of Žižek's favorite terms). For Lacan, what we experienced as "reality" is no way close to Reality as such (which he terms as the Real): "reality" is articulated in the symbolic level, through language; however, symbols and words can never fully capture the totality of the Real. Yannis Stavrakakis summarizes Lacan's view in the following way:

> The central feature of language, of the symbolic, is discontinuity: something is always missing in language, the symbolic itself is lacking. [...] As

> Lacan points out in *Television* (1973), language cannot say the whole truth. The words to do it are missing; it is *materially impossible* (these are Lacan's exact words) to achieve it and this is a source of alienation in which what emerges is the lack in every representation. This is also why entering into the field of linguistic representation permits the development of our desire and a certain structuration of our identity; but this identity can never be full since the symbolic is never full. Entering into language entails a loss of immediacy, the loss of a direct unmediated fulfilment of need. It entails symbolic castration. (Stavrakakis 1999: 51–52)

Hence, what characterizes "reality" — a symbolic order indeed — is *lack*, due to the impossibility for symbols and words to fully cover the Real.[16] Also, what fundamentally characterizes us (as speaking beings) is *lack* as well, owing to our incapacity of access to our own body without the mediation of language (hence, "symbolic castration"). In this sense, lack (often phrased by Lacanian theorists as the fundamental Lack) is the product of symbolic castration as the primordial violence of human socialization. We have to undergo this primordial *alienation* to be able to fully emerge in our symbolic world. "The very existence of the human *qua* being-of-language stands thus under the sign of an irreducible and constitutive lack" (Žižek 2005a: 206). In this precise sense in Lacanian psychoanalysis, people as speaking beings are referred to as the "barred subject."[17]

[16] Lacan thus defines the Real as "the impossible" (Lacan 1979: 167). "The closest we can get to that pre-symbolic or non-symbolisable real," as Stavrakakis notes, "is through the points of failure of the symbolic" (Stavrakakis 1999: 49).

[17] Lacan uses the symbol "$" (read as the barred subject) to refer to speaking beings. Bruce Fink explains the emergence of the barred subject as follows: "In Lacan's concept of alienation, the two parties involved, the child and the Other, are very unevenly matched, and the child almost inevitably loses in the struggle between them. By submitting to the Other, the child nevertheless gains something, he or she becomes, in a sense, one of language's subjects, a subject 'of language' or 'in language'." (Fink 1995: 49) In other words, it is through alienation as the result of symbolic castration, that one is able to fully emerge in "reality," into the intersubjectively shared symbolic space. This gaining something (i.e. "subjectivity") nonetheless entails the total disappearance of that which is the subject's *own* (namely, his/her own desire): "in his or her confrontation with the Other, the subject immediately *drops out* of the picture. While alienation is the necessary 'first step' in acceding to subjectivity, this step involves choosing 'one's own' disappearance." (Fink 1995: 51)

For Lacan, both the subject and the Other (i.e. the symbolic order)[18] are barred, meaning that they are both fundamentally characterized by the lack — the lack of access to the Real. In Lacan's work this fundamental lack, as Bruce Fink remarks, "has, to a certain extent, an ontological status" (Fink 1995: 52). Owing to its lack of the Real, "reality" or "social reality" as a symbolic world can never be whole or full. "As experience and ontological reflection show, the full Other does not exist; the guarantee of the Other is missing" (Stavrakakis 1999: 46). This ontological status opens up the subjective experiences of "reality": social reality cannot be "objective" because it lacks the ultimate guarantee in the Real. Reality entails transcendentally a subjective point of view: it is accessible only through the primordial act of looking awry. This "anamorphic view" is yet responsible for so many of our choices and actions in everyday life. The very target psychoanalysis aims at changing is precisely this fundamental vision of the analysand's (in Lacanian terms, what psychoanalysis endeavors to achieve is "the traversing of the fantasy"). After the proper psychoanalytic process, "what changes is only the 'perspective,' the position of the subject" (Žižek 2005a: 54).[19] Despite being "only the perspective," *the very way we relate ourselves to reality* changes (to put in Lacanian terms, what changes is our very relation to the Other).

Now it is no longer difficult to decode the following (in)famous Lacanian formulae: "the big Other does not exist" (which means, "reality"

Thus, Lacan's anti-Heideggerian thesis is: people are not directly "thrown" into the world; rather, they have to undergo the violent operation of castration to be "included" in the world. Different from Heideggerian existentialist phenomenology, psychoanalysis takes the following situation into its account: in some rare case, children have vanquished the Other in the "primordial struggle"; that is to say, they have survived the symbolic castration. The psychoanalytic name for these people is psychotic subjects. They do not experience lack. They also do not have the "sense of reality." As Dominique Heqc notes, "the psychotic has neither access to symbolization, nor to the judgment required for this experience to be inscribed in the symbolic" (Heqc 2001: 71). They are entirely "foreclosed."

[18]Lacan idiosyncratically calls the realm of language and law the big Other. Hence, the Other refers first to a place or locus — that of language and law (i.e. the symbolic order), and second to a subject "occupying" this place and thus "embodying" the Other for another subject. It is the mother who first occupies the position of the Other for the child. The castration complex is formed when the child discovers that this Other is not complete, that there is a lack in the Other (see Evans 1996: 133).

[19]See also Fink 1997: 70.

does not *Really* exist); and, "there is no Other of the big Other" (the decoded message of which is that "reality" does not have any ontological ground, it thus cannot be "objectively there").

"Reality" in this counter-Real sense, designates "a *totality* set on effacing the traces of its own *impossibility*" (Žižek 1989: 49, emphases modified). Reality is lacking ("not-all") and, at the same time, attempting to cover this lack up. Now comes the crucial question: *How* does it efface its own impossibility? *How* does reality effectively hide its own fictionality, and make itself appearing "real" to people? The Lacanian answer is: through the magical operation of fantasy. "The construction of reality, the illusion of the world as a well-structured whole, would not be possible without the intervention of this element of fantasy" (Stavrakakis 1999: 62).

What we experience as "reality" (or "social reality"), which does not have ontological dignity, has indeed a structure of fiction: its coherence relies on *narrative fabrications*. "Reality," like all fictions, entails an *imaginary* dimension. As we — as readers of fictions — all know very well, even a great deal of "true statements"[20] are included in a fiction, the big *scenario* — for which those statements are organized to support — is nonetheless of an imaginary character. Similarly, the consistence of our sense of reality, is also sustained by a fundamental imaginary scenario. The Lacanian name for such imaginary scenario is *fantasy*, the extremely crucial piece of imagination without which "we experience the 'loss of reality'." Thus, fantasy is called by Lacan "absolute signification": "it constitutes the frame through which we experience the world as consistent and meaningful" (Žižek 1989: 123). We need fantasy to stage for us the fundamental stories about our everyday reality, about the (consistent) meaning of our lives, etc. In this sense, fantasmatic narratives are *constitutive* of our lives. Our social construction of reality acquires its ontological consistency, and finds it only in the fantamatic scenarios (instead of in the Real). Fantasy is the very device that veils the lack in the Other. What makes such narratives special, different from other "ordinary" narratives, is not that they entail some intrinsic quality in themselves. Rather, these

---

[20]The author may mention, for example, that "there is a lot of snow in Greenland," or that "human beings typically have two ears," etc. (cf. Terry Eagleton 1991: 22). Even science-fiction writers need to include a great deal of "true statements" in the fiction.

narratives are special due to *the structural space they occupy* — the invisible, "spectral" space at the intersection of intimate imaginations with symbolic processes. Such "spectral" space enables one's fundamental fantasy to organize all kinds of other narratives, grand or trivial, into its framework, and by doing that, make the symbolic realm appear to him/her as a consistent Whole.[21] Thus with the shattering of the fundamental fantasy, people experience the loss of "reality."

Reality therefore is *structured like a fiction*: around one big plot all other detailed narratives are organized. Such main plot functioning as the fundamental frame of reality, is the fantasmatic narrative. It sustains and supports our experience of reality by endowing it with (illusionary) consistency and fullness. Unbearable trauma — namely, the traumatic experience of the loss of reality, of the inexistence of the Other — emerges once such narrative (the fundamental plot) collapses. We learn from our everyday living experiences that many narratives can be "deconstructed," without driving people to feel "our world falls apart" or inflicting any serious effect upon the existing order. This profound difference between symbolic and fantasmatic narratives, between our everyday symbolic universe and its fantasmatic support, can also be approached from mundane observations of, say, the different reactions from an average (atheist) Chinese person and an American Evangelical towards the statement "Jesus Christ was not born from Immaculate Conception," or the different effects that the statement "Santa Claus is a fabrication" would have respectively on teenagers and five-years-old kids.

This difference between symbolic and fantasmatic narratives renders clear the deconstructionist motto "Everything is textual" its inherent limit, which is, its failure to tackle *the fantasmatic core of our being*.[22] Rather than immediately engaging in deconstructing the Centre (*qua* Presence), Lacanian psychoanalysis emphasizes instead that "supplement is the

---

[21] Bruce Fink links the Lacanian fundamental fantasy to what Freud calls the "primal scene," a scene that fundamentally constitutes the analysand's sexuality and life in general. The Freudian point is: the primal scene "is not so much a real scene witnessed by the child at a particular moment in time, as a construction by the child — perhaps based on numerous scenes observed, overheard, and/or imagined" (Fink 1997: 57, 70).

[22] A Žižekian response towards this deconstructionist attitude is: true, everything is textual, but where is your hamster (the fetish object without which one's entire symbolic universe collapse)?

condition of possibility *and* the condition of impossibility of the Centre" (Žižek 2005a: 210). Symbolic Centre is essentially framed and sustained by its fantasmatic supplement. Žižek's next anti-Derridean point is: far from being tantamount to symbolic Presence, what can be properly deemed "the Center" in fact resides in a supplementary, "spectral" space. For Lacan, every totalization has to rely on a fantasmatic "master-signifier" (Žižek 2001: 101). As the supplement to the "ordinary" signifying chain constituting a symbolic totality, the master-signifier functions precisely as that which creates and maintains the illusion that the existing signifying chain constitutes a totality. "It is the signifier to which all other signifiers represent a subject. Should this signifier be missing, none of the other signifiers represents anything at all." (Fink 1995: 74)[23] Once the fundamental fantasy epitomized by the master-signifier is traversed, the whole symbolic universe collapses. In other words, the master-signifier (the Centre) is precisely the weakest spot within the linguistically constituted realm experienced as "reality." Hence, "the Centre Derrida endeavors to 'deconstruct' is ultimately the very supplement which threatens to disrupt its totalizing power" (Žižek 2005a: 210).

Žižek argues regarding "Derrida's failure to acknowledge fully the ultimate identity of supplement and Master-Signifier":

> Derrida's "deconstruction" aims at undermining the authority of the central signifier that pretends to totalize the texture of traces, and thus to restrain its dissemination – again and again, he emphasizes how this central signifier is always subverted, displaced, by what it is supposed to dominate; how it depends structurally on its effects, and so forth. It might seem, therefore, that the supplement and the Master-Signifier are opposites whose tension provides the contours of the textual process: the supplement us the undecidable margin that eludes the Master-Signifier. Lacan, however, locates this undecidability in the very heart of the Master-Signifier: with reference to the series of "ordinary" elements, the Centre is by definition an excessive, supplementary element whose place is structurally ambiguous, neither within nor without. (Žižek 1994a: 196)

[23] As Fink further makes it very clear, the master-signifier is "a positional notion," which "simply designates a signifier which is isolated from the rest of discourse" (Fink 1995: 77).

Lacan's name for this master-signifier is, of course, the (in)famous "phallus."[24] Hence, Derrida's criticism of Lacanian psychoanalysis as "phallogocentric" is valid within his deconstructive logic — how can there be such a thing as a "privileged signifier," given that every signifier is defined only by its differences from other signifiers? It is a sound critique in terms that Lacan does privilege "phallus" as a signifier that is not included in the set of all signifiers, and that designates the signification process itself. However, from Lacanian viewpoint, the key point Derrida nonetheless misses here is *the fantasmatic dimension of language*. The master-signifier is "privileged" because of the "structurally ambiguous place" it occupies (which makes it both the central and "weakest" spot within social reality): the master-signifier is not defined by its differences from other signifiers since it is *a fantasmatic signifier*, which signifies nothing but the supplement/excess that, by standing in and covering up the empty ground of the Other, holds all other signifiers into a differential system.

Hence, the crucial lesson of Lacanian psychoanalysis, according to Žižek, is that the linguistic realm is *not merely* tantamount to the whole complex of signifying practices and symbolic processes. This is Lacan's challenge (or, contribution) to the Saussurian-oriented (post)structuralist school. True, in Lacan's theory it is the order of the Symbolic which constitutes this matrix of social reality. This symbolic order governed by the Law[25] is also a "big Other" in terms that it is a totalizing system of

---

[24]This naming is rather arbitrary — at best culturally and disciplinarily valid. As Bruce Fink notes, "Psychoanalytic practice suggests, as do other practices, that in Western cultures in general, that signifier is the phallus. Though many claim that that is no more than a preconceived notion, psychoanalysis claims that it is a clinical observation, and as such contingent. It is verified time and again in clinical practice, and thus constitutes a generalization, not a necessary, universal rule. There is no theoretical reason why it could not be something else, and there perhaps are (and have been) societies in which some other signifier plays (or played) the role of the signifier of desire." (Fink 1995: 102) I will further discuss why the master-signifier is also the signifier of desire in Chapter 1.

[25]In Lacanian psychoanalysis, emphasis is placed on language as structuring the Law of social exchange. The Law in Lacan's work (which Lacan often writes with a capital "L") refers not to a piece of legislation, but to the fundamental principles which underlie all social relations. As Dylan Evans points out, Lacan's discussions of the Law owe much to the work of Claude Lévi-Strauss. For Lacan, "the law is the set of universal principles

regulatory institutions that shape our behavior, though its power of operation is purely symbolic and has no normative force outside of collective behavior (i.e. it lacks any ontological foundation in the Real). Lacan himself quite often suggests that any aspect of subjective experience which has a linguistic structure pertains to the symbolic order. This totalizing, all-encompassing effect of the symbolic order leads Lacanian theorists to often speak of the Symbolic as "a universe." Once the symbolic order has arisen, it creates the sense that it has always been there, since "we find it absolutely impossible to speculate on what preceded it other than by symbols" (Lacan 1988: 5).

Žižek's works nonetheless further remind us: in addition to its symbolic dimension as the underlying matrix of reality, language, according to Lacan, also has *an imaginary dimension.* Lacan argues: "there is something in the symbolic function of human discourse that cannot be eliminated, and that is the role played in it by the imaginary" (Lacan 1988: 306). In her *Žižek: A Critical Introduction*, Sarah Key offers a very good succinct summary regarding this aspect of Lacan's theorization of the Symbolic and the Imaginary: "The Symbolic is the domain of structure, difference and gap, as realized in the signifying chain; whereas the Imaginary provides the illusion of stability, content and wholeness" (Key 2003: 169). However, this argument of Lacan's has been largely overlooked. Just as Dylan Evans observes, "One common misconception of Lacan is that language is synonymous with the symbolic order" (Evans 1996: 100). As a consequence, Lacan's theorization of the imaginary dimension of language (for example, narratives generated in the fantasmatic space) had literally no influence in the structuralist and poststructuralist movement of the last century. This intellectual legacy of Lacan's makes Žižek's works fundamentally incompatible with the poststructuralist camp. For Žižek, fantasmatic narratives are crucial to the process of the subjective constitution of reality because they make the symbolic Law *accessible.* "Contrary to the common-sense notion of fantasizing as

---

which make social existence possible, the structures that govern all forms of social exchange, whether gift-giving, kinship relations or the formation of pacts. Since the most basic form of exchange is communication itself, the law is fundamentally a linguistic entity — it is the law of the signifier." (Evans 1996: 101) indulging in the hallucinatory realization of desires prohibited by the Law, the fantasmatic narrative does not stage the suspension-transgression of the Law, but is rather the very act of its installment" (Žižek 1999b: 94). In other words, fantasy is an essentially *constitutive* element of reality. It is fantasy that, by staging an imaginary scenario in which the Real can be achieved, guarantees the coherence and fullness of reality.

Herein also resides the central thesis of Žižek's politics: "If we are to overcome the 'effective' social power, we have to first break its fantasmatic hold upon us" (Žižek 2005a: 251). This is so because, as noted above, the fundamental fantasy occupies both the central and weakest spot in the construction of our social reality: it stands in and covers up *the empty place* functioning as the "void ground" of the Other. Žižek argues: "It is necessary to introduce the crucial distinction between 'symbolic signification' and its own place, the empty place filled by signification" (Žižek 2005a: 47). The function of the fundamental fantasy is exactly *to cover up the primordial emptiness of this place*: by providing a coherent "primordial narrative," it offers us a *necessary alternative* to the traumatic acknowledgement that our sense of reality is *groundless*, that there is no Other of the Other. As Stavrakakis remarks, "Fantasy attempts to remedy the fundamental deficiency (impossibility) of the big Other, to 'restore' the fullness of the Other" (Stavrakakis 1999: 47). The fantasmatic supplement is needed precisely because "the central feature of language, of the symbolic, is discontinuity: something is always missing in language, the symbolic itself is lacking" (Stavrakakis 1999: 52). Social reality as the symbolic order is ontologically *lacking* — the lack of its fullness, of its ultimate guarantee in the Real. The "cruel" fact about the Real is that it is by definition non-symbolic and unsymbolizable.[26] It "accounts for the failure of all symbolic representations of objective reality." Reality is itself revealed as lacking because, as Stavrakakis puts it, "it attempts the impossible, that is to say, the representation of something ultimately unrepresentable. Representation is the representation of a real fullness which is always beyond our grasp." (Stavrakakis 1999: 38, 68) Fantasy is thus also needed for covering up — or to put it more figuratively, "stitching up" — the very *abyssal gaps* witnessing and marking the failure of symbolic representations.

---

[26]Lacan defines the Real as *that which resists symbolization.*

According to Lacan, "fantasy is an imaginary involved in a signifying function (seminar of 21 May 1958)" (quoted from Stavrakakis 1999: 46). By *telling stories about those issues people find troubling, uneasy, disturbing* (such as the story of a beneficent Dragon (China) being bullied by vicious enemies intruding from the West, which I will discuss in Chapter 1), and *staging scenarios in which such troubling issues are imaginarily resolved, or rendered solvable*, the function of fantasy is to project a coherent "reality," and at the same time, to obscure its own operations (the fictionality of reality thus "magically" disappears…). Fantasy does not *Really* solve any profound issue — such issue is from the Lacanian psychoanalytic view *partial embodiment* of the irreducible gap between reality and the impossible Real; rather, it merely generates the framework necessary for perceiving the troubling issue as being resolved, or solvable (i.e. not an *issue* any more). Žižek thus argues that "fantasy constitutes the primordial form of narrative, which serves to occult some original deadlock." When the "reality" falls apart because of a traumatic experience, the subject encounters what Žižek calls the "uncanny absolute proximity of trauma and fantasy" (Žižek 1998: 196; 2003: 283).

This Lacanian viewpoint of fantasy can indeed be of great use apropos of tackling the unique "intensified" style of intellectual polemics in contemporary China — academic arguments are quickly overwhelmed by personal attacks; opponents in a debate quickly become sworn enemies; intellectual groups are easily turned into warring factions. In the following chapters of this book, I will discuss various discourses emerging in the post-Maoist Chinese intellectual landscape including the New Enlightenment, postmodernism, liberalism, the New Left, nationalism, the China model, etc., which altogether have produced continuous vehement debates — very often, in the form of "spitting wars" (*koushui zhan*, a term frequently employed by contemporary Chinese intellectuals to refer to the hostility of these exchanges) — among intellectuals and intellectual camps. When Chinese intellectuals engage passionately in debating issues of China's reform or "Chinese problems," from a Lacanian perspective they are involved in a *clash of fantasies* that take place in what might best be described as a fantasmatic space. In terms that people's divergent sense of reality is framed and sustained by fantasy, truly as Žižek notes, "war is always also a war of fantasies" (Žižek 1994a: 78). Their conflicting definitions of "China's reality" and identification of "Chinese problems," in this view are the productions of individual acts of "looking awry." Hence, Chinese intellectuals' intensified writing and debating style, which is frequently featured with emotional statements, moral accusations, even nasty personal attacks, can be explained from this Lacanian psychoanalytic point of view: by telling and defending their different stories and visions about China, contemporary Chinese intellectuals are actually defending their own sense of reality. If one "loses" to his/her rival(s) in an intellectual debate, (s)he encounters not merely the common psychological experience of "losing face" (*diulian*), but fundamentally *the ontological experience of subjective disintegration* (the loss of reality). This is the true stake embedded in Sinophone critical inquiry, which is however much less intense — if not largely absent — in its Anglophone counterpart.

Why and how, then, do clashes of fantasies emerge? How do we take account of such strong effect caused by them (e.g. turning intellectual circles into deadly battlefields)? According to Žižek, the ability to fantasize is the one unique thing about each of us because fantasy provides the structure of our personal experiences of reality: fantasy makes us individuals because it allows us to have our subjective view of reality. Reality therefore is not an "objective existence"; consequently one can only get access to reality through the anamorphic screen of "looking awry." As such, our fantasies are extremely sensitive to the intrusion of others: when a fantasmatic scenario is shattered and wrecked by such intrusions, what we encounter is the shock that comes of having our subjective sense of reality challenged. Fantasy in this sense serves as the *protective shield* against intrusions that threaten our experience of reality. The collision of two opposite fantasies produces what Žižek calls the "uncanny absolute proximity of trauma and fantasy." In Lacanian psychoanalysis, the acute pain or torment felt by a subject when the horrible experience that (s)he has successfully repressed, disavowed or foreclosed becomes linguistically exposed is termed as "trauma." In other words, trauma is the unbearable ordeal emerging at the moment when *what is repressed, disavowed or foreclosed by the subject at the point of its assumption of a position in language* disrupts the subjectively constituted reality. Trauma emerges, for example, when "the story the community has been telling itself about itself" no longer makes sense (to paraphrase Richard Rorty). Trauma thus very often appears to be a way of holding the subject to the past, gripping them so that they cannot move beyond it.[27] Žižek particularly links trauma to the (mal)operation of fantasy and argues that "[t]here is always something utterly traumatic about directly confronting one's fundamental fantasy — such a confrontation, if not properly managed by the analyst, can easily lead to complete subjective disintegration" (Žižek 2003: 283). Fantasy therefore not only provides the fundamental support for our sense of reality, it is also the psychological remedy for the unbearable experience of trauma. Thus, *when the space of fantasy is trespassed or intruded, trauma emerges*; and only by *renewing the fantasmatic narrative* can the subject regain his sense of reality and keep himself from "complete subjective disintegration" (i.e. *aphanisis*).

In short, what Žižek calls the "fundamental fantasy" of a subject functions as a defensive shield that covers up the inconsistencies of the symbolic order. Trauma erupts if such a fantasy fails to sustain our subjective access to reality. In terms of its defensive functioning, fantasy is not an unrealistic hallucination, but the very constitutive ground of (one's sense of) reality. In relation to the symbolic Law that confines our experience of reality to a given set of coordinates, fantasy does not stage the breaking of the Law, but rather the establishing of it.

From this Lacanian–Žižekian elaboration of fantasy then, we can view the Confucian endeavor of "establishing peaceful and harmonious order everywhere under Heaven" (i.e. rectifying the existing order) as a fantasy endeavor at its purest for it attempts to establish a symbolic order in accordance with the ultimate *Dao* (the ontological Real) of Heaven. It is precisely such intellectual tradition that produces what Davies calls Sinophone preference for "linguistic certitude" — Chinese thinkers tend to presume that "language represents 'what is *really* happening out there'," thus there can be a harmonious congruence between the field of the Real and the field of linguistic signification. *The attempt aiming at such congruence is an act of fantasy in the precise sense that it is not regarded as mere hallucination.* From the viewpoint of Confucianism, the ultimate social Harmony can be realistically achieved. Such a view is utterly fantasmatic because, to recall the Lacanian idea of fantasy, there is

[27] Cf. Žižek 2005a: 256; Ian Parker 2004.

no social harmony *per se*, only *projections* of social harmony. The Confucian project of achieving social harmony, thus, is a fantasy at its purest: Confucian scholar-officials since the time of Confucius have not succeeded in actually realizing this ideal; what they have effectively achieved and have been really good at, though, is to generate the framework necessary for perceiving such ideal as achievable, and to provide stories in which the ideal has been already achieved (by past Confucian Sage-Kings such as ancient legendary/fictional figures like Emperor Huang, Yao, Shun, Yu, as well as historical figures like Emperor Taizong of Tang Dynasty…). Fantasy is indeed a "promise of fullness," "an imaginary promise as an answer to the anomaly emerging at the intersection of this symbolic and the persisting real" (Stavrakakis 1999: 45, 47). By promising an imaginary mastery of the impossible Real, fantasy attempts to suture the ontological gap between the Real and reality, and creates the delusion that the real fullness can be — and/or already has been — achieved. The key point regarding such operation of fantasy is: the actual realization of the promise is nonetheless *always deferred, or (perceived as) halted by some external intrusions or obstacles*. In this sense, the Confucian attempts to establish a social order in congruence with the *Dao* of Heaven are *structurally* doomed to fail. The "causes" of failure are in Chinese history often attributed to the "fatuous emperor" (*hunjun*), the "little people" (*xiaoren*) near the emperor who control the government power, the invasion of barbarians… [28]

Indeed, it is a fantasy, in this precise Lacanian sense, in which the topic of Western military and cultural invasions since the Opium Wars (1839–1842) is described as a lethal intrusion that led ultimately to the

[28] What is noteworthy here is Daoism, arguably the biggest intellectual rivalry of Confucianism in Chinese intellectual history, also shares with Lacan in the idea that the Real (its counterpart in Daoist terminology is *Dao*) is radically beyond the field of signification. It is unpresentable, unreachable, and utterly eludes and resists any symbolization. As Lao Zi puts it in the beginning of *Dao De Jing*, "*Dao* that can be put into words is not really *Dao*" (see Roger Ames and David Hall's recent translation of *Dao De Jing* 2003: 77). Against Confucian doctrine, classical Daoist theorists such as Lao Zi and Zhuang Zi reject the idea that by endeavors of human agents, the congruence between *Dao* and the social order of humans can be achieved. In this sense (and only in this sense), Lao Zi and Zhuang Zi were achronologically Lacanian thinkers.

disintegration of the Confucian view of China as *Tianxia* ("all under Heaven"). A proper Lacanian reading would exactly turn the story around: it is the invasions of the West that *retroactively* enabled late Qing and twentieth-century ("modern") Chinese thinkers to write about the integrity of Chinese civilization and to imagine a former harmonious social order that they seek to recover. Such psychoanalytic view is helpful in explaining the frequent references to traumatic experience in late-nineteenth and twentieth-century Chinese writings. For instance, in the frequently quoted words of Li Hongzhang (1823–1901), one of the most influential scholar-officials of the late Qing Empire: "(what we have encountered is) an enormous change unprecedented in the last three thousand years" (*sanqian nian weiyou zhi bianju*). Li used "three thousand years" to express the acute nature of China's crisis. By implying that in the last three thousand years, China was relatively unchanged, Li created the fantasy of a once stable ("eternal") Chinese realm now perceived as under threat — the (fantasized) fullness of Chinese civilization was shattered by the intrusion of the West. The paradox here is the lost object — the fullness of Chinese civilization — *is retroactively constructed precisely by what is identified as the cause of its loss.* Stavrakakis explains this point as follows,

> The lost object is an object which is not lost as such but is posited as lost *après coup.* What does that in effect mean? It means that it is lack that introduces the idea of fullness and not vice-versa. It means that it is an act of power, an act of exclusion, that retroactively produces the fullness we attribute to what was excluded, to that unknown impossibility. No doubt, it is common sense to think that something was there before exclusion, otherwise exclusion would make no sense at all; the only problem is that we can't really know what it was. To think that it was a state of fullness is a retroactively produced fiction. (Stavrakakis 1999: 43–44)

What Li Hongzhang evoked is exactly such a fantasmatic fiction of an unchanged Chinese civilization, which is possible to be talked about and taken for granted only by means of the intrusion of the West, the perceived "external cause" responsible for the destruction of the original harmony of Chinese civilization. Similarly this expression of the loss of Chinese civilization in Li Hongzhang's slogan is echoed strongly in the famous expression of the prominent scholar Wang Guowei (1877–1927) — "What we love we can no longer believe in; and what we can believe in is not what we love" (*keai zhe bu kexin, kexin zhe bu keai*). The former refers to the status of Chinese knowledge — though severely discredited or even broken down, it is yet still held so dear by Wang; and the latter to the opposite status of Western knowledge. Wang Guowei committed suicide by drowning himself in Kunming Lake in Beijing's Summer Palace in 1927. Wang left a note carrying his last words to his son: "I am fifty years old, and have experienced everything except death; after experiencing that the world has changed I do not want to be humiliated again" (*wushi zhinian, zhiqian yisi, jingci shibian, yi wu zairu*). In his "Eulogy for Wang Guowei," Wang's colleague and friend Chen Yinque (1890–1969), another influential scholar, claimed that it was Wang's traumatic feeling about the loss of Chinese civilization that eventually drove him to suicide. Chen wrote:

> I was asked about the reason of Wang's suicide. My reply is: scholars recently started to bring forward theses on Oriental culture versus Western culture. What is at stake is not how to demarcate these two cultures, or which is the better one. What can be presumed as true is the following condition: When a culture enters a phase of decline, people who were cultivated by such culture inevitably feel torment. The more the extent of such culture being integrated into personal life is, the deeper the agony erupts. When this traumatic feeling goes extremely deep, there is nothing that can pacify one's heart and make life right except suicide. (Chen Yinque 2005)

This excerpt shows that Chen's eulogy for Wang locates the cause of Wang's suicide as a sense of trauma that overcame him. Chen's explanation indeed accords with Žižek's psychoanalytic observation that "[t]here is always something utterly traumatic about directly confronting one's fundamental fantasy — such a confrontation, if not properly managed by the analyst, can easily lead to complete subjective disintegration."[29]

[29] In this sense, I contend that it is promising and intellectually rewarding to rewrite Joseph R. Levenson's master piece *Confucianism and Its Modern Fate* from the psychoanalytic approach focusing on the operation of fantasy.

Although contemporary Chinese intellectuals have not personally suffered such trauma, they however write *as if* they had collectively suffered the same trauma that Chen Yinque attributed to Wang Guowei. Such "as if" is precisely a key feature of the Lacanian Imaginary — the realm of narcissistic identification and fantasmatic (mis)recognition: a man fully becomes a (symbolically recognized) father once he acts *as if* he is one. By the same token, a man truly becomes a member of modern Chinese intellectuals once he writes *as if* he had personally suffered the traumatic deprivation of China's civilizational essence. That which supports this "as if" operation is, of course, fantasmatic narratives — such as the story, mentioned briefly earlier and substantially later, of a beneficent Dragon being bullied by vicious enemies intruding from the West. Such stories ground personal identities (e.g. a Chinese) and frame subjective experiences (e.g. trauma), by staging a consistent scenario in which all troubling issues disappear, and everything makes "sense." To evoke a line very commonly employed in Hollywood spy thriller films — "you have been framed!", indeed, contemporary Chinese intellectuals (as "barred subjects" deprived of their *own desire*) *have been framed* — framed by such fantasmatic stories about China.

Many contemporary Chinese intellectuals write *as if* they were contemporaries of Li Hongzhang, Wang Guowei, Chen Yinque, etc. This is effectively enabled by the following fantasy-operation: the dominant narratives about "modern China" have been setting their opening prologue at the Opium Wars (the 1840s) or the "May Fourth" (the late 1910s). Through such fantasmatic frame, contemporary intellectuals can imagine themselves *in the same scenario* with those late-Qing to early-Republican authors. Recently, the Beijing-based public intellectual Zhu Yong published a book, which even tries to set the date much earlier. Entitled *The Trauma of the Empire*, Zhu's book is a historical study of several historical events from Zheng He's voyages to the West (*Zhenghe xia xiyang*, which occurred between 1405 and 1433) in the early Ming dynasty to Japanese invasion in the 1930s. In the opening line of the book's "preface" Zhu writes: "Chinese history of recent centuries is a painful history. This is acknowledged by every Chinese person." In statements that echo Li Hongzhang and Wang Guowei, Zhu writes heavily about "the trauma of China" and "the tragic change of Chinese history." He proposes that "if it is appropriate to compare ancient China to a structurally stable and systematically sophisticated machine, then it is the interventions of the outside force that changed the physical settings of that machine" (Zhu Yong 2009: i).[30] Zhu assumes that every contemporary Chinese person feels the same torment about the Chinese past, that everyone is suffering the same traumatic blow caused by the "outside force" of the West. Thus, Zhu writes *as if* he were experiencing the same trauma as late Qing scholar-officials and early twentieth-century intellectuals. *Such rhetoric creates an imaginary trauma, which is then experienced as "real" via a fantasmatic window*. In other words, what contemporary authors such as Zhu share with late-Qing figures such as Li and Wang is not the trauma *per se*, but the fantasmatic scenario which produces such traumatic effects stemming from the deprived object (China's greatness, the fullness of Chinese civilization). That this type of writing does not appear odd in present-day Chinese intellectual discourse shows that the rhetoric of such traumatic experience nonetheless prevails *despite* the imaginary nature of the experience itself. It is precisely narratives like the one Zhu told, that allow fantasmatic views of history that "distort" the past in particular ways.

Such trauma staged in the fantasmatic scenario not only can be experienced as utterly "real," but also can be extremely intense and unbearable. The prominent Beijing-based literary critic Yu Hong (1957–2007) posted an essay entitled "A Century for a Person" in his personal blog three months before he committed suicide by jumping out of the window of his apartment. In this essay (which is the last update of his blog, thus widely viewed as his last words), the author wrote: "To choose to keep on living in this disastrous century of Chinese history — living with dignity instead of merely living, means that one has to bear numerous unbearable moments, to deal with tremendous unspeakable agonies." And Yu's own final "choice" is: "It is not easy to commit suicide; but it can be much harder to keep on living" (*zisha buyi, huozhe gengnan*) (Yu Hong 2007). The tone of Yu's last words is reminiscent of that of Wang Guowei's, who took the same choice eighty years ago. (Another uncanny coincidence is

[30]By "a structurally stable and systematically sophisticated machine" Zhu echoes the influential thesis of "the ultrastable system" made by two leading New Enlightenment intellectuals Jin Guantao and Liu Qingfeng in the 1980s. This famous thesis of Jin and Liu's will be discussed in Chapter 2.

that both Wang and Yu took their lives at the age of fifty.) Together with "A Century for a Person" Yu posted another piece entitled "China and Me," which was the text of his speech given at the academic conference "The Problem of China and the Original Production of Theory" held in Hangzhou, December 2006. Yu contended in this essay that many Chinese thinkers locate the "problem of China" in the relationship between China and the world; what is ignored is the relationship between "China and me." Yu urged the intellectual community to post this following question to itself: What has constituted and sustained the relationship between China and an individual Chinese person? (Yu Hong 2006) The author left the question unanswered (or answered with his final suicidal act). The Lacanian answer to Yu's question is, of course: it is fantasy that constitutes, regulates and sustains the very "relationship" between the big Other and the subject by staging an imaginary scenario for the latter to gain access to the former. Also from Lacanian psychoanalytic angle, Yu was only one step away from what Lacan calls "traversing the fantasy" or "going through the fantasy," which is for Lacan the final goal of psychoanalytic treatment. The individual cases of Wang Guowei and Yu Hong show the critical psychoanalytic lesson that *what happens in the fantasmatic space has Real effect* — indeed, they have been "framed"! This leads us back again to the question of why Chinese intellectual discussions and debates often turn quickly into nasty spitting wars. By defending their arguments and theses on the problem of China and its solution, Chinese intellectuals are in fact defending something much deeper, something personal, intimate, and *existential*. Chinese intellectuals' frequent violent attacks on fellow authors are, from the psychoanalytic view, the very attempts of protecting themselves from "complete subjective disintegration."[31]

The New Enlightenment movement of the 1980s can be thus, from such Lacanian viewpoint, seen an intellectual response to "the tragedy of Chinese history." This is because, in China, the history of modern China

[31] Žižek has used many examples from popular literatures and films to illustrate the point that the intrusion of one's fantasmatic space can lead to violent acts, especially when such intrusion triggers the sudden disintegration of one's fundamental fantasy. See, for example, Žižek 1991b: 8–9.

is always presented as a traumatic experience endured by different generations of Chinese from the Opium Wars onwards. Interestingly, the trauma of the Cultural Revolution of the late 1960s and early 1970s (the massive destruction of lives and property, the willing or forced betrayal of loved ones, etc.) is often presented as a continuation of suffering and as evidence of a fundamental problem in Chinese society. The collapse of the Maoist paradigm produced *a revival of the language of trauma* in the post-Maoist "new era." For example, the writings of what was called "scar literature" or "literature of the wounded" (*shanghen wenxue*) in the late 1970s expressed abundantly the "spiritual trauma" (*jingshen neishang*, a phrase used by the Beijing-based writer Liu Xinwu in *The Class Teacher*, a novel regarded as the pioneer of scar literature) of the Chinese people at that moment. New Enlightenment thinkers of the 1980s such as Jin Guantao and Liu Qingfeng contend that the "ultrastable" (*chao wending*)[32] structure of Chinese culture (Maoism is regarded as a recent (re)production of such structure) is the primary cause of the spiritual trauma of the Chinese people. The task of achieving enlightened vision is thus described by New Enlightenment intellectuals as an unfinished project of "China's Enlightenment" initiated during the May Fourth movement (1917 to 1927). Xu Jilin remarks that the New Enlightenment movement of the 1980s "in some ways was another 'May Fourth'" (Xu Jilin 2000: 169). However, what makes it comparable or even "identical" to the May Fourth movement goes beyond the contents of conscious imitation of May Fourth propositions and slogans. Fundamentally, May Fourth thinkers of the late 1910s and New Enlightenment thinkers of the late 1980s shared the belief that by importing ideas from the West, they would be able to improve Chinese society, give people a real sense of identity, and restore China as a great civilization. Yet, as argued above, the idea that China must be "saved" is a byproduct of China being imagined as facing imminent doom. The fantasy of a "traumatized" people creates its own solution in the form of an "awakened" people capable of resolving all of the nation's problems. It is as if the nation, or China, or Chinese civilization, is

---

[32] Jin and Liu borrow this term from contemporary physics theories (such as the theory of control, the theory of system, etc.) to indicate the historically steady character of social and cultural structures.

imagined as a lost object (what Lacan has called *objet petit a*), awaiting recovery. In Lacanian theory, fantasy creates an imaginary illusion of (the possibility of) attaining or recapturing the lost object (i.e. the *objet petit a*), and thus with the support of fantasy, the lack in the symbolic order disappears, or at least becomes bearable. Hence, what fundamentally characterizes both intellectual movements is, from this Lacanian psychoanalytic perspective, the fantasmatic promise of the fullness. The highly popular song "Descendants of the Dragon" composed by Hou Dejian who sang this song in Tiananmen Square during the 1989 student protest movement, presents us with an effective way of understanding this fantasy. The song, examined in Chapter 1, is the reason why I have called Chinese intellectual tendencies a "Great Dragon fantasy."[33]

Also, in this Lacanian view, various post-1989 (or so-called "post-Enlightenment") narratives of China's paths or Chinese problems can be seen as competing attempts to restore (the fantasmatic promise of) China's fullness. The Tiananmen incident of 1989 — the killings in the streets of Beijing — was commonly regarded as what marked the end of the New Enlightenment movement. This tragic event powerfully allows contemporary Chinese intellectuals to link their traumatic experiences with those of the late Qing generations as well as those of the Cultural Revolution generations. Their post-Tiananmen writings, in this sense, can also be regarded as their endeavors to cope with the psychical trauma. While the proponents of various post-1989 intellectual discourses ("postmodernism," "nationalism," "liberalism," "the New Left," "the China model," etc.) debate against each other vehemently (and very often viciously), they nonetheless all share a common fantasmatic frame in their discourse, which is, a fantasy of healing old wounds through adopting the right type of knowledge.

After 4 June 1989, there was a crisis of consciousness among Chinese thinkers that led them to search for alternative paths to modernization, against the Western-style path to liberal democracy that was passionately endorsed by New Enlightenment intellectuals (and for a time, even by the advisors to Zhao Ziyang). Xu Jilin's use of the phrase "the fate of

[33] I will elaborate it by engaging in a detailed analysis of "Descendants of the Dragon" in Chapter 1.

Enlightenment," is a sentimental reference to the collapse of the "homogeneity" (*tongyixing*) of the Enlightenment discourse (both the May Fourth Enlightenment as well as the New Enlightenment).[34] When Xu presents the New Enlightenment movement as collapsing owing to "some inescapable historical destiny" he implies the impossibility of "rescuing" China from the status quo of one-party rule (Xu 2000: 186). Furthermore, when equating the collapse of the New Enlightenment movement with the "fate of May Fourth Enlightenment movement" (Xu 2000: 186), Xu's argument reflects ironically a sense of shared Chinese belonging. What emerged after the collapse of the Enlightenment discourse was a series of heated debates. While the participants of these debates disagreed with each other, their arguments shared a common *generative mechanism* — their writings were represented as intellectual responses to the crisis of the collapse of the fundamental fantasy brought by "traumatic events" (the invasions of the West, the horrible turbulence during Cultural Revolution, the blood spilled in the streets of Beijing ...).

What also needs to be noted here is that during the 1980s New Enlightenment movement there were already several competing intellectual groups. In the 1990s, they developed further around concepts such as "postmodernism," "nationalism," "liberalism," "the New Left," "the China model," etc. Despite their differences, they all share the fantasy of healing China through adopting the right type of knowledge. As noted earlier, in Žižek's view, fantasies are what make people individuals. Through their fantasmatic vistas, people see and experience reality differently; when they act in accordance with their own sense of reality, conflicts, inconsistencies, and clashes take place. With regard to Chinese intellectual inquiry, diverse proposals for a better future for China, by the same token, inevitably divide Chinese intellectuals into several mutually hostile camps. The poststructuralist concept of "multiple, dispersed subject-positions," according to Žižek, can be properly understood as the product of the operation of fantasies. Similarly, one can better understand the fierce intensity embodied in contemporary Chinese intellectual inquiry via an

---

[34]Wang Hui first employed the term "homogeneity of attitude" in his study of the May Fourth Enlightenment movement, and Xu Jilin re-adopted this term to characterize the 1980s New Enlightenment movement (Xu Jilin 2000).

analysis of how differently China's problems and the solutions to the problems are presented by different groups. The vehement debates (often involving personal attacks) among these groups reflect a pathology. The nastiness suggests that the participants of those debates have deeply held beliefs towards which they cannot afford any serious questioning. They are not prepared to heed any criticism. Instead, they view criticisms as a threat to their sense of reality and react violently to protect themselves from losing this reality. This accords with the psychoanalytic explanation of fantasy as the framing and sustaining mechanism of reality, and as a displacement of trauma. From the Lacanian psychoanalytic view, when confronted with messages discordant to their sense of reality, people often react violently in order to protect themselves from the traumatic experience of the loss of their reality.

As I have argued thus far, Žižek's Lacanian elaboration of fantasy is helpful in illustrating that, when Chinese intellectual debates revolve around distinguishing "good" from "poor" scholarship, the authors of different arguments are actually defending their own versions of reality. Thus, contemporary Chinese critical inquiry is not only intellectual and academic, but also personal and "existential": it is about how to understand the present reality of China as into which those authors are "thrown" (to borrow Heidegger's famous phrase). To paraphrase the concern of the U.S.-based literary critic Zhang Xudong, it is about "how to live as a Chinese person today" (*women jintian zenyang zuo Zhongguoren*) (Zhang 2005: i). From such Lacanian psychoanalytic angle, the writings of contemporary Chinese intellectuals can be viewed as projecting fantasmatic visions (of China's reality, of its past, present, future) that are based in "multiple, dispersed subject-positions," which, in turn, leads to clashing "realities." In this sense, truly as Žižek emphasizes, "the status of reality *is* precarious: it depends on a delicate balance between reality-testing and the fantasy-frame" (Žižek 1993: 89). When this balance is severely disturbed, i.e. too much of reality-testing/challenging is inflicted upon the fantasy-frame, we experience the loss of reality — "our world falls apart." Trauma, in Lacanian psychoanalysis, is the outcome of such clash of fantasmatic visions of reality.

In illustrating such "clash of realities," here I would like to take the Beijing-based economist Cui Zhiyuan's critique of the 1980s cultural fever as an example.[35] As a young scholar who acquired his PhD degree in the U.S., and emerged in the Sinophone intellectual scene in the mid-1990s, Cui was later labeled by his detractors as a "New Leftist" for his open criticisms towards the 1980s New Enlightenment movement and the discourse of liberalism of the 1990s. In his widely reprinted and circulated essay published originally in the influential Hong-Kong based journal *Twenty-First Century* (*Ershiyi shiji*) in 1994, Cui criticized the participants of the cultural fever of the 1980s for abstractly idealizing Western ideas and wrongfully embracing the "systems of developed Western nations" (*xifang fada guojia de zhidu*) with neither sufficient attention to the social contexts of China, nor to the discursive as well as socio-political contexts in which these Western ideas had appeared and these systems had developed (Cui 1994). While Cui accused his discursive rivals for lacking concrete experiences of contemporary China's social reality, Cui himself was accused for the same flaw. In her observation of Chinese intellectual inquiry of the 1990s, Liu Qingfeng, one of the leading figures of the New Enlightenment movement who stayed in Hong Kong after 1989 and co-founded the journal *Twenty-First Century* with Chen Fong-ching and Jin Guantao, mentioned that in the late 1990s "a friend on the mainland explained the situation to me in a letter as follows: Cui Zhiyuan is only in his thirties and does not understand China one bit because he is too young. When he was living in China he was still in his early twenties and thus he saw China in passing like someone taking a train ride. Although he returns to China every year he now lives in the United States and has become someone who looks out at China from the window of an airplane. He is incapable of having any real sense of China's problems." (Liu Qingfeng 2001: 53, discussed in Davies 2007: 72) (Is not the clash of fantasies, though, precisely *the clash of the visions seen through windows of different airplane on which each individual has taken?*) In commenting on this debate between liberals and "New Leftists," the prominent philosopher Li Zehou who fled to the U.S. after the Tiananmen incident, criticized both camps for being out of touch with China's present reality (*xianzhuang*) by claiming that the

[35] In the following section in which I use the controversies around Cui Zhiyuan's work as an exemplary case, I am indebted to Gloria Davies' discussion of Cui's work (Davies 2007: 72–75).

proliferation of texts the debate had produced showed few signs of "an organic association (*youji jiehe*) with Chinese reality or Chinese tradition" (quoted from Davies 2007: 87).

In contemporary intellectual debates, there are many examples of this in which the author unabashedly attacks the proposals of his opponents as "unrealistic" or accuses them of being unable to see "the reality of China" clearly. Another recent example is a 2005 debate between the Shanghai-based literary critic Wang Xiaoyu and the Beijing-based historian Wang Hui. The latter is a leading member of the "New Left" intellectual camp. From 1996 to 2007, Wang Hui was one of the two chief editors of *Reading*. First published in April 1979, *Reading* can be said to be the most influential intellectual journal in post-Maoist China. In an essay published in *Dongfang zaobao* (*Oriental Morning Post*), Wang Xiaoyu criticized Wang Hui for wrongly praising the *Reading*-organized activities as "the only real hope of our world." For Wang Xiaoyu, Wang Hui's statement implies an announcement that the works of other intellectuals are all "useless works" (*wuyong gong*). In Wang Xiaoyu's view, this kind of "the-only-real-hope-of-our-world" activities and works are indeed "ultra-fantasies of 'critical intellectuals'" ("critical intellectuals" is a term Wang Hui promotes to replace the label "New Leftist intellectuals"), if not "farces" (*naoju*) or "swindles" (*pianju*) (Wang Xiaoyu 2005). Wang Hui's rebuttal essay entitled "The Fantasy of Reality and the Reality of Fantasy" is equally fierce: "We need to ask him [Wang Xiaoyu] — What on earth does he want? What is his 'reality'? From the logic of his essay, his answer would be this existing 'order' and the 'procedures' that protect this 'order'!" Wang Hui avers that Wang Xiaoyu and other liberal intellectuals in mainland China such as Zhu Xueqin belong to the group of intellectuals whose only job is to protect the existing socio-political order, the group who jump up and stamp their feet (*tiaochulai duojiao*) only when the great leaders of such an order start to feel "uncomfortable": "When will these people feel comfortable? It is probably the time all critical intellectuals are expelled to that so-called 'fantasy' field. Only by so doing they can prove that their 'reality' is the only reality. [...] In terms of the perception of 'fantasy' and 'reality,' those people who accuse [the works of] 'critical intellectuals' as 'ultra-fantasy' indeed live in an entirely different reality from the one I live in." (Wang Hui 2005)

Although this extremely unfriendly exchange between Wang Xiaoyu and Wang Hui went nowhere except with the result that both authors became sworn enemies afterwards, it nonetheless shows that *the subjective "perception of 'fantasy' and 'reality'" is what drives contemporary Chinese intellectuals into engaging in fierce — sometimes even extremely nasty — debates.* As Žižek remarks, "Fantasy intervenes (serves as a support) precisely when we draw the line of distinction between what is merely our imagination and what 'really exists out there'" (Žižek 1999b: 122). When Wang Hui and Wang Xiaoyu both blamed each other for "lacking touch of reality," they equally viewed the other's problem (i.e. trapped in fantasy) *through their very own fantasy-windows.*[36] Accusing one's opponent of "lacking touch of reality" is a form of personal insult in Chinese intellectual debates.[37] It is this type of criticism that often elicits a nasty reply from the accused. Hence, debates are turned into "spitting wars." Today, intellectuals who belong to different camps are like combatants on a "battlefield" (see Davies 2007: 2–3, 11) who contend fiercely with each other over "Chinese problems" and "China's reality." In fact, I have often been reminded by intellectuals and scholars based in mainland China that in order to organize an academic conference (sometimes, even social events like a dinner), one must have a (frequently renewed) map of the current intellectual factions. This is in order to avoid inviting people who refuse to be in the same room with each other.

This type of hostility is not only the result of the conflicting fantasmatic visions about China's reality among Chinese intellectuals, but also that of intellectual work in China being frequently associated with a form of moral responsibility. As discussed earlier, the instrumentalist logic embedded in Chinese scholarship since its classic (Confucian) phase forms a moral confirmation of the need for intellectual work to guide social change. This moral dimension is represented in the Chinese intellectual tradition as the intellectuals' personal responsibility. Within such

[36] For a more detailed analysis of this debate between Wang Hui and Wang Xiaoyu, see Wu Guanjun 2006: 189–196.

[37] In fact, one of those critiques frequently made by mainland China-based authors against Anglophone Sinology and China studies, is also the latter's lack of concrete "sense" of China's reality. See, for example, Liu Dong 2001.

tradition, to engage in intellectual inquiry is not simply to provide excellent scholarship but to first and foremost see the correct way or truth (*Dao*). The same tradition also produces the deep belief that intellectual endeavors must achieve a harmonious congruence between the *Dao* of Heaven and the social order of humans. (The "modern mutation" of this belief is that intellectual endeavors must achieve China's perfection.) However, following Lacan and Žižek, it can be said that such a belief is actually nothing other than a fantasy: the goal that is proposed is nothing but a fantasmatic "promise." In this regard, there is truly a psychological ambivalence embedded in the Sinophone instrumentalist approach toward knowledge: though "ostensibly" taken as a tool to achieve the ideal order in congruence with *Dao* (or, to achieve China's perfection), however, knowledge (*sixiang* or *xueshu*) is nonetheless overwhelmingly used as an effective instrument for Chinese intellectuals to defend their own sense of reality, protecting themselves from the traumatic experience of *aphanisis* (subjective disintegration). In this sense, Chinese intellectual inquiry can be characterized as *altruistic and selfish at the same time*. This duality is suggested in the orthodoxy of Confucianism: the aim of intellectual and scholarly practice is not only to achieve the welfare for *Tianxia* (all under Heaven), but also to "settle down properly one's own lives" (*anshen liming*, a very commonly used Confucian phrase). This orthodox Confucian teaching thus already renders clear the characteristic ambivalence still embedded in contemporary Chinese intellectuality, namely, its altruistic morality's deep entwinement with the intimate fantasy that supports one's sense of reality.

Hence, Davies is certainly right when she observes that Chinese intellectuals "write as if they are representing the collective interests of the Chinese people rather than defending their own informed preferences" (Davies 2007: 20). Using a Lacanian perspective, one is further able to see that (1) the assumption of representing the interests of others enables Chinese intellectuals, at a profound psychological level, to regard their writings as the defense of "the truth," and more crucially that (2) their views of "China's reality" and the "correct way" ahead, far from being grounded in extralinguistic truth or *Dao*, are indeed entirely framed and sustained by their own fantasy. It is within the fantasmatic space that altruistic morality, in its most selfless form (e.g. worrying about China and the

Chinese people), directly coincides with its very obverse — the (inner) most selfish interest (e.g. protecting oneself from subjective disintegration). By targeting the operation of fantasy, psychoanalysis offers a useful tool in understanding the psychical features, obvious and hidden, of Chinese intellectuality. Such psychical features have so far not been discussed in studies of contemporary Chinese ideas.

Intellectual Inquiry from the "New Era" to the "Post-New Era"

In this section I will discuss briefly the theme of each chapter of book. During the 1980s cultural fever, intellectual inquiry reflected a largely univocal style. It was termed as the New Enlightenment movement because "May Fourth Enlightenment" was used as the model. The movement of the late 1910s and early 1920s was widely perceived as having a common anti-Confucian purpose. In the 1980s, however, it was Maoism (especially the radical ideas of the Cultural Revolution of the 1960s and 1970s) that was being opposed, not Confucianism. Hence, the various New Enlightenment intellectual projects were unified by a common anti-Maoist purpose.

However, something deeper unified the various intellectual activities — from the scientism-inspired *Towards the Future* book series, the *Culture: China and the World* (*Wenhua: Zhongguo yu shijie*) book series that featured various modern and contemporary Western ideas, to the activities of the Confucian-flavored "national studies" (*guoxue*) conducted by the Academy of Chinese Culture. From the viewpoint of Lacanian psychoanalysis, one could say that in the writings of the 1980s Chinese intellectual elite there was a shared idea that if people were liberated from the former ideal of the "socialist new man" (*shehuizhuyi xinren*) regarded now as a delusion, they would be able to see the true reality of China. "Descendants of the Dragon," one of the most popular songs in mainland China of the 1980s, reflects this assumption very well. In this song, China is depicted as a great dragon that has unfortunately been suffering from poor-sightedness for more than a century. One should bear in mind that "Enlightenment" is figuratively represented in Sinophone discourse as an act of seeing clearly: for both May Fourth Enlightenment and the 1980s New Enlightenment thinkers, "Enlightenment" is deemed as an urgent task in that a clear vision of China's reality is urgently needed. The lyrics of "Descendants of the Dragon" offer a coherent narrative which links those two moments together and constructs fantasmatically a Chinese past in which all those successive failures, from the military defeats of Qing Empire to those much more recent social catastrophes under Mao's rule, were caused by the lack of clear vision. The song suggests that, because of its poor-eyesight, China still has not yet been able to see clearly, and therefore not yet chosen the correct path for its future. Hence, the song ends with a passionate call for the great dragon to "rub and open its eyes," which strongly echoes the May Fourth call for acquiring an enlightened vision. I will discuss the lyrics of this pop song from a Lacanian psychoanalytic angle in Chapter 1.

The idea of "enlightening" China was mostly synonymous with "modernizing" China in the 1980s New Enlightenment discourse. The project had two aspects. The Party-state's official campaign of "four modernizations" was accompanied by the campaign for "cultural modernization" proposed by the participants of the New Enlightenment movement. The appearance of "unity" allowed intellectuals to imagine a "homogeneity of attitude"[38] among them. Despite the shared attempt of enlightening China's vision, Chinese intellectuals nonetheless do not share the same view about *what* should be seen after "the dragon rub and open its eyes." One can thus say that in the 1980s, the differences were concealed by the rhetoric of unity.

In recent years, this 1980s fantasy of officials, intellectuals and citizens working to realize a common modernization "dream" has been nostalgically recalled in the writings of several mainland intellectuals as a "golden age." This trend of reminiscing about the 1980s began in the mid-2000s and reached a peak with heated debates in 2006. Such writings were immediately called a "fever for the eighties" (*bashi niandai re*). As we all know, the expression "golden age" structurally entails the implication that such an "age" has long since gone. The "new era" under Deng Xiaoping's rule ended in the year 1989, and the post-Tiananmen era is very often

[38]As mentioned earlier, this influential phrase was first coined by Wang Hui in his early studies on the May Fourth movement. Later Xu Jilin borrowed it to characterize the 1980s New Enlightenment movement. See Xu Jilin 2000: 177.

referred to as the "post-new era" (*hou xin shiqi*) by Chinese intellectuals. Together with the blunt halt of the New Enlightenment movement after the Party-state's purge of the 1989 protest movement (during the Tiananmen protest the song "Descendants of the Dragon" became an anthem), the "homogeneity" among Chinese intellectuals also quickly ended.

In the early 1990s, the control over intellectual writings was much tighter than in the late 1980s. Under such an ideological atmosphere, some participants of the New Enlightenment movement started to reflect upon the proximity of intellectual work to socio-political transformations which have been featured in New Enlightenment writings, and suggested a separation of scholarly works from "vacuous" (*kongshu*) proposals for socio-political change, and correspondingly that intellectuals should withdraw themselves from contemporary debates over China's path or China's problems (i.e. from "worrying about China") and concentrate instead on the pursuit of scholastic research and the establishment of the system of "academic norms" (*xueshu guifan*), in order to "join rails" (*jiegui*) with the institutionally established model of Western intellectual inquiry. During the first few years of the 1990s, a series of scholastic journals were successively founded in mainland China including *Scholar* (*Xueren*), *China Social Sciences Quarterly* (*Zhongguo shehui kexue jikan*), *Scholarship Collection* (*Xueshu jilin*), *Original Studies* (*Yuanxue*). As this trend of professionalization of intellectual life was not a natural outcome of the development of Chinese intellectuality, it did not last very long. After Deng Xiaoping's "Tour of the South" (*nanxun*) in 1992, intellectuals embraced a gradual loosening of political controls, and the space for expression was reestablished. Although the topic of "June Fourth" was banned, there were heated discussions and debates over topics related to Chinese problems, China's reality and its perfection, and others such as the "loss of the humanistic spirit," "postmodernism," "globalization," "liberalism." There was also a call for academic standardization, and some reacted to it by describing the tendency as weakening intellectual life. For instance, the prominent New Enlightenment thinker Li Zehou claimed that what differentiates the early 1990s from the 1980s is that "thinkers fade out while academicians come to prominence" (*sixiangjia danchu, xuewenjia tuchu*), implying that the 1989 Tiananmen event killed not only students on the street, but also true Chinese thought, smothered intellectual praxis of any weight. This counter-movement of academic standardization and professionalization has clearly gained the upper hand since the late 1990s. Especially around 1998, intellectuals who publicly identified themselves as "liberals" (*ziyouzhuyizhe*) or "liberal intellectuals" (*ziyou zhishifenzi*) openly appealed for "bearing the torch of Enlightenment" and claimed that their intellectual endeavor was to carry on the unfinished project of Enlightenment and China's modernization.[39]

In fact, the discussions over the "loss of the humanistic spirit" (*renwen jingshen de shiluo*) initiated by several Shanghai-based intellectuals in 1994, already manifested a strong reaction against academic professionalization, as well as the related current of cultural commercialization. As Xu Jilin remarked in a 2003 essay, this discussion signifies an attempt "to reestablish the publicness of the intellectual and to reassert the intellectual's responsibility for guiding society" (quoting from Davies 2007: 90). In another essay penned earlier Xu directly commented on the professionalization of intellectual life: "Rather than public engagement they [the advocates of academic professionalization] preferred to find a peaceful niche as specialists within the disciplinary structure of the Party-state's academic establishment" (Xu Jilin 2000: 183). To comply with the Party-state's establishment is seen in post-Tiananmen Chinese intellectual sphere as a shameful moral corruption (during the debate between "liberals" and "New Leftists" in the late 1990s, both camps accuse their "discursive enemies" as defenders of the existing order).

As discussed above, embedded deeply in the self-understanding of contemporary Chinese thinkers, is the notion that intellectual works are not just mere knowledge production that can be developed into an industry in an institutionalized academic marketplace, but are also burdened with the urgent (and selfless) task of finding proper solutions to China's problems and shedding a light on the picture of a better future for the Chinese people. It is this unique intellectual tradition running deep over centuries in China which highlights a moral dimension of intellectual works that held back any trend of "joining rails" with the professionalism featured in Western humanities and social sciences and thus from blossoming in the

[39]The primary texts written in the early to mid-1990s by proponents of academic standardization can be found in Deng Zhenglai ed. 2010.

Chinese intellectual world. After this short debate over what Xu Jilin called the "rift between 'the engaged' and 'the academic'" had happened in the early 1990s, it is apparent that Chinese intellectual inquiry of the 1990s followed its own highly engaged tradition, though, after the "homogeneity of attitude" was out the picture, taking a completely different outlook from that of the 1980s.

In post-Tiananmen China, the question of which path China should take became much more urgent. The blood in the square made many participants of the New Enlightenment unable to keep their support to the official ideology of modernization. Quite a few intellectuals started to reflect the New Enlightenment project of China's modernization. For them the urgent questions are: Where would this ongoing "transformation" and official modernization campaign lead China to? What is the picture after China fully "modernizes" itself?

With this context, some intellectuals started to employ "postmodern" terms and jargons to depict the picture and claim an "end of modernity," while others sought to re-define modernization in much clearer and liberal-flavored terms, and openly appealing for constitutional rule, representative democracy, and human rights. In the view of these Chinese liberals, the New Enlightenment failed because it focused too much on "cultural" modernization instead of political modernization. In 1999, ten years after the June Fourth Tiananmen incident, the leading figure of Chinese liberal intellectuals, Li Shenzhi (1923–2003), who was a party official (Vice-President of the Chinese Academy of Social Sciences till 1989) and accompanied Deng Xiaoping on his visit to the U.S. serving as adviser to the delegation, even wrote a public letter to the then General Secretary of CCP Jiang Zemin immediately after the grand ceremony at Tiananmen Square celebrating the fiftieth anniversary of the People's Republic, urging him to be a "clear-sighted man" (*mingbai ren*) and use his power to install parliamentary democracy in China, as well as to allow non-party owned newspapers and opposition political parties to form (Li Shenzhi 1999). Meanwhile, a few other intellectuals (some also active participants of the 1980s New Enlightenment movement) started to turn their attention to various contemporary leftist or Marxist discourses and suggested alternative paths to embracing and merging into today's capitalist-inflected globalization. These intellectuals, because they all held a critical attitude towards liberal-flavored modernization and appealed for non-capitalist reform, were labeled by their "discursive enemies" as "New Leftists." In the historical and ideological context of mainland China, the term "New Leftist" implicates a compliance with Party theory, and thereby for those labeled by it, this term is associated with a strongly pejorative connotation. In order to avoiding being simply discredited as a return to Maoist politics, some of those intellectuals such as Wang Hui thus employed another term to refer to their group — "critical intellectuals" (*pipan de zhishifenzi*).

Besides those "postmodernist," "liberal," "New Leftist" discourses, the discourse of "nationalism" has been also very active since the mid-1990s. Though, as we discussed before, contemporary Chinese intellectual inquiry, generally speaking, is structured around a powerful nationalistic longing — a longing for the ultimate achievement of China's perfection (the fullness of Chinese civilization), the term "nationalism" in China however refers specifically to a type of discourse that attributes the causes of contemporary "Chinese problems" solely to the bullies from the West (primarily the U.S. and Japan) — e.g. its vicious ideological denigration or demonization of China, various implicit or explicit interventions, and so on. Intellectuals who publicly identify themselves with "Chinese nationalists" generally hold a vehemently hostile attitude towards the 1980s New Enlightenment intellectual enterprise as well as the discourse of liberalism of the 1990s, and characteristically advocate the empowerment of China from the angle of military (instead of cultural or political) modernization. Many extremely violent and vulgar linguistic deployments can be found in the discourse of "China's new nationalism" (to borrow Peter Gries' phrasing). In parallel to this rather vulgar trend of "new nationalism," there also emerged an "elite" discourse of "new Confucianism" (see Daniel A. Bell 2008), as well as the passionate appeal for the construction of China's "civilizational subjectivity." This intellectual trend, featured by fashionable terms such as "Chinese values," the "China way," the "China model," etc., has been extremely influential since 2003, a time that China's stunning economic development effectively propelled its "rise" as a new world power. Thus, in short, the unified (at least at an ostensible level) New Enlightenment movement of the 1980s was quickly replaced by various small, mutually hostile intellectual fractions in the following two decades.

In terms of the operation of Lacanian fantasy, these mutually hostile intellectual camps can be read as antagonistic attempts to repair or reinvent the fantasmatic frame that was severely damaged and sabotaged by the 1989 Tiananmen incident: while liberal intellectuals attempt to repair the old broken "modernization fantasy" by filling in a series of clearly-stated "liberal elements" such as constitutional rule, parliamentary democracy, market economy, etc., postmodernist intellectuals, and leftist "critical intellectuals" choose to reinvent — or in Cui Zhiyuan's term, "systematically renovate" (*zhidu chuangxin*) — the idea of modern China, attempting to create different new socio-political projects to achieve national perfection; exponents of China's "civilizational subjectivity," on the other hand, reject all together the horizon of "the modern" (modernization is disparaged as a "self-castrated" path), and suggest instead a "confident" return to China's culturo-civilizational *root* (*gen*, the Chinese character carrying an extra explicit connotation of male genital). Chinese intellectuality of the post-new era is characterized, from this Lacanian view, by antagonistic fantasies engaging in a fierce struggle for hegemony.

Žižek's elaboration of violent acts as a product of the collisions between fantasies is illuminating in understanding the extensive heatedness embodied in contemporary Chinese intellectual debates. In Chapter 2, I will explore the 1980s New Enlightenment enterprise of China's modernization. In Chapter 3, I will move to the discourse of "postmodernism" arising in Chinese intellectual arena in the mid-1990s via a detailed analysis of Chinese adoptions and interpretations of Richard Rorty's works. I will then devote myself in discussing in length about the debate between Chinese liberals and leftist critical intellectuals in Chapter 4. The post-Maoist trends of Chinese nationalism, in turn, constitute the object of my critical examination in Chapter 5. In Chapter 6, I will first investigate the discourse of China's civilizational subjectivity, then turn to a critical examination the recent "fever for the eighties" in the Chinese intellectual world.

Perhaps, the last topic requires further elucidation. As noted earlier, after many fierce fights filled with lots of personal attacks and condemnations against each other, quite a few eminent Chinese intellectuals (from both liberal and New Left camps) engaged passionately into a reminiscence of the "golden" 1980s. Whilst contemporary Chinese intellectuals seem unable to find a common fantasmatic ground to unify their "sense of reality" and their vision of China's "future" path, they choose instead to engage together in *fantasmatically constructing a "past" when they were united into one intellectual movement.* The reason I start my discussion about Chinese intellectual inquiry from the 1980s New Enlightenment movement and stop at the recent acts of reminiscing (fantasizing) the 1980s is the following one: the way Chinese intellectuals attempt to re-install and defend their sense of "reality" is very similar to the way they attempt to re-gain their access to the "past." It is the same psychical mechanism — the operation of fantasy in Lacanian psychoanalysis — that produces the following phenomenon in the Sinophone intellectual scene: whenever Chinese intellectuals tackle the issues over the "correct" path for China, it is always important for them to sort out at the same time a "correct" interpretation of China's historical past. An exemplary case which I will discuss in Chapter 2 is that the narrative of "modernization" characteristic of the 1980s New Enlightenment intellectual discourse, not only created a powerful scenario of China's ultimate perfection, but also functioned as the fantasmatic frame via which one is able to get "proper" access to China's past.

It is important to note here that although the space for intellectual discussion has been significantly enlarged in the post-Maoist era, publications remain under strict state censorship. Topics about China's present reality, as well as China's future path, are still highly politically sensitive. In some cases, the interpretation of China's historical past can also become sensitive and thus dangerous for intellectuals to write about. One recent case is the violent reaction of the Propaganda Department of the CCP Central Committee towards the Guangzhou-based historian Yuan Weishi's essay on modern Chinese history published in *Zhongguo qingnian bao* (*China Youth Daily*) in 2006, which led to the temporary ban of the journal and the dismissal of its two chief editors. In general, contemporary Chinese intellectuals are still continuously punished by the Party-state for writing and publishing their views in those sensitive "zones," ranging from being expelled from their institutions to being arrested and jailed. Some well-known examples include the Beijing-based political theorist Liu Junning who was expelled from the Chinese Academy of Social Sciences and prohibited from traveling abroad for his studies on liberalism as well as his public endorsement of liberal ideas in 2001; the Guangzhou-based economist and prominent public intellectual He Qinglian was fired by her former employer *Shenzhen fazhi bao* (*Shenzhen Legal Daily*) in 2000 for her critical observations of massive corruptions and other social problems and later left China for the U.S. in 2001, not to mention the total ban on dissidents such as Yu Jie for publicizing forbidden topics such as the June Fourth killings in Beijing, 1989.[40] Thus, one should, when discussing contemporary Chinese intellectual inquiry, bear in mind that it is produced under an authoritarian one-party rule that is still intolerant of dissenting voices, especially those of intellectuals. This is primarily because Chinese intellectuals still follow the Confucian teaching of assuming personal responsibility to search and adopt ideas in order to guide social change.

Hence, contemporary intellectuals, whether liberal, "New Left," or otherwise, still engage in a perilous enterprise, and some take the risk of offending the powerful. Under state policing, intellectuals' employment of heavy scholarly jargons and technical terms can also be read as a standard strategy to avoid censorship while maintaining their engagement in critical inquiry. Institutionally organized academic debates often serve in mainland China as a coded way to debate China's present reality and its future. From this angle, the appeals for "professionalization" in those years shortly after the massacre of June Fourth can also be read as Chinese intellectuals' attempt, in the darkest days of post-Maoist China, to retain some space for independent expression and academic autonomy.

I fully agree with Davies' argument that to simply dismiss those unique styles of contemporary Chinese intellectual writings from a supposedly professional or academic angle as "naïve," "unprofessional," or "inappropriate" to the task of critical inquiry, is to indeed "miss the crucial subtext of Chinese intellectual unease over a perceived widening gap between knowledge production and its immediate social relevance within the

[40]Following more than a year of house arrest, Yu Jie emigrated to the U.S. with his family in January 2012. Yu was arrested and allegedly tortured in 2010 for his friendship with Liu Xiaobo and a critical biography of Prime Minister Wen Jiabao entitled "China's Best Actor." Though having been awarded the 2010 Nobel Peace Prize, Liu Xiaobo is still in jail for his participation with the *Charter 08 manifesto*.

public sphere" (Davies 2001: 4, 11–12). After all, we have to understand that intellectual work for Chinese authors is not simply knowledge production, but much more importantly and intimately a fundamental way to, to recall the Confucian phrase, "settle down properly their own lives." This instrumentalist feature of Chinese intellectuality, approached from a Lacanian interpretation, reveals the fundamental role of fantasy in understanding Chinese reality.

Chapter 1

"Descendants of a Blurry-Eyed Dragon"

The Dragon That Lost Its Glory

By the late 1980s, a pop song called "Descendants of the Dragon" (*Long de chuanren*) had arguably become "the best-selling pop song ever marketed in China. Everyone knew the words."[1] Hou Dejian, the former Taiwanese pop star who wrote the song in the late 1970s, left Taiwan and went to live in mainland China in the early 1980s. This led the Taiwanese Government to ban his music. But in 1989, after the purge of the Tiananmen student protest movement in which "Descendants of the Dragon" became something of an anthem, Hou was expelled by the Chinese government back to Taiwan for his active participation in the movement. The lyrics of "Descendants of the Dragon" contain the following three verses:

> In the far east, there's a river;
> *Changjiang* (Yangtze River) is its name.
> In the far east, there's another river;
> *Huanghe* (Yellow River) is its name.
> Although I haven't seen the beauty of *Changjiang*,
> In my dreams I'm often sailing in its waters.
> Although I haven't heard the roar of *Huanghe*,
> In my dreams I often see its strong waves.
>
> In the ancient east flies a dragon;
> *Zhongguo* (China) is its name.
> In the ancient east resides a group of people;

---

[1] Quoted from the documentary film *The Gate of Heavenly Peace* (1995). The film transcripts are available online at <www.tsquare.tv/film/transjune2.html> (accessed on 12 March 2010).

They are all descendants of the dragon.
I grew up beneath the feet of the great dragon,
I'm a descendant of the dragon.
With black eyes, black hair and yellow skin,
I'm forever a descendant of the dragon.

It was one hundred years ago on a quiet night,
The deep dark night before the great changes.
The bursting rumble of guns and cannons broke the peace of the night.
What was besieged was a cowardly sword.
After so many years, the guns and bombs are still rumbling;
So many years and so many years more.
Great dragon, great dragon, please rub and open your eyes.
For now and ever more, open your eyes.
Great dragon, great dragon, please open your eyes.
For now and ever more, rub and open your eyes.[2]

Zhongguo, the "middle kingdom," has long been symbolized as the "(great) dragon" (*ju long*). "Descendants of the dragon" and the "sons and grandsons of the dragon" (*longzi longsun*) are idiomatic expressions in Chinese that remain popular to this day. As a traditional symbol for China, the dragon (*long*) in traditional Chinese culture is clearly not the image of the monstrous dragon in Western mythology. Rather, the Chinese *long* is a beneficent, immortal, omnipresent, and unconquerable beast, capable of plunging into watery depths, and soaring aloft to the highest heavens.[3]

[2]This is mostly my translation, in which a few lines were taken from the transcription of the documentary film *The Gate of Heavenly Peace*. (See <www.tsquare.tv/film/transjune2.html>)
[3]In the Introduction of *In The Eyes of the Dragon: China Views the World*, Yong Deng and Fei-Ling Wang describe the Chinese dragon in the following way, which can shed some light here in understanding it: "The dragon became the totem of the Chinese nation two thousand years ago at the latest. The dragon, as the Chinese interpret it, is an almighty, unpredictable, and eternal creature. It is not necessarily bad-tempered and is not an evil monster, as Europeans might believe. In appearance, the dragon is a mixture of boar, deer, lion, snake, horse, lizard, and fish." (Deng Yong and Wang Fei-Ling eds. 1999: 19; see also He Xin 1989) A succinct introduction of China's dragon culture and the evolution of the image of the Dragon in English can be found in Roy Bates 2002.

According to Sima Qian's *Historical Records* (*shiji*), Confucius once said to his disciples that:

> Of the bird, what I know is that it can fly; of the fish, that it can swim; of the quadruped, that it can walk. An animal that walks can be caught in a net; one that swims can be caught with a line; one that flies can be caught with an arrow attached to a wire. But of the Dragon, I can know nothing: supported by the wind and the clouds, it rises in to the sky... (Quoted in François Jullien 1995: 155)

The Chinese idea of the dragon, according to the influential philosopher and sinologist François Jullien, "symbolizes a dynamism never visible in concrete form and thus [is] unfathomable." It is the "Void" in the human world and the "Beyond" of the mundane order (Jullien 1995: 151, 161–162). Thus, the dragon in Chinese culture is regarded as an infinite, quasi-divine being, representing the highest good and sovereign power, to form a symbolic bridge between the Heaven and human beings. In short, it functions as a figurative representation of *Dao* or *Tian-Dao* (The Way of Heaven) in the popular culture. Thus, in the following, I will represent the dragon using the capital letter D for it shares the same cosmic importance as *Dao* and Heaven.

For these reasons, as Jullien argues, the "Dragon motif" of dynastic China — from the Qin era (221–206 B.C.E.) to the Qing era (1644–1911) — became symbolic of imperial rule, indicating the legitimate rule of *Tianxia* (all under Heaven). The national flag of the Great Qing Empire (used officially since 1888), the first national flag in China's history, is named "Yellow Dragon Flag" (*huanglong qi*) — a flag with a blue Dragon on plain yellow background, with a red pearl at the upper left corner. While yellow has long been the royal color of Chinese emperors (the legendary first emperor of China was known as the Yellow Emperor or *Huangdi*), the Dragon has been a symbol of the imperial power and strength (in Chinese culture a flaming pearl is frequently shown together with the Dragon, representing wealth, good luck, and prosperity).[4] Thus,

[4]I thank Josef G. Mahoney for bringing the national flag of the Qing Dynasty to my attention.

in dynastic China the Dragon was a reference to the Emperor, the Son of Heaven (*tianzi*) and, by extension, his empire; political legitimacy was understood in terms of acknowledging the Son of Heaven as "the true Dragon," reflected in the traditional saying — *zhenlong tianzi* (a true Dragon as the Son of Heaven). This means that the legitimate Emperor, symbolized as a true Dragon, is supposed to bring about a harmonious congruence between the ways of society and the Way of Heaven. Owing to its significance in the political symbolism of dynastic China, using the Dragon to refer to someone other than the reigning emperor or to a regime other than the ruling house was regarded as treason. According to recent literary studies, it was only from the early Republican era onwards that the traditional symbolism of *long* became adapted to represent China as a civilization.[5] Of course, this Dragon motif is also the cultural reason that many contemporary Chinese male movie stars feature the character *long* in their stage names, such as Li Xiaolong (known in the English speaking world as Bruce Lee and also as Lee Siu Loong), Zun Long (John Lone), Cheng Long (Jackie Chan), Di Long (Tommy Tam Fu-Wing), Shi Xiaolong (Ashton Chen), Liang Xiaolong, and so on. The use of the character *long* in the names of these movie stars implicitly engenders a sense of being the "master" (often, the "master" of Chinese martial arts).

Since the late 1970s, traditional symbols like the Dragon, the Yellow River, the Yangtze River and the Great Wall have gradually replaced the symbols of Marxism–Leninism. The symbolism of the Maoist era such as the Little Red Book has long been commercialized. To many Chinese, the song "Descendants of the Dragon" that has become highly popular since the 1980s is a celebration of their historical and cultural uniqueness. That is, the song is about being Chinese. The lyrics of the song explicitly carry a dense agglomerate of national pride — "China" is (the name of) *the* great Dragon, and the Chinese people today are still the descendants of the Dragon. The song also suggests that China was once and will be again a

[5]For example, in his essay entitled "There is no doubt that we are descendants of the Dragon," the Beijing-based literary critic Duan Baolin points out that "Since the 1911 revolution, the image of the Dragon has ultimately freed itself from the feudalist fetter. 'Descendants of the Dragon' thus became the symbol for Chinese identity and has done so ever since." (Duan Baolin 2002: 130)

great civilization, as long as it awakens to its true nature. The figure of the Dragon is used to suggest an eternal, quasi-divine being, which indicates the greatness of the Chinese civilization. The expression that "we are descendants of the Dragon" thus reflects *a deep longing for a Chinese identity imagined as whole and consistent.* Hence, an old nationalistic theme, drawn on the Republican use of the Dragon to symbolize Chinese civilization, is revived in Hou's song. We should note that this return to traditional themes effectively bypasses Mao Zedong and the revolutionary images of the Maoist era.

One of the most interesting characteristics about this song is that it was originally written by an artist who was born in Taiwan. Hou Dejian offers three reasons in the lyrics as to why he, as well as many Taiwanese, should be considered as legitimate "descendants of the Dragon": First, as he puts it, Hou grew up "beneath the feet of the Great Dragon," a reference to his birth in Taiwan, an island to the southeast of mainland China (thus the Yangtze River and Yellow River are not far away…). Second, Hou writes of sharing the same genetic features with people living in mainland China — "black eyes, black hair and yellow skin." Hou's lyrics emphasize the importance of the shared cultural memory of people living in Taiwan and mainland China in the form of historical events that happened "a hundred years ago on a quiet night." Hou is referring to the Western military invasions of China during the Opium Wars (1839–1842). He also implies, through lines such as "after so many years, the guns and cannons are still blaring," that things still remain somewhat unchanged even in the present — because China is still not *fully itself* in a world dominated by the West. The strong sentiments of racial belonging in Hou's song, to a large extent, are produced by recalling historical humiliations inflicted on China since the Opium Wars. Thus, the song encourages the people of Taiwan and mainland China to work towards the common aim of awakening themselves: because their shared history is one of defeat and humiliation, they must reclaim the power of the "Great Dragon."

Owing to the popularity of "Descendants of the Dragon," Hou Dejian received a very warm welcome when he first visited China. In 1983, *Outlook Weekly* (*Liaowang*), a politically influential magazine owned by *Xinhua News Agency* (*Xinhuashe*), published a special essay to welcome Hou Dejian's "return" to China. The essay, titled "A 'Descendant of the Dragon' Returns to the Homeland of the Dragon," begins with words of passion:

> The heartfelt voice (*xinsheng*) of all Chinese people can be heard in "Descendants of the Dragon." Today, this song has already become extremely popular in Taiwan, Hong Kong, and mainland China, as well as in all other places where "descendants of Emperor Yan and Emperor Huang" (*Yan Huang zisun*) dwell. (Tang Hua and Chen Lian 1983: 14–15)

Though Hou was expelled from mainland China after 1989, his song has not been banned. This is surprising as it was frequently sung by the protesting students on Tiananmen Square in 1989. To this day, it is still highly popular and often sung as part of official or civic festive celebrations. Also, many pop stars such as Tan Yonglin, Wang Lihong, have chosen to record their versions of this song in the 1990s and 2000s.

Expressions such as "rubbing and opening one's eyes" from the song form part of what Gloria Davies describes as "a Sinophone vocabulary of national empowerment." A powerful instance of this vocabulary is Mao Zedong's famous announcement that "The Chinese people have stood up" (*Zhongguo renmin zhanqilaile*) at the founding moment of the People's Republic of China. Mao meant that the history of China's defeat and humiliation was over and that China had regained its power. The popularity of Hou Dejian's "Descendants of the Dragon," in this regard, can be seen as a symbolic manifestation of a need to re-invent in the post-Maoist era a "new vocabulary of national empowerment." Especially, at the time when protesting students sang "Descendants of the Dragon" in 1989, they were opposing the Chinese government and were calling on the government to introduce reforms to strengthen the nation. The song's call for urgent action — "rubbing and opening one's eyes" has since become an integral part of the Sinophone vocabulary of national empowerment.

Hou Dejian's "Descendants of the Dragon" was by no means the only bestselling nationalistic pop song in post-Maoist China. "The Great Wall Will Never Fall" (*Wanli Changcheng yong budao*) was also very popular in the 1980s. This song shares much of the symbolism of "Descendants of the Dragon" and includes such lines as: "After sleeping deeply for hundreds of years, the Chinese people have gradually awakened. Oh please, open your eyes, and look carefully"; "The Great Wall will never fall, the water of Yellow River will always flow." It explicitly calls for "China's resurgence" and states that China "does not look like it has already caught a severe disease."

The historical theme of China's former humiliation and defeat in both these songs is intended to urge the Chinese people to attain clear-sightedness and to recover China's lost glory. Another highly popular song "My Chinese Heart" (*Wo de Zhongguo xin*) asks people to develop a sense of cultural pride. The lyrics state that "Although I wear Western-style clothes, my heart remains a Chinese heart. Every inch of my body has been branded by my ancestors with the stamp of China." The reference to "Western-style clothes" implies that the Chinese people are still borrowing from the West and that people have yet to fulfill the wishes of their "Chinese heart." The song "My Chinese Heart," like the other two songs discussed earlier, also uses such symbols as the Great Wall, the Yangtze River and the Yellow River to represent China. These are symbols of grandeur that *project an image of an eternal China*. They thus imply that China "will never fall" as long as one continues to remain faithful to China. Another interesting feature worth noting is that these songs were all originally written and sung by Taiwan and Hong Kong pop stars before they became extremely popular in mainland China. In this regard, the sense of cultural pride that these songs convey appears to be shared across the Chinese-speaking world.

As an image, the "awakened Great Dragon" derives from the vocabulary of national awakening of the late nineteenth and early twentieth centuries. It has remained popular to this day. In fact, the expression in Hou's song of "rubbing and opening one's eyes" echoes the call of the late Qing scholar-official Wei Yuan (1794–1857) that the Chinese should "open their eyes to see the world" (*fangyan kan shijie*). Wei's phrase remained popular throughout the twentieth century. It is not surprising that Hou's song has become so popular since the 1980s, a time when mainland China started to separate itself radically from its Maoist period and undergo enormous social and economic changes.

From 1978 onwards, Chinese intellectuals were able to publish much more of their opinions and concerns. According to the Shanghai-based historian Xu Jilin, the year 1984 marked "the appearance of a public intellectual sphere" owing to the fact that several intellectual groups and organizations were established in that year (Xu Jilin 2000: 173–174). In the enormous number of publications that Chinese intellectuals produced in the mid- to late 1980s as part of what came to be called "cultural fever" or "New Enlightenment," phrases such as "rubbing one's eyes," "awakening," "opening one's eyes," and "seeing with new eyes," made a frequent appearance. There was also a deliberate attempt to recall the language of the 1920s, or the discourse of May Fourth intellectuals. The term "New Enlightenment" is a direct echo of the importance that May Fourth intellectuals accorded to the notion of enlightenment. Writing nostalgically of the 1980s New Enlightenment movement, Xu Jilin remarks that it "in some ways was another 'May Fourth', but of course a contemporary one." Xu also notes that "in fact, some participants in the New Enlightenment were to employ just such a transhistorical evocation when they claimed that their efforts in the 1980s were a revivification of the May Fourth era." Xu points out in the same article that after Fourth June 1989, Chinese intellectual life changed dramatically. Thus, he distinguishes between two phases of post-Maoist intellectual discourse: (1) the New Enlightenment discourse of the 1980s which Xu characterizes as showing a "homogeneity of attitude" (*taidude tongyixing*), and (2) the post-1989 range of writings that reflect a discourse of what Xu calls "divergence" (*fenhua*). It is, in Xu's view, the "homogeneity of attitude" that made intellectual activities in the 1980s a rather unified "movement." And by "divergence" Xu means the disappearance or destruction of this "homogeneity of attitude" among Chinese intellectuals in the post-Tiananmen 1990s. As he writes: "A unified intellectual sphere in which people can engage in profitable dialogue no longer exists. The consensus of the New Enlightenment has collapsed, very much in the way that it did during the original May Fourth movement." According to Xu, this "homogeneity of attitude" characteristic of the New Enlightenment discourse of the 1980s first and foremost manifests itself in a commonly shared desire to "revaluate all values." This form of revaluation also reflects the popularity of philosophical language in the 1980s. Xu argues that the 1980s intellectual discourse can be viewed as a relatively unified movement insofar as its producers all genuinely believed that they should assist in China's modernization (Xu Jilin 2000: 169, 176–177, 181, 186). In this regard, even though the concept of

New Enlightenment was being expressed in the philosophical terms of a radical revaluation of all values, it reflected the same idea that was expressed in Hou Dejian's pop song of getting the Great Dragon to "rub and open its eyes."

In those reminiscent discussions in the 2000s by intellectuals who were active during the 1980s, expressions involving an act of "seeing (clearly)" remain in frequent use. For instance, the Beijing-based philosopher Xu Youyu recently wrote nostalgically about the 1980s: "At that time, everyone saw the similarity between the 1980s and the May Fourth era, and engaged him or herself in the new cultural movement and the pursuit of Enlightenment." Xu explicitly notes that "our plan was to first open our eyes widely to see the world as it really was, and then to devote ourselves to studying China" (Xu Youyu 2006). Liu Zaifu, a leading figure of the 1980s New Enlightenment movement who went to the U.S. after 1989, avers that the most important change that happened in China during the 1980s was that "China started to face the world with new eyes and with a new attitude." According to Liu, what the 1980s New Enlightenment movement produced was "a great cultural legacy, namely, the soul that makes the Chinese nation shine again with vigor" (Liu Zaifu 2006). One can see from these recent statements that nearly two decades after the 1980s New Enlightenment movement, prominent participants such as Xu Youyu and Liu Zaifu still place the emphasis on getting the Chinese people to "open their eyes." They also believe that the New Enlightenment is an unfinished project which intellectuals must continue to shoulder as their responsibility: this is evident in their use of phrases such as "opening one's eyes," or "seeing with new eyes." Liu is especially keen to promote a collective will — a "soul" (*linghun*) — developed out of the 1980s New Enlightenment, and his vision of the Chinese nation as one that will "shine again with vigor" indicates how clearly he imagines such a collective will. The explicit use of phrases related to clear-sightedness in these recent statements by prominent intellectuals shows the continued significance of this type of wording.

Suffice it to say that from the May Fourth era onwards, in Sinophone critical inquiry, "Enlightenment" (*qimeng*) has often been reified metaphorically into an act of "seeing clearly." The question is: Why is it necessary for the Chinese people to "see clearly"? To return to the song

"Descendants of the Dragon" as an exemplary popular instance of Sinophone Enlightenment discourse, the first thing we should note is that Enlightenment presupposes a preceding state of blindness or myopia, a loss of the clear-sightedness. Thus, because the Dragon (as China and the Chinese people) *lacks* clear vision, it must seek to become conscious of "blind zones" in its horizon and then proceed to remove the obstacles that prevent it from seeing things clearly. The same idea, transposed into an intellectual idiom, becomes the call to "revaluate all values."[6] This Nietzschean slogan in China is, in an interesting way, tightly associated with Enlightenment discourses (both May Fourth and New Enlightenment discourses) featured by the act of "opening eyes and seeing clearly." That is to say, for Enlightenment intellectuals, to revaluate all values (Maoist-socialist values, Confucian values, etc.) is to see clearly.

Moreover, because the Dragon must rub and open its eyes in order to see things clearly, this symbol for the Subject (as Chinese civilization) is depicted as being in a dysfunctional state. Thus, a remedy is urgently needed. In this sense, what "being Chinese" (being "descendants of the Dragon") involves is not merely a demand for international recognition of Chinese identity (whether conceived of as national or cultural), but also a commitment to rescuing China (as the Great Dragon) from its current dysfunctional state.[7] Thus, people exhort each other to achieve national and civilizational perfection in order to return China to its former greatness. In this regard, the Sinophone discourse of Enlightenment turns on the metaphysical presupposition that there is a Chinese essence to which one can remain true. It is in this way that the Enlightenment discourse can posit this presumed genuine Chinese nature as something lost that needs to be recovered. For this reason, the discourses of the May Fourth era and the 1980s share the same assumption that China is in a dysfunctional state.

---

[6]The Beijing-based philosopher Zhou Guoping's book on Nietzsche had great influence on the 1980s cultural discussion. This also made Zhou a leading figure in the New Enlightenment intellectual movement (see Zhou Guoping 1986).

[7]This sense of China being in a dysfunctional state is reflected not only in pop songs such as "Descendants of the Dragon," but also very powerfully in the official national anthem — "March of the Volunteers" (*Yiyongjun jinxingqu*), whose lyrics announcing that "the Chinese nation has arrived at its most perilous time."

In her recent work, Gloria Davies describes contemporary Chinese intellectual discourse as acts of worrying about China, of "worrying about problems that prevent China from attaining perfection, not only as a nation, but also as an enduring civilization" (Davies 2007: 1). Through a thorough examination of post-Maoist Sinophone inquiry (form the 1980s to 2000s) with a focus on its linguistic characteristics, Davies notes that in this discourse

> China [is] imagined as something that is constitutive of the self as well as being the "home" that one seeks through language to renovate, reconstruct, or strengthen in any number of ways. This metaphysical presupposition is one that many Chinese intellectuals imbibe when they describe their inquiry in terms of fulfilling an obligation to their nation or their culture of China, as if these terms constitute a spiritual "presence" dependent on the toil of intellectuals for its ongoing maintenance and ultimate perfection: a presence imagined as the eventual return to civilizational grandeur. (Davies 2007: 20)

I would like to further add that "Enlightenment" in Sinophone critical inquiry presumes clear-sightedness in order that people can see and understand what "being Chinese" means. The Dragon motif is symbolically powerful in popular Chinese culture for the same reason. This is because the immortal, omnipresent, and quasi-divine character of the Dragon as *long* allows China to be extolled as such a metaphysical "presence." Similarly, in Sinophone critical discourse, as Davies points out, there is a similar desire to envisage "a genuine China that awaits discovery or rediscovery." Davies contrasts contemporary Sinophone critical inquiry to its Anglophone counterpart — what she calls "the self-reflexive form of EuroAmerican critical inquiry" exemplified by Jacques Derrida's critique of the "metaphysics of presence." In this context, with regard to Sinophone inquiry, Davies observes a "characteristic indifference to the metaphysics inherent in anticipating a truth to be 'discovered' about China." The metaphysical presupposition of Sinophone inquiry is precisely that there is "a truth to be 'discovered' about China." The longing for clear-sightedness — to see clearly China's true nature — constitutes the very core of "being Chinese" today, as Davies puts it, "the metaphysics of 'being Chinese' conjures up China as a powerful metaphysical presence — the object of inquiry and perfection," as if it were "a self-evident entity" (Davies 2007: 20–40).

This unique character of Chinese Enlightenment — the Sinophone preoccupation with "recovering" or "discovering" the original, authentic nature of China — leads to what Davies calls "an instrumentalist logic" prevailing in Sinophone mode of inquiry: ideas and theories, especially Western ones, are reduced to tools to serve the purpose of advancing China's civilizational perfection. According to Davies, "habits of writing that evolved out of worrying about China have resulted in a discourse dominated by formulations that are aimed at evaluating the pros and cons of particular sets of ideas in the common higher interest of improving Chinese society and culture." Davies traces this "instrumentalization of theories" back not only to China's most prominent modern writer Lu Xun who, when talking about adopting foreign ideas in his famous text titled "Appropriatism" in 1934, urged his readers to choose only those ideas that were suitable for the national interest, but also to the *Mencius*, which proposed the influential Confucian idea of knowing "what to adopt, what to discard" (*qushe*). Since the 1980s, various Western ideas and theories — ranging from modernization theories to postmodernism — have been introduced to the Sinophone world when they are viewed by Chinese intellectuals as useful in advancing China's national and civilizational perfection (Davies 2007: 11, 24, 30, 192).

This "habitual appropriation of Western theory in the instrumentalist sense of its value to Chinese thought" observed by Davies has been a distinctive feature of Sinophone inquiry from the 1910s till the present day. Contemporary Chinese intellectual praxis is still fundamentally dominated by the *telos* of reviving China's civilizational grandeur (Davies 2007: 8). After 1989, even those who have expressed themselves as critical opponents of the 1980s New Enlightenment discourse still nonetheless affirm their passionate desire to resuscitate China's lost glory. For example, Wang Hui, an influential Beijing-based historian who was one of the New Enlightenment intellectuals in the 1980s and viewed as a leading figure of the "New Left" camp since the late 1990s, explicitly speaks about such a desire: "I rejoice that I was born in China since what could be more heartbreaking and also more exhilarating than the glorious revival of a decaying civilization of which so many generations of people have dreamed? And what could be more thrilling than to watch and experience the minutiae and process of this collective dream?" (Wang Hui 1994: 21–22; translation quoted from Davies 2007: 53) There is a clear resonance between this intellectual attitude and such phrases as "we are descendants of the Dragon," keen to show "[our] Chinese heart." In fact, Wang also notes that "I believe that the glorious revival of Chinese civilization relies on the rational efforts of several generations" (Wang Hui 2000b: 473). Though Wang has been highly critical of the 1980s New Enlightenment movement, his post-1989 writings nonetheless still move within the teleological horizon of Sinophone Enlightenment discourse, which reflects the metaphysical presupposition that there is a truth to be discerned about China and that it is only through having clear-sightedness that one would be able to contribute to "the glorious revival of Chinese civilization." Hence, although there are clear differences between 1980s Chinese intellectual discourse and the discourse of the 1990s and 2000s, both nonetheless share two presuppositions.

These presuppositions are: (1) there is an essential truth about China — a metaphysics of "being Chinese" — and it is the role of the intellectuals to attempt to draw ever closer to that truth in their writings; (2) this presumed truth about China has been lost and has yet to be "recovered" or "discovered." As I have noted, the same presuppositions are also implicit in such pop-songs as "Descendants of the Dragon." In likening Chinese intellectual discourse to the lyrics of a pop song, I am not trying to denigrate the ideas that have been produced. Rather, I am attempting to highlight the prevalence of the desire within Chinese society for China's national or civilizational renaissance.

The point to be made is that the idea of such a metaphysical "presence" acquires symbolic power through written works, pop songs, and films. In other words, ideas like China's true nature or the essence of Chinese culture are always imaginary. They are products of fantasy (in Jacques Lacan's use of this term) that are constructed retroactively. Of the two presuppositions discussed above, the second one needs the first one as its necessary condition. So, if this shared belief that China was and still is by its very nature "great" is merely a fantasy retroactively constructed, we then need to reconsider what "being Chinese" means today. In contemporary Sinophone discourse, "being Chinese" is presented *metaphysically*, and in turn involves a task of, to recall Wang Hui's words, achieving the "glorious revival of Chinese civilization" through the "efforts of several generations."[8] But what if this metaphysics of "being Chinese" can only ever remain a mere fantasmatic construction?

The Fantasmatic Core of Clear-Sightedness

So far, we have seen that to be Chinese involves, as the song "Descendants of the Dragon" indicates, a commitment to the goal of making China great again in a world in which China's civilizational superiority is no longer acknowledged. In the song, the act of "rubbing and opening one's eyes" (enlightening oneself and revaluating one's values) is supposed to achieve "clear-sightedness." This, however, also implies that there is a "blind zone" in the Dragon's present field of vision preventing it (and its descendants) from seeing properly. Moreover, since it is the Chinese people who make up the Dragon, the song suggests that *everyone* will see *the same reality if they were to achieve enlightened vision*. This presupposition reflects a desire to capture the ultimate truth by means of which one can "revaluate all values" in aid of China's national empowerment, and this was a desire that many Chinese intellectuals expressed in their writings, especially in the 1980s. To achieve national and civilizational perfection is at the core of the Sinophone Enlightenment discourse, and broadly speaking, Chinese critical inquiry in general. "This national-culturalistic tendency of Chinese critical inquiry is," as Davies observes, "deeply haunted by the rhetoric of awakening to the pain and fear of cultural and spiritual loss that the language of worrying about China has produced since the Opium Wars." Even in the post-Tiananmen intellectual discourse

[8]Richard Rorty's thought offers a different way of "being Chinese" (being "ethnocentric"): instead of a *metaphysical* way, there is a *pragmatic* way of being Chinese, which does not rely on any metaphysical "foundation," or "essence." However, this post-foundational ("post-philosophical") approach of Rorty's is highly incompatible with Sinophone preference on "linguistic certitude," and thus attracted vehement rejection when introduced into the Chinese intellectual world. I will discuss in detail the Chinese reception of Rorty's thought in Chapter 3.

characterized by what Xu Jilin calls "divergence," most Chinese intellectuals remain deeply proud of being Chinese and regard themselves as having the responsibility of recovering China's lost greatness. Sharing this passionate desire to perfect China — "a powerful desire to produce a new or originary truth about China," as Davies puts it, post-1989 Chinese intellectuals nonetheless "have come to be divided over the proper way ahead for China's perfection." Thus, it is appropriate to describe the key characteristic of contemporary (post-Maoist) Sinophone critical inquiry as showing a metaphysical presupposition that there is a truth to be discovered about China (Davies 2007: 30–31, 43). I will discuss the ways in which participants in the 1980s intellectual movement identified their pursuit of truth as a continuation of the May Fourth intellectual legacy of the 1910s and 1920s in Chapter 2, and those post-1989 intellectual disputes over finding the correct way forward in Chapters 3 to 6. For now, I will focus on how this "powerful desire to produce a new or originary truth about China" functions in Sinophone intellectual discourse.

The pop song "Descendants of the Dragon" remains my primary text for analysis, mainly because of its huge influence in contemporary China. The song's popularity makes it a useful device for examining what the Lacanian philosopher Slavoj Žižek calls the relationship between fantasy and (what we experience as) "reality."

Let us get acquainted once again with the basic contour of Lacanian thought and the psychoanalytic conceptions of fantasy and reality. A basic premise of Lacanian psychoanalysis is that there is no way for the subject to have direct access to Reality as such (which Lacan calls "the Real"). According to Lacan, people cannot "see" anything unless they are provided with a frame that structures the whole configuration of what is to be "seen." This frame is what Lacan terms "fantasy." Lacanian theorists also often use the term "the fundamental fantasy" to refer to the kind of primordial narrative that structures and guarantees people's access to something called "reality," which is not the Real, but dependent on a given structure of seeing. As Stavrakakis puts it, "reality is articulated at the symbolic level and the symbolic is lacking; reality can only acquire a certain coherence and become desirable as an object of identification, by resorting to fantasy" (Stavrakakis 1999: 46). Fantasy plays a fundamental role in constructing "reality" and creating the necessary illusion of the world as a well-structured Whole. It is such fundamental fantasy that enables people to imagine that they occupy the same "reality."

In the Maoist era, the CCP was successful in providing people with a fundamental "dream." This was a fantasmatic scene that allowed people to translate their words and deeds into "revolutionary" acts that they could then imagine as contributing to the perfection of a communist society in which all problems of exploitation and oppression will have been resolved. In short, it promised metaphysically China's perfection (at least in the foreseeable future). However, the violence that accompanied the promotion of Mao's revolutionary path led to its rapid disintegration after Mao's death in 1976. The popularity of the pop song "Descendants of the Dragon" in mainland China in the 1980s is representative of the type of fantasmatic narrative that appealed to Chinese people in the post-Maoist era. It was a way of bypassing the Cultural Revolution era to affirm Chinese cultural identity through recalling historical scenes of national humiliation. Expressions such as "After so many years, the guns and cannons are still rumbling," thus form part of the symbolic coordinates of the Chinese people's experience of a shared reality. What is important to note about this symbolism is that it revolves around the attempt to fill a gap and to heal a trauma in Chinese culture, figured as the blurry-eyed Dragon.

According to Lacanian psychoanalysis, the traumatized person is drawn to fantasize in order to cope with the traumatic experience. In simplest terms, a happy person tends to see life or reality as complete while a traumatized person will tend to see gaps or a lack of coherence in their life. Lacanian psychoanalysis allows us to posit that "reality" is the effect of some or other fantasy at work, and that it is only when a trauma occurs that the traumatized person deviates from his/her fantasmatic vision which has previously endowed him/her with access to see "reality." As long as the fantasy works, the fissures of "reality" can remain concealed, and the person who has not experienced a trauma has no need to question what he takes to be real. Let me here extend Žižek's Lacanian reading of Soviet society to China under Mao. The fantasy of achieving communist perfection was not only an inspiration for the majority of Chinese people in the 1950s but considered to be *the* future reality that people were working towards. When the gap between people's everyday lives and Party doctrine grew too big, the fantasy could no longer be sustained. So what matters is not whether this act of fantasizing can ultimately bring curing effects, since none of us has access to "the Real" as such, but *what type of fantasy is being promoted in the name of enlightened vision.*

In brief, fantasy is not opposed to "reality." Fantasy is not an imaginary scene functioning as an "exit" for people to "escape" from the "raw reality." On the contrary, it is the vista *enabling* people to "see" and claim a reality. As Žižek writes,

> With regard to the basic opposition between reality and imagination, fantasy is not simply on the side of imagination; fantasy is, rather, the little piece of imagination by which we gain access to reality — the frame that guarantees our access to reality, our "sense of reality" (when our fundamental fantasy is shattered, we experience the "loss of reality") (Žižek 1999b: 122).

What this means is that without a fundamental "fantasy frame," people are left with no access to "reality" at all. In the years immediately after Mao's death, there was a rapid dismantling of "Mao Zedong Thought" and related ideas such as the "socialist new man." Within mainland China, the call for "rubbing and opening one's eyes" put forward in the pop song "Descendants of the Dragon" became an implicit reference to the end of the Maoist era. It was an appeal to the "descendants of the Dragon" to replace Mao's socialist vision with a different fantasmatic vision of China, one that would accord with the economic reforms introduced under Deng Xiaoping's leadership. Thus, as "socialism with Chinese characteristics" was being promoted, a new fantasy was being constructed through words and images. As Žižek writes, "far from simply deranging/distorting the 'proper balance of things,' fantasy at the same time *grounds* every notion of the balanced Universe" (Žižek 2000: 86).

In this regard, people are always doomed to be "poor-sighted": without the corrective lenses of the fundamental fantasy, they cannot "see" at all. Thus Žižek asserts that people can only "look awry" — that is, they cannot see reality as such. Reality is possible *only because of the "blind spot" in one's vision.* The belief that with enlightened eyes, we can see reality clearly for what it is, is fantasy at its purest. Owing to the fact that people cannot communicate their experience of reality without recourse to language, Lacan uses the term "the Symbolic" or "the symbolic order" to designate what we perceive as "reality," and the term "the Real" to designate the domain of whatever subsists outside symbolization (one can also understand "the Real" as "experience" prior to language). The Symbolic cancels out the Real and creates what we experience as "reality," i.e. a universe which is named and ciphered by language and can thus be thought, interpreted ("deciphered"), talked about, and shared through acts of communication. To "understand" is a phenomenon located within the horizon of an already meaningful "reality." Thus, symbolization is the process by means of which reality "becomes what it is" (Žižek 1996: 226). By becoming "speaking beings," we lose our access to the Real, which only manifests itself when "our sense of reality" is in crisis. Encountering the Real is the moment of trauma. Sean Homer offers a concise explanation of this close relationship between the Real and trauma, "[T]rauma is *real* insofar as it remains unsymbolizable and is a permanent dislocation at the very heart of the subject. The experience of trauma also reveals how the real can never be completely absorbed into the symbolic, into social reality. No matter how often we try to put our pain and suffering into language, to symbolize it, there is always something left over. In other words, there is always a residue that cannot be transformed through language. This excess, this 'X' as Lacan will call it, is the real." (Homer 2005: 84)

In comparing contemporary Chinese critical inquiry with its EuroAmerican counterpart, Gloria Davies observes that what prevails in the former is "a general Sinophone preference for certitude in the use of language (demonstrable, among other things, in the frequent recourse to axiomatic statements), which lies at odds with the contemporary Anglophone emphasis on linguistic contingency (or the ways in which statements relate to other statements rather than to meanings, truth or a reality 'out there')." Contemporary EuroAmerican approaches (Lacanian theory included) to critical inquiry are basically a product of what has been generally called "the linguistic turn" in humanities and social sciences. As Davies writes: "The linguistic turn in late twentieth-century EuroAmerican scholarship was effected by individuals who interrogated, in the discourses of different disciplines, the ways in which institutionalized habits of speaking and writing came to shape what we are accustomed and primed to receive and (re)produce as 'knowledge'." However, as Davies continues to point out, contemporary Sinophone inquiry is nonetheless still dominated by what can be properly described as "linguistic certitude," by which she means "an *effect* of assuming that one 'knows what the words mean' and relies on the presupposed correspondence of word to thing": Chinese writers are still writing in such a way "as if the words that one enlists for the description of things and feelings, or indeed 'reality,' carry an inherent truth that must be restored against the adverse influence of the 'wrong' kinds of ideas." "[T]his style of writing," as per Davies, "presupposes in positivistic fashion that the gap between language and reality, or between word and thing, could be progressively narrowed by the use of ever-more precise formulations" (Davies 2007: 26, 238, 11, 101). The gap between language and reality (or in Lacanian jargons, between the Symbolic and the Real) is often regarded as merely a technical problem in the writings of contemporary Chinese intellectuals.

What, then, fundamentally supports this positivistic logic of Sinophone inquiry? Here, Lacanian psychoanalysis stands out from other EuroAmerican approaches in providing critical insights, for the dual structure of language and reality is not what Lacan was willing to settle.

As discussed earlier, the Lacanian response to this question is the projection of fantasy that supports symbolization. It is fantasy that sutures this irreducible gap between the field of signification and the Real (the unrepresentable X, that which is beyond signification), and supports the positivistic view of reality. In this regard, we must note, following Žižek, that the symbolic order ("reality") is *a priori* "not all," which means, there is always some unfathomable (thus horrifying) Thing outside the realm of the Symbolic, resisting symbolization. Reality is always *lacking*. The Real takes the form of a "blind spot" in the subject's vision of "reality," which becomes revealed in a crisis. This is because the "blind spot" marks out the inconsistencies of the symbolic order. Fantasy, on the other hand, is the very defensive device that prevents such "blind spots" from being encountered. Through the operation of fantasy the gap between signification and the Real is effectively concealed, covered up. Fantasmatic narratives do not have to be "beatific" (e.g., life is meaningful, certain; my works have purpose; tomorrow will be another beautiful day; etc.). On the other hand, it can well include — like many Hollywood science-fiction films did — the horrifying, disturbing Thing, for the very act of including the disturbing elements in the imaginary scenario, rendering them with ghostly images, horrifying stories, etc., is precisely an effective operation to cover up "blind spots." Within such fantasmatic space the unfathomable *is* being symbolized (images, stories); hence, with the support of fantasmatic narratives, nothing is radically *alien* (to recall the famous movie series) any more. That is also why Sinophone inquiry featured by "linguistic certitude" entails structurally a fantasmatic supplement. Davies is right to argue: "What the articulation of a particular set of 'Chinese problems' provides is an ordering of reality within the framework of these problems, rather than an omniscient revelation of *reality* as such" (Davies 2007: 40). What I would like to further add in this argument is that fantasy is the very device that enables — indeed, frames — a particular way to perceive "Chinese problems" (e.g. as "problems" caused by the intrusions of the West). What I call the "Great Dragon fantasy," in this sense, has been playing a fundamentally crucial role in the production of post-Maoist Chinese intellectual discourse. Although the "Great Dragon fantasy" includes intensely traumatic elements ("the bursting rumble of guns and cannons [that] broke the peace of the night," etc.), it nonetheless effectively makes the reality of the Chinese people "coherent." It sets up an imaginary scenario (to recall lines like "It was one hundred years ago on a quiet night," "After so many years, the guns and bombs are still rumbling," "I'm forever a descendant of the Dragon," etc.) that connects contemporary Chinese people with those who lived (at least) one century before them, organizing them into one coherent narrative. Just like in many spy films the heroes were "framed," "set-up" into some secret plot, contemporary Chinese people are framed into this fantasmatic scenario. Through such fantasmatic narrative, people living in the post-Maoist era not only have effectively identified *what the cause of their trauma is* (the intrusions of the West), but also learned *what to desire* (the greatness and fullness of Chinese civilization). The desire of the Other (its desire to be full), through the scenario staged by the "Great Dragon fantasy," turns magically into the subject's desire (to be "Chinese," to acquire a full identity).

Let us move one step further now. How is this "Great Dragon fantasy" able to ensure Chinese people to experience the same "reality"? To put in Davies' term, how is fantasy able to ensure "linguistic certitude"? Sean Homer's remark that "fantasies are never a purely private affair but circulate in the public domain through such media as film, literature and television" (Homer 2005: 85) is worth repeating here. Through media such as film, literature, television, and pop music, fantasy operates at the intersubjective level, that is, it is neither "subjective" nor "objective," as Žižek puts it, it belongs to the "bizarre category of the objectively subjective" (Žižek 2000: 83). Precisely owning to its "objectively subjective" characteristic, fantasy not only enables but ensures that a group of people can share the "same reality." Fantasy can thus be said "are at once universal and particular" (Homer 2005: 85). Illustrated strongly by Hou Dejian's pop song and many other texts discussed earlier, the "Great Dragon fantasy" is clearly such an objectively subjective fantasy. This fantasmatic narrative, which not only provides a coherent tragic story, but also effectively organizes and utilizes the "Dragon motif" and other traditional symbols (the Yangtze River, the Yellow River, the Great Wall, and so on and so forth) in supporting this story, powerfully shapes people's "insights" into *"China" as a flawed presence* (a blurry-eyed Dragon), enabling them to perceive a *shared* reality. Through the "Great Dragon fantasy," "China" as a signifier is magically turned into a metaphysical presence. This in turn produces what Davies detects as "linguistic certitude" embedded in and characteristic of Sinophone critical inquiry. By enabling Chinese authors to regard signifiers (e.g. "China," "Chinese civilization," "Chineseness") as metaphysical Entities, and thence allowing them to write in positivistic fashion, the "Great Dragon fantasy" effectively "patches up" or "fills in" the gap between signification and the Real. Because of its "essential" role played in the fantasmatic space, "China" (or "Chineseness," "Chinese civilization") functions precisely as what Lacan calls the master-signifier, the fantasmatic signifier above all other "ordinary" signifier, which "subjugates" the subject, and in so doing, guarantees his/her very identity (his/her symbolic title-mandate).

Within Lacanian psychoanalysis, the failure to merge into "reality" is understood as the reason for momentary or permanent psychosis. Psychotics are people who are not properly "anchored" in the symbolic order.[9] They do not "see" the same "reality" as other people. For psychotics, "reality" as a totalizing symbolic order *does not exist.* A "psychotic breakdown" happens when one falls into an abyssal black hole or "void" that cannot be accounted for by the existing symbolic co-ordinates. That is why fantasy has "healing" effects: by stitching up the gap between language and the Real, fantasy prevents "psychotic breakdowns" and provides the subject with a meaningful frame to "see" reality as a coherent Whole. However, Lacanian psychoanalysis does *not* acclaim the "healing function" of fantasy (hence the famous Lacanian motto "the bid Other does not exist"). Rather, one of the main purposes of the Lacanian psychoanalytic treatment is to *traverse the fantasy*, to disclose its arbitrary and unfounded character.

To elaborate on this point, we need to understand that Lacanian theory claims that there is no "world" before the emergence of language (in a hypothetical pre-linguistic state, entities would continue to be, but they would not be disclosed within a horizon of meaning). Furthermore, there is no *consistent*, *totalized* "world" before the establishment of a fundamental fantasy. Fantasy is the very embodiment of what Lacan calls "symbolic castration" (the primordial installment of the symbolic universe, of the Law): one gains a coherent vision of "the world" through his/her fantasy-window. Thus, fantasy is a (relatively) stable way of veiling the fundamental lack in the Other. After the destruction of such fantasmatic screen, what one encounters is not "objective reality," but the terrifying intrusion of the unintelligible Real. Within this context, the song "Descendants of the Dragon" can be read as offering a fantasmatic scenario in which Chinese people, symbolized as descendants of the Great Dragon, acquire an identity as builders of a better future for China. The song urges them to acquire the enlightened vision to perform this task. Against Lacan's thesis of the Real as pre-linguistic and unintelligible, the call for the Dragon to rub and open its eyes, if taken *literally*, become

---

[9]Bruce Fink rightly notes that "Psychosis, according to Lacan, results from a child's failure to assimilate a 'primordial' signifier which would otherwise structure the child's symbolic universe, that failure leaving the child unanchored in language, without a compass reading on the basis of which to adopt an orientation" (Fink 1995: 55).

futile: "clear-sightedness" would produce psychosis and expose a terrifying void!

The fact that this theme of acquiring enlightened vision structures so much of the 1980s Chinese intellectual discourse is important to consider. The writings of New Enlightenment intellectuals of that era revolved around such terms as self-awareness and self-awakening and were always directed towards discovering or recovering an ultimate truth. The function of this fantasy is to imagine that China would become strong once its people have been cured of their "poor-sightedness." But as the Lacanian argument I have presented so far indicates, there can be no cure for such poor-sightedness since we can only see reality by "looking awry" (to recall Žižek's phrase). In this regard, the New Enlightenment project is best understood as an *impossible* mission. In the language-mediated realm, there is no "objective truth or reality" to be derived from symbolic representation because any attempt to derive such a "truth" produces yet another symbolic representation. This is what Lacan formulates as "there is no Other of the Other": there is no ultimate guarantee (e.g. an ontological truth) of the symbolic order. Within the Lacanian terrain, this negative thesis could be rearticulated in positive way: one can find the *only* (limited) support that the Other can get *in the fantasmatic space*. The narrative of rubbing one's eyes to see clearly is a fantasy of the post-Maoist era that implies that there is a proper path to recover China's lost greatness and fullness. It is in fact an act of "looking awry" that sought to replace the discredited Maoist vision with the desire for a new form of enlightenment. In the 1980s, this New Enlightenment discourse was embodied in the large-scale campaign of China's modernization. What those various post-Tiananmen Chinese intellectual discourses (including those anti-(New)Enlightenment discourses such as Chinese postmodernism, the "New Left," nationalism, the China model, etc.) offer, in the similar sense, are *different fantasmatic narratives competing each other for hegemony*. The vehement debates in the Chinese intellectual arena are decisively about *what type of fantasy* should be elevated in the name of enlightened vision. The function of these fantasmatic narratives is also to keep (re) producing a positive vision of the nation, and thereby reinforcing the positivistic mode of thinking that Davies has observed (i.e. what she calls "linguistic certitude").

"There Is No Such Thing, Yet It Is True!"

Let us now further explore the complex relationship between fantasy and desire. According to Lacanian psychoanalysis, the relation of fantasy to desire is vital insofar as people do not desire "naturally," or "spontaneously." Rather, they are taught to desire.[10] Far from being a result of one's unfulfilled desire, fantasy is the very (objectively subjective) device that teaches people what to desire, and how to acquire enjoyment in the existing symbolic order (Lacan 1977: 313). Žižek writes in explaining this feature of the psychoanalytic notion of fantasy:

> [W]hat is fantasy? As everybody knows, fantasy is a hallucinatory realization of desire. In principle, this is true; however, [...] not "realization" in the sense of fulfilling it, but rather "realization" in the sense of bringing it forth, of providing its coordinates. It is not the case that the subject knows in advance what he wants and then, when he cannot get it in reality, proceeds to obtain a hallucinatory satisfaction in fantasy. Rather, the subject originally doesn't know what he wants, and it is the role of fantasy to tell him that, to "teach" him to desire. (Žižek 2005a: 304)

In this very sense, fantasy is the *setting* — rather than a result — of desire: one learns what object (s)he desires through fantasmatic stories. It is the very device through which desire is organized and structured, and rendered effectively as "ones' very own." Desire strings from lack; desire and lack are "coextensive" (Fink 1995: 54). It is symbolic castration, the very operation turning us into subjects of language (i.e. "speaking

[10]Lacan differentiates desire from need. Need is a purely biological instinct, an appetite which emerges according to the requirements of the organism and which abates completely (even if only temporarily) when satisfied. However, Lacan lifts the concept of desire completely out of the realm of biology. Desire is shown to be distinctively human. It is directed either toward another desire, or to an object which is perfectly useless from the biological point of view. Unlike a need, which can be satisfied and which then ceases to motivate the subject until another need arises, desire can never be satisfied; it is constant in its pressure, and eternal. The realization of desire does not consist in being "fulfilled," but in the reproduction of desire as such. A good discussion of the Lacanian conception of desire can be found in Evans 1996: 37–38.

beings") and instituting the fundamental lack (the lack of full *jouissance*),[11] that initiates the self-perpetuating movement of desire. Hence, "language [is] ridden with desire and desire [is] inconceivable without language; [desire is] made of the very stuff of language" (Fink 1995: 50). Only the barred (castrated) subject desires: (s)he desires for the "missing piece," desires to be "full." For Lacan, desire is thus always the desire to acquire what is perceived as the missing piece by the hold of which one is eventually able to (re)install fullness. However, this is "a fullness which is desired exactly because it is posited as lost/sacrificed" (Stavrakakis 1999: 44). The function of fantasy is to promise the retrieval of fullness upon obtaining the lost (desired) object: by clinging to this missing object (called by Lacan the *objet petit a*) the barred subject is able to sustain an illusion of wholeness, and in turn, able to ignore his/her alienated status.[12] The Lacanian point is, however: what this promise of fantasy effectively covers up is the fact that desire can never be satisfied. Why is so?

In the following passage Stavrakakis powerfully explains this Lacanian view of desire,

> Desire is illusory, says Lacan in *Anxiety*, precisely because it is always addressed elsewhere (seminar of 15 May 1963), exactly because the imaginary signified can never become real. [...] Desire, the element that keeps everything going, is animated by the quest for a lacking/impossible fullness, around the promise of encountering *jouissance* — and *jouissance* always has "the connotation of fullness." Whenever we reach the object of our desire, any *jouissance* we get is nothing compared to what we were expecting. [...] If no object can provide us with our lost/impossible

---

[11] As Fink rightly notes, "Lacan's notion of castration focuses essentially on the renunciation of *jouissance* and not on the penis, and therefore that it applies to both men and women insofar as they 'alienate' (in the Marxist sense of the term) a part of their *jouissance*" (Fink 1995: 99).

[12] Lacan formalizes fantasy with the "matheme" $\$ \diamond a$, which is to be read: the barred subject in relation to *objet petit a*. Fantasy is that which embodies the specific relationship between the subject and his/her desired object. It is in the subject's relation to this object that (s)he achieves a fantasmatic scene of wholeness. Also in this sense, as Fink argues, *objet petit a* "is the subject's complement, a fantasmatic partner that ever arouses the subject's desire" (Fink 1995: 61).

> *jouissance*, it follows that the fragile equilibrium of desire can only be maintained by the continuous displacement from object to object: strangely enough it is the prevention of *jouissance* that sustains desire, a prevention which keeps the dream of attaining it alive (seminar of 17 December 1958). It is this repetition of failure that sustains desire as a promise to attain the mythical *jouissance*; if the realization, the full satisfaction of desire is impossible, then the promise of this realization becomes necessary; without it no desire can be sustained. (Stavrakakis 1999: 45)

Desire is a crucial element in sustaining the mundane running of our everyday life (i.e. "the element that keeps everything going"). The primary goal of fantasy is to keep desire always alive. Since desire withers after satisfaction (after getting what you want, you do not desire it any more), there are only two ways to keep desire alive: (1) "teaching" the subject to desire other objects (hence the Lacanian statement that "desire *is* a metonymy," see Lacan 1977: 175); (2) keeping the object of desire forever out of the subject's grasp. Hence, fantasy as *the* operation of staging desire, is indeed a *perverted operation* in that it (1) specifies the desired object for us, and at the same time (2) keeps us from obtaining it. It promises us the final achievability of the lost object ("the missing piece of our life"), and also tries as much as it can to spare us from the ultimate disappointment ("still, that's not *it*!"). Since as speaking beings we are forever excluded from full *jouissance* (i.e. the theses of "symbolic castration" and the "barred subject"), what fantasy brings to us is thus an empty promise, whose "realization" it has to simultaneously obstruct. Through the operation of fantasy, the fundamental lack — not only the lack of full *jouissance*, but also the lack in the Other[13] — is magically turned (reduced) into some positively identified lost object, and an imaginary scenario is created to sustain the necessary illusion that such object can be eventually obtained (ergo, the encounter of full *jouissance*). It is however the very

[13]These two lacks actually occur exactly at the same place — as Fink writes, "*the subject has lodged his or her lack of being in that 'place' where the Other was lacking*" (Fink 1995: 54, emphases in original). For Lacan, what constitutes both the social and the subject is the same kind of *lack* — the lack of access to the Real. Hence, both the subject and the Other are *barred*.

same operation that obstructs the eventual attainment of the lost object by keeping it always *metonymic* or *elusive*. The Lacanian term *objet petit a*, stands for this inherently metonymic/elusive object of desire around which a fantasy is constructed. It is the kernel of fantasy. Desire can never be satisfied because it is indeed not a relation to an object, but a relation to lack; and *objet petit a* is the "little object" that fantasmatically embodies the fundamental lack, and for that reason forever eludes our final grasp (what we can empirically obtain is always a "sham"). This fantasmatic object, appearing as *agalma* (hidden treasure), is ontologically speaking nothing but *an abyssal structural spot*; and because of this very reason, it is *the* only one object of desire, a "spectral object," which can be metonymically represented by a variety of empirical objects. As Žižek puts it insightfully, this little object is "not what we desire, what we are after, but rather that which sets our desire in motion, in the sense of the formal frame which confers consistency on our desire" (Žižek 1998: 214).

Fantasy constructs a narrative by means of which *objet petit a* is perceived as attainable. As such, fantasy as the narration and enactment of desire, organizes a specific way for us to enjoy. As Sean Homer writes, "The pleasure we derive from fantasy does not result from the achievement of its aim, its object, but rather from the staging of desire in the first place" (Homer 2005: 87). For this very reason, such pleasure or enjoyment can never be full, or real. For Lacan, the production and circulation of such enjoyment is what Freud means by "the pleasure principle," whose sole function is in fact to prevent the subject from the encounter of full enjoyment (*jouissance*).[14] That which was forever sacrificed after the subject's emerging in the symbolic world, is termed by Lacan as *jouissance* (the French word for enjoyment, which English translations of

[14]Žižek repeatedly differentiates *jouissance* from pleasure: "[E]njoyment (*jouissance, Genuss*) is not to be equated with pleasure (lust): enjoyment is precisely 'Lust in Unlust'; it designates the paradoxical satisfaction procured by a painful encounter with a Thing that perturbs the equilibrium of the 'pleasure principle.' In other words, enjoyment is located 'beyond the pleasure principle'." (Žižek 1993: 280) This is why, as Evans has noted, the pleasure principle was originally phrased by Freud as the "unpleasure principle." And for Lacan, the pleasure principle is "nothing else than the dominance of the signifier." "The function of the pleasure principle is to make man always search for what he has to find again, but which he will never attain" (see Evans 1996: 148–149).

Lacan's texts often leave untranslated): "Desire comes from the Other, and *jouissance* is on the side of the Thing" (quoted from Fink 1997: 207). Symbolic castration means for Lacan exactly the loss of *one's own desire* (termed often separately as "drive"), and its satisfaction (*jouissance*). It means that as speaking subjects, we are doomed to taking the Other's desire as our own (i.e. *alienation*). Emerging into the symbolic world violently turns — castrates — us into the "barred subjects." Lacan explains the relationship between *jouissance* and desire in the following way: "*[J]ouissance* is forbidden to him who speaks, as such." Thus, "Castration means that *jouissance* must be refused, so that it can be reached on the inverted ladder of the Law of desire" (Lacan 1977: 319, 324).[15] And the function of fantasy can be understood as "compensating" the sacrificed *jouissance* by enabling the subject to "enjoy" himself/herself through endlessly chasing his/her desired object (*objet petit a*).

However, this "enjoyment" organized by fantasy is nothing close to *jouissance*. This enjoyment is, as Carmela Levy-Stokes notes, "a little compensation in the form of what is allowed of *jouissance*, a compensation for [...] the loss which has occurred in the forbidding of *jouissance* of the Other" (Levy-Stokes 2001: 104). Differently put, it is — to quote Bruce Fink this time — "the mere pittance of pleasure left after the drives have been thoroughly subjected [...] to the symbolic" (Fink 1995: 120). The Lacanian name for such enjoyment is "phallic *jouissance*" (or "symbolic *jouissance*"). The ontological lack in the Other constitutes the place where, through the operation of fantasy, some "lost object" appears, standing in for the sacrificed *jouissance*, and creating a link between the Other and *jouissance*. This is why fantasy can also organize us to gain access to some specific type of enjoyment — the phallic *jouissance*. "Phallus" for Lacan is not tantamount to "penis" as the actual male genital organ; it is but the signifier of desire (hence, the signifier of the Other's

---

[15] I thank Josef G. Mahoney for pointing out to me the similarity between Lacan's contention on the inaccessible *jouissance* against the Law of desire (i.e. that of the Other's desire) and the first chapter of *Dao De Jing*, "*Dao* that can be put into words is not really *Dao*; and naming that can assign fixed reference to things is not really naming. The nameless is the fetal beginnings of everything that is happening, while that which is named is their mother" (see Ames and Hall's translation 2003: 77). I would like to argue here that one can understand properly the Lacanian notion of the (m)Other exactly in this Daoist sense.

desire) (Lacan 1977: 289–290).[16] "Phallus" is thus also the signifier of lack since desire is always correlated with a lack.[17] The enjoyment deriving from the play of this signifier is therefore called by Lacan "phallic *jouissance*." Reversely speaking, phallus is "the signifier that has no signified, the one that is based, in the case of man, on phallic *jouissance*" (Lacan 1999: 81). As Fink has put it, "Man's pleasures are limited to those allowed by the play of the signifier itself," and "phallus" as the very symbol for the Lacanian master-signifier, "functions for a man as a limit to his range of motion and pleasures" (Fink 1995: 106, 107). The phallic function is in this sense equivalent to the function of castration, the alienating function of language, which causes the primordial loss — i.e. the fundamental lack — of *one's own desire* (drive) *and its satisfaction* (*jouissance*).[18] The phallic function leaves — at least seems to leave — the subject no other option but to take the Other's desire as his/her own (this is why Lacan calls it the "forced choice").[19] Fantasy, through providing certain "lost object" to stand in for the fundamental loss, organizes phallic *jouissance*.

In contrast to "raw" *jouissance*, phallic *jouissance* can be linked to the Freudian pleasure principle, which functions precisely as a limit to enjoyment, and commands the subject to "enjoy as little as possible." Thus, phallic *jouissance* for Lacan is nothing but "the *jouissance* of the idiot" (Lacan 1999: 81). Hence, as Fink suggests, we should understand "phallic" as "fallible": "Phallic *jouissance* is the *jouissance* that fails us, that disappoints us." He further explains:

[16]As Evans notes, different from Freud, "Lacan generally prefers to use the term 'phallus' rather than 'penis' in order to emphasize the fact that what concerns psychoanalytic theory is not the male genital organ in its biological reality but the role that this organ plays in fantasy" (Evans 1996: 140).

[17]The phallus can be also seen as the name given to what the (m)Other lacks.

[18]As Fink puts it, "Whereas castration refers to a primordial loss which sets the structure in motion, the phallus is the signifier of that loss" (Fink 1995: 102).

[19]Although the expression "the forced choice" is itself an oxymoron, its employment is crucial for Lacan's theorization of the relationship between the subject and the Other. As Fink has perceptively noted, "The choice of submission [to the Other] is necessary *if* one is to come to be as a subject, but it maintains its status as a choice since it is nevertheless possible to refuse subjectivity" (Fink 1995: 50).

> There is a barrier between my desire for something as formulated or articulated in signifiers (S) and what can satisfy me. Thus, the satisfaction I take in realizing my desire is always disappointing. This satisfaction, subject to the bar between the signifier and the signified, *fail* to fulfill me — it always leaves something more to be desire. That is phallic *jouissance*. Just like one cannot take the lack out of Lacan, one cannot take the failure out of the phallus. Phallic *jouissance* lets one down, comes up short. (Fink 2004: 159–160)

This phallic *jouissance* is indeed a sham, a fantasmatic counterfeit. Fantasy stages symbolic castration, separating the subject from *jouissance*, and at the same time veils it by turning the Other's desire into the subject's. Since then, the barred subject only "enjoys" through the simulating and stimulating channel of fantasy — fantasy literally teaches the subject *what* to desire, and *how* to desire. Actually it does not directly "reveal" to the subject what his/her "missing piece" is. It operates via a "detour": by creating an imaginary scenario, fantasy first provides an unambiguous answer to the enigma of the Other's desire, transforming the mysterious object of the Other's desire into some very specific object; it then turns this object of the Other's desire into that of the subject's by "revealing" to the subject what the Other wants from him/her, and more specifically, by telling what his/her "ego-ideal" should be.[20] The fundamental fantasy thereby turns uncertain fragments in our life (fragmented pieces of everyday mundane life, things yet without senses, etc.) into a clean, consistent story. It removes our anxieties — the Heideggerian *angst* — by giving us directions and meanings of our life, of everything we do and teaching us how to enjoy our life. Hence by doing so fantasy proffers us imaginary access to *jouissance* through its empty promise of fullness. Since the type of "enjoyment" it provides is but only a counterfeit which

[20] Žižek explains the Lacanian understanding of ego-ideal and superego: "Ego-Ideal is the agency whose gaze I try to impress with my ego image, the big Other who watches over me and impels me to give my best, the ideal I try to follow and actualize; and superego is this same agency in its vengeful, sadistic, punishing aspect, [...] the cruel and insatiable agency that bombards me with impossible demands and then mocks my botched attempts to meet them, the agency in whose eyes I am all the more guilty, the more I try to suppress my 'sinful' strivings and meet its demand" (Žižek 2006b: 80).

is *a priori* "fallible," the operation of fantasy requires "structurally" the aid from the superego agency whose imperative is in fact nothing but "Enjoy!" — the inability to "enjoy" is a sign (indeed a "symptom") of betrayal of one's very fantasmatic core of being. Losing your desire is a crime in the gaze of the superego, since it means that you are unable to enjoy any more, that the fantasmatic support of your life starts to lose its effective hold. Desire is the very way in which the Other (as "reality," the symbolic world) appears meaningful to you (what it wants from you). Losing desire is a dangerous sign of what Freud calls the "death wish" (the Thanatos, translated preferably by Lacanian theorists as "death drive"). The ethics of psychoanalysis is, precisely contrary to the superego as the ethical agency, to never let the Other's desire take precedence over one's *own* desire (drive).[21] For Lacan, the only thing one can be guilty of is to give in one's own desire. *The* ethical question he poses is: "Have you acted in conformity with *the desire that is in you*?" (Lacan 1992: 314, emphasis mine) This is why Žižek emphasizes repeatedly that for Lacan every drive is a death drive, because what its repetitive movement eventually leads to is a blind and persistent break-up with the "obscene circle of enjoyment" (the Freudian pleasure principle) organized by fantasy and commanded by the superego agency.[22] The goal of Lacanian psychoanalysis — the traversing of the fantasy, means nothing other than the radical separation from the Other's desire, the stubborn insistence upon "the desire that is in you." The crucial technique of such traversing is thus to extract the fantasmatic kernel of enjoyment, and in turn render visible the gap between the imaginary access to enjoyment (which is nothing but an empty promise) and the sacrificed *jouissance* — i.e. to render clear the "fallible" character of the enjoyment supported by fantasy. Hence as

[21] Žižek rightly emphasizes that from the Lacanian psychoanalytic view, the superego is precisely "the anti-ethical agency, the stigmatization of our ethical betrayal" (Žižek 2006b: 80).

[22] Dylan Evans notes that one big difference between Lacan's concept of the death drive and Freud's is that, whereas Freud opposed the death drive to the sexual drives, Lacan insists that the death drive is not a separate drive, but is in fact an aspect of every drive. "Hence, Lacan writes that 'every drive is virtually a death drive' (Ec, 848), because [...] every drive is an attempt to go beyond the pleasure principle, to the realm of excess *jouissance* where enjoyment is experienced as suffering" (Evans 1996: 33).

Lacan emphasizes, "Our technique involves handling desire, interfering with it, and even rectifying it" (quoted from Fink 1997: 42).

What the lyrics of the pop song "Descendants of the Dragon" that has been extremely popular in the Chinese-speaking world since the early 1980s effectively offer, is a consistent fantasmatic narrative — phrased in this study as "the Great Dragon fantasy" — about China and its modern fate: in the scenario the song stages, the present Chinese people as "descendants of the Dragon" are organically connected with the traumatic events that happened one hundred years ago. Hence, this fantasmatic narrative produces the desire to restore the fullness of Chinese civilization (to put into the words of the lyrics, to resuscitate the greatness of the Dragon by rubbing its eyes), by offering the object of desire — the deprived fullness and greatness of China. "[I]n the fantasy-scene the desire is not fulfilled, 'satisfied,' but constituted (given its objects, and so on) — *through fantasy, we learn 'how to desire'*" (Žižek 1989: 118). In this very sense, the Dragon that is unfortunately blurry-eyed is not the result of this unsatisfied desire, but it is the very symbol that is utilized to generate the desire for the lost fullness of China. Understood within a Lacanian framework, we can say that the primary function of the Dragon serves "to remedy the fundamental deficiency (impossibility) of the big Other, to 'restore' the fullness of the Other" (Stavrakakis 1999: 47), by rendering in the fantasmatic space the Other with a symbol, an image, and a story. The "Great Dragon fantasy" makes it possible to evoke a holistic idea of Chinese civilization and nationhood and to enrich the idea through other symbolic associations.

This fantasmatic narrative also posits the Dragon in a dysfunctional state, with the loss of the clear-sightedness. What effectively springs from this "original loss" is, of course, the desire to (re)gain full eyesight. (This desire is indeed the Other's desire and it is through the operation of the "Great Dragon fantasy" that it turns into the subject's "own desire.") Such "original loss" — which stands in for, in psychoanalytic terms, the primordial loss created after castration — gives rise in the fantasmatic space the elusive *objet petit a*. This is what Žižek calls the fundamental paradox of the Lacanian *objet petit a*: it emerges as *being-lost*. However, as Žižek further emphasizes, "(fantasmatic) narrativization occludes this paradox by describing the process in which the object is first given and then gets lost" (Žižek 1998: 199). Fantasy in this sense is strictly correlative to the Kantian transcendental illusion: it is a necessary illusion for it enables us "to (mis)perceive the object which gives body the primordial lack as the object which is lacking, which was lost (and consequently, possessed prior to this loss); this illusion sustains the longing to regain the lost object, as if this object has a positive substantial identity independently of its being lost" (Žižek 2001: 68). The "Great Dragon fantasy" precisely functions as such transcendental illusion: it not only posits the desired object which is lacking, but also orchestrates the illusion of such object being a metaphysical presence. What the "Great Dragon fantasy" effectively utilizes is precisely a set of symbols — the Dragon, the Yellow River, the Yangtze River, the Great Wall, etc. — that imply an unchanging essence of Chinese civilization. Through its fantasy-screen an image of an eternal China is projected. Symbols such as the Great Dragon become the objects of desire precisely because they *present and represent* the (imagined) fullness of Chinese civilization.

How to make something ordinary worthy of our desire? The Lacanian answer is: by entering the framework of fantasy, by being included in a fantasy-scene which gives consistency to the subject's desire (cf. Žižek 1989: 119). Once being organized in the "Great Dragon fantasy," the Yellow River, the Yangtze River, the Great Wall — the list can almost infinitely go on: panda, chopstick, Confucian temple, *gongfu/wushu* (Chinese martial arts), *hanfu/tangzhuang* (Chinese closing), *weiqi* (encircling game), Sun Wukong (the Monkey King), and so on and so forth — are suddenly turned into objects of desire, magically elevated into something which are "more than themselves." The Lacanian term for such magical change is "sublimation" — the process in which an ordinary object is elevated to the dignity of the Thing. As Dylan Evans notes, "The sublime quality of an object is thus not due to any intrinsic property of the object itself, but simply an effect of the object's position in the symbolic structure of fantasy" (Evans 1996: 201). Here, Žižek's analysis of Alfred Hitchcock's *Rear Window* did a fantastic job in explaining the operation of sublimation in the fantasmatic space. This "rear window" through which James Stewart (portraying a disabled photographer confined to his wheelchair) gazes continually is precisely a (cinematic demonstration of the) fantasy-window, since "his desire is fascinated by what he can see through the window." The heroine played by Grace Kelly, by suggesting against spying on neighbors with binoculars and a telephoto lens (she asks her boyfriend, "Whatever happened to that old saying, 'Love thy neighbor'?"), first appears to Stewart only as a stain disturbing his view through the window. Thus, as Žižek notes, instead of being aroused by her beauty, the heroine becomes literally an obstacle of desire. "How does she succeed, finally, in becoming worthy of his desire? By literally entering the frame of his fantasy; by crossing the courtyard and appearing 'on the other side' where he can see her *through the window*. When Stewart sees her in the murderer's apartment his gaze is immediately fascinated, greedy, desirous of her: she has found her place in his fantasy-space." (Žižek 1989: 119) Isn't what happened in the cultural scene of post-Maoist China exactly the same operation — something ordinary (the Yellow River etc.) is magically lifted up into the object of desire when it enters the fantasmatic window through which contemporary Chinese people see the "reality"? Fantasy, in its "magical operation" of sublimation, literally tells you *what* to desire.

To pursue this Lacanian line of inquiry, we could read the Dragon, the Yellow River, the Great Wall, etc. as images that "stand in" for China, precisely because the narrative of the "Great Dragon fantasy" permits people an access to the "reality of China" through the projection of such images: when people in the 1980s invoked a sense of "being Chinese," they called up such a fantasmatic scenario heavily utilizing and promoting such images. The way fantasy operates is: it sutures those (ontological) "black holes" of our symbolic universe by "offering us the object as a metaphor of our lacking fullness." "By promising an always absent fullness, [fantasy] positivizes symbolic lack" (Stavrakakis 1999: 47). The term the "Great Dragon fantasy" is coined precisely because one of the most successful metaphors for the Other's lacking fullness in post-Maoist China is, of course, the Dragon. Actually, pop songs like "Descendants of the Dragon," "The Great Wall Will Never Fall," and "My Chinese Heart," provide us with excellent examples of the Lacanian argument that it is only through fantasy that the commonality of "a people" becomes symbolically meaningful to speak, experience and desire. The images conjured up of the Dragon, the Great Wall, the Yellow River, the "Chinese heart," and so on, provide the symbolism of "being Chinese" expressed in song.[23] The popularity of these songs thus enables a powerful fantasy to determine the contours of people's desire: this fantasy is one that fosters national pride about "being Chinese." Since the "new era" what is experienced as the "reality of China" is itself fundamentally framed and sustained by the "Great Dragon fantasy" (no longer by the Maoist-communist fantasy that sets up the ego-ideal as being a "socialist new man"). It is through its "magical operation" that there emerges something about China, which is "in it but more than itself." This something is the alleged *deprived essence* of Chinese civilization, functioning as the Lacanian evasive *objet petit a.*

By promising the recovery of clear vision, Chinese intellectual discourse reflects a similar desire to the one powerfully expressed in Hou Dejian's song. Both revolve around the notion of China restored to wholeness or fullness. As Gloria Davies writes of contemporary Chinese intellectual discourse, it reflects "a powerful desire to produce a new or originary truth about China," a desire to produce "a presence imagined as the eventual return to civilizational grandeur." The 1980s New Enlightenment discourse and its calls for clear-sightedness is the fantasy of China's path back to greatness. In this sense, the New Enlightenment discourse can be seen as one specific embodiment of the "Great Dragon fantasy." The fantasmatic narrative gives the ontological lack (the fundamental lack) a positivistic image — a great nation/dragon deprived of clear-sightedness. Thus, by the act of "rubbing and opening eyes," it could be able to completely get rid of the identified (positivized) empirical obstacle that prevents itself from being great. The "Great Dragon fantasy," as any narrative functioning as the fundamental fantasy, is a defense veiling people's lack of access to the Real (speaking beings as the "barred subjects"). This fundamental lack is embodied *in the inability of contemporary Chinese people to "understand" who they are without resorting to fantasmatic stories about being "descendants of the Dragon" and so on.*

Since contemporary Sinophone intellectual inquiry, as well as many pop songs discussed earlier, all reflect the *strength* of the desire to be Chinese (descendants of the Dragon), then the questions we need to track

---

[23] The official national anthem "March of the Volunteers," also appropriates such symbolism as the Great Wall.

are: Why is the desire to be Chinese so strong in the present day? What makes "being Chinese" such a big deal? With these questions in mind, let us turn to a general analysis of what sustains a "nation."

"A nation *exists*," argues Žižek, "only as long as its specific *enjoyment* continues to be materialized in a set of social practices and transmitted through national myths or fantasies that secure these practices" (Žižek 1993: 202). The socially shared historical narratives of a community — i.e. what are now fashionably termed as "collective memories" — are part of these social practices sustained by fantasy. These narratives ("memories") are thus stories people tell themselves in order to confirm themselves as members of a historically constituted community. History, as Žižek argues, is nothing but "the set of explicit mythical narratives and ideologico-ethical prescriptions that constitute the tradition of a community — what Hegel would have called its 'ethical substance'." But what sustains a "national" community is not symbolic history alone; Žižek reminds us that one has to be attentive to the obscene supplement of the "symbolic history" — the "fantasmatic history" (Žižek 2000: 64). For Žižek, to emphasize in a "deconstructionist" mode that nation is "a contingent discursive construction, an overdetermined result of textual practices" is not enough; nation is a fantasmatic construction at its purest (Žižek 1993: 202, 232). In our case, what essentially and effectively holds Chinese people together as a nation is, rather than a series of historical narratives, the *enjoyment* of fantasizing about China as a great (even the greatest) civilization. When "symbolic history" (e.g. the historical narratives of China's defeats and humiliations since the Opium War) is not sufficient to hold together a "national" community, fantasy comes in. People in the post-Maoist era choose to use "fantasmatic history" constituted by images like "the Great Dragon" to affirm their "national" identity. Though expressions such as "we are descendants of the Dragon" are, in the eyes of "outsiders," completely "explicit mythical narratives," they are nonetheless emotion-laden expressions that can produce the binding force to bind strangers into a community: the "Great Dragon fantasy" allows one to console oneself with the idea that although China unfortunately encountered severe crises and humiliations in the last one and a half centuries, it was once the greatest civilization.

Hence, we could say that: *what essentially holds and sustains "China" as a (modern) "nation" is the fantasy of its (premodern) greatness, retroactively formed.* The effort to become "descendants of the Dragon" is itself the very fantasmatic operation of creating an "imagined community" (to recall Benedict Anderson's famous phrase). It is from this fantasmatic domain that the passionate desire to be Chinese and to restore China's glory grows. The "Great Dragon fantasy" offers a specific way of celebrating China as a nation of people descended from a common ancestor. This enjoyment derived from this fantasy, as Homer notes, "does not result from the achievement of its aim, its object, but rather from the staging of desire in the first place." Hence, the enjoyment that people achieve when engaging in the self-assigned task of restoring China's lost civilizational greatness does not result from the actual fulfillment of their task, but from the "Great Dragon fantasy" that makes the idea of this task imaginable in the first place. Such enjoyment is precisely what Lacan calls "phallic *jouissance*" in that it is purely organized and sustained by fantasy. The signifier "China" (indeed, a phallic "master-signifier"), along with images such as the "Great Dragon" and all sorts of fantasmatic historical images associated with "China" (both its glorious and humiliating moments), gives body to and "materializes" this specific enjoyment (what Žižek would have called "obscene enjoyment"), and then sets in motion the passionate desire to achieve the "glorious revival of Chinese civilization" (to recall Wang Hui's phrase).

What is interesting with regard to the "Great Dragon fantasy" is that everything is already quite clear and does not require any arduous "ideological analysis": "descendants of the Dragon" *is already an obvious fantasy*, one hundred percent myth, within which an imaginary "greatness" is embodied. Nonetheless, it still operates very well and functions as an underlying (pseudo-)Hegelian "ethical substance" that fundamentally frames and sustains the "reality" of the contemporary Chinese people. In short, the "Great Dragon" is a nonexistent entity which nonetheless continues to assert its symbolic efficiency as the binding force of "reality." It is this "Great Dragon fantasy" *qua* the "ethical substance" of the Chinese nation that fundamentally sustains the metaphysics inherent in the anticipation of a truth to be discovered or recovered about China. Žižek tells a story with regard to the Jewish tradition, a story of a rabbi narrating to a young pupil the legend of a prophet to whom a divine vision appeared; when the youngster eagerly asks him, "Is this true? Did it really happen?", the rabbi answers: "It probably didn't really happen, but it *is* true" (Žižek 2000: 64). The "Great Dragon" is another example of "there is no such thing, yet it is true." Fantasy is "a 'primordial lie,' a screen masking the fundamental *impossibility*" (Žižek 1998: 205). Since we as speaking beings (the barred subjects) *ontologically fail* to reach the Truth in the Real, fantasy steps in and produces truths for us, with the logic "there is no such thing, but it is true."

Herein resides the paradox of fantasy as the underlying structure that frames "reality": instead of being directly perceived as the actual support of "reality," fantasy is narcissistically invented at first as a *conscious lie* in order to make people's lives seem better than the cruel "raw reality"; then, people *end up believing their own lie*, and in this way, fantasy starts to operate effectively as the support of "reality." Thus, with regard to the operation of fantasy, the empirical proof of "hard facts" does not matter. To recall the classical Marxian critique of religion, fantasy functions like "opium": the actual existence of the "Great Dragon" does not actually matter at all; one needs it simply to make one's life bearable, experienced as a consistent, meaningful Whole. This idea of a necessary lie is explored in one episode of the highly popular sitcom *Seinfeld*. In a dialogue between Jerry Seinfeld and George Costanza (played by Jason Alexander), Jerry has been asked by his new girlfriend who is a policewoman to be tested using a lie detector. So Jerry goes to George for help: "How do I beat this lie detector? George, you got the gift! You're the only one who can help me." George answers, with a serious face: "Jerry, just remember: it's not a lie if you believe it." George's "secret recipe" of lying that appears to be ostensibly vulgar and cynical in fact reveals the hidden ideological operation underlying cultural and religious beliefs, even the most sincere ones. The same logic is at work in Hou Dejian's pop song. Being descendants of the Great Dragon is a fantasy that many people enjoy as a vital part of their own identity. Fantasy effectively covers up the perverse splitting between knowledge and belief by explicitly invoking the Costanzaian logic "it's not a lie if you believe it." Fantasy organizes "the way things 'truly seem to me,' although I never effectively experience them in this way" (Žižek 2005a: 113). With the support of the "Great Dragon fantasy," contemporary

Chinese people experience the "historical reality" of China before the Opium Wars *as if* they had lived it (a harmonious *Tianxia*, an innocent group of people "with black eyes, black hair and yellow skin," a great civilization, etc.). The enjoyment they achieve through such fantasy-scene can only be described as — I cannot resist the temptation to borrow the Žižekian phrase — *obscene*. One never enjoyed (the Harmony, the full *jouissance*), and through fantasy, (s)he feels *as if* (s)he enjoyed.[24] Bruce Fink's observation from the angle of clinical psychoanalytic practice is totally relevant here: "The pleasure given up seems all the more valuable now that it is lost (it seems we didn't know we had it so good)" (Fink 1997: 67). Providing obscene enjoyments is only just half the job that fantasy does for us. Via the same operation, fantasy also effectively augments the traumatic experience of losing such Harmony/Wholeness/Innocence. Although Chinese people in the post-Maoist era do not experience the kind of trauma that late-Qing scholar-officials and early twentieth-century intellectuals experienced, they nonetheless act *as if* they are experiencing the same trauma by connecting the breakdown of Maoism with that of Confucianism into a coherent historical narrative. The lyrics of "Descendants of the Dragon" explicitly tell such a narrative — a narrative about a fundamental "loss" (the loss of vision). The era of Opium Wars and the post-Maoist era are key elements of the fantasmatic frame that the song constructs. In assuming that Chinese people of different historical eras share the same sense of not seeing clearly, the song constructs Chinese identity as a trans-historical will to restore true knowledge (sight). The demonstration of a willingness to participate in this task hence becomes a definition of "being Chinese." Thus, the myth of an original state of harmonious unity symbolized by such terms as the "Great Dragon," "All under Heaven" (*Tianxia*), the "Great Unity" (*datong*), and so forth can be thought of as an objectively

[24]In this sense, the function of fantasy is very similar to the "canned laughter" frequently embedded in American situation comedies: even you do not enjoy the TV show, it enjoys for you; through its "magical operation," you feel *as if* somehow you also enjoyed. This is exactly Žižek's point when he calls canned laughter, which was invented by American sound engineer Charles Douglass, "the greatest American contribution to the world": "So even if, tired from a hard day's stupid work, all evening we did nothing but gaze drowsily into the television screen, we can say afterwards that objectively, through the medium of the other, we had a really good time" (Žižek 1989: 35).

subjective fantasy. As Stavrakakis states, "The lost object is an object which is not lost as such but is posited as lost" (Stavrakakis 1999: 43), the wholeness and greatness of Chinese civilization is posited fantasmatically in the post-Opium Wars era, and served as an effective means of fostering a national identity.

Such operation of fantasy as the constitutive force of the nation can be found in many cases. There is some similarity between this type of Chinese construction of a national or civilizational identity and the idea of empire that Stavrakakis examines in relation to Thomas Richards' work *The Imperial Archive: Knowledge and the Fantasy of the Empire.* Stavrakakis states,

> There is no doubt that no nation can close its hand around the whole of the world. In that sense an empire is always, at least partly, a fiction. Absolute political control is impossible due to a variety of reasons, such as the lack of information and control in distant parts of the imperial territory. This gap in knowledge (in the symbolic constitution of the empire) and control, was covered over by the fantasy construction of the imperial archive, "a fantasy of knowledge collected and united in the service of state and empire." In that sense "the myth of imperial archive brought together in fantasy what was breaking apart in fact" and was thus shared widely; it even had an impact in policymaking. This imperial archive was not a real museum or a real library, it was not a building or a collection of texts, but a fantasy of projected total knowledge: it constituted a "collectively imagined junction of all that was known or knowable, a fantastic representation of an epistemological master pattern, a virtual focal point for the heterogeneous local knowledge of metropolis and empire." In this utopian space, disorder was transformed to order, heterogeneity to homogeneity and lack of political control and information to an imaginary empire of knowledge and power. (Stavrakakis 1999: 81–82; quotations within the passage from Richards 1993: 6, 11)

Like the "Great Dragon fantasy," the imperial archive that was not a real museum or a real library, neither a building nor a collection of texts, but a fantasy of projected total knowledge, functions effectively as the binding force of the national identity of the British.[25] Without such fantasmatic narratives, the sense of Britishness, like that of Chineseness cannot be sustained.

In our case, the fantasy of being descendants of the Great Dragon — as a contemporary desire for an authentic Chinese identity — requires two things: (1) ways of "seeing" China as a grand entity, and (2) ways of experiencing a desire to belong to that grand entity. The analysis I have presented so far indicates that it is fantasy that enables people to endow China with the symbolic significance of, for instance, the "Great Dragon" and to desire the awakening of that Dragon as their *own* awakening. In this regard, China *exists* as a "nation" only insofar as it has acquired necessary symbolism of nationhood, and a fantasy-frame that powerfully connects such symbolism with the idea of "China" (*qua* the master-signifier), and makes it meaningful within the realm of the Symbolic. "China" or "Chineseness" is thereby often described in terms of a set of cultural and historical properties. However, these properties alone are far from sufficient to engender a passionate desire to be Chinese and to restore the fullness of China. What makes "being Chinese" desirable today exceeds the properties attributed to China. What fundamentally produces such passionate desire can be located only in the fantasmatic field. The pop song "Descendants of the Dragon" encourages people to fantasize about having an authentic Chinese identity. Even though it is a myth (from an empirical perspective, the "Great Dragon" and its "descendants" are mere imaginary fabrications), *it is nonetheless "true"* (same as the case with the imperial archive as "the fantasy of empire"). In this regard, the notion of "descendants of the Dragon" serves as what Žižek calls the fantasmatic core of nationalism as a "nation-Thing." He argues that this is akin to some vital "spectral property" — the mystical X in the "nation" which is "more than

[25] Stavrakakis also quotes Stuart Hall's analysis of Thatcherism to illustrate the same point: "'What Thatcherism as an ideology does, is to address the fears, the anxieties, the lost identities, of a people. [...] It is addressed to our collective fantasies, to Britain as an imagined community, to the social imaginary.' (Hall 1988: 167) The same applies to nationalism, to millenarian redemption, as well as to Disraeli's 'One Nation' and to Blairism." (Stavrakakis 1999: 82)

itself" — that enables our desire to become fixed on a given object. For Žižek, the crucial element that holds together a given community never resides in the symbolic level: the bond linking together its members always implies a shared fantasy, i.e. a fantasmatic relationship toward a Thing. That is to say, the idea of what is essential to the nation "can be perceived only by a gaze 'distorted' by desire" (Žižek 1991b: 12, 162; 1993: 201). In this precise sense, "China" cannot be exhausted by a collection of features and properties precisely because at its very "heart" there is always someThing more eluding the collection. "Being Chinese" is thus not only the desire to embody or to actualize a set of positively identified/identifiable properties but the affirmation of the "spectral property" at the very core of "China" — the "essence" that makes the idea of China imaginable in the first place. Expressions such as "although I wear Western-style clothes, my heart remains a Chinese heart; every inch of my body has been branded by my ancestors with the stamp of China" (from the lyrics of the pop song "My Chinese Heart" discussed earlier) thus cannot be discussed in "positive" or "empirical" terms; it can only be perceived as "true," as Žižek suggests, from "a gaze 'distorted' by desire." This Chinese heart, someThing about "China" but more than itself, which cannot be found anywhere, but nonetheless is the "truth," is therefore a fantasmatic object at its purest. Žižek has perceptively pointed out: "The national Thing exists as long as members of the community believe in it; it is literally an effect of this belief in itself" (Žižek 1993: 202). In this precise sense, the Chinese heart "truly" exists.

This Chinese heart (and other symbolism of the Dragon, the Great Wall, and so on) as the "spectral property," along with the stories about several-thousand-years civilization, constitute a fundamental fantasy-ground, where the set of "usual properties" associated with China is effectively transformed altogether into a desired object — the lost fullness and greatness of Chinese civilization. Within such fantasmatic frame, trivial cultural details (such as *zhenjiu* (acupuncture), *gongfu*) can be magically turned into fascinating icons or "national heritages," usual historical figures (such as the Song-era military general Yue Fei) into idols or "national heroes." Let us recall here Žižek's analysis of such "sublimation" operation through the case of *Rear Window*: *the* precondition for an ordinary object to be worthy of desire, is its entering the window of our fantasy. To analyze what Žižek calls "the sublime object of ideology" (i.e. *objet petit a* as the object-cause of desire), one thus *has to* move beyond discourse analysis (textual and historical analysis), and step into the fantasmatic ground. Symbols such as the Great Dragon, the Yellow River, etc., sustain the idea of China as a fantasy that can be perpetuated as long as people are capable of "seeing" and identifying with them, to the (truly astonishing) extent that even though people know that they could not possibly have been descended from a fabulous creature like the "Great Dragon," the myth is sufficient to sustain their sense of common belonging. In this regard, we can say that what the act of "rubbing and opening one's eyes" offers is the vision of an ideal China that is always already a fantasy. What the act conceals is *the terrifying prospect of there being no "China" (or the "Great Dragon") with which to identify.*

Like the logic of the song "Descendants of the Dragon," the standard historical narrative about modern China's rise since the collapse of the Qing dynasty in 1911 revolves around the need for the reconstruction of the harmonious order that was destroyed. At the core of this story is the assumption that one is not "being Chinese" (i.e. being a "descendant of the Dragon") unless one has internalized the loss of China's glorious civilization. The loss of China's civilizational greatness is exactly what makes "being Chinese" so important. Žižek describes the mechanism that sustains the motion of desire:

> [W]hat sets human desire in motion is a short circuit between the primordially lost Thing and an empirical, positive object, that is, the elevation of this object to the dignity of the Thing — this object thus fills out the "transcendental" void of the Thing, it becomes prohibited, and thereby starts to function as the cause of desire (Žižek 1996: 190).

In the narrative provided by the "Great Dragon fantasy," it is precisely the imaginary "loss" of "Chineseness," of the fullness of Chinese civilization, that takes the place of the "primordially lost Thing," and in turn elevates "China" or "Chineseness" (or any object once perceived as partial embodiment of "Chineseness") to the "dignity of the Thing," positing it in the structural spot of the abyssal object-cause of desire (*objet petit a*). The mysterious X, that which is "in the object but more that itself," far from being a set of positively identified or identifiable properties, is structurally enabled by the short circuit between the empirical object and the primordially lost Thing. The psychical mechanism that enables the object of our desire (whether a pony or China as the nation-Thing) appearing so fascinating to us, thus always entails a two-layer structure: (1) the loss in terms of some object being (perceived as) missing, and (2) fantasy which allows this loss to take the place of the fundamental lack. So what happens to "the motion of our desire" is always one of the following two ways: either that we eventually get the desired object, and find it not as good as we expected (the enjoyment achieved is nothing compared to what was expected), then some other object start to attract us (thanks to fantasy that tells us what to desire), the movement of desire continues; or, that the object is forever out of our reach (also thanks to fantasy that obstructs its attainment), and desire persists. In both ways, it is fantasy that keeps our desire always alive.

Through fantasy that stages symbolic castration, we lose access to our very own desire (drive), and take the Other's desire as our own. This is exactly what the "Great Dragon fantasy" does: it magically turns the Other's desire to be full (China's fullness) into the desire of contemporary intellectuals to "be Chinese." As Žižek emphasizes, "The Other's desire provides the minimum of fantasmatic identity to the subject" (Žižek 1998: 196). The desire to "be Chinese" (to be "descendants of the Dragon"), in this sense, is purely a product of fantasy. Fantasy ensures that we desire an object only insofar as it is desired by the Other by telling us what we are for the Other, what the Other wants from us. It is the fantasmatic scenario that connects us to the socio-symbolic reality. Let us recall what we have discussed in the Introduction with regard to the 1980s "fever for intellectuals": Chinese intellectuals in the "new era" publicly command social respect once they are able to see themselves once again as leaders of social change, assuming (resuming) their personal responsibility for China's perfection. Isn't this a perfect exemplary case of the operation of fantasy: the subject finds his/her position in the symbolic universe once (s)he is certain about what the Other wants from him/her? What ego-ideals — from the Maoist model of the "socialist new man" to the post-Maoist revivification/re-adaption of the traditional moral-political figure of the *shi dafu* — entail is precisely the fantasmatic message about what the Other wants from you.

Let us approach this fantasmatic relationship between the subject and the Other from the theoretic angle. In Lacanian psychoanalysis, the Other is structurally divided into two parts: the barred Other and the *objet petit a*. In parallel to alienation *qua* the operation that divides the subject into the barred subject and the drive and its sacrificed *jouissance*, the Lacanian name for the operation dividing the Other is separation (see Fink 1995: 118). The feature shared by both the subject and the Other is thus what Lacanian theorists call "the fundamental lack": just like the barred subject, the Other is deficient in its relation to the Real; both of them are castrated. Alienation and separation are in this sense two "sides" of the operation of castration, turning the primordial child–mother unity into a fantasmatic relationship between the barred subject and the barred (M)Other: fantasy becomes the *constitutive medium* that tells the subject what the Other wants from him/her by specifying for him/her what the Other actually lacks and thus desires. The operation of castration takes place entirely in the "spectral" space of fantasy. Working together, alienation and separation as fantasmatic operations produce barred subjects, guarantee their access to "reality" (the barred Other), and organize the specific (fallible/phallic) way they enjoy their lives through the endless and fruitless pursuit of the missing piece (the *objet petit a*). The crucial element of this process is to replace the subject's own desire with the Other's desire (i.e. to replace the pre-fantasmatic drive with desire as the product of fantasy). While alienation "cuts off" the subject's own drive, the operation of separation is responsible for the emergence of desire: the barred Other in its pursuit of the *objet petit a* in order to be "full." The fundamental fantasy further connects the barred subject to the barred Other by turning the Other's desire into the subject's, instituting what Bruce Fink calls "the *overlapping* or *coincidence* of two lacks" (Fink 1995: 53).

The "Great Dragon fantasy" lays out clearly what the Other lacks (its clear-sightedness and fullness), and in turn magically makes "being descendants of the blurry-eyed Dragon" desirable. Hence, the narrative it tells does a very good job in turning the Other's desire into the subject's, and in doing so, connects the individual persons tightly to a shared "China's reality." This is why it has the capacity to become quickly "hegemonic" in the fantasmatic space in the post-Maoist era, a time when the fantasy of communist construction has significantly lost its capacity to turn the Other's desire into the subject's, and therefore its capacity to guarantee people's access to reality. The prominent historian Wang Hui's famous passage is worth quoting here again: "I rejoice that I was born in China since what could be more heartbreaking and also more exhilarating than the glorious revival of a decaying civilization of which so many generations of people have dreamed? And what could be more thrilling than to watch and experience the minutiae and process of this collective dream?" (Wang Hui 1994: 21–22) It is crystal clear from such passage how fantasy — exemplified by the "Great Dragon fantasy" *qua* the "collective dream of many generations of the Chinese people" — first posits/identifies the lack, then spurs the desire (the Other's desire turned into the subject's) and organizes (limited access to) enjoyment. From the Lacanian psychoanalytic perspective, Wang's experience of "rejoicing" is precisely the kind of enjoyment that is fallible (phallic) and obscene. To answer the questions posed earlier (Why is the desire to be Chinese so strong in the present day? What makes "being Chinese" such a big deal?), it is clear that what I call the "Great Dragon fantasy" is indeed responsible for making "being Chinese" such a big deal.

The desire to be Chinese, from this psychoanalytic view, is thus entirely pathological, because it is based on a fundamental misrecognition which takes place in the fantasmatic space. Such misrecognition suggests that "identity and alienation are strictly correlative" (Žižek 1989: 24). Contemporary Chinese authors frequently write, to paraphrase Žižek, *as if* the determination of "being Chinese" were a "natural" property of the person of a Chinese, *as if* they all do have a "Chinese heart." For example, Zhang Xudong, a former PhD student of Fredric Jameson and a prominent self-styled postmodernist, posed in the 2000s his influential question to the entire Sinophone intellectual world which is perceived as having been dominated by Western ideologies of globalization and universalism since the 1980s — "How to live as a Chinese person today?", with the implicated suggestion that Chinese intellectuals should be wary towards the "specific set of values [i.e. "Western values"] which disguises itself in the name of the universal" (Zhang Xudong 2005: i–viii). What Zhang's question fails to problematize, however, is precisely the metaphysics of being

Chinese and the pathological desire to be Chinese, for the Chinese identity ("live *as* a Chinese person") is presupposed by him as self-evident.[26] Hence, I cannot help but follow Žižek's idiosyncratic questioning here: "How can one not remind oneself here of the famous Lacanian affirmation that a madman who believes himself to be a king is no more mad than a king who believes himself to be a king" (Žižek 1989: 25). Lacan rewrote Descartes' motto "I think, there I am" as "I am the one who thinks 'therefore I am'." Žižek emphasizes that these two "ams" in the formulation are radically different: the second am is purely fantasmatic (Žižek 2005a: 266). Hence, we should rephrase "I am Chinese" as "I am the one who thinks 'therefore I am Chinese'." Through such Lacanian rephrasing, the fantasmatic core of the Chinese identity becomes visible. What also becomes prohibited in the contemporary Chinese desire for an authentic Chinese identity is any self-interrogation of images such as "descendants of the Dragon." This is because the "authentic Chinese identity" is constructed only through such fantasmatic images. Hence, to paraphrase Lacan and Žižek: a "madman" who believes himself to be a "descendant of the Dragon" is no more mad than a man who believes himself to be a Chinese.

The West That Makes the Chinese "Chinese"

The "Great Dragon fantasy," by offering us the story of the greatness of China (the Dragon) being deprived by vicious intrusions of the West, sets up the desire to be Chinese — which simultaneously means, to resuscitate China's greatness and fullness — in motion. This "loss" (deprivation, prohibition) of the object, which stands in for the unfathomable Thing (i.e.

[26] In *Worry about China*, Davies discussed the work of the prominent "New Left" economist Yang Fan. When being asked in a 2004 interview why he was critical of the liberal position held by many leading Chinese intellectuals, Yang defended his critique by asserting that "we have patriotism, nationalism, and traditional Chinese culture in our very bones. This is unlike the kind of individualism that liberalism advances which takes American culture as 'universal culture'." That the rhetoric of "in our very bones" is very common within the writings of self-styled "critical intellectuals" suggests, as Davies insightfully points out, that "China"/"being Chinese" is posited as an unquestionable, self-evident "metaphysical presence" in the language of Sinophone critical inquiry (Davies 2007: 20–21).

the Lacanian Real that appears always as a void or an abyss in the Symbolic), is the *necessary condition* for the desire to emerge. As we have discussed earlier, although the primordial Real is an *a priori impossible* for speaking beings, the specific missing "object" — the transitional, temporary "embodiment" of *objet petit a* as the object of fantasy, in our case, China's lost greatness and fullness — that fills out its void gives it an imaginary "body," through which "the primordially lost Thing" can be thought of to be eventually achieved. This turning the inaccessible Thing into an ordinary missing object (or, to put it reversely, the elevation of an ordinary object to the dignity of the Thing), is precisely the "magical" operation of fantasy.

The trick here, however, is that the "loss" itself presupposes that there is "something" *originally there* (to be lost) in the first place. Since this "something" (e.g. the greatness and fullness of Chinese civilization) is itself always fantasmatically constructed, its "loss" is nothing but an illusionary experience of "something" missing or being taken. It is fantasmatically posited as the "lost object." *Objet petit a* can "cause and perpetuate desire only if it is lacking, making the satisfaction of this desire impossible (when the object embodying the *objet petit a* function is acquired then desire is fixed on another lacking object)" (Stavrakakis 1999: 49). Desire is stimulated by the object fantasmatically perceived as the missing piece. In other words, the actual acquisition of the *objet petit a* has to be always deferred. Desire can never be fully satisfied or fulfilled. In this sense, *objet petit a* represents the *lack* in the symbolic order "not in the sense of a specific object that is lacking but as lack itself." It is "'objectively' speaking, nothing. It only exists as something in relation to the desire that brings it about." (Homer 2005: 87–88) The "greatness of the Dragon" as the object of fantasy is thus absent *ontologically* instead of *historically*: it is not stolen or lost; rather, it is a product of fantasy, retroactively constructed through stories, pop songs, films, etc. What is embodied in contemporary narrative like Hou Dejian's "Descendants of the Dragon" is a fantasmatic operation, whose product is a foreclosed story of a traumatic "loss." The narrative about "the bursting rumble of guns and cannons that broke the peace of the night," fantasmatically and retroactively allows people to imagine that there was a "peaceful, harmonious China" before the intrusions of the West broke it. The existence of an essential Chinese civilization or "Chineseness" only becomes imaginable *once it was perceived as being deprived.* It is this fantasmatic "loss" that triggers a passionate desire to acquire the "lost object," though this "loss" is, as Žižek puts it, "in itself a lure, a 'primordial lie' destined to deceive the subject by providing the fantasmatic foundation of his or her being" (Žižek 2000: 70). The hidden assumption is that if this missing or lost "something" is (re)gained, life would be once again whole.[27]

Lacanian psychoanalysis offers us a useful way of seeing that such belief about an eventually achievable wholeness/fullness is an unavoidable fantasm: such picture is perceived "only by a gaze distorted' by desire." Through the operation of fantasy, "reality" becomes imaginable and the idea of "national unity" then turns on one or another "object of desire" to suggest that even though we have not yet achieved that national unity in its fullness, we can identify its properties. Precisely through such acts of identifying its "properties" (which utilize as many elements as it could locate ranging from traditional Chinese ideas such as the Great Unity, Harmony, *Dao*, *Tianxia*, all the way down to trivial cultural formations such as *gongfu*, *zhenjiu*), an essential China or Chinese civilization is fantasmatically constructed. Once an ordinary object "accidentally" enters the screen of the "Great Dragon fantasy," it is magically elevated into a fascinating "sublime object," an object of desire. So from the psychoanalytic perspective, it is utterly futile to argue with a Chinese person whether gunpowder or compass or any other item was first invented by Chinese (the claim might well be true, founded on "historical facts"); what should be addressed and critically tackled instead are the following

[27] Homer is thus right to suggest to understand *objet petit a* as an everyday "sense" that constantly and fundamentally bothers our lives: "The *objet a* is not, therefore, an object we have lost, because then we would be able to find it and satisfy our desire. It is rather the constant sense we have, as subjects, that something is lacking or missing from our lives. We are always searching for fulfillment, for knowledge, for possessions, for love, and whenever we achieve these goals there is always something more we desire; we cannot quite pinpoint it but we know that it is there. This is one sense in which we can understand the Lacanian real as the void or abyss at the core of our being that we constantly try to fill out. The *objet a* is both the void, the gap, and whatever object momentarily comes to fill that gap in our symbolic reality. What is important to keep in mind here is that the *objet a* is not the object itself but the function of masking the lack." (Homer 2005: 87–88)

questions: Why do those "past inventions" make such a great deal to a Chinese person? What makes contemporary Chinese people so fascinated about those "historical records"? What mechanism turns inventing gunpowder or compass into matters that concern the very core of being Chinese? As the way Lacanian analysts investigate what makes the analysand so fascinated about a specific woman or obsessed with a certain fetish-item (Žižek's analysis of *Rear Window* also serves an exemplary practice), we have to step into *the space of fantasy* to investigate the contemporary mechanism that magically connects certain trivial historical details to China's national-civilizational building (i.e. the construction of an essential Chinese nation/civilization). In exactly the same way, in claiming that the loss of the fullness of Chinese civilization is a product of fantasy, we do not need to dismiss lightly those unfair treaties the Western powers have inflicted on China since the Opium War of the 1840s. The Lacanian suggestion is rather: what we should investigate into is the very way these unequal treaties are organized in supporting the existence of a harmonious, essential China before such events. Žižek is right to emphasize: "[W]hen a certain historical moment is (mis)perceived as the moment of a loss of some quality, upon close inspection it becomes clear that the lost quality only emerged at this very moment of its alleged loss" (Žižek 1998: 199). What enables China to be perceived as once a Whole, a harmonious Entity, is precisely this kind of powerful fantasmatic narratives epitomized by Hou's "Descendants of the Dragon" which effectively utilizes all sorts of cultural and historical (even racial) details at its disposal in organizing a coherent narrative about the traumatic "loss" of the Fullness/Essence/Harmony. Instead of being trapped in debating over "historical records," the truly critical task is to examine *how such historical records are organized in the fantasmatic space into a fundamental story that permits and supports contemporary Chinese people's very access to "China's reality."*

Let us further our discussion. In his 1996 article entitled "Fuck Chineseness: On the Ambiguities of Ethnicity as Culture as Identity," Allen Chun observed that "Chineseness in terms of material culture, ethnicity, or residence was never clearly defined." He did not further discuss why this is so, but nevertheless perceived this as a distinctive problem of "the Chinese rendition of nationalism" (Chun 1996: 114).[28] Similarly, in commenting Deng Xiaoping's slogan of "building socialism with Chinese characteristics," Lucian W. Pye noticed that Deng nonetheless "has trouble identifying those characteristics," and saw it as a salient evidence of the inherent flaw of the post-Maoist state-nurtured nationalism, namely, "the problem of lack of [normative] content" (Pye 1993: 127). Both authors however did not engage in tackling the mechanism that produces such characteristic lack of clear articulation of "Chineseness" (or "Chinese characteristics") in contemporary Sinophone discourse. Lacanian psychoanalysis indeed offers a powerful theoretical tool to analyze this issue. The Lacanian distinction between *any* given object of desire and *the* object-cause of desire is as follows: *once the desired object is fully defined or described in positive terms to become empirically achievable, it starts to lose its "magical appeal."* Yet it is that "magical appeal" that constitutes the object-cause of desire (as opposed to a given object of desire). We will see in Chapter 2 that once the "Great Dragon fantasy" is given detailed elaboration in the discourse of modernization construction, it creates only intellectual divisions rather than the unity that is posited as a goal. In other words, once the fantasmatic scenario is articulated as something that can be positively defined, portrayed, and empirically achievable, it nonetheless starts to lose its "magical power" to unite a people. This trick can be encountered and observed very frequently in our everyday lives — for example, the "spoiler" that ruins the fun: *once* you know about the story-line of a novel, you lose the appetite to actually read it (even you previously so desired to read it). By the same token, the lack of clear definition or articulation of "Chineseness" is precisely necessary in order for it to remain as a collectively desired object: a clear definition would amount to the "spoiler" that kills its "magical appeal" enabling it to function as the *objet petit a*. What is really worthy

[28]An example of Chun's observation can be found in a recent interview of Gan Yang, conducted in 2006. Since the early 2000s, Gan has become a leading figure calling for a reconstruction of China's "civilizational subjectivity." (I will discuss this intellectual discourse in detail in Chapter 6.) However, when he was asked about the positive content of "Chineseness" or Chinese civilization, Gan nonetheless replied in an elusive tone: "I rather remain it as an open question. I don't want to define it. My reason is simple: once defined, Chinese civilization would be inevitably narrowed, fixated." (Gan 2012a: 159–160)

of people's desire, cannot be positively specified, fully articulated: once the content of the fantasmatic object is positively articulated, its limitations will be revealed, and hence, its "magical appeal" will vanish. Moreover, people always search for fulfillment and *whenever* they achieve these very objects they pursue (e.g. love, power, knowledge, or, more specifically, a romantic partner, fancy car, clothes, house, etc.), there is always something *more* they desire... Thus, once the *objet petit a* is specified and becomes empirically attainable, it starts to lose its "sublime" status as the desired object. Human desire is in this sense always the desire for something that is "mysteriously still missing" and thus involves a constant search for the missing object. Žižek uses Einstein's theory of relativity to illustrate the movement of *objet petit a* as the object-cause of desire:

> The starting point of the theory of relativity is the strange fact that, for every observer, no matter in what direction and how fast he moves, light moves at that same speed; in an analogous way, for Lacan, no matter whether the desiring subject approaches or runs from his object of desire, this object seems to remain at the same distance from him. Who doesn't remember the nightmarish situation from dreams: the more I run, the more I stay rooted to the spot? This paradox can be neatly solved by the difference between the object and the cause of desire: no matter how close I get to the object of desire, its cause remains at a distance, elusive. (Žižek 2006b: 76–77)

In short, the object-cause of desire exists — or, rather, persists — in a kind of curved space: "The nearer you get to it, the more it eludes your grasp (or the more you possess it, the greater the lack)" (Žižek 2000: 24). To apply these ideas to the symbolism of Chinese nationhood, through the operation of the "Great Dragon fantasy" China's lost greatness and fullness occupies the place of the *a priori* inaccessible Thing: the former positivizes the latter through such symbols as the Dragon, the Great Wall, the Yellow River, etc. There can only ever be *proposals* as to how Chinese people can "open their eyes" to retrieve China's lost glory, not one *solution as such*. This is because there can be no ideal comprehensive proposal capable of completely filling this experience of loss. In this regard, every proposal is always limited in its effects, insofar as the attainment of the "desired" object — for instance, the goal of "reform and opening up" (*gaige kaifang)* as defined in one or another way — can only ever reveal new gaps hindering the attainment of that goal. More generally, *the idea of China as a civilization that has lost its former glory and fullness remains crucial even when China has enjoyed enormous economic growth.* Only in this way can the idea of China's lost glory function properly as the object-cause of people's desire to affirm their Chinese identity. The object of fantasy has to remain absent, lost. That is why the "Great Dragon fantasy" works only as an act of "rubbing and opening one's eyes." It fosters an expectation of a better future for China but *it leaves the positive content of the clear-sighted vision empty.* In fact, once the content of a given insight is specified, that insight will reveal its limitations. As such, *every insight will thus always require further acts of "clear-sightedness."* In this context, the secret of a successful fantasmatic operation is that it has to keep the missing object forever "missing." Let us take the Maoist vision of a communist society as an example: the moment the communist society is announced as something that was in the process of *becoming reality*, it began to expose itself as a fantasy. The importance that the Maoist state accorded to the role of propaganda, together with its active coercion of Chinese citizens into showing public support for Party doctrine, reflects the importance of fantasy as the primary setting of desire. The Maoist state had to keep the communist fantasy alive in powerful ways in order that people would willingly support the goals that the Party had set out. Though the shift from the communist fantasy of the Maoist era to the "Great Dragon fantasy" of the post-Maoist "new era" marks an important change in terms of the way of "being Chinese," the very structure of the fundamental fantasy nonetheless has to remain the same way for it to be operative.

Furthermore, although the passion for revolution of the Maoist era is very different from the passion for material wealth and success in the post-Maoist era, the discourses of both eras share a common preoccupation with imagining (and fantasizing) the arrival of a powerful China. In order for this desire to be kept alive, there has to be something missing — a "lost object" — that is always just out of one's reach. In order for the "lost object" maintaining always "lost," there must always be an obstacle to the realization of the fantasy. In the settings of the post-Maoist "Great Dragon fantasy," *the* obstacle which blurs the Dragon's eyesight is indeed not hard to locate — "the West." In the Maoist era, the same obstacle was cast in terms of "Western imperialism." In fact, in any standard story of "modern China," "the West" is depicted as the key obstacle to the actualization of China's national strength and civilizational glory. In this story, China always appears as a flawed present, awaiting its transformation in the future.[29]

In contemporary narratives of "being Chinese" such as Hou Dejian's pop song, "the West" is often cast in the role of a violent force. By this means, China can thus appear as a flawed present that needs to recover its ancient glory through acquiring a powerful modern character. "The West" thus becomes imaginable not only as the cause of China's decline and the destruction of Chinese culture, but also as a force that needs to be accounted for, understood and studied.

In this regard, the idea of "Chinese reality" is understood as one that was formerly structured around Confucianism and the set of traditional values that developed out of Confucianism. The collapse of Confucianism as the orthodoxy of dynastic China is thus equated with the destruction of China's harmonious order. In this way, the idea of a return to China's harmonious order requires "the West" to play the role of both destroyer and savior. Since the greatness and fullness of Chinese civilization is itself *retrospectively constructed*, it matters mainly as a *feeling* of loss rather than the loss of something actual. It is this feeling of loss that helps to sustain the idea of "China" as a "national" community. This ironic logic is what Žižek has in mind when he claims that "the modality and direction of our search participate in the creation of the object for which we are searching" (Žižek 1996: 228). In other words, the desired object that one claims to be lost "exists" only as long as the effort to recover it continues to be reified in a set of narratives and social practices.

Therefore, the search for the "lost object" (e.g. China's civilizational fullness) is always already a "transcendental" failure, *not because of some external obstacles that hinder the search, but the inherent impossibility of the search itself*: the "lost object" is itself a fantasmatic construction, a product engendered retroactively by the search for this very object. When

---

[29] Similarly, in the hegemonic fantasmatic formation prevailing in dynastic China — the fantasy of *Tianxia* as a harmonious order, this necessary element functioning as the obstacle to the final realization of harmony is, of course, "the barbarians" (*yi*) situated on the periphery of *Tianxia*. In this precise sense, at that time it was the (perceived) "barbarians" who made the Chinese "Chinese" (*xia*, or *huaxia*).

one "successfully" gets rid of the external obstacles (e.g. "the West"), what (s)he gets is not the fulfillment of the search, but the exact opposite — its total breakdown: (s)he directly confronts the traumatic core of the desired "lost object," which is, its "transcendental" emptiness. Žižek is right when he points out that "*external hindrances that thwart our access to the object are there precisely to create the illusion that without them, the object would be directly accessible* — what such hindrances thereby conceal is the inherent impossibility of attaining the object" (Žižek 1996: 189, emphases in original). In our case, what "the West," understood as destructive force, creates is the illusion that China would recover its greatness if it could tame the destructive powers of the West. The inherent impossibility is obscured in the fantasmatic scenario by a positively identified external obstacle. Thus, the West functions in various modern Chinese narratives as a "constitutive obstacle," that enables the idea of China's lost civilizational greatness to appear as the collectively desired object. Fantasy's job is to provide "an answer to the anomaly emerging at the intersection of this symbolic and the persisting real" (Stavrakakis 1999: 47). The clear answer, the one the "Great Dragon fantasy" provides, is the West ("the bursting rumble of guns and cannons [that] broke the peace of the night"): it is the intrusion of the West that destroys the original harmony and fullness of Chinese civilization, and deprives it of greatness. In turn, the promise of the "Great Dragon fantasy" is that once this external obstacle is removed, China can retrieve its lost fullness and greatness.

Žižek, and Stavrakakis following Žižek's elaboration of fantasy, distinguish two modalities of fantasy: the one that offers a beatific harmonious picture, and the one that projects an unpleasant, humiliating, even horrific situation. Why is the latter also necessary for fantasy to properly function? It is because in people's everyday lives, they have the constant sense that something is lacking or missing from their lives. But they do not know what it is or how such lack happened. In a time of crisis, this ontological uncertainty produces unbearable anxiety (*angst*). The key problem is thus "not so much that the Other is lacking, but that we do not know why he is lacking. Fantasy provides a solution to this uncertainty, a solution which is nothing but a compromise. In that sense, it reduces anxiety and creates a semblance of harmony but this harmony may depend on a picture of the Other as demanding something horrible and unpleasant. For the subject — the neurotic subject — even this horrifying picture of the Other is preferable from the state of uncertainty regarding the lack and the desire of the Other." (Stavrakakis 1999: 151) In fact, these two modalities of fantasy are inherently entwined: "beatific fantasy (the vision of the state of things 'before the Fall') is supported by a disturbing paranoiac fantasy which tells us why things went wrong (why we did not get the girl, why society is antagonistic)" (Žižek 1998: 209–210).[30] The fantasmatic narratives of the West in modern China can be seen as such an unpleasant, disturbing fantasy: while bringing experiences of grave trauma to Chinese thinkers from the late Qing onwards, it nonetheless provides them an "answer to the anomaly," offering an explanation for why the Other is lacking. To produce an unpleasant fantasmatic scenario that provides a clear solution as to what is preventing one from attaining one's desire is preferable to acknowledging the impossibility of such a realization. Fantasy thus is first of all a scenario that obfuscates the true horror of a situation that there is ontologically no such thing as Fullness, Perfection, Harmony, the omnipotent "Dragon" (as the embodiment of the *Dao* of Heaven), etc. in the first place. In this sense, what Gloria Davies terms as acts of "worrying about China" is also an effect or a product of this fantasy: instead of directly confronting the emptiness/void of "the Great Dragon" (as a master-signifier, a signifier without signified), contemporary Chinese intellectuals *prefer* to worry about the Dragon, to identify what causes the loss of the Dragon's greatness, and, to quote Davies, to ceaselessly identify "problems that prevent China from attaining perfection." The "Great Dragon fantasy" thus turns on the promise that once these problems and obstacles have been removed, the perfection of Chinese civilization can be achieved. However, as the Lacanian argument I have presented so far indicates, this promise can never be fulfilled and the attainment of the goal must always be postponed. The "Great Dragon fantasy" is forever articulated as a promise of attaining fullness in the *future*: *once* the Dragon rubs and opens its eyes, it is able to regain its lost greatness and fullness. Within the settings of this fantasmatic scenario, what constantly denies the realization of fantasy in the present is

[30]This dual character of fantasy applies even to the most intimate fantasy — sexual fantasies, as Žižek notes, "Fantasy is thus not simply the fantasy of a successful sexual relationship, but rather the fantasy of why it went wrong" (Žižek 1998: 210).

positively identified as the intrusion or intervention of "the West." Instead of recognizing the constitutive impossibility of realizing its promise, fantasy allows the subject to always blame "someone else."

On the other hand, however, the West is also ambivalently imagined as a force of salvation. In this regard, Davies writes:

> [The] Sinophone suspicion of the unknown and dangerous potency of foreign ideas, which has facilitated the production of nationalistic Sinophone formulations, cannot avoid admitting that the very language in which it is given frequent articulation is already indebted to or parasitic on foreign ideas. But this Sinophone suspicion is also unsurprising inasmuch as foreign ideas, whatever their content, were certainly not composed within the reassurance of worrying about China. The historically antecedent problem of modern Chinese intellectual discourse coming *after* the West and its modernity might be likened to a second sibling forever envying the once only child, the sibling that preceded it. Whatever the case, it is the difficulty of achieving that uncontaminated development in the face of so much foreign thought that is clearly *not* worrying about China that leads to a position of heightened alert and suspicion of the Other, a position that is forever in competition with the other side of the equation and that is, to be in competition with the very hope that the other, the stranger, does indeed have something to offer that is of value to China. The historical injustices of coerced trade concessions and the Treaty of Versailles aside, this in itself is a powerful structure of contemporary Chinese discourse inherited from an older poetics and unanimously persuasive across the political spectrum of contemporary Chinese intellectual positions. For our purpose, this discursive structure is one that raises the problem of precisely how much hospitality should be shown to the foreign, and, what does it mean when others show "too much"? (Davies 2007: 47–48)

With this in mind, we can better understand the ambivalent and significant position that "the West" occupies in the calls for China to achieve national perfection. The *necessity* of this ambivalent relationship to the West can be elaborated through Žižek's comment that: what may appear as an obstacle to a certain enterprise is in fact its constitutive element, by the full elimination of which, the very enterprise itself immediately fails, or breaks down. That is to say, what is perceived as the *obstacle* to the full actualization of X, is actually *the very condition* of X's functioning (see, for example, Butler, Laclau, and Žižek 2000: 93–94).[31] Hence, what is experienced as the obstacle that hinders us from getting to the desired object actually effectively makes this object always desirable *by permanently postponing its empirical realization.*[32]

"The West" is, in this precise sense, the symbolic embodiment of what makes the task of perfecting China always incomplete, of what suspends its completion. It is the traumatic *presence* of "the West" (incarnated as a totalizing culturo-military power) that turns "being Chinese" (which entails the search for China's lost greatness) into a desirable object. In the "reality" of "modern China" framed by the "Great Dragon fantasy," "the West" is effectively a fantasmatic domain: it cannot be located in geography. In fact, this fantasmatic West often includes Japan, as Peter Gries notes in his *China's New Nationalism*, "Japan is not geographically west of China, but Chinese often include Japan in both the noun and adjective '*Xifang*' — 'the West' and 'Western'" (Peter Gries 2004: 35). Thus, "the West" is a "category" that Žižek calls "an imaginary cartography" (see Žižek 2000: 4).

[31] Herein resides Žižek's key criticism of the classical Marxism: the old Marxist attempts to get rid of capitalist social conditions and yet keep its unbridled, self-increasing productivity cannot be actually realized because "if we abolish the obstacle, the inherent contradiction of capitalism, we do not get the fully unleashed drive to productivity finally delivered of its impediment, we lose precisely this productivity that seemed to be generated and simultaneously thwarted by capitalism — if we take away the obstacle, the very potential thwarted by this obstacle dissipates..." (Žižek 2000: 17–18)

[32] One of Žižek's favorite examples is: in the usual love story in a patriarchal society, two young people fall in love and their parents, owning to some "rational" considerations (wealth, social status, family background and history, even physical matters such as looking, health...), forbid them to see each other. During the process of striving to be together, the love between the two becomes so strong that they eventually choose to die together (in this way, no one can separate them). In this typical tragic story of love versus parental power, the latter which appears as the external obstacle to the realization of the former is nonetheless what sustains the former and makes it strong. If this obstacle is successfully removed or there is no such obstacle in the first place, the love cannot reach this intense level that makes two persons choose to die together. That is to say, without the interference of this patriarchal power as the external obstacle, most likely after "consummation," the love itself subsides (when the desired object is directly achieved, this object itself starts to lose its appeal). Thus, the point to be made is: what is experienced as the obstacle that hinders us from getting to the desired object actually effectively makes this object always desirable *by permanently postponing its empirical realization.*

Moreover, the "external obstacle" is not only constitutive of the desired object, but also, as Žižek writes,

> stages the most elementary "short circuit" in the subject's relationship to the primordially missing object-cause of his desire: what "bothers" us in the "other" (Jew, Japanese, African, Turk...) is that he appears to enjoy a privileged relationship to the object — the other either possesses the object-treasure, having snatched it away from us (which is why we don't have it), or he poses a threat to our possession of the object (Žižek 1994a: 71; also 1999a: 201; 2000: 8).

Thus, the Chinese hostility towards "the West" since the Opium Wars cannot be adequately conceived without reference to the "magical appeal" of the object-cause of desire, in the form of "something" (a national or ethnic Thing, as Žižek would put it) imagined as lost. In this regard, Chinese civilization becomes perceived as the precious, unique "substance" (without which there can be no Chinese national identity) that is always under threat from an "external enemy" who not only poses a threat but appears to enjoy "what we lack." Davies' comment that Chinese intellectual discourse revolves around the question of "how much hospitality should be shown to the foreign, and, what does it mean when others show 'too much'?" is in accord with the basic paradox of the object-cause of desire that Žižek identifies.[33] "The West" is precisely this kind of "external obstacle," a foreign body, whose intrusion, intervention, or even its very presence mortifies Chinese people significantly, deprives them of their precious civilizational "greatness" and corrupts the original "harmony" of their lives, but nonetheless at the same time makes them "Chinese" (i.e. makes it "meaningful" to be Chinese), evokes and accelerates the search for China's lost "substance." In this precise sense,

---

[33]The point Žižek stresses is, to be concise, that our national or ethnic Thing — the precious, unique "substance" *qua* the object-cause of our desire to attain a national identity — is menaced, and at the same time also constructed retroactively, by "them," an "external enemy" who, by means of their excessive enjoyment, pose a threat to our "way of life": "the 'other' wants to steal our enjoyment (by ruining our 'way of life') and/or it has access to some secret, perverse enjoyment.... The basic paradox is that our Thing is conceived as something inaccessible to the other and at the same time threatened by him." (Žižek 1991b: 165; also 1994a: 71)

when contemporary narratives, represented popularly by Hou Dejian's "Descendants of the Dragon," evoke a self-glorifying passion of "being Chinese," what is simultaneously rendered is, ironically, the very message that undermines this self-glorifying passion: "Chinese" people *structurally* need the humiliations brought by "the West" in order to be fully "Chinese." Davies reveals this point in her following argument which is very sharply put:

> If we choose to crystallize the self-reflexivity of EuroAmerican critical inquiry through Hans-Georg Gadamer's notion that "We are all others, and we are all ourselves," then the positivity of Chinese critical inquiry could be said to reflect the following contrary claim: "Because we have been othered, we must now learn once more how to be ourselves." (Davies 2007: 240)

"The West" as the "evil force" has "othered" the Chinese people, and is experienced as still "othering" them. This is a necessary element for the "Great Dragon fantasy" to be operative, since China's essence or "greatness" *has to* be experienced as lost, namely, deprived or stolen by the fantasmatic figure of "the West." Again, to acknowledge this is not to deny that China was forced to sign unfair treaties with the Western powers after the Opium Wars and was subjected to economic exploitation and some loss of sovereignty; but to urge us to re-examine how "the West" is represented in Sinophone discourse and how such representation in turn has constitutive force on forming the national identity of the Chinese people. It urges us to pay attention to what Lacanian psychoanalysis describes as the operation of fantasy. In the case of what I have called the "Great Dragon fantasy," "the West" has thus acquired a highly complex symbolism as the cause of China's insufficiency, and in turn, been posited as that which has stolen — and is stealing — Chinese people's enjoyment. Through the fantasmatic operation of identifying an external force obstructing the acquisition of full enjoyment, the fundamental lack (the inability of accessing to *jouissance*) is effectively covered up.[34]

---

[34]Lacan's point apropos of the Oedipus complex (the incest taboo) is exactly the following one: this symbolic prohibition of enjoyment is a prohibition of something which is already

What we encounter here is thus a typical "victimization" scenario: the Subject of the fantasy is a victim (a handicapped "Dragon") whose precious treasure has been taken by a violent force intruding from outside. Those heterogeneous popular symbols such as "descendants of the Dragon," "the Chinese heart," etc. utilized in projecting this fantasy are thus inevitably organized to re-produce *a fundamental split between a presupposed metaphysical "Chinese self" and its equally presupposed "non-Chinese other," an evil "them."* The pursuit of an "authentic" way of "being Chinese" has to rely on the use of those symbols that can convincingly "stand in" for the "nation-Thing" in the fantasmatic space, for such "nation-Thing" — the essence or substance of "Chineseness" — is ironically in itself always an ontological void.

To sum up, as elaborated in the light of Žižek's analysis of desire, the point to be made is that the desire to pursue and resuscitate the "authentic" way of "being Chinese" is itself at the same time corrupted and sustained by a fantasmatic foreign body, a "non-Chinese other" symbolized as "the West." Thus, such questions as "What essentially constitutes Chineseness" are, therefore, what Žižek would have called the *"post-question,"* which is to say: they are themselves *a part of the problem*. The question "What essentially constitutes Chineseness" itself already presupposes that there is a metaphysical "Chineseness" out there. Similarly, the question famously posed by Zhang Xudong — "How to live as a Chinese person today" — already presupposes a metaphysics of "being Chinese." Thus, these questions themselves need to be problematized in the first place, rather than trying to seek answers for them.

Hence, a proper Lacanian analysis of the post-Maoist discourse shows that "China" or "Chineseness" functions not only as *the master-signifier*, for it is the one signifier representing the subject for all other signifiers, an empty signifier with no clear definition or articulation ("The more the signifier signifies nothing, the more indestructible it is," Lacan 1993: 185), but also as *the nation-Thing* (*the sublime objet petit a*, the "master-signifier" of the master-signifier), for it entails following features: (1) it

a priori impossible. The function of the incest taboo, which is perceived as being shared by all "civilized societies," is precisely to sustain the fantasmatic illusion that enjoyment would be attainable if it were not forbidden (see Evans 1996: 92).

appears to be ours, something "accessible only to us"; (2) despite this, it is constantly under threat by "them" who try to steal our Thing; (3) it appears as what gives meaning and vivacity to our life, and hence defines fundamentally our identity; and (4) we can only ever describe it in terms of "empty tautology," or through recourse to mythical stories (see Žižek 1993: 201). In short, "China" or "Chineseness" is both an empty signifier (phallic master-signifier) that signifies nothing, and a fantasmatic object functioning as the cause of desire. As noted earlier, in Lacanian psychoanalysis the big Other is structurally divided by the fantasmatic operation of separation into the barred Other, which is associated with the signifier, and the *objet petit a* as the object-cause of desire. Viewed from this theoretic angle, "China" indeed plays simultaneously two crucial roles through the "Great Dragon fantasy": "China" as the master-signifier signifying nothing but a lacking Presence, and "China" as the desired object, the nation-Thing (China's essence, "Chineseness"). In both its roles, "China" is sustained by fantasy: the narrative of the "Great Dragon fantasy" enables it to be regarded as a metaphysical Entity and at the same time desirable. The recognition that there is no big Other, i.e. the recognition of the non-existence of China (the Great Dragon), thus amounts to the moment of the traversing of the "Great Dragon fantasy."

As I have argued so far in this chapter, the "Great Dragon fantasy" functions as a "make-believing" machine, enabling people to believe that the signifier "China" contains some lost essence — the X that made China great and glorious; and this belief in turn enables the idea of "being Chinese" to make sense. The passionate desire to achieve the "glorious revival of Chinese civilization" is dependent on this "Great Dragon fantasy." This fantasy does not have to deal with revealing what this X is (that is, what constitutes China's lost substance); for its smooth functioning, it only needs an "external obstacle" to "negatively" forge "Chineseness": people do not have to know anything about the lost treasure in order to engender a desire to retrieve it; the idea of an "outsider" taking away their treasure alone is sufficient enough to form a "national" community. Specifying positively the content of "Chineseness," on the contrary, would only weaken the desire to pursue it. What this "Great Dragon fantasy" attempts to "normalize" and "harmonize" is not only the past, but also, even more importantly, *the present*. Žižek insightfully notes that "our present can be conceived only as the outcome (not of what actually happened in the past, but also) of the crushed potentials for the future that were contained in the past" (Žižek 2000: 90). In this precise sense, China's crushed essence (contained in the past) is the very fantasmatic settings out of which the Chinese present is experienced: the "identity" as "Chinese," the contemporary passionate desire to revive China's lost greatness, etc. are all caused and stimulated by this "Great Dragon fantasy."

Within the fantasmatic domain, empirical proofs ("hard facts," "historical records," etc.) do not matter. Indeed, there are two modes of "facts-do-not-matter": to paraphrase Žižek (1992: 261), (1) the subject "lies" about the factual (or propositional) content of his/her utterances, yet this very lie on the level of enunciated brings forth *the truth of his/her desire*, his/her authentic subjective position of enunciation; and (2) the subject speaks "the truth and nothing but the truth" in order to conceal *the falsity of his/her subjective position*. The crucial point also not to be missed here is that these two modes are usually both embedded in a fantasmatic formation. With regard to the "Great Dragon fantasy," one can detect clearly that both these two modes are at work. (1) Even though the "Great Dragon" is a mythical figure (no empirical proof regarding the existence of such quasi-divine creature), a one hundred percent obvious lie, the statement that "we are descendants of the Dragon" is nonetheless "true" not only in terms of its (objective) effectiveness, but also with regard to what people (subjectively) believe. (2) Reversely, even though some specific propositions (such as "gunpowder was first invented by Chinese") are empirically founded, the very frame that organizes them together into a coherent narrative fundamentally supporting the "Chinese identity," is nonetheless a "primordial lie," covering up the *a priori* impossibility/inability of restoring the authentic way of "being Chinese."[35] The function of *objet petit a* explains how this "primordial lie" works in the fantasmatic domain: endlessly stimulating the subject's desire through the fantasy-frame, the *objet*

[35] Let us recall the argument that "reality is structured like a fiction" discussed in the Introduction — what defines a fiction is the following feature: even including many empirically true statements (like "there is a lot of snow in Greenland," or that "human beings typically have two ears," to quote Eagleton), the whole narrative is nonetheless fictional.

petit a — "Chineseness" as *agalma*, the deprived substance of Chinese civilization (and thus, of the "Chinese identity") — is the "fantasmatic 'stuff of the I'" (Žižek 1992: 262) filling out the barred subject's *void kernel*, turning it magically into "a Chinese heart." These two modes — ostensible and primordial lies — fundamentally characterize the life supported by fantasy: one lives in lies ("descendants of the Dragon," "the Chinese heart," etc.), which nonetheless constitute *the* "truth" of his/her life.

For Žižek, this is a "tragic mode of existence": the subject endeavors to sustain his/her fidelity to *the* mission which gives meaning and consistency to his/her life — e.g. "China" as the phallic master-signifier, as the *objet petit a* — to the end, and his/her attempt ultimately fails because of the fantasmatic ground of such mission (i.e. it lacks Real/ontological ground); in Žižek's own words, it necessarily fails because of "the remainder [i.e. the Real] that resists the master-signifier" (Žižek 2000: 43). The problem which this study sets out to address is precisely this "tragic mode of existence" of contemporary Chinese intellectuals: what if, the final goal of their self-assigned mission of achieving — to use again Wang Hui's words — the "glorious revival of Chinese civilization" through the "efforts of several generations" is itself a mere fantasmatic construction, which *in the first place endows them with such goal but at the same time is determined to prevent its actual realization*?

One of the most influential contemporary attempts of controlling the national destiny of the Chinese and resuscitating China's lost grandeur is embodied in the project of "cultural modernization" (*wenhua de xiandaihua*), an enterprise aiming at transforming (traditional, or, "communist") China into a (modern, "capitalist") "nation," put forward and advanced in the 1980s New Enlightenment intellectual movement. The problems that arise when "fantasy" is treated as "fact" ("reality") is what we will explore in the next chapter, in relation to the 1980s intellectual project of "cultural modernization."

Chapter 2

New Enlightenment as Modernization

Many Chinese intellectuals who were active during the 1980s now refer to that decade as a "golden age." In recent years, reminiscing about the age of the 1980s has become something of an intellectual fashion. Around this topic, numerous essays and books have been produced since the late 2000s (especially in 2006 and 2007). Participants of the 1980s Chinese intellectual scene like Gan Yang now describe the intellectual discussions of that era as "pure, sincere, simple" (see, for example, Gan Yang 2006b: iii). In Chapter 6, I will discuss how this retrospective view of the 1980s as a "golden age" offers a new kind of fantasy within Sinophone intellectual discourse of the 2000s. In this chapter, let me first note that this nostalgia for the 1980s is intended to send the message that the 1990s and the 2000s cannot compare with the intellectual activities in the eighties. In this context, the eighties is being retroactively constructed as unique and unusually vibrant. Xu Jilin observes that the distinctive characteristic of the 1980s intellectual movement is the "homogeneity of attitude towards culture" (*wenhua taidu de tongyixing*). According to Xu, it is precisely this "homogeneity" that makes the intellectual activities of the 1980s a unified "movement" (which has been termed as the "New Enlightenment movement") (Xu Jilin 2000: 177).

As noted in Chapter 1, from the May Fourth era onwards, "Enlightenment" has often been described in Sinophone texts in terms of "seeing clearly." The "homogeneity" of the New Enlightenment can be viewed as crystallized in anticipation of an "enlightened" vision that will enable everyone to gain the capacity to *see* the Real. In other words, an ultimate truth is presupposed by the intellectuals who identify with the New Enlightenment: they do not necessarily agree with each other about the actual content of this ultimate truth, but they *all* assume that there *is* an ultimate truth out there that will enable people to discover the answer to restoring China as a great civilization. Thus, in the 1980s, although intellectuals were actually engaging in different projects — some were advancing a Westernized modernization whereas others were searching for a "creative transition" of traditional Chinese culture, they were nonetheless to a large extent "united" with a "homogeneous attitude" supported by the fantasmatic promise of seeing reality clearly. Thus, they formed a unified movement. This "homogeneous attitude" is evident in the frequent calls for "cultural modernization" in the 1980s New Enlightenment intellectual discourse. This phrase was extremely popular in the mid- to late 1980s. The first person to use the phrase was the philosopher Gan Yang who was a prominent New Enlightenment thinker in the 1980s, and who since then has remained very active in the Chinese intellectual landscape. Among other things, when Gan described the New Enlightenment during the 1980s, he referred to "a historic onrush that merges the whole nation into one heart committed to marching towards socialist modernization" (Gan Yang 1987a: 5). "Socialist modernization" is the official reformist ideology of Deng Xiaoping's era. The "homogeneous attitude" of the New Enlightenment is embodied in this "one heart committed to marching towards socialist modernization." In Gan's account, "cultural modernization" is a crucial dimension of "socialist modernization."

From the late 1970s onwards, the post-Maoist Chinese Communist Party launched an official project of modernization (*xiandaihua jianshe*) which includes four aspects — the modernization of agriculture, industry, national defense and science-technology.[1] Having replaced Maoist socialist construction with modernizing China through market reform, the post-Maoist state allowed and encouraged Chinese intellectuals to pursue "cultural modernization" as well. In Chinese, the idea of cultural modernization is regarded as complementary to the official campaign of the "Four Modernizations." Xu Jilin notes that "[T]he New Enlightenment thinkers were at pains to avoid talking too much about the politically sensitive dichotomy of capitalism versus socialism. Instead they availed themselves of what were then fashionable theories of modernization and

---

[1] Zhou Enlai, the premier in Mao's era, had first proposed in 1964 a program for the "four modernizations." He renewed the proposal in 1975. It is until 1978 that the modernization project was formally approved in the 3rd plenary session of the 11th Central Committee of the Communist Party of China, with the political rise of a new leader, Deng Xiaoping.

developmentalism in China." Xu also points out that for those New Enlightenment thinkers, this is much more than just "strategic" thinking. The intellectuals of the 1980s were "homogeneous" in the aspect of "longing for the ultimate prospect of modernization: although this prospect varied drastically among different intellectuals, it was understood teleologically and viewed as the universal truth" (Xu 2000: 177). This is a very important point with regard to the 1980s New Enlightenment movement: although there were many different proposals for modernization, these generally proceeded along one of two directions — either towards the goal of a fully Westernized culture, or, towards the achievement of a "creative transition"[2] of traditional Chinese culture. Thus, despite their differences, New Enlightenment thinkers were still united under the same banner of "cultural modernization." The term "modernization" was the organizational theme of the New Enlightenment intellectual movement.

In Lacanian terms, the project of "China's modernization" (that is, of imagining China as a nation on the road that will lead towards a bright future), can be described as the shared fantasy of officials and intellectuals in post-Maoist China. Indeed, the narrative of modernization can be regarded as a specific embodiment of the "Great Dragon fantasy" discussed in the previous chapter, because it claims to offer a clear view of the future of China. It promises that by following the path of modernization, China can be great again. Modernization hence functions as a fantasy that works only by projecting a future towards which the present will lead. In other words, the realization of its promise — the elevation of China into a clear-sighted, fully enlightened, modernized nation — structurally resides in the *future*. In this juncture, a distinctive phenomenon with regard to the 1980s intellectual discourse is thus noteworthy: though the term "modernization" was widely employed by intellectuals and became a keyword of the 1980s, the term "modernity" was hardly used. It was not until the mid-1990s that "modernity" became a frequently used term in Sinophone intellectual discourse.[3] The crucial difference between these two terms is: while

[2] This term is used by Gan Yang in his various texts written in the 1980s, see, for example, Gan Yang 1987a: 18.

[3] Xu Jilin specifically notes in a recent essay on contemporary Chinese thought that "[I]t was not until 1994 that the term 'modernity' became widely used" (Xu Jilin 2007: 21).

"modernization" refers to the very course heading towards the "modern society," "modernity" is used to signify a set of standard attributes of the "modern societies." In this regard, "modernity" presents the ultimate prospect of "modernization." In 1990s China, the development of a discourse based on the concept of modernity posed a significant challenge to the modernization discourse that first appeared in the 1980s and continued to remain popular in the 1990s and since. Here, we can evoke once again the Lacanian argument that the "ultimate prospect" must always remain vague or evasive: once it is positively defined, portrayed, and empirically achievable, it loses its "magical power" to unite a people.

As noted in Chapter 1, what is crucial in terms of the smooth operation of fantasy is that *the desired object must remain unattainable*: *the moment the object is fully achieved, it can no longer be desired.* In the 1980s, the desired object created by the fantasmatic narrative of "modernization" — i.e. a fully modernized China — enabled the discourse of the New Enlightenment to function *as if* it were true for the majority of Chinese intellectuals. In other words, "modernity" had not yet been attained and thus, New Enlightenment could be discussed as the means to achieve that goal. In the operation of this fantasy of modernization, the "modernity" that would arrive once the process of modernization had been completed remained barely conceived. What mattered most to intellectuals of the 1980s was that they should be advancing China's modernization. They had yet to quarrel with each other over the different visions they had of what a fully modernized China should look like. Thus, in a discourse which is fundamentally structured by the fantasmatic window of modernization, the ultimate prospect of [Chinese] "modern society" (i.e. the content of "modernity") must be concealed and kept in an unproblematized and unthematized way. The emergence of a different discourse in the mid-1990s — one that challenged the assumptions of the modernization discourse and effectively ended the ostensible "homogeneity" of New Enlightenment discourse — precisely started itself by posing the question regarding "modernity" (see Zhang Yiwu 2000[1994]; Wang Hui 1997, 1998, 2000b; Han Yuhai 2002).

We will examine the 1980s modernization discourse in this chapter, and the use of the term "modernity" in the 1990s as a critique of the modernization discourse in Chapters 3 and 4.

"Modernization" as a Fantasmatic Window

As noted in the previous chapter, Lacan argued that fantasy is a defensive and necessary device for creating a sense of reality. Without it, what one experiences is not reality itself, but on the contrary, the total collapse of any sense of reality. Trauma, which results in subjective disintegration, is the effect of the mal-function of this fantasy device. In this precise sense, "fantasy constitutes the primordial form of narrative, which serves to occult some original deadlock" (Žižek 1998: 196). If we apply this Lacanian argument to the narrative of "modernization construction" supported and propelled by the post-Maoist CCP, it is possible to say that this narrative offers an alternative fantasy to the failed Maoist fantasy of communist construction.

The 1980s New Enlightenment intellectual discourse was an unambiguous endorsement of the CCP's official modernization discourse. As mentioned in the previous chapter, the symbolism of modernization in the 1980s Sinophone intellectual discourse is similar to the idea in Hou Dejian's pop song of restoring China's greatness as a clear-sighted Dragon. According to Xu Jilin, the New Enlightenment discourse was unified and homogeneous because different groups of intellectuals in the 1980s all believed that it is absolutely necessary for China to modernize/enlighten itself.

In the 1980s New Enlightenment discourse, there were two types of binary thinking at work: (1) the temporal binary of tradition versus modernity and (2) the spatial one of China versus the West. For some New Enlightenment thinkers like Jin Guantao and Liu Qingfeng, these two dichotomies were overlapping ones, but to many others, they were not. Thus, we can find in many 1980s texts, exemplified especially by Gan Yang's works, that "modernization" was endorsed while "Westernization" was frequently criticized. We should note that the idea of "cultural modernization" itself was and remains ambiguous. Some people (represented by both Gan Yang and Jin Guantao) understood it as modernization in the cultural and intellectual fields (as different from fields of agriculture, industry, national defense, science-technology, etc.). Some others (e.g. Tang Yijie) understood it in terms of the modernization ("modern transition") of Chinese culture. Because of this ambiguity, various participants in the intellectual enterprises of the 1980s — ranging from those who were importing all sorts of new intellectual ideas from the West, to those who were rediscovering the Chinese philosophical and intellectual tradition — were tempted to identify themselves with the "cultural modernization" label, thus forming an ostensible "homogeneity." Though Gan Yang recently labeled the 1980s as "pure" and "simple," as one can clearly see here, it is however neither "pure" nor "simple."

Xu Jilin comments with regard to the intellectual discourse of the 1980s,

> There was a basic intellectual premise, a commensurability that made conversation possible and the contestation was one that took place between equals standing on level ground. Thus sincere and honest exchanges and highly emotive debates were commonplace during the New Enlightenment. (Xu Jilin 2000: 178)

It is precisely this "basic intellectual premise" which produced a commensurability or homogeneity among the New Enlightenment intellectuals of the 1980s, that can be described in Lacanian psychoanalytic terms as the objectively subjective fantasy. The editorial of the first issue of the New Enlightenment journal, *Culture: China and the World*, puts its editorial task this way: "As China moves towards becoming part of the world, it is understandable that Chinese culture will also have to become international. As China works to achieve modernization, it is a corollary that 'cultural modernization' will also be on the agenda. This is the shared belief of all people of conscience (*youshi zhi shi*) in the 1980s. This is an inevitable and logical part of China's historic take-off." (Gan Yang 1987b: 1)[4] The author of this text, Gan Yang, who was the chief editor of the journal, further stated in his essay published in the same journal issue that "Modernization ultimately is 'cultural modernization.' [...] Therefore, the basic assignment for contemporary Chinese intellectuals is to use their *imagination* to

---

[4]The translation I adopt here is taken from Geremie R. Barmé and Gloria Davies' translation of Xu Jilin's essay "The Fate of an Enlightenment: Twenty Years in the Chinese Intellectual Sphere (1978–98)," with some slight revisions. See Xu Jilin 2000: 174.

explore and inaugurate modern Chinese culture." (Gan Yang 1987a: 7; emphasis added) In Gan's view,

> Chinese culture before "May Fourth" is a form of premodern culture. "May Fourth" marks the historical starting-point of the radical shift of Chinese culture from its premodern to its modern form. The fundamental task of the 1980s cultural discussions in China is to decisively complete this historical shift, and to truly establish the system of modern Chinese culture. That is to say, the task is to wholly realize the "modernization of Chinese culture." (Gan Yang 2012b[1985]: 25)

Gan's view can be seen as representative among intellectuals of the 1980s in the sense that, as noted above, people who had disagreements about a lot of issues nonetheless all identified their works with this task of realizing the modernization of Chinese culture. Even though they differed with regard to the "imagined" content of "modern Chinese culture," they had this "shared belief" that through "(cultural) modernization" they could effectively, to borrow Gloria Davies' phrasing, "improve the quality of the nation's Thought and Life" (Davies 2007: 19). That is to say, through the fantasmatic window of "modernization," "China" is cast in the role of a Subject advancing towards *the future*. It is exactly because of such modernization fantasy that the Chinese people in the 1980s appear as a homogenized subject. Moreover, the (imagined) "modern Chinese culture" that is the goal of this Subject is understood as the outcome of a modernization that China has so far been unable to fully achieve.

Gan Yang coined an influential slogan in the 1980s — the "struggle between the ancient and the modern" (*gujin zhi zheng*) — to emphasize the difficulty of achieving cultural modernization, translating the inherent vagueness of "cultural modernization" into external difficulties. Moreover, Gan's slogan reflects both the assumption of linear progress and the perception of modernization as a path of struggles. For Gan Yang, the urgent task for Chinese intellectuals is not to defeat the "evil force" of "the West," but to get rid of China's own "traditional form of culture." This is what Gan perceives as the most difficult part in the process of achieving cultural modernization. To defeat the influential force of China's tradition is posited as the crucial struggle that all contemporary Chinese intellectuals should undertake (Gan Yang 1987a: 18). During the May Fourth era of the 1910s and 1920s, "Westernization" was one of the central proposals in order to regain China's greatness. In the 1980s, the project of modernization took its place.

In the above cited paper entitled "A Few Issues Concerning the 1980s Cultural Discussions," which was an influential text of the 1980s New Enlightenment, Gan argues that many people involved in the ongoing "cultural discussions" wrongly perceived the "struggle to be one between China and the West"; instead, people should be focusing on the "struggle between the ancient and the modern" (Gan Yang 1987a: 8). Gan argues that the "spatial" dichotomy between "China" and "the West," should be replaced by the "temporal" dichotomy between "the ancient" (or "the traditional") and "the modern." He states that:

> The key problem is that this geo-cultural difference between Chinese and Western cultures is usually emphasized and unconditionally accepted that we often neglect the more substantial, more fundamental problem of the difference between traditional and modern cultures, of Chinese culture itself having to undergo a transition from an older paradigm to a modern form (Gan Yang 1987a: 18).

Gan calls this "paradigm shift" from traditional Chinese culture to its modern form the "great theme of the last century" (*bainian da keti*). Gan attempted to get his readers to see that these efforts to strengthen China in the last one hundred years should not be viewed as attempts to advance "Westernization." Rather, he argues, these were efforts that sought to advance *China's own* modernization. By this substitution of "modernization" for "Westernization," Gan identifies the 1980s intellectual discussions as key to understanding the "great theme of the last century." "[T]he discussions on China's culture in the 1980s," writes Gan, "certainly is a continuing and deep reiteration of cultural debate of the last one hundred years but at a higher level. This historical continuity is endorsed by the evidence of the historical course China undertook in the last one hundred years. In one sense it is a phase of preparation for China's modernization." (Gan Yang 1987a: 5–7) Gan criticizes many eminent Chinese thinkers from the late Qing onwards, such as Kang Youwei (1858–1972), Liang

Qichao (1873–1929), and Liang Shuming (1893–1988), for presenting their ideas in the framework of China versus the West.

Meanwhile, Gan argues that only Feng Youlan (1895–1990), a renowned philosopher and historian of Chinese philosophy who was often viewed as a representative of "cultural conservatism" or "modern neo-Confucianism," recognized the need to move beyond the China/West dichotomy. Gan further quotes Feng's words to illustrate the necessary replacement of the old "Westernization" argument with the correct framework of "modernization": "What was usually regarded as the difference between the East and the West is actually one between the ancient and the modern. [...] What was usually viewed as Western culture is in fact modern culture. So-called 'Westernization' is actually 'modernization'." (Gan 1987a: 16) From his quotation of Feng's argument, what Gan has in mind when he speaks about the "modern form of Chinese culture" becomes clear: Gan's concept of "cultural modernization" is in fact no more than a new way of discussing social and cultural reform but without using the term "Westernization." Thus, when Gan quoted Feng's word that "So-called 'Westernization' is actually 'modernization'," one can also read it inversely with regard to the 1980s New Enlightenment discourse of "cultural modernization": so-called "modernization" is actually "Westernization." What Gan suggests in his proposal for "cultural modernization" is not an internal reconstruction of classical Chinese culture and thought. Rather, what he calls the "modern form of Chinese culture" is none other than the "modernized," "enlightened" ideas of which he approves, that have been imported from "the West."

In short, the "modern form of Chinese culture" in Gan's account is an alias of contemporary Western culture. Gan claims that in the contemporary discussion of "cultural modernization," what should not be neglected is the "fact that there is a difference between a traditional stage and a modern one within Western culture itself"; China thus must go through the same "paradigm shift" in order to modernize itself (Gan Yang 1987a: 8–18). Gan further writes:

> If we really want to carry forward (*fayang guangda*) Chinese culture, we should not speak all the time about "those ancient sages, or a hundred schools of thought, or of Confucianism, Buddhism, and Daoism." Rather,

> we should explore in a down-to-earth manner the path that would lead Chinese culture towards its modern cultural form. If we really care about Chinese culture, we should first of all not worry about the sustainability of Confucianism, but ask from time to time whether or not our cultural form is still *outside* today's universal modern culture. If we really have cultural confidence and national pride, then instead of fantasizing blindly that "the world's future culture must be the revival of Chinese culture," we should be pondering this issue: whether the *present* Chinese culture is actually capable of getting rid of its traditional form, of transforming itself into its modern form. (Gan Yang 1987a: 18, emphases in original)

Clearly, at the core of Gan Yang's account of the "struggle between the ancient and the modern" is the teleological argument that the "modern" (modern society, modern culture, etc.) is *the* common future of all enlightened people in the world: for him as well as many other New Enlightenment thinkers of the 1980s, "modernization" is that which *must* be "advanced," and "Chinese culture must get rid of its traditional form and run towards its modern form." When writing of "getting rid of the traditional form of Chinese culture" Gan means that it should be completely eliminated, for he claims that this process involves a "most thorough, fundamental, complete and profound change." "Modern culture" in Gan's account is a universal paradigm, and perceived as the only way for Chinese people to revive China's lost "cultural confidence and national dignity." Gan thus claims that in order to perfect China, the Chinese people must create what China's traditional culture does not have, by which he means the imported ideas from the West (see Gan Yang 1987a: 2, 17–18, 24–25).

In this sense, "cultural modernization" in Gan's account is actually an alias of the old concept "Westernization." The question is: Why did Gan Yang claim that "Westernization" must be discarded when his arguments were in fact very similar to the discourse of "Westernization"? The explicit reason, as Gan indicates in his argument, is that "Westernization" has the effect of making China seem inferior. By substituting "modernization" for "Westernization," Gan thus sought to "neutralize" the perceived inequality between the West and China, to locate the "struggle" for modernization within China itself as one "between the ancient and the modern." In doing so, Gan does not discard the framework of the China versus the West dichotomy. Rather he has given it a new name but without changing the underlying structure of this dichotomy one bit. For New Enlightenment intellectuals like Gan Yang, the May Fourth "anti-traditionalist" spirit is something necessary, crucial (though he does not endorse its "Westernization" proposal): it must be defended in order for the present Chinese culture to radically break from its "traditional form" and move rapidly towards a "modern cultural form." Hence, New Enlightenment intellectuals often linked their intellectual activities in the 1980s back to the May Fourth movement as the origin of "China's Enlightenment movement." They perceived their own enterprise as a "New Enlightenment" — a continuation and an improvement of the May Fourth enterprise.

A perhaps more important reason for New Enlightenment intellectuals such as Gan Yang to replace the discourse of "Westernization" by using the term "modernization" is that this notional replacement allows them to describe their work as the revival of *Chinese civilization.* This is why Gan places a special importance on regaining China's "cultural confidence and national pride." In encouraging people to modernize traditional Chinese culture, Gan Yang claims that it is important to affirm one's Chinese identity. Gan stresses that discarding traditional Chinese culture will not affect contemporary people's identity as "Chinese." As he puts it,

> In comparison with those common historical changes, the "change" caused by modernization is the most thorough, fundamental, complete and profound kind, for it requires *a complete change of social structure, cultural form, and psychological structure*. When we are engaged in advancing modernization, it is simply the process of *self-consciously pushing forward* this kind of overall "change(s)." To block this "change" is to block the progress of modernization. We do not [have to] "worry" (*youhuan*) at all whether, after going through the comprehensive change(s) caused by modernization, the Chinese people are still Chinese or whether Chinese culture is still Chinese culture. This is because, in our view, no matter how intense and deep this change is, it is still *a change made by the Chinese people themselves, a change of the Chinese culture itself, which is,* the *self-transformation of the Chinese people and the self-development of Chinese culture*. Therefore, after this change, no matter how drastically different *the future* would be from *the past*, it is still a development of the Chinese

> people themselves and a creation of the Chinese culture itself, thus *internally becoming a "traditional" part of the Chinese people or the Chinese culture.* (Gan Yang 1987a: 25, emphases in original)

Gan's argument that what the Chinese people collectively choose as the path of modernization is "Chinese", simply because of their cultural and national identity, is clearly very simplistic. Nonetheless, it allows him to claim that when the Chinese people collectively choose a set of Western ideas, the ideas chosen would cease to be "Western" and become "Chinese" ideas instead. This is what Gan means when he writes that "modernization" is none other than the "self-development of Chinese culture." Gan views China's traditional culture as the very obstacle of China's modernization; thus, modernization as "a complete change of social structure, culture form, and psychological structure" requires the thorough annulment of China's tradition. However, this thorough annulment of China's tradition is, according to Gan, by no means a thorough annulment of China's culture; instead, this thorough annulment is "internally" a part of Chinese culture as its self-development. Following this reasoning, Gan therefore presents his conclusion in a paradoxical way: "the most powerful way of inheriting and glorifying the tradition is 'anti-tradition'" (Gan Yang 1987a: 35). This statement shows clearly that the sole aim of cultural modernization for New Enlightenment thinkers such as Gan is to resuscitate China's lost grandeur, to achieve its civilizational perfection. Thus, though in terms of their normative content, "modernization" and "Westernization" are almost interchangeable, nonetheless this notional replacement of the latter by the former is of great significance for New Enlightenment intellectuals, for what they endeavor is to "carry forward Chinese culture" and revive China's lost "cultural confidence and national pride." From this one can see that the fantasmatic narrative of modernization complements or indeed "embodies" the "Great Dragon fantasy" discussed in the previous chapter, in terms of their common assumption that the Real (the ultimate Truth of China) itself is attainable, and once China is modernized (the Dragon regains its clear sight), it can resuscitate its lost glory and once again becomes a great civilization.

Gan Yang's argument of a "struggle between the ancient and the modern" was representative of the 1980s New Enlightenment intellectual discourse. In his study of the 1980s intellectual movement of China, Zhang Xudong noted that "In Chinese scholarship [of the late 1980s], the critical focus has shifted from the binary of East–West conflict to that of a tradition-modernity transformation" (Zhang Xudong 1997: 60). What this comment fails to acknowledge is that this "shift" is purely a notional one, with no substantial change of the underlying structure. As is evident in Gan Yang's argument, the only change was rhetorical, involving the substitution of the dichotomy of "traditional" versus "modern" for the dichotomy of China versus the West. In the 1980s, New Enlightenment thinkers like Gan believed that they were not only renewing the Enlightenment discourse of the May Fourth era but rescuing it as well from the old "wholesale Westernization" ideology which was dominant in the 1920s. The goal of the New Enlightenment enterprise of cultural modernization was not to Westernize Chinese culture, but to revive its lost grandeur by advancing its "self-development."

The "New Enlightenment" Interpretations of China's History

Let us now move to another aspect of the New Enlightenment movement: namely, the tendency of New Enlightenment intellectuals to imagine an ongoing process of modernization in which they appear as pioneers of new knowledge about China. There is also a "homogeneity of attitude" in this aspect of their work insofar as they all sought to re-interpret history from the *teleological* perspective of advancing China's modernization.

Luo Rongqu, an influential historian who is regarded as a specialist in modernization theory, states in the preface of his book *A New Discussion on Modernization* (which was written in the late 1980s and published in 1993) that "modernization" is not a term recently imported from the West. It can be traced back to the "Hundred-Day Reform Movement" (1898), which, in Luo's view, "was in its original sense a movement advancing China's modernization." He argues that this movement later inspired May Fourth intellectuals to search for "the road of China's modernization," and shaped the later "heated discussions" of the 1930s. The War of Resistance (1937–1945), according to Luo, interrupted "this big topic of modernization." This interrupted "big topic" was resumed thirty years later. Luo writes that "after the state fully shifted onto a new developmental path that took the realization of socialist modernization as its main content," modernization once again became a "heated topic." Luo claims that the importance of "studying China's modernization over nearly a century" as an "intellectual movement of Enlightenment" is that it will provide lessons to "today's search for the road towards the socialist modernization with Chinese characteristics, especially the road towards the reconstruction of Chinese culture" (Luo Rongqu 2004[1993]: iii, viii–ix).

Luo's account of Chinese history of the last one hundred years clearly resonates with Gan Yang's view of modernization as a "big theme of the last century," though Luo does not regard "cultural modernization" as a total cancellation of Chinese traditional culture. Instead, Luo borrows the CCP's official ideological slogan — "socialist modernization with Chinese characteristics" — to indicate that Chinese cultural characteristics should be kept and reconstructed during the course of modernization. Luo's account of modernization is also similar to Gan's in using the dichotomy of "traditional" versus "modern" to present a teleological view of modernization. In this sense, Luo's (re)interpretation of the history of China's twentieth century is, just like other New Enlightenment works like Gan Yang's writings in the 1980s, essentially framed by the "modernization fantasy."

The teleological view of modernization is even more striking in the work of Jin Guantao and Liu Qingfeng, two historians and leading representatives of the New Enlightenment. Jin and Liu co-authored an influential and well-received book, *Prosperity and Crisis: On the Ultrastable Structure of Chinese Society*, in which they systematically reinterpreted Chinese history in order to provide answers to the questions they raised: "Why did modern China drop behind? Why is the obstacle that [Chinese] tradition presented to modernization so huge?" (Jin Guantao and Liu Qingfeng 1992[1984]: 8) Unlike Luo Rongqu who focused on the century from the 1890s to the 1990s, Jin and Liu dealt with the whole of China's dynastic history from the Qin to the Qing (221 B.C.–1911 A.D.). Their study of "pre-modern" China, like Luo Rongqu's study of the history of "modern China," is also organized around modernization. This is because Jin and Liu sought to tell a coherent story of the Chinese past through the model of Western-style modernization as the yardstick for the re-description of two thousand years of China's "pre-modern" history.

According to Jin and Liu, there is an "ultrastable" structure that shaped and sustained the "circular changes" in Chinese society throughout the premodern dynastic centuries and that also affected developments in China's twentieth century: so-called Chinese Marxism is in their view simply this old structure with a new outlook. In other words, the "ultrastable structure" was also responsible for the sinicized (*Zhongguohua*) Marxism that took the form of Mao Zedong Thought. In their view, "it is traditional Chinese culture that distorted Marxism-Leninism, and caused the disastrous Cultural Revolution." They claim that despite the apparent difference between Chinese society under Mao and traditional society, the two shared a deep connection. They saw it as their task to identify the cause of China's "feudalist" culture and to locate the "traditional genre of Mao Zedong Thought" (Jin Guantao and Liu Qingfeng 2000: 5). For this reason, they refer to both Confucianism and Maoism as part of the one tradition evolved out of the "ultrastable structure" of Chinese society. In this context, they call Confucianism the "old tradition," and Maoism the "new tradition."[5] For Jin and Liu, China as the Nation-Subject was impaired due to this ultrastable structure, which they argue has prevailed into the twentieth century in the hybrid form of sinicized Marxism. Modernization (especially the "cultural modernization") is necessary for China to acquire "enlightened" vision because it is by definition *the* project that can achieve a radical break from the "traditional" Chinese culture. In this sense, Jin and Liu's historical analysis resonates strongly with Gan Yang's thesis on the need for a thorough negation of the traditional form of Chinese culture.

In a book published in 2000, Jin and Liu extend their theory of China's "ultrastable structure" from the domain of socio-historical studies to the field of Chinese intellectual history. They claim that the same ultrastable structure has shaped the ways in which Chinese thought has been produced for over two thousand years. According to Jin and Liu's study, "Mao Zedong Thought" is by no means unique or a radical departure from Chinese tradition. Rather, they see it as reflecting the structure of traditional Chinese culture using Marxist terminology. In this book Jin and Liu

[5]The articulation of the "old" and "new" traditions can be found in many other New Enlightenment intellectuals' discourses (for example, Tang Yijie 2001b: 130–131).

sought "to show that Chinese thought from Han dynasty down to the Cultural Revolution is actually organized by a simple logic." They claim that Chinese history which is usually divided into different phases or periods is actually a consistent whole. Chinese Marxism, which "emerged after the May Fourth Movement, in essence, is a certain slightly altered structure (*biangou*) of the main tradition of Chinese culture" (Jin and Liu 2000: 56). What emerges from this "altered structure" is in their view merely the old untrastable structure with a new appearance, decorated by Marxist–Leninist terminology. Therefore, in Jin and Liu's argument, modernization promises a radical change which breaks not only with the persistent ultrastable tradition of Chinese culture but with the intrinsically traditionalistic structure of Maoism.

In Jin and Liu's argument, "history" is posited as an agent-subject who is capable of "choosing" what it "needs." For example, they claim that "from our point of view, the fact that the doctrines of Emperor Huang and Lao Zi (*huanglao zhi xue*) emerged in the early period of Han dynasty, manifests the historical need of the unification structure, which is, the dominant ideology must be provided with the structure of the unity of Heaven and human" (Jin and Liu 2000: 28).[6] In this sense, they actually do not discuss the "unification structure" (a term they use interchangeably with the "ultrastable structure") they claim to have discovered in China's history as simply an analytical concept; rather, they treat it as a Subject which fully "knows" its own "needs" in order to keep functioning properly. Thus, in Jin and Liu's articulation, this ultrastable structure, in order to maintain its proper function during different historical epochs, "chose" Confucianism, and later Maoism, in order to meet its own "need." The problem with this kind of theorization is that the ultrastable structure then becomes a kind of trans-historical force by means of which Chinese history evolves. Evidence of such a structure remains a hypothesis even though Jin and Liu use a lot of historical data to "prove" their argument. This is because, in their analysis, they select data that conforms to their claims about the existence of an "ultrastable structure" shaping the development of Chinese history. The teleological approach that Jin and Liu adopt leads them to write about history *as if* it had and

[6] One can find other similar examples at, for example, Jin and Liu 2000: 25–26, 52, 60.

knew its own "end" or "need."[7] This "ultrastable structure" is, from Lacanian psychoanalytic view, therefore precisely a fantasmatic construction — even its "historical needs" cannot be backed up by empirical studies (an apparent fabrication indeed), *yet they are the "truth."* Tradition — no matter whether Confucianism as the "old tradition" or Maoism as the "new tradition" — has to be shattered in order for the project of modernization to start up, a project that would, viewed by Jin and Liu through their fantasmatic vista, lead Chinese people "towards *the* future" (this phrase itself is the title of a very influential book series for which Jin Guantao served as its co-chief editor). The function of this fantasmatic narrative about China's "pre-modern history" is, in the light of this Lacanian angle, nothing but providing the following self-posed questions "Why did modern China drop behind? Why is the obstacle that [Chinese] tradition presented to modernization so huge?" a satisfying answer, and then in turn, affirming the (new) "historical need" of modernization (as the project of removing this identified obstacle). What is interesting is that Jin and Liu criticize Marx, Weber and neo-liberal theories for using one simple mechanism — such as the surplus value of labor, the rationalization of society, or the mechanisms of the market economy — to provide a grand blueprint of human history (Jin and Liu 2000: viii–xi). Clearly, they do not see that they are also providing a blueprint of Chinese history, using an equally simple mechanism of the "ultrastable structure."

Tang Yijie, the philosopher who headed the Academy of Chinese Culture in the 1980s, also contended that there was a structural resemblance between traditional Chinese thought and Mao Zedong Thought. Like Jin and Liu, Tang also used the phrase "old tradition" to describe Confucianism, and "new tradition" to describe Chinese Marxism and Maoism (see Tang Yijie 2001b: 130–131). In his essay entitled "The 'Cultural Fever' and the 'Craze for National Studies'," Tang notes that in the May of 1985, a

[7] Such theorization is Hegelian and anti-Hegelian at the same time: it is Hegelian in terms of "history" being posited as a Spirit or Mind moving towards its own end, and strongly anti-Hegelian in so far that this Spirit does not *move dialectically* towards its end — it either remains "ultrastable" (no "movement" at all) or moves linearly (from traditional "ultrastable structure" to modernity).

conference called "Symposium on Cultural Matters" was held in Shenzhen, which he believes set the tone for the "cultural fever" that ensued ("Cultural fever" is synonymous with New Enlightenment). In that conference, according to Tang, scholars from Beijing, Shanghai, Wuhan, Xi'an, and Shenzhen made a collective announcement, in which they claimed that "modernization should not be limited to the scientific-technological dimension. Rather, it should be complemented by deep cultural modernization, including values, ways of thinking, and reflections on our old and new traditions, and so forth" (Tang Yijie 2001a: 113). Tang and those scholars who attended that conference clearly echoed Jin Guantao and Liu Qingfeng's thesis on China's "dual traditions." Their ways of formulating modernization show the importance they placed on "cultural modernization" as the key to the overall transformation of China's "old tradition" (Confucianism) and "new tradition" (Maoism).

At this juncture, it is worth noting that many of the participants in the 1980s New Enlightenment conceived of this intellectual movement as guided mainly by three major groups of intellectuals: (1) *Towards the Future* book series editorial board headed by Bao Zunxin and Jin Guantao; (2) another editorial committee led by Gan Yang, which was responsible for several book series under the name of *Culture: China and the World*; as well as (3) a group of intellectuals associated with the Academy of Chinese Culture, a non-official academic organization that made a significant contribution to the "cultural fever" in the mid- and late 1980s (see Chen Fong-ching 2001: 72; also Xu Jilin 2000: 178–181). The above analyses of Gan Yang, Jin Guantao and Liu Qingfeng, and Tang Yijie, the respective leaders of these three groups, show that their attitudes towards modernization were indeed quite "homogenous." Their constant calls for cultural modernization reflect the teleological structure of their arguments: it is described as a linear progression towards *the future* (as the name of the New Enlightenment book series *Towards the Future* suggests).[8] In this

[8] This image of ongoing progress was also common in the writings of many other Chinese intellectuals during the 1980s, and even in the 1990s. For example, the influential book *The History of China's Modernization* co-edited by Xu Jilin and Chen Dakai and published in 1995 can be seen as a continuation of the New Enlightenment interpretation of China's history (see Xu Jilin and Chen Dakai 1995).

sense, they imagine "China" fantasmatically as a Subject advancing towards the future, in pursuit of an "elusive" modernization that it has so far been unable to reach.

When I stated earlier that the New Enlightenment discourse about cultural modernization could be described in Lacanian terms as a fantasy, I was primarily focusing on the ways in which New Enlightenment intellectuals believed that it was possible not only for everyone to see the same reality but for everyone to share the same set of values and ideas and to shape the destiny of the Chinese. Through the analyses of those leading figures of the 1980s New Enlightenment, one can see that this modernization fantasy is clearly at work, functioning as the underlying ground of the New Enlightenment thinkers' discussions of China's past, present, as well as its future, and thereby forming a "homogeneity of attitudes" among them. The use of the word "struggle" is important in their discourse, indicating a tough break between "traditional" (China's past) and "modern" (*the future* of China) that has not yet been actualized; which is to say, China has not fully "opened its eyes," and thus needs a further Enlightenment. Gan Yang's slogan of the "struggle between the ancient and the modern" was highly popular in the 1980s precisely because it accorded with the popular fantasm of China as a collective Subject on the arduous road towards the realization of "cultural modernization."

In fact, Luo Rongqu reflects the use of such language in his *New Discussion on Modernization* when he writes that "China has had more than one hundred years' tough struggle in exploring its own road of modernization." Luo treats the historical period from the 1860s to the 1940s as "China's hard course toward modernization" and links this "hard course" to the present "socialist modernization" as the "tough struggle of more than one hundred years" (Luo Rongqu 2004 [1993]: 119, 249–403). This "modernization" rhetoric is thus the means by which modernization is represented as an ongoing struggle. Jin Guantao and Liu Qingfeng's works which mainly focus on the "feudal" history of China reflect the same preoccupation with the challenge of overcoming China's "ultrastable structure." In this regard, they attempt to read the past from the perspective of the future — that is, to read it through a specific teleological lens. What is crucial here is that Jin and Liu — as well as other New Enlightenment intellectuals like Gan Yang, Luo Rongqu — have already presupposed a specific concept of *change* as linear progression. They have also defined a path (based on Western modernization studies) and then applied this path as the criterion by which to judge China's progress towards modernization. When Jin and Liu criticize Maoist socialism as the intrusion of a malignant aspect of "feudal" China returning in the twentieth century to disrupt the fragile social structure of a newly modernized China, they rely, like Gan Yang, on the dichotomy between "tradition" (or "feudalism") and "modernity"[9] to make their case.

From New Enlightenment to River Elegy and "Confucian Capitalism"

What emerges from these 1980s intellectual discourses of Chinese history is hence a new, (supposedly) "enlightened" version of "reality" framed through the conceptual model of cultural modernization, which fantasmatically re-articulates the last one hundred years as a consistent "course," and China's "pre-modern" history as "ultrastable." In this framework, the West is not featured as a hostile force. Rather, it is the historical period of Maoist construction (throughout the 1950s till the 1970s) that is conceived of as an obstacle to modernization. By describing the Maoist era as the obstacle to cultural modernization, the New Enlightenment discourse of the 1980s thus conforms to the official economic project of modernization to provide a new way of seeing China's historical past and the present-day reality using a new set of concepts (that are opposed to the revolutionary rhetoric of the Maoist era) such as "rationality," "industrialization," "market," "democracy," "science," "enlightenment," "human rights," and so on and so forth. From a Lacanian perspective these concepts can be said to organize and shape what we might call the 1980s' fantasmatic vista of modernization. These are concepts that enable China to be imagined as a harmonious system or a coherent symbolic order. They stand for New Enlightenment and thus for "cultural modernization" that seeks to take the best from the "old tradition" of Confucianism while rejecting the worst

[9]As mentioned earlier, "modernity" as a noun was rarely used in the 1980s New Enlightenment discourse. Instead, what those New Enlightenment intellectuals employed was "modern."

aspects of the "new tradition" of Maoism. Thus, in Lacanese, modernization discourse is a fantasmatic narrative at its purest, contributing to a powerful illusion of social harmony. What this illusion produces is the promise of the social harmony in the future. The costs associated with securing social harmony are not taken into account.

The New Enlightenment discourse of the 1980s became known as "cultural fever" because it elevated intellectuals to new social heights. In fact, it was also referred to as a "fever for intellectuals." Leading intellectuals in the New Enlightenment movement saw themselves as heroic figures who were working to discover the ultimate truth so that they might lead the nation towards a bright future. Thus, once "the critical focus has shifted from the binary of East–West conflict to that of a tradition-modernity transformation" (to recall Zhang Xudong's comment cited earlier), the "heroes" of modernization were able to claim that they were working to resolve the antagonism between socialism (China) and capitalism (the West) and that China's modernization would be realized through overcoming the obstacles of undesirable aspects of Chinese tradition. In a recent interview on the topic of the 1980s intellectual movement conducted two decades later, Gan Yang still uses words like "famous figures," "celebrities," and "talented people" to describe himself and his peers as leading participants of the 1980s intellectual movement (Gan Yang 2006c: 203, 208–209, 215, 219).[10]

This is why the New Enlightenment intellectuals often regard the 1980s intellectual movement as another May Fourth movement. As Xu Jilin notes, "Some participants in the New Enlightenment were to employ just such a transhistorical evocation when they claimed that their efforts in the 1980s were a revivification of the May Fourth era" (Xu Jilin 2000: 169, 176). May Fourth was a time when intellectuals pictured themselves as playing a significant and heroic role in changing the ideological co-ordinates of social reality (see, for example, Lin Yü-sheng 1979). To this day, many leading intellectuals active in the 1980s like Gan Yang and Xu Youyu continue to claim that what they were doing in the 1980s was tantamount to discovering the truth about modernization for the entire nation. For example, Xu Youyu, who was associated with Gan Yang in the

---

[10] I will discuss Gan Yang's writings in the 2000s in Chapter 6.

Culture: China and the World group, claimed in 2006 that when members of his group "strongly advocated 'wholesale Westernization'," they were doing the right thing (Xu Youyu 2006). Xu Youyu is, unlike Gan, happy to describe modernization as Westernization, and to affirm the legacy of the May Fourth movement as a project of Westernization that would reap benefits for China. As noted earlier in this chapter, Gan's substitution of "modernization" for "Westernization" is purely discursive, and, to some extent, strategic. Thus, Xu's retrospective account is closer to the actual direction of the 1980s New Enlightenment discourse. This direction is much clearer in the famous 1988 TV series *River Elegy* (*He Shang*), which sought to embody the New Enlightenment spirit.

River Elegy has been very often viewed as the crucial mediator connecting the "cultural fever" to the socio-political movements of the late 1980s.[11] This socially influential six-episode television series was produced by several self-claimed New Enlightenment intellectuals including Su Xiaokang, Wang Luxiang and Xie Xuanjun. Jin Guantao was invited to serve as a main consultant, and other leading representatives of the New Enlightenment intellectuals like Liu Qingfeng, Li Yining, and many others appeared in the show as interviewees. *River Elegy* was aired on CCTV (China's Central TV) twice in June and August of 1988. As a commentator notes, through this popular TV series, "the cultural movement [in the 1980s] finally found its voice in the true mass media of the day" (see Chen Fong-ching 2001: 81).

Using the analogy of the Yellow River, China was portrayed in *River Elegy* as once at the forefront of civilization, but subsequently dried up due to isolation and conservatism. *River Elegy* contrasts the "yellow civilization" represented by China with the "blue civilization" represented by the West and Japan, proclaiming that the revival of China must come from the explorative, open cultures of the "blue civilization." Following the model that Jin Guantao and Liu Qingfeng's historical studies have

---

[11] For example, in their coauthored essay entitled "China's Intellectuals in the Deng Era: Loss of Identity with the State," Merle Goldman, Perry Link and Su Wei contend that *River Elegy* represented a new "stage" (the last stage) of the 1980s intellectual movement, which led directly to the democracy movement of 1989 and its bloody suppression (Goldman, Link and Wei 1993). Chen Fong-ching (2001) also holds a similar view.

produced, *River Elegy* specifies two targets of the "anti-traditionalist spirit" of the New Enlightenment — Confucianism (i.e. the "old tradition") and Maoism (i.e. the "new tradition"). Furthermore, it spreads the message of the New Enlightenment using the dragon symbolism that, as we saw in Chapter 1, was already highly popular as a result of Hou Dejian's pop song. Two illustrative quotes from the transcript of *River Elegy* follow:

> The psyche of our nation is suffering. All trauma is located in the fact that our civilization has waned. [...] Today, it is time to thoroughly awaken it. [...] What we, descendants of the dragon, need to create is a brand-new civilization. (cited from the first episode of *River Elegy*)
>
> [The tragic turbulence in the Cultural Revolution period] is a tragedy for the whole nation. If China's social structure remains un-renewed, Chinese politics, China's economy, culture and Chinese ideas will remain in an un-modernized state. Could we assure ourselves that the tragedy will not return? (cited from the fifth episode)[12]

In the Introduction I discussed Chen Yinque's eulogy for Wang Guowei in which Chen explained the cause of Wang's suicide in 1927 as the trauma of witnessing the decline of Chinese civilization. Sixty years later, *River Elegy* echoes this view of Chen and uses psychoanalytic terms to describe the "wane of our civilization": in the eyes of the producers of *River Elegy*, the decline of Chinese civilization is a "fact," and this fact has never stopped producing traumatic feelings in "the psyche of our nation." Even in the post-Maoist present, still "[t]he psyche of our nation is suffering." Only by "creating a brand-new civilization" (which means, a thorough change of China's social structure) can this trauma embedded in the psyche of the Chinese people be released.

By identifying "us" (*women*) as "descendants of the Dragon," the narrative of *River Elegy* also echoes Hou Dejian's pop song. However, whereas Hou's use of the dragon symbolism is mainly to create a sense of

[12] Quoted from the narration of the TV series *He Shang*.

belonging, the use of the same dragon symbolism in *River Elegy* is to provide an argument in favor of democratization. Democracy is the key topic addressed in the final episode of *River Elegy*. The "thorough modernization" (including cultural, economic, and political aspects) that *River Elegy* advocates was seen by many intellectuals in the 1980s as a confirmation of their views. In fact, in the early 1990s, many would claim that the TV series provided inspiration for the 1989 Tiananmen student protest (after the Tiananmen incident, some of the people who worked on *River Elegy* were arrested and others fled mainland China). For example, in his book entitled *China in Growth* published in 2002, the Beijing-based political scientist Fang Ning writes: "The 'stream' of *River Elegy* which flows in the hearts of young students and young intellectuals [...] was not confined to the intellectual field; it, unfortunately, developed into a 'political incident'" (Fang Ning, Wang Bingquan and Ma Lijun 2002: 66). What has to be noted here is that strict censorship in post-Tiananmen mainland China forbids any public discussion of the 1989 student protest. Fang Ning is able to go as far as to suggest that a "political incident" occurred in 1989 only because the view he presents in *China in Growth* accords with the official verdict about the 1989 student protest movement.[13] Fang echoes the official view when he condemns the student movement as a "painful" turbulence that was "conceived and manipulated by a certain small anti-revolutionary group."[14]

In the Hong Kong-based scholar Chen Fong-ching's view, the New Enlightenment intellectual movement of the 1980s not only led directly to the production of *River Elegy*, but also contributed to the emergence of the 1989 student movement and hence the June Fourth Tiananmen event. New

---

[13]For Fang, who stands quite closely towards CCP's official ideology, views that "[T]he result of this long-term intellectual development [from the New Enlightenment to the 1989 student movement via the 'stream' of *River Elegy*] is obviously very painful" (Fang Ning, Wang Bingquan and Ma Lijun 2002: 66).

[14]We can also find the discussions of the causal relationship between the New Enlightenment intellectual movement (especially its voice in mass media represented in *River Elegy*) and the 1989 social movement in the works of some commentators who are sympathetic to the 1989 protest movement. Unfortunately, these discussions can be only found in the publications outside mainland China. See, for example, Chen Fong-ching 2001: 81.

Enlightenment intellectuals not only influenced students in their thinking, but became themselves involved in numerous demonstrations and protest activities (Chen 2001: 81–82). The June Fourth incident — the killings in the streets of Beijing — was a traumatic event for most mainland intellectuals and halted the 1980s New Enlightenment movement. Some New Enlightenment thinkers such as Liu Xiaobo were severely punished by the authorities; others such as Bao Zunxin, Jin Guantao, Liu Qingfeng, Gan Yang were fortunate enough to flee the mainland but were prevented from returning for many years. Most of them, however, visited China in the late 1990s. However, there were many who kept their institutional positions (such as Li Yining and Tang Yijie).

The discourses of the 1990s that became known as "post-New Enlightenment," featuring such concepts as postmodernism, the "humanistic spirit," liberalism, the "New Left," new nationalism, the "China model," etc., can also be regarded as various ways of coping with the trauma caused by state violence in 1989. The presumed "homogeneity of attitude" of the New Enlightenment could no longer be imagined in the post-Tiananmen intellectual world.

In this sense, the intellectual activities of the Academy of Chinese Culture headed by Tang Yijie are quite unique. The Academy organized a series of lectures from the mid- to late 1980s, focusing primarily on classical Chinese philosophy as well as Chinese culture in general. Scholars from overseas were invited to give lectures, such as Tu Wei-ming, a U.S.-based Chinese philosopher and prominent representative of contemporary "neo-Confucians." These activities of the academy raised a range of ideas and issues sweeping across the Chinese intellectual sphere at that time and eventually led to what has been called the "craze for national studies" (*guoxue re*) in the early 1990s. Thus, in terms of anti-traditionalism, the intellectual activities of the Academy of Chinese Culture were not as radical as those of the other two New Enlightenment intellectual groups. This group of intellectuals also turned politically active in 1989. The signatories of the open appeal to the government initiated by poet Bei Dao in February 1989 included not only Bao Zunxin, Jin Guantao, and Liu Qingfeng of the *Towards the Future* group, but also the leading representatives of the Academy of Chinese Culture such as Tang Yijie, Yue Daiyun, and Zhang Dainian. However, although the Academy of Chinese

Culture was suspended for several years after 1989, its leading figures did not receive harsh suppression. Indeed, the intellectual influences of the Academy still thrived and generated in the early 1990s a "craze for national studies."

In the name of reviving "national studies" which seems a counter-trend of the dominant anti-traditionalism of the New Enlightenment movement, "modernization" nonetheless played a key role in the Academy's activities. As Tang Yijie wrote retrospectively about the Academy's activities, "We expected our nation to undergo 'full-scale modernization'" (Tang Yijie 2001a: 114). The members of this group viewed modernization as the guiding principle of their revaluation of traditional Chinese thought. A widely discussed topic in the late 1980s was the question of how Chinese culture could be transformed into a force of modernization. This argument was famously formulated by the U.S.-based historian Lin Yü-sheng as a "creative transformation of Chinese tradition" (Lin Yü-sheng 1988). Lin's phrase became widely used in mainland Chinese intellectual circles in the mid- to late 1980s. The rapid economic development in Singapore, Taiwan, Hong Kong, and South Korea at that time (also known as the "four small dragons in East Asia") served as successful examples of the "modern transformation" of Confucianism. The label of "four small dragons," which draws on the same symbolism as Hou's song, establishes a geo-cultural connection between China (the "Great Dragon") and these four Asian countries and cities (the "four small dragons in East Asia"). The Weberian approach of another U.S.-based historian Yu Ying-shih (Yu Yingshi) became influential in China in the late 1980s. Yu's work focuses on the positive connection between "China's modern religious ethics" and "the spirit of merchants" (Yu Ying-shih 1987: 441–579). In addition, a third U.S.-based historian Ray Huang (Huang Renyu) was also widely read. Huang's method of examining China's "macro history" via the lens of modernization was translated into Chinese in the mid-1980s and made a deep impression on many young scholars (Ray Huang 1981; 1988).

The works of these U.S.-based scholars were introduced to mainland China primarily through the activities organized by the Academy of Chinese Culture. Meanwhile, the concept of "Confucian Capitalism," also appeared in the 1980s to become the explanation for the success of the "four small dragons." For many Chinese intellectuals of the 1980s, this was a persuasive argument that successfully combined China's traditional thought and Western approaches to modernization. In sponsoring lectures and seminars on all of these Confucian-related themes, the Academy contributed key traditional elements to the 1980s discourse of modernization.

Gadamer Versus Huntington

The above analysis of the 1980s Chinese intellectual discourse shows how different individuals and groups sought to articulate, in the name of "(cultural) modernization," a range of goals for China. There were various kinds of social reform agenda advocated by the *Towards the Future* group and the *Culture: China and the World* group,[15] as well as projects of the "creative transformation" of Chinese culture and Confucian-derived "capitalism" presented by the Academy of Chinese Culture group. Despite their evident differences, all these groups shared a positive fantasy of national progress through modernization.

By attempting to advance China's modernization through ideas, New Enlightenment intellectuals in the late 1980s reflected their need for a theoretical framework that would support their goal of a harmonious cross-cultural fusion. Some found the ideas of the German philosopher Hans-Georg Gadamer to be very useful in this regard. Several of Gadamer's major works, such as *Truth and Method*, *Philosophical Hermeneutics*, were successively translated into Chinese in the late 1980s and early 1990s. The systematic introduction of hermeneutic thought however can be traced back to 1983 when a series of lectures on "Post-Analytic Philosophy" was organized by the Institute of Foreign Philosophy at Beijing University, where many New Enlightenment intellectuals including Gan Yang were studying at that time. This intellectual trend of

[15]The members of these groups were largely intertwined. Knowledge background is regarded by commentators as the major difference between *Towards the Future* intellectuals and *Culture: China and the World* intellectuals: most members of the former group adopt scientific approach, while members of the latter group base their knowledge-background in humanities. See Chen Fong-ching 2001: 76–77; also Xu Jilin 2000: 179–180; Liu Qingfeng 2001: 48.

Gadamerian hermeneutics soon spread into the areas of philosophy, history, and literary criticism. At the peak of the "cultural fever," a conference on "Philosophy and Hermeneutics" was held in Shenzhen in 1987. Hermeneutics was explicitly adopted by Gan Yang and many members of the *Culture: China and the World* group as their main theoretical framework. Zhang Xudong, a U.S.-based literary critic and then a young participant in the 1980s New Enlightenment movement (as a member of the *Culture: China and the World* group) addresses this phenomenon in his 2003 essay "Revisiting the 1980s," arguing that "hermeneutic theory as a mode of thinking and a cultural stance [of many New Enlightenment intellectuals] is of crucial significance in that cultural discussion" (Zhang Xudong 2003: 108). Zhang elaborates this argument in his two-volume study on the 1980s Chinese cultural discourses, *Chinese Modernism in the Era of Reforms*:

> The hermeneutic approach marks the preliminary maturity of the Chinese cultural discussions initiated in a new historical and discursive situation. It is not a methodological achievement of any particular school or individual, but rather a general reorientation in a way of thinking. [...] As far as the discursive logic of the Great Cultural Discussion is concerned, hermeneutics was at the very kernel of the cultural reorientation. (Zhang Xudong 1997: 60–61)

Since this "hermeneutic approach" played such a significant role in the 1980s intellectual movement, let us first have a brief look at the "discursive logic" of Gadamerian hermeneutics. To simplify it to the uttermost, Gadamer's account of dialogue has three distinctive features: it embraces the possibility of dialogue between texts; it takes dialogue to be the most effective model of language; and it aims at a "fusion of horizons" which implies that dialogue, when successful, resolves itself in such a fusion.[16] This Gadamerian "fusion of horizons" received warm acceptance in Chinese intellectual circles of the 1980s and also the 1990s. It was used to present theoretically the prospect of a cross-civilizational fusion between

[16] See David Vessey, "Gadamer and the Fusion of Horizons."

China and the West. Tang Yijie for instance, regarded "finding the converging point in these two cultures [i.e. Western and Chinese cultures]" as a primary task of post-Maoist intellectuals (Tang Yijie 2001a: 68). Similarly, Li Shenzhi, an influential Chinese social scientist and public intellectual, averred that "the fusion of all cultures has already begun," and in China this fusion took place through the project of modernization (Li Shenzhi 2000a: 178, 180).

With regard to the influence of Gadamer on the New Enlightenment discourse, Zhang Xudong further comments:

> Gadamerian "fusion of horizons" serves as both a critical *bridge* across tradition and the modern, and a *fruitful conflation* between an emerging Chinese cultural discourse and a "Western" paradigm of human sciences understood as essentially a critique of modernity. [...] Hermeneutics here is a critical reinvention serving the ends of engaging the new situation with a radically contemporary stance while remaining self-conscious of the historical determination of Chinese society and culture, or at least of the pertinence of one's national, regional, and individual circumstances. All these, to be sure, are articulated in *a painstaking detour through Western texts as an immediate modernity*. It is understood only too well that the real question for the Chinese contemplators is "not in what way being can be understood but in what way understanding is being," as Gadamer says about *Being and Time.* (Zhang Xudong 1997: 60–61, emphases added)

Zhang reads New Enlightenment thinkers such as Gan Yang as successfully employing Gadamerian hermeneutics to serve the end of bridging "tradition and the modern" though he notices that this successful fusion ("fruitful conflation") between traditional Chinese culture and modern "Western" paradigm is still a "painstaking detour." Zhang does not specify what he means by this nor does he explain how the Gadamerian "fusion of horizons" was adapted by New Enlightenment intellectuals. As noted earlier, the New Enlightenment substitution of "modernization" for "Westernization" is purely discursive and strategic. This cross-civilizational "fusion" is in this sense *itself actually an "immersion"* (into Western civilization), *entailing a total cancellation of the Chinese culture/civilization.* In this sense, what Zhang Xudong describes as "a painstaking detour through Western texts as an immediate modernity" is not a detour at all.

A successful "fusion" or "fruitful conflation" of the East ("yellow civilization"/Confucianism) and the West ("blue civilization"/capitalism) in the vision of the New Enlightenment intellectuals is therefore no more than a pure illusory (mis)recognition, for they failed to take into account during their adoption of Gadamerian hermeneutics the frequently expressed experiences of deep trauma and torment in the Chinese discourse since late Qing. As I have argued in Chapter 1, when the West is discussed in Chinese public discourse as a source of destruction, it becomes a thing to be feared. Those "cross-civilizational" encounters with the West thus take on what Lacan calls a traumatic form, with China being cast in the role of a victim of the abusive West. Discussions of the West in this form are a *constitutive* element in the narrative of Chinese nationhood. In the 1980s New Enlightenment discourse, however, "China" is not presented as a victim. Rather China is represented as a home to be modernized by heroic figures who are able to guide it towards this goal. The trauma (of China as victim), which was a feature of Maoist discourse as well as discourses of Republican China, is evaded in the 1980s New Enlightenment discourse. The "fruitful conflation" between China and the West preached by the New Enlightenment intellectuals is thus a fantasmatic "bridge" that obscures the "trauma" of violent encounters with the West that earlier discourses of the Maoist and Republican eras highlighted. That is to say, in the 1980s New Enlightenment discourse, the idea of China as victim is displaced by the adoption of a new vision of "fusions of horizons" that understands modernization as *the* common "path" of all civilizations. This also explains why it was theoretically crucial for New Enlightenment thinkers such as Gan Yang to put the dichotomy of "traditional" versus "modern" above (or prior to) the dichotomy of China versus the West: "civilizational discord" was perceived as secondary in order for "a fruitful conflation" to be imagined as the correct way forward. The point is that this "fruitful conflation" rests on nothing more than a fantasmatic scene.

The Lacanian explanation would be that the notion of a "fruitful conflation" between China and the West is itself the result of "looking awry." In other words, the viewer is not seeing reality as such but a version of "reality" perceived from a specific horizon — namely, the fantasy of modernization. Lacanian psychoanalysis tells us that in spite of the denial of an existing problem or emotional disturbance through the operation of fantasy, the problem or disturbance does not go away. Instead, it poses the constant threat of disrupting the "reality" constructed to avoid it.[17]

With regard to what comes after the emergence of critical challenges to the dominant social fantasy, the heated responses to Samuel P. Huntington's 1993 essay "The Clash of Civilizations?" by contemporary Chinese thinkers can be of some help: they are excellent for helping us to understand the fantasmatic function of the New Enlightenment advocacy of a "fusion of horizons" — it allowed people to avoid having to explain the enormous cultural and political differences between China and the West. What Huntington's formulation of civilizational clash evokes in Sinophone intellectual world is exactly the disruptive encounter of some counter argument of the civilizational fusion thesis: Huntington's antagonistic argument clashed directly with the kind of fantasy that China's New Enlightenment intellectuals proposed. Besides the Sinophone debate on Huntington's thesis of "clash of civilizations" in the early 1990s, the heated debate on "postmodernism" in the mid-1990s and the one under the label "liberalism versus the New Left" in the late 1990s can also be analyzed in light of this Lacanian argument on the operation of fantasy. Let us first start with the Huntington debate and follow with the other two debates in Chapters 3 and 4.

The Chinese translation of Huntington's essay was first published in the nineteenth issue (October 1993) of *Twenty-first Century*, a Hong Kong academic journal that was very influential in the post-1989 mainland Chinese intellectual world.[18] Dozens of Chinese intellectuals and scholars from various disciplines responded to Huntington's argument about the "clash of civilizations." Parts of the essays were collected into a book in 1995 entitled *Civilization and International Politics: Chinese Scholars Discuss Huntington's Account of the "Clash of Civilizations,"* edited by

---

[17] In Lacanian psychoanalysis, only in the moment that the (unconscious) fantasy is disruptively challenged, it manifests itself as fantasy (instead of reality).

[18] The editor-in-chief of *Twenty-first Century* is Liu Qingfeng, who went to Hong Kong after 1989, and established *Twenty-first Century* with Jin Guantao, Chen Fong-ching in 1991.

the Beijing-based political theorist Wang Jisi. In the "preface' of the book Wang notes,

> Among the responses [to Huntington's essay by Chinese intellectuals] I have read so far, most of them are critical. Only a few partly agree with Huntington. No one fully endorses his view. [...] A foreigner who studies politics but knows nothing about China has unexpectedly touched a nerve among Chinese intellectuals — the issue of whether there is a clash or a fusion between Chinese and Western cultures is a sensitive topic in China and has remained so for over one hundred years. (Wang Jisi 1995: 178)[19]

Wang's comment highlights the importance that is accorded to the question of the relationship between China and the West in contemporary Chinese intellectual discourse. Let us illustrate a few responses from Chinese thinkers here. In his essay entitled "Remarks on Huntington's 'Clash of Civilizations'," Tang Yijie writes: "The clashes caused by culture are just temporary, and the assimilations and fusions among cultures are dominant" (Tang Yijie 2001a: 60). He Xinquan, a specialist in the field of political philosophy and Confucianism, in responding to Huntington, avers that "culture is not the origin of world-clashes; rather, it is the starting-point of the world-fusion" (He Xinquan 1993: 7). Similarly, Qian Chengdan, a prominent historian argues from the perspective of "world history" in an essay entitled "Clash of Civilizations? In conversation with Huntington": "Civilization develops necessarily through fusion. There will be no civilization if there is no fusion." (Qian Chendan 1995: 338)

These responses of contemporary Chinese thinkers to Huntington (who might even not have had the chance to read these Chinese essays) reflect a defense of fusion that suggests their refusal to accept any other alternative point of view. The strong opposition they showed to Huntington's argument suggests that they are deeply opposed to the idea of a clash between Chinese and Western civilizations. That is to say, they do not engage with Huntington's argument about the "clash of civilizations" but seek from the

[19] Regarding the Sinophone response to Huntington's thesis, Gan Yang's recent comment can also be of a proof: "I might be the only one in the Sinophone academia around 1995, who highly praised Huntington's book. All people held negative views toward that book." (Gan Yang 2012a: 155)

outset to prove it wrong. This indicates that Huntington's argument *projects a "reality" that Chinese intellectuals found unacceptable.*

The essays of these contemporary Chinese thinkers show that they are not disputing the facts Huntington provides or examining his assumptions and flaws. Rather, they were "fighting" in the discursive space against an enemy of their modernization fantasy. Huntington, ironically, was *absent* from the "battle zone" — he was not involved in any actual debate with his Chinese critics. The readers whom these Chinese intellectuals addressed, in this sense, were obviously their own group — those who read Chinese academic journals where these publications appear. In opposing Huntington, these Chinese intellectuals were thus writing to *reassure themselves* about the intellectual enterprise they have been engaging in, or, to put in psychoanalytic terms, to protect their "modernization fantasy" from becoming regarded by their readers as inauthentic. They thus effectively did *not* require Huntington's response for such a defense. They were writing for themselves in the sense that Žižek describes when he quoted Lacan's famous definition of the unsent letter as "A letter [that] always arrives at its destination," one that people write/send to assure themselves.

Hence, what is interesting in the Sinophone reactions to Huntington's thesis is the anxiety they showed in their defense of their own preferred picture of a harmonious "cross-civilizational fusion." It would seem that they were so committed to projecting an image of Chinese modernization as the fusion of civilizations that they found any contrarian view to be intolerable. Although New Enlightenment intellectuals claimed to be endeavoring to "open their eyes," what we find in their strong opposition to Huntington's thesis is their unwillingness to take a serious look at views that contradict the one they deeply held.

Thus, regarding contemporary Chinese intellectuality, it is not surprising that the search for the truth of Chinese cultural identity has tended to hark back to symbols that are well-established such as "descendants of the Dragon." Huntington's thesis played the role of the fearful intruder who threatens the "harmonious" vision of cultural fusion that New Enlightenment intellectuals believed China could attain, so long as they and other Chinese citizens kept improving their ability to see clearly. In this sense, Huntington embodies what the fantasmatic vision of civilizational fusion represses — namely, the prospect of an irresolvable clash.

Thus, the promoters of "fusion" are led to criticize Huntington's argument as unreal in order to claim that they stand on the side of the real. Yet, the problem is that any discussion of what is real or what is reality is dependent on the language used to convey a sense of reality. Reality is, in this sense, symbolic. As Žižek puts it,

> (What we experience as) reality is not the "thing itself", it is always-already symbolized, constituted, structured by symbolic mechanisms — and the problem resides in the fact that symbolization ultimately always fails, that it never succeeds in fully "covering" the Real, that it always involves some unsettled, unredeemed symbolic debt. *This Real (the part of reality that remains non-symbolized) returns in the guise of spectral apparitions.* [...] Spectral apparitions emerge in this very gap that forever separates reality from the Real. (Žižek 1994b: 21)

Hence, for contemporary Chinese thinkers of the New Enlightenment, Huntington's thesis is akin to a negation of their modernization discourse since it upsets the symbolic order of things on which the modernization argument depends. *The extent to which they attack a view that contradicts their own is an indication of how deeply they feel threatened by that contradiction.* While many were critical of Huntington's "clash of civilizations" argument, *they did not condemn him outright.* Their criticisms of "postmodernism" and the "New Left" were far stronger and the attacks that New Enlightenment intellectuals and their followers launched against their peers who held these alternative views led to deep divisions among Chinese intellectuals from the mid-1990s onwards. Once the "Great Dragon fantasy" (the promise of "the eventual return to civilizational grandeur," of the return of the Great Dragon) is positively articulated in the terms of the discourse of modernization construction, it also becomes vulnerable by opening itself to alternative challenges against modernization theory. In this sense, various post-1989 intellectual discourses can be seen as competing narratives emerging to produce new fantasmatic pictures in which the object of the "Great Dragon fantasy" (the elusive *objet petit a*[20]) — China's fullness and greatness — is projected as achievable.

[20] Recall that the Dragon in Chinese culture functions as a figurative representation of the *Dao* of Heaven.

With regard to what follows the emergence of the challenge to the dominant fantasmatic narrative, let us turn to the short story "Black House" by the American writer Patricia Highsmith. Žižek recounts this story to illustrate how a deeply held view can be likened to a fantasy, and the consequence if such a view is severely challenged. The story follows a young man who has just moved into a small American town. In the saloon he listens to the local men recount tales from their youth of their adventures in and around the black house on the hill. This house is a desolate building which, they claim, is either haunted or inhabited by a homicidal maniac or, in some other way, malevolent. Determined to verify this, the young man goes to the house the next evening and finds nothing but an old ruin devoid of any threat, supernatural or otherwise. When he returns to the saloon to inform the men of his findings, they are horrified. One of them then attacks the young man, an act which ultimately results in his death. The reason for this violent behavior, according to Žižek, is that the black house functioned as a fantasmatic screen upon which the local men could project their nostalgic desire. By empirically proving that the house was just an old ruin, the young stranger inadvertently intruded upon the fantasy space of the townsfolk and caused them deep anguish. Their violent reaction is caused by the young man annulling "the difference between reality and fantasy space, depriving the men of the place in which they were able to articulate their desires" (Žižek 1991b: 9; also see Tony Myers 2003: 103).

Just like those townsfolk in Highsmith's story, those New Enlightenment intellectuals were deeply troubled by Huntington's thesis of a "civilizational clash," for it challenges the fantasmatic scenario where China is on the path of modernization leading to a harmonious "cross-civilizational fusion." This heated Sinophone debate over Huntington reflects the kind of threat that the advocates of New Enlightenment want to dispel. In this regard, contemporary Chinese intellectuals who perceive themselves as "heroic" figures defending New Enlightenment toward China's modernization reveal themselves to be highly vulnerable to criticism and challenge.

One can see this even more clearly from the later heated debates on "postmodernism" in the mid-1990s, and the "debates between liberalism and the New Left" in the late 1990s: the way that defenders of the New

Enlightenment reacted to postmodernism and the "New Left" is very similar to the way that the townsfolk in Highsmith's story reacted to the young stranger. This suggests that their vision of China is one that cannot tolerate any contrary points of view. In the next two chapters, I will examine how the discourse of New Enlightenment dealt with the contradictions posed by "postmodernism" and the "New Left." The American philosopher Richard Rorty and the Beijing-based historian Wang Hui are respectively my key case studies in Chapters 3 and 4. Although their arguments bear no similarity to Huntington's, nor to one another, both Rorty and Wang Hui acquired a similar status to Huntington in the 1990s' mainstream discourse of Chinese modernization: they too touched a "nerve" by disrupting the fantasy of modernization as the harmonious fusion of China and the West.

Chapter 3

"Traumatic" Encounters with Postmodernism

The Arrival of a "Post-New Era" and the "Loss of the Humanistic Spirit"

The works of contemporary Western thinkers such as Fredric Jameson, Jean-François Lyotard, Michel Foucault, Jacques Derrida and Richard Rorty have been introduced and translated into Chinese since the mid-1980s. Jameson and Rorty visited mainland China in the mid-1980s and had extensive intellectual exchanges with Chinese thinkers. However, it was not until the early 1990s that a group of Beijing-based literary critics such as Wang Ning, Zhang Yiwu, Chen Xiaoming, Wang Yichuan, Zhang Fa, Wang Zhihe, and so on, started to use their works to promote postmodernism in China.

Zhang Yiwu, in an essay entitled "The End of 'Modernity': An Unavoidable Topic" published in 1994, declared that with the emergence of postmodern discourse in the Western intellectual world, the "myth of modernity has been deconstructed," and consequently, for Chinese intellectuals, "stepping out of 'modernity' means a new path of development and the emergence of a new cultural strategy" (Zhang Yiwu 2000[1994]: 230). According to Zhang and other self-named "Chinese postmodernists," this "new cultural strategy" is the thriving popular commercial culture that quickly developed after Deng Xiaoping's statement "to get rich is glorious" unleashed a tidal wave of commercial euphoria in China. The quick emergence of a "consumer society with socialist characteristics" after Deng Xiaoping made his famous "Tour of the South" in January 1992 brought deep social changes. The cultural and value shifts caused by commercialization were depicted by Chinese promoters of postmodernism as the emergence of a promising postmodern culture and the end of modernity; and they saw the emergence of postmodern culture as a "new path of development" (Zhang 2000: 231). Because the 1980s is often called the "new era" in the post-Maoist official as well as intellectual discourses to demarcate the Party-state's new agenda of modernization from its Maoist past, the post-1989 era was labeled by Zhang Yiwu and other Chinese post-modernists as the "post-new era." By this, they meant an era that embraces the end of modernity. As Gloria Davies pointed out, "When Zhang and others coined the term 'post-New Era,' they sought to cast a postmodern aura over the expanded scope of intellectual and cultural practices that had flourished in mainland China since the 1990s as a consequence of cultural commercialization." Chinese postmodernists defined the "new era" as one that sought to achieve China's modernization through market reforms; and by using the prefix "post" to distinguish the 1990s from the 1980s, they signaled that contemporary Chinese culture had in fact entered into post-modernity (Davies 2007: 139).

Although Zhang Yiwu did not find many allies willing to celebrate the arrival of postmodernism in China, his announcement of the end of modernity in China certainly hit a nerve among mainland Chinese intellectuals. As its result, a heated debate on "postmodernism" started. Writing as an ally of Zhang's, Chen Xiaoming described this debate as unbalanced: he observed that there were only a few people on the side of "postmodernism" but there was a huge army on the opposing side. In an essay Chen published in 1994, he claimed that the discourse of post-modernism in China showed enormous potential: "Although postmodern studies in contemporary China are just 'a few drops of rain,' nonetheless it has already caused general panic and fierce attacks, from which we can see its potential." According to Chen, critics of postmodernism in China were deliberately overlooking the fact that "Daily life in China and Chinese popular culture are already postmodernized" (Chen Xiaoming 2000[1994]: 177–178).[1] Ten years later in 2004, Chen compiled a book entitled *Postmodernism* which includes a large number of essays written by contemporary Chinese authors in the mid-1990s on the topic of postmodernism. In the editorial preface of the book, Chen mentioned another reason for the "unbalanced" nature of the debate: he

[1] In parallel to the term "modernization," the term *houxiandaihua* ("postmodernization" or "postmodernize") is also very often used in Chinese in the 1990s.

claimed that whereas advocates of postmodernism were only able to publish their essays in rather insignificant journals, their adversaries could easily make their voices heard in influential ones (Chen Xiaoming 2004: 4).

Among the critics of postmodernism, the majority were famous participants of the 1980s New Enlightenment movement. For example, Xu Youyu published several essays in different journals to criticize the "postmodernist challenge to contemporary Chinese culture." Xu rejects the Chinese postmodernists' depiction of present-day Chinese society:

> What those postmodern theorists are unwilling to admit is that China is still in the pre-modernized and pre-industrialized phase. Thus, the path of modernization is still valuable to China. Modernization should be advanced, not discarded, for it is still an unfinished enterprise in China. I understand that a few literary theorists and artists are fond of avant-garde experiments. However, postmodernism should not become a direction for societal development, or the standard for cultural criticism. There is a national consensus that China needs to be modernized. (Xu Youyu 1999[1996]: 354, also, 250–251)

Xu stresses that China's social condition (*guoqing*) was totally different from that of the contemporary Western "post-industrial" societies in which postmodern discourse originated and thrived. He argues that in the West, postmodernism was a "utopian reaction" towards the negative consequences of modern industrialization. Thus, it was not suitable for China because the country "has not yet solved the basic problems of adequate food and clothing (*wenbao wenti*)." Xu further claims that because the negative consequences of industrialization in the West were not the same as in China, postmodernism was a luxury that China could not afford. It had, in Xu's view, no constructive value and offered the wrong kind of criticism because China was not yet fully modernized (Xu Youyu 1997[1996]: 192). In an essay entitled "'Post-ism' and Enlightenment," Xu defines postmodernism, along with other alleged "post-ist discourses" (including postcolonialism, poststructuralism, "postphilosophical" culture and "post-new era"), as a counter-Enlightenment discourse. By "Enlightenment," Xu certainly does not merely mean an abstract philosophical discourse originated in the seventeenth-centuries Europe; rather he means the 1920s May Fourth Enlightenment movement and the 1980s New Enlightenment movement in China. In Xu's depiction, "Enlightenment" is "a sublime, necessary, and unfinished enterprise; it is especially so in China." He argues that the two Chinese Enlightenment movements of the 1920s and 1980s were halted not because they had run their course, but because they were violently suppressed. Hence, "Enlightenment in the eighties was clearly not excessive. In fact, it was insufficient." (Xu Youyu 1999[1997]: 364–365) On this basis, Xu concludes: "I am afraid that to embrace postmodernism in today's China is a kind of acute disease. [...] The postmodernist experiment in China is a suicidal act which would bury the experimenters themselves." (Xu Youyu 2004[1995]: 150–151) What should be stressed is that in offering this conclusion, Xu claims that he is not only expressing his personal view but representing a "national consensus."

Indeed, Xu Youyu is representative of many Chinese intellectuals who are opposed to postmodernism and who express a deep concern for China's modernization project. Similarly, a group of Shanghai-based intellectuals, including the literary critic Wang Xiaoming, the philosopher Zhang Rulun, the historian Zhu Xueqin, also claim that the emergence of postmodernism in China had caused great damage. They went further than Xu Youyu. They claim that postmodernism had not only handicapped China's modernization but brought about a disastrous "loss of the humanistic spirit" (*renwen jingshen de shiluo*). They regard postmodernism as intellectual endorsement for the rapid rise of China's consumer society and its commodity-oriented popular culture. In 1994 and since, these Shanghai-based intellectuals have published their discussions on this issue in the influential intellectual journal *Readings* (*Dushu*). They claimed that they were defending the dying "humanistic spirit."

In one of these discussions, Zhang Rulun states that "because we are not satisfied with the current cultural condition, we start to pursue the lost humanistic spirit. Though the elements which caused this general dissatisfaction are diverse, fashionable 'deconstructionism' is undoubtedly one of these elements. [...] It is however 'deconstructionism' itself that needs to be deconstructed." (Zhang Rulun *et al.* 1996[1994]: 72–73) One of Zhang's interlocutors, the Shanghai-based literary critic Gao Yuanbao went even further. He says that "The intellectual unity featured in [the intellectual movement of] the new era [i.e. the 1980s] was deconstructed in the post-new era. But who deconstructed it? Deconstructivists? Avant-garde artists? Postmodernists? It seems to be none of them." (Gao in Zhang Rulun *et al.* 1996[1994]: 74) What Gao implies in this passage is, within the social context, quite unambiguous: it was political oppression by the state that put an end to the "new era" of the 1980s New Enlightenment movement. Thus, it is not, as Chinese postmodernists proclaimed, the arrival of postmodernism in China that ended the Enlightenment and modernity. In the same conversation, another interlocutor, the Shanghai-based literary critic Ji Guibao stresses that as various new post-ist theories such as Rorty, Jameson etc. flooded into the Chinese intellectual world, the significance of Chinese culture itself had become effaced. For Ji, "the direction of the 'cultural fever' in the 1980s had the positive and conscious effect of [making] cultural contributions." He notes that this movement was eventually suppressed because the cultural realm in China was still not independent. He claims that it needed to be separated from the political and the economic realms. (Ji in Zhang Rulun *et al.* 1996[1994]: 77–78). In their discussions, those Shanghai intellectuals regard the "humanistic spirit" as the lost essence of Chinese civilization. They claim that that was what the 1980s "cultural fever" tried to resuscitate. They then accuse postmodernism of nihilism, claiming that it dismissed this valuable cultural spirit and impeded the "realization of a true 'fusion of horizons'" (Zhang Rulun *et al.* 1996[1994]: 76–82).

In his rebuttal of this call for resuscitating the "humanistic spirit," Chen Xiaoming avers that this so-called "humanistic spirit" is just an "illusion" (*huanjue*). He claims, in a rather sarcastic tone, that those intellectuals who are "so sublime and so responsible" invented the phrase "humanistic spirit" to offer a new "grand narrative" after the "modernization" discourse started to lose its attraction in the post-1989 era; and they invented the discourse of "humanistic spirit" not because they were concerned about China's reality or tried to carry forward the moral responsibility of keeping cultural essence alive. Rather, they were just used to speaking and writing about this kind of "meta-narrative." Chen also claims that these guardians of the "humanistic spirit" were using this new discourse to attack postmodernist theory, in their attempts to assert their "discursive hegemony." Chen further stresses that the rapid rise of postmodernism indicates its inevitability, and he regards it as a new direction for China. He states that it was precisely because this rise was so rapid that the defenders of the New Enlightenment generation had no time to become familiar with it; thus "they feel that they have been truly abandoned by history" (Chen Xiaoming 1996[1994]: 120–128).

Zhang Yiwu's rebuttal was less subtle and more nationalistic than Chen Xiaoming's. Zhang calls the discourse of "humanistic spirit" the "last myth." He writes: "Observed from within the historical context of contemporary China, the pursuit of the 'humanistic spirit' is actually a pursuit of cultural 'universality'; thus it is the result of submission to and identification with Western centralism." Hence, Zhang claims, the "humanistic spirit" discourse is nothing but a strengthened version of the 1980s New Enlightenment discourse that drew in turn on the myth of China's "merging with the world" and with Western centralism. For Zhang, the subjectivity (the subjectivity of Chinese civilization) embodied in this "humanistic spirit" is not a true subjectivity, but "an impotent and inferior Other of the Western world." Zhang's diagnosis is that "Against the utter defiance of current Chinese culture [constitutive of postmodernism], what the 'humanistic spirit' discourse provides is the last resort to return to the old subjectivity. [...] This is an illusionary goal of modernity. This discourse enables those Enlightenment intellectuals to keep occupying the central point of the discursive arena. It is thus nothing but a utilitarian strategy, a power-oriented operation." (Zhang Yiwu 1996[1995]: 139–140)

Chen Xiaoming and Zhang Yiwu regard the 1990s' "humanistic spirit" discourse as a new version of the outdated 1980s' "Enlightenment discourse" which they claim had little relevance in "post-new era" China. For them, the "paradigmatic" transition from modernity to postmodernity is an irreversible process and they claim that the "humanistic spirit" discourse shares an outdated paradigm with the 1980s Enlightenment discourse. Chen and Zhang's provocative writings intensified the debate. For example, in reply, the Beijing-based critic Zhang Zhizhong states that postmodernism itself is also a "myth"; and he claims in turn that "Chinese postmodernists" were also attempting to establish their own "discursive hegemony." Zhang Zhizhong comments that he refuses to use the phrase "post-new era" to describe China after 1989. He argues that since China had already begun the process of modernization it cannot revert to some sort of cultural "hermeticism" in order to become liberated from "Westernization." Zhang further contends,

> Those Chinese post-ist thinkers confuse theory with reality. They import various weapons from the West, and believe that they have chosen the newest and best theory. They think that, by using these weapons they can conquer anything. [...] However, they have not studied the object they attempt to deconstruct, they have no idea the harm this theory will bring to China. They attempt to destroy all "others" (*tazhe*) which impede the rise of postmodernism. What they do to the "humanistic spirit" discussion is merely one of those vicious and destructive acts. (Zhang Zhizhong 1996: 179–180)

Similar to Xu Youyu, Zhang Zhizhong's conclusion is that what postmodernism brings to China is nothing but an irreparable disaster. Among the many vehement Chinese responses to the emergence of postmodernism in the mid-1990s, Xu Youyu and Zhang Zhizhong's responses are actually rather modest. There were others who accused postmodernism (or more broadly, "post-ist discourse") of being a "theoretical magic show and a crazy cultural rant" (Zhang Dexiang 2004[1994]: 105), a "collective spiritual retreat" (He Yi 2004[1995]: 123). From this we can see that the debate between Chinese postmodernists and their opponents was not a polite academic disagreement but a fight between two camps that both believed they were defending the truth about their society: those who supported the New Enlightenment were convinced that China's modernization project is well underway and must not be disrupted; at their opposite side stood the "post-ist" conviction that "China has already entered into postmodernity and the paradigm shift from modernity to postmodernity is an unstoppable new direction." The intensity of this debate reflects a situation similar to the one presented in the preceding chapter. People held a given view so strongly that they denounced all opposing views that posed the threat of undermining their "sense of reality." The strength of this conviction in a given view of reality can be illustrated in the attacks made on the works of Richard Rorty. In the section below, we shall see how the defenders of New Enlightenment turn Rorty, who is viewed in China as a prominent postmodern thinker, into an object of criticism.

Richard Rorty Must Leave!

The reasons I have picked Rorty are two-fold. First, by comparison with the innumerable Chinese writings on Fredric Jameson, Michel Foucault, and Jacques Derrida, writings about Rorty are comparatively modest: there have been two monographs and roughly three dozen papers on Rorty's ideas by Chinese authors since the 1980s. This makes a thorough discourse analysis possible.[2] Second, in spite of the modest number of Chinese commentaries on Rorty's work, the symbolic influence of Rorty is nonetheless quite deep. Rorty himself visited China twice (1985 and 2004) and each time aroused broad controversies in the Chinese intellectual world. And most of his works, as well as many studies of Rorty's thought by Western scholars have been translated. In contrast, the introduction and translation of the works of other thinkers who are identified in mainland China as "postmodernist," such as Jean-François Lyotard, Jean Baudrillard, and Jacques Lacan, are less salient because they are not much discussed. Quite interesting though, Rorty suggests that "we must be ethnocentric" because there are always great difficulties in understanding an alien culture, so that there is nothing to be said if we move outside "a given society — *ours*" (Rorty 1991: 26, 23). Even if Rorty was not much interested in his "fantasmatic images" produced in China, nonetheless he acquired a unique symbolic significance for contemporary Chinese intellectuals.

In my analysis, I will continue to draw on Slavoj Žižek's ideas and argue that when certain Chinese intellectuals insist that China does not need postmodernism, they are reacting against the threat of a "trauma-maker," to borrow Žižek's term. In other words, they oppose postmodern discourse because it undermines and negates the vision of China's modernization that they defend. They regard postmodernism as unrealistic but do not see that their project of modernization — their scheme of getting China from an unsatisfactory "here" to a fully developed "there" — is equally fantasmatic. In their writings, these promoters of modernization tend to claim that the idea of the "post-modern" is unnecessary and irrelevant for China.

---

[2]This is 2004 data made before Rorty's second lecture tour in China during which I served as his translator.

Yet because postmodernism is a widely known concept in the West, they argue that it only has a relevance there and make use of Rorty to illustrate this point.

Sometime in the early 1980s, Rorty was bestowed with a Chinese name — "Luo Di." Since then, his works have been introduced, interpreted and discussed in mainland Chinese scholarship and intellectual circles using this Chinese name. However, "Luo Di" is in no way a transparent mirror of Rorty. The difference between these two names is more than merely linguistic. If we accept that every language is made up of a unique network of signifiers and that what Lacan calls the symbolic order is composed of signifying chains that shape our perception of reality, then the process of translating ideas from English to Chinese will lead those ideas to become subject to the symbolic order that constitutes "reality" as it is perceived in the Chinese language. In this regard, "Luo Di" is a product of Sinophone discourse and it is inevitable that "Luo Di" should differ from Rorty and how "he" sounds and is received in English.

Rorty's thought has been interpreted by Chinese intellectuals as an important aspect of Western postmodernism. The identification of Rorty with postmodernism has been widespread since the 1980s. Zhang Guoqing, one of the main Chinese translators and interpreters of Rorty's works, has written a monograph, *The Spiritual Condition in the Non-Foundational Era*: *An Intellectual Study of Rorty's Philosophy*, in which he avers: "Postphilosophical culture is undoubtedly a kind of postmodernist culture. Although Rorty himself uses the term 'postmodern' in a very cautious way, the postphilosophical culture that Rorty advocates is obviously a kind of postmodern culture." (Zhang Guoqing 1999: 391) Disregarding Rorty's own cautiousness in relation to the term "postmodern," Zhang employs adverbs of a definite tone, such as "undoubtedly" and "obviously," to label Rorty's thought as "postmodern." This rather arbitrary labeling could be found in many other Chinese writings on Rorty. The intellectuals in contemporary China who regard Rorty seriously as a "postmodernist" are greater in number than those who regard him as a "pragmatist" or an "ironist," though Rorty far more frequently called himself the latter rather than the former (see Guo Guichun 1994: 25–33; Liu Kui 1995: 102–127; Zhou Tiejun and Wang Chuanxi 1995: 27–32; Chen Huaxing 1997; Guo Guichun and Li Hong 1997; Tan

Zhongyi 1998: 16–20; Hong Xiaonan 1999; Xiao Feng 2000. Also cf. Wang Yuechuan 1992: 198–228; Wang Zhihe 1993; Sheng Ning 1997: 106–128; Guo Guichun 1998: 151–178; Yao Dazhi 2000: 268–301; She Biping 2000: 115–127; Chang Shiyan 2001: 222–240).

Houxiandai, the Chinese translation of the "postmodern," as noted before, is frequently understood and debated by Chinese thinkers in comparison with "modernization" (*xiandaihua*). It was also in the 1980s that ideas under the label "postmodernism" were introduced into the Chinese intellectual world; and this trend of introducing Western postmodern thought reached its zenith in the mid-1990s. In his 1998 monograph on postmodernism, Zhang Guoqing explains the rise of postmodernism in China as follows:

> Postmodernist thought came to China in the early 1980s and gradually became a fashionable cultural and social phenomenon in China. In the beginning, this trend of thought was prudently introduced by Chinese scholars. Later on, it gradually became a heated topic which produced discussions in Chinese theoretical circles and cultural circles. [...] Many Chinese authors started trying intentionally to produce postmodernist works. These authors wrote with a visible postmodernist intention and began to attract people's attention and comments. Today, it seems that this "cultural bubble" (*wenhua paomo*) which was raised by many artists, litterateurs, philosophers and critics in the field of humanities has become quite prevalent in China. (Zhang Guoqing 1998: 1)

After providing a general survey of the trend of postmodernist thought in the contemporary Chinese intellectual world, Zhang uses the metaphor "cultural bubble" to refer to this "fashionable" postmodernist trend. Zhang's negative attitude toward the "postmodern" is rather obvious. In the conclusion of his book, Zhang asserts,

> Some postmodernists' denial of humanistic spirit and rejection of modernity clearly show that postmodernist thought, in general, runs counter to the basic course of modern society. Modernization does not need postmodernism. Fundamentally speaking, postmodernism has no way out at all in today's China. (Zhang Guoqing 1998: 261)

In Zhang's writing, the humanistic spirit is apparently something close to modernity. He regards it as the ultimate goal of modernization. In his teleological map of China's modernization, postmodernism therefore has no relevance. Moreover, Zhang's statement that "modernization does not need postmodernism" (which is also the title of the final chapter of the book) places "modernization" in the symbolic place of an autonomous subject who knows and is able to choose what it "needs." This kind of writing is very prevalent among New Enlightenment intellectuals. In the large-scale intellectual discussion on subjectivity and humanistic spirit and in the mid-1990s, *the autonomous subject* (*zizhu de zhuti*) has gained the sovereign symbolic position in contemporary Sinophone intellectual discourse; namely, it is posited as a sovereign end. Thus, in Zhang Guoqing's account, modernization is not only a means to an end. By affirming China's modernization rhetorically as *an autonomous subject*, Zhang totally rejects the postmodernist trend in China and concludes that it "has no way out at all in today's China." In Chapter 2 where I discuss Jin Guantao and Liu Qingfeng's historical formulation of what they call the "ultrastable structure," I pointed out that in their writings, "history" is posited as an agent-subject who fully "knows" and is capable of "choosing" what it "needs." Herein we can see the discursive similarity between Jin and Liu's writings in the mid-1980s and Zhang's writings in the mid-1990s. This is because Zhang's anti-postmodernist argument, just like Jin and Liu's in the eighties, is articulated through a totalizing vision of modernization.

Because China's modernization constitutes the basis of Zhang Guoqing's project, he evaluates all other ideas and intellectual trends using the criteria of modernization he has chosen. As discussed in Chapter 2, whenever there is an inconsistency that threatens the "fantasy" of China's modernization, it is generally dismissed, negated or discredited. Postmodernism occupies this negative role in the writings of pro-modernization intellectuals like Zhang. Postmodernism is thus dismissed as unreal or unrealistic. Zhang's use of the phrase "cultural bubble" to describe "postmodernism" as a passing fad is unintentionally ironic, and reveals Zhang's own concerns about the realism of the modernization project he supports. On the one hand, he dismisses postmodernism as a bubble; on the other hand, however, he implies that this "cultural bubble" is dangerous enough to put the modernization enterprise at risk of failing.

The way Zhang responds to postmodernism ironically reflects the significant extent to which he regards it as disruptive and contrary to the modernization he imagines for China.

Among Chinese commentators of Rorty, it is not only Zhang Guoqing *alone* who has expressed strong disapproval of postmodernism and sees it as a disaster for China. In the preface he wrote for Jiang Jingsong's monograph on Rorty's thought, *From the Mirror of Nature to the Web of Beliefs: A Commentary on Rorty's Philosophy,* the well-known Beijing-based philosopher Liu Dachun made very similar comments (Zhang Guoqing and Jiang Jinsong's books are the two best-known works on Rorty by Chinese authors):

> The real problem of present-day China is that: on the one hand, it remains basically in the pre-modernization phase and must undertake modernization; on the other hand, since the world is still advancing and has developed much more than China, the Chinese people who have not yet modernized cannot be regarded as post-modern. That is to say, the Chinese people encounter attacks from both the front and the back (*qianhou jiaji*), and they face two mutually contradictory challenges: first, they must try and acquire formal reason and the positive spirit [toward knowledge] that our tradition lacks; second, they must deal with the fashion of post-positive knowledge and postmodernism at the same time. [...] We have just started on the road that the West has already travelled. We must make up for the lessons we missed. Some people may feel frustrated about this and they may feel tired of learning these things and want to discard the lessons. In other words, there have been many problems [with modernization] that have been exposed. They [the postmodernists] thus do not take those things as ideal goals, and do not wish to pursue them without hesitation. However, we must firmly take this step [towards modernization], disregarding the double objections from both the power of tradition and the force of postmodernism. There is no future without modernization. (Liu Dachun 1998: iii–iv)[3]

In this excerpt, Liu Dachun uses the terms "premodernization," "modernization" and "postmodernization" (or postmodernism) and understands

[3] "Post-positive knowledge" is a term coined by Liu himself to refer to the postmodernist version of epistemology, especially the type of epistemology Rorty endorses.

them as three stages along a linear, progressive process. He sees the Chinese people as moving toward the "second phase" — modernization. Although Liu does not see modernization as the final goal (the New Enlightenment vision of "the future"), he nonetheless regards it as the very "ideal goal" present-day China needs to undertake. Modernization is the necessary "step" for the Chinese people to move forward. In this sense, China's modernization project also constitutes Liu's fundamental horizon, enabling him to argue that "there is no future without modernization." Liu thus explains the objections put forward by the postmodernists as fatally mistaken. This is because his image of modernization (or his "modernization fantasy") cannot accommodate postmodernism. The announcement made by Chinese postmodernists that the enterprise of modernization should be discarded is completely incompatible with Liu's fantasmatic vision. Based on this "fashion of post-positive knowledge and postmodernism" in China that threatens the modernization fantasy he shares with Zhang Guoqing and many other Chinese intellectuals, Liu avers that postmodernism will not help Chinese people to move towards "the future." And in order to reestablish a sense of order, and restore the coherence of working towards a fully modern Chinese society of the future, Liu stresses that only by undertaking modernization, *despite its pitfalls*, would improve the situation in China. He sees it as the only way ahead for China.

Lacanian analysis allows us to consider the psychic foundation of Zhang Guoqing's assertion that "Modernization does not need postmodernism" and Liu Dachun's statement that "There is no future without modernization." As developed by Žižek, Lacanian analysis explores the symbolic elements (symbols, images, myths, stories, etc.) that are within a given culture and society, in a particular time, that are used to create a coherent fantasy. The important thing about such a fantasy is that it is used to defend a particular view of life and thus avoids or denies what poses a threat to its coherence. Thus, when such a threat is encountered, it must be explained as unrealistic or absurd. To those who insist on modernization as the only way forward, the Chinese discourse of the "postmodern," in terms of its opposition towards the "modern," embodies this type of threat. Thus, they explain that postmodernism is not suitable for China and that it constitutes a violent break from the path that post-Maoist China should follow. If we compare this defense of modernization to the

Lacanian notion of fantasy, we can see more clearly its strong opposition to postmodernism as based in deeply held beliefs rather than in facts.

As discussed in Chapter 2, many Chinese thinkers in the post-Maoist era see modernization as the only way for China to regain its cultural and economic power in the contemporary world. In his monograph on Rorty's thought, Jiang Jinsong posits teleologically the idea of achieving a "modern industrial civilization" as the only desirable prospect for the Chinese people. He regards the establishment of this "modern industrial civilization" as the result of continuous endeavors made by great Chinese thinkers since the nineteenth century:

> Since the gunboats of Western powers dragged China into the modern world arena, those great men who persisted in changing the poor and feeble appearance of China have begun to look for the weaknesses of the Chinese traditional culture. They did so in order to revive the nation through cultural reconstruction. After repetitive deliberations and discussions in the last one hundred years, Chinese philosophical circles have basically reached an agreement: although Chinese traditional philosophy has many unique merits, it has inherent deficiencies not only in relation to logic and epistemology but also in the construction of theoretical systems and the division of disciplines. Moreover, it lacks the non-utilitarian spirit that is required in the field of academic inquiry. These deficiencies blocked the establishment and development of a modern industrial civilization in China as well as the introduction and development of the democratic institutions of such a civilization. Over the last century and more, Chinese philosophy has mostly advanced in the direction of this goal. (Jiang Jinsong 1998: 227)

Jiang Jinsong describes "traditional China" as a false idea, claiming that it was considered to be a harmonious system, which has nonetheless showed itself to lack the knowledge that made Western nations powerful. Among the elements of this knowledge, he listed: logic and epistemology, the construction of theoretical system, the division of disciplines, and a non-utilitarian spirit of pure research. He claims that the most important contribution of "those great men who persisted in changing the poor and feeble appearance of China" was to introduce these forms of Western knowledge into China. Jiang's description shows that China's modernization project, which appears in his description as an enduring historical project of the "establishment and development of a modern industrial civilization and its democratic institutions," occupies the place of an evident truth. This is because it has been the subject of "repeated deliberations and discussions over the last hundred years" by distinguished scholars and intellectuals. This is an act of positing China as a subject in its own right, with representative "great men" acting on its behalf to help its progress toward modernization. When Jiang assumes that he is discussing the consensus reality, the fantasmatic nature of his account becomes evident. For instance, he describes the goals of modernization as having been arrived at as "a basic agreement" among great minds.

Jiang's arguments move within the binary frame of "tradition" versus the "modern," and since the May Fourth era the former is conceived in totalistic terms by many Chinese intellectuals and scholars as dark, bad, negative, backward. Conversely, the latter is upheld in equally totalistic terms as bright, good, positive, advanced and thus desirable. The modern thus represents hope and is synonymous with the idea of "the future." Hence, this binary is actually a specific embodiment of the linear and progressive view of history that Chinese intellectuals acquired approximately between the 1890s and 1910s. It could also be described as the alias (or justification) for promoting modernization. In this regard, Jiang's imagining of China's modernization as the result of a continuous endeavor on the part of progressive Chinese intellectuals is representative of a large number of writings in mainland intellectual discourse today. The basic assumption is that Chinese intellectuals have *a particularly important role* to play in advancing China's modernization and it would seem that intellectuals like Jiang derive a great deal of pleasure from writing about their self-appointed mission. To use Žižek's vocabulary to describe this approach, this is a screen of fantasy that allows Chinese intellectuals to accord symbolic meaning to their own work as representatives of the "Chinese people" today. It is this fantasmatic core that creates and supports the sense of a "we" in contemporary Chinese discourse (using phrases like "descendants of the Dragon").

On this basis, Jiang Jinsong criticizes Western postmodern thinkers for contradicting China's path toward modernization. He writes: "The viewpoints of Rorty's and other postmodern thinkers' place us in the dilemma of not knowing whether to go left or right (*zuoyou weinan*). We want to learn from the West, but it seems that what we need to learn has now become something that the West wants to criticize and discard." (Jiang 1998: 227) In Jiang's description, Rorty and other postmodern thinkers are described as people who may lead China astray. They are accused of threatening the vision of China's continuous modernization and are thus described as posing a dilemma for Chinese intellectuals — "the dilemma of not knowing whether to go left or right." Liu Dachun refers to a similar "dilemma" when he describes the Chinese as placed in the difficult position of facing "attacks from both the front and the back" (*qianhou jiaji*). Using Žižek's vocabulary, we could say that Rorty and other postmodern thinkers in Jiang's description are intruders, people from outside who trespass the fantasmatic space field of the "Chinese people" (Recall Patricia Highsmith's story "Black House" discussed in Chapter 2). This is because the arguments of "the postmodernists" vehemently disrupt the fantasy of modernization, revealing its flaws. Instead of engaging with the postmodern critique of modernization, Jiang instead asserts that it would lead China to a disastrous path. This indicates that Jiang regards his argument as the only kind of truth that China should accept. The writings of Liu Dachun and Jiang Jinsong reflect the general argument held in mainstream Chinese intellectual discourse and are thus constrained by the assumptions of this argument. Their argument is best described as a creed because it rests on the assertion that since the late Qing era, China's future depends on its capacity to transform itself into a modern society by learning from the West in order to resist it.

Post-modernization, or, Traditionalization?

In the twenty-first century version of this approach, as Liu's and Jiang's indicate, the problem is not only of "learning from the West" but of choosing the correct Western knowledge, especially in a situation where the latest Western ideas appear to encourage people to turn away from the discourse of modernization.

In his monograph on Rorty, Jiang notes that "It seems that the ancient Chinese culture is quite similar to the 'postphilosophical culture' dreamed by Rorty" (Jiang 1998: 227). This claim turns "traditional" Chinese culture, which used to be regarded as backward, into something that is new and postmodern. Thus, since in the Chinese intellectual world the postmodern is often understood in a linear framework as a more advanced stage than the modern (which is casted as a middle "phase" between the premodern and the postmodern), then the traditional culture of China already reached this advanced stage.

David L. Hall, who significantly shares Richard Rorty's views, provided a more sophisticated argument in the early 1990s that classical Chinese culture is more advanced than "modern culture." In his paper on "Modern China and Postmodern West," Hall avers that Chinese culture held the philosophy of difference; which means that the basic elements of classical Chinese thought is remarkably "postmodern." Hall suggests, therefore, that the Chinese should not change themselves to adapt to modernization and that it is much better for them just to go back to the original classical-postmodern culture. "It is unnecessary for the Chinese to reject their classical past in order to enter the modern age," writes Hall. Instead of the New Enlightenment project of "cultural modernization," *the* correct way for the Chinese is thus to return to their "postmodern" past (David Hall 1991: 50–70). In Hall's formulation, modernization is what contemporary people — both in the West and East — should leave behind and replace with classical Chinese culture. In ascribing postmodern qualities to classical Chinese culture, Hall implies that it would be of value to both China and the West.

Hall's formulation was taken up in China around the mid-1990s. Zhang Yiwu, together with other two self-claimed "Chinese postmodernists" Zhang Fa and Wang Yichuan, coauthored an influential paper published in 1994 in which they advocate a paradigm shift from "*xiandaixing*" (modernity) to what they phrase as "*Zhonghuaxing,*" whose literal translation is "Chineseness."[4] These authors aver that China's modernization had undergone five phases since the mid-nineteenth century — (1) the period of the dominance of technology, (2) the period of the dominance of regime,

[4]See Zhang Fa *et al.* 1994: 10–20 (2000[1994]: 232–256). A critical response — in defense of the "modernization fantasy" — could be found in Shao Jian's lengthy paper published in the same journal eleven months later. See Shao Jian 1995.

(3) the period of the dominance of science, (4) the period of the dominance of sovereignty, (5) the period of the dominance of culture — and it "moved to an end" (*zouxiang zhongjie*) in 1989. According to them, the 1980s New Enlightenment (the "cultural fever") represents this last phase of China's modernization — the period of the dominance of culture. They argue that the discourse of the "ultrastable structure" advanced by Jin Guantao and Liu Qingfeng is a meta-narrative that depreciates China's tradition as a low-grade and inferior civilization whilst endorsing Western modernity as the universal model. "By adopting this radical stance, Western meta-discourse instead of Chinese traditional meta-discourse is posited as the fundamental direction or standard of 'the oriental revival'." The three authors claim that although New Enlightenment was still influential in the Chinese intellectual world in the 1990s, and was reflected in discussions about subjectivity and the cultivation of the humanistic spirit, China's modernization project had already run its course. They define the course of modernization as consisting of the five stages mentioned in the preceding. Echoing Hall, the three authors claim that "the normative and dominant elements of the original Chinese culture," were actually very postmodern (Zhang Fa *et al.* 2000 [1994]: 233–241, 249–250). Despite their ostensible "rejection" of a linear picture of history, these self-styled "Chinese postmodernists" also imply that the "postmodern" follows the "modern" in temporal sequence and is thus more advanced than the "modern." In calling for a "paradigm shift" from modernity to "Chineseness," they are claiming that "Chineseness" is synonymous with "postmodernism."

Modernization is the cherished dream of many Chinese intellectuals. I refer to this dream, in psychoanalytic terms, as a fundamental fantasy because it revolves around the story of making China rich and powerful, and by achieving that, recovering the lost greatness of Chinese civilization. Such fantasmatic vision of modernization, however, is contradicted by the alternative vision of the Chinese postmodernists who argue that China attained its "postmodern" (advanced) status in ancient times. Although those Chinese intellectuals — modernization advocates and postmodernism promoters — hold exactly opposite views, *they nonetheless share a utilitarian style of argument that seeks to identify causes of progress and regress*. Thus, when Jiang Jinsong writes that intellectuals now face "the dilemma of not knowing to go left and right," he highlights the importance of having the correct approach to the future. It is not surprising that he assesses Rorty's work for its usefulness and decides that Rorty's argument — especially his postphilosophical defense of liberal ideas — can be used to promote a clearer image of what a "fully modern" China would look like. "But what must be noted here is that although objecting to logocentrism, Rorty nonetheless does not elevate the cultures of the Third World, especially the ethical and political aspects of these cultures [as a new paradigm which has the potential to replace the paradigm modernity]" (Jiang Jinsong 1998: 227). Rorty, as Luo Di, becomes in Jiang's view someone who can be described as an advocate of modernization because this Chinese scholar judges all cultures (including thus traditional Chinese culture) against the standards of modern Western liberal values. Jiang implies that these are the values that are crucial for China's modernization. Hence, Jiang believes that Rorty's thought, when carefully used can help to defend the goals of modernization.

Jiang thus provides a confused image of Luo Di as someone who has caused a postmodern dilemma on the one hand yet has provided on the other hand liberal values that could help Chinese intellectuals resolve the "dilemma of not knowing whether to go left or right":

> The resemblance, to some extent, between traditional Chinese culture and postphilosophical culture should not become an excuse for our returning to traditional culture without criticizing it. It is correct to compare these two cultures and to examine the similarities and differences between their characteristics (*huxiang canzhao, huxiang jiejian*). On the one hand, over the historical long-term, the achievements and deficiencies, as well as the experiences and lessons, of traditional Chinese culture have provided rich and vivid precedents for understanding postphilosophical culture. On the other hand, the theoretical explorations that are part of postphilosophical culture can also provide new ideas and approaches for reviewing and revaluating traditional Chinese culture. As different cultures meet (*jiaohui dian*) along the Chinese nation's path of modernization, confrontations and dialogues between the traditional culture and the postmodern culture will definitely produce fruitful achievements and will surely inspire the development of human culture as a whole. (Jiang Jinsong 1998: 228)

This argument resembles the typical New Enlightenment appropriation of Gadamer's notion of the "fusion of horizons" which was first made popular by Gan Yang and the *Culture: China and the World* group in the late 1980s. The "meeting point" of different cultures has always been imagined in terms of the "convergence" of China and the West as a necessary aspect of China's modernization. Jiang writes in the style of a manifesto when he names a correct way forward in the convergence between "traditional Chinese culture" and (Rortyan) "postphilosophical culture"... This "correct way" (of modernization) according to Jiang can free people like Jiang himself from "the dilemma of not knowing whether to go left or right." By referring to the convergence and mutual interaction of cultures, Jiang implies that there are superior and inferior ways of learning from the West. He suggests that his vision of modernization is the best way of learning from the West when he figures it as the meeting point of traditional Chinese culture and postphilosophical culture. Jiang then discusses what is wrong with both "traditional Chinese culture" (as the "Chineseness" advocated by Chinese postmodernists), and "postphilosophical culture":

> We must remain very cautious about the deficiencies of traditional Chinese culture. Modern Chinese intellectual history has illustrated time and again that the traditional culture is of great temptation (*youhuoli*) — some people who were originally revolutionists and enlighteners were tempted to become old-fashioned and regressive (*luowu tuibu*) later. The huge inertia of thousands of years of Chinese culture, plus the inadequate social progress and civilizational development, the various underdeveloped and premodern social existences greatly constrained the liberation of our thinking. Therefore, we cannot underestimate the negative influences of the traditional culture. Our mission is to modernize philosophy, to modernize people's thinking, and to reconstruct traditional Chinese philosophy. These are still our long-term goals and the task is difficult. We must definitely not let contemporary Western postmodern thought influence the fulfillment of our stated goals. (Jiang Jinsong 1998: 230–231)

In the above statement, by rejecting both "traditional Chinese culture" and "contemporary Western postmodernist thought," Jiang attempts to "repair" his vision of China's modernization. This vision illustrates the Lacanian argument that a fantasy is sustained by ensuring that everything that contradicts it is perceived as a "fatal threat." The fantasmatic space has not to be "trespassed." Thus, Jiang presents a set of "stated goals" that he claims to be the truth that is in danger of being undermined by the intrusion of "contemporary Western postmodernist thought." Moreover, by equating postmodernism with "traditional Chinese culture," Jiang is able to describe both with ambivalence as having achieved some merits but as ultimately hindering the "social progress and civilizational development" required in modernization. He does this to imply that those who are on the correct path, the true "revolutionists and enlighteners" of the May Fourth era, would see in postmodernism the same flaws as Chinese tradition. Rorty can thus be described as causing a negative reaction among Chinese intellectuals who fantasize about modernization in vague terms but who are nonetheless very committed about their vision. Thus, Jiang warns his readers in the conclusion to his monograph on Rorty that "We must remain very cautious" and "should not let it influence the realization of our stated goals." This is because, as he puts it, Rorty's postmodernist thought poses "a dead end and offers no way out" (*qiongtu molu, cilu butong*) (Jiang Jinsong 1998: 229). "Luo Di," considered against Jiang's complete image of modernization, is *forced* to play the strange role of an ambivalent advocate of modernization. He is portrayed as negating traditional Chinese culture while offering Western liberalism in ways that would help to modernize Chinese culture.

In the first chapter of his monograph, Jiang Jinsong criticizes Zhang Guoqing's elaboration of Rorty's thought as being too "sympathetic," though he thinks that Zhang's interpretation is basically "correct" and "clear." Of Zhang's book on Rorty, Jiang writes that "There is too much adoration and praise and hardly any analysis and critique" (Jiang Jinsong 1998: 19). To some extent, Zhang did make rather positive evaluations about Rorty's thought by comparison with Jiang's evaluations. Zhang claims:

> Postphilosophical or post-foundationalist culture provides significant inspiration for China's current cultural construction and the project of modernization. At present, the discussions about cultural issues in Chinese scholarship become more and more intense, but significant progressive developments are barely visible. There are many reasons for this. One is

> that cultural discussions in recent years have not been able to get rid of the influence of the Western foundationalist culture that has been prevalent since the [May Fourth] Enlightenment. We believe that Rorty's postphilosophical culture will provide a new perspective to advance our present cultural discussions. It shows that the foundationalist culture since the Western Enlightenment has been constrained by complicated conflicts between the natural sciences and the human sciences. The tensions between the natural sciences and the human sciences tend to become intensified in China's present stage of modernization. The recent discussions about the loss of humanistic spirit in Chinese scholarship reflect, to some extent, the intensity of these tensions. Therefore, although postphilosophical or post-foundationalist culture started in contemporary Western developed countries, it still provides significant guidance and inspiration for our ongoing modernization campaign, especially in relation to cultural projects. (Zhang Guoqing 1998: 207–208)

In this paragraph, Zhang Guoqing praises Rorty's postphilosophical (or post-foundationalist) culture with reference to the present discussions in contemporary Chinese scholarship. However, Zhang is producing a different type of "Luo Di" and one that is just as totalistic and fantasmatic as Jiang's. In Zhang's view, Rorty is described as a contemporary Western thinker whose thought could "provide significant references and critical inspirations to our ongoing modernization campaign." In other words, whereas Jiang's "Luo Di" is ambivalently discussed but ultimately dismissed as "a dead end" and as offering "no way out," Zhang's "Luo Di" is praised as a valuable intellectual resource.

What is ironic here, then, is that the two opposite evaluations seek to assess whether Rorty's thought is useful for the Chinese people, specifically, whether Rorty can help Chinese intellectuals promote the modernization project. In Jiang Jinsong's view, Rorty's thought is potentially harmful to China's current modernization project and he urges "extreme caution" such that "[we] should not let it influence the realization of our stated goals." Zhang Guoqing is less harsh in his judgment, noting that although the "postphilosophic culture that Rorty advocates is obviously a kind of postmodern culture," it is nonetheless useful and could provide some aid to China's modernization project in terms of the liberal values it offers. But he does not state this explicitly and goes only so far as to say that "Postmodern ideas are not as entirely useless as some people think. They could offer us some points [upon which we can reflect our current projects]" (Zhang Guoqing 1998: 8). Both Jiang and Zhang develop their philosophical thinking and evaluate contemporary Western ideas through arguments that are ultimately hostile to ideas that threaten their deeply held conviction about China's modernization. Thus, even though Zhang offers modest praise for Rorty's liberal values, he is also suspicious of postmodernism.

In fact, Zhang Guoqing is actually more strongly opposed to postmodernism than Jiang Jinsong. Let us recall Zhang's radical rejection of postmodernism cited above: "Modernization does not need postmodernism. Fundamentally speaking, postmodernism has no way out at all in today's China." This is the concluding statement of his 1998 monograph on postmodernism. Zhang also claims in the preface of that book:

> Postmodernist thought shows that present Western society is undergoing a significant or perhaps catastrophic change or decline. Therefore, fundamentally speaking, postmodernism is neither a goal to be pursued by human beings, nor a model to be followed by countries that have started late on the modernization process, especially developing countries that are still lagging behind. (Zhang Guoqing 1998: 6)

What emerges from this description is that postmodernism is, for Zhang, something radically negative, a "catastrophic change or decline," for it "runs counter to the basic course of modern society." "Modernization process" as the "basic course of modern society" is the yardstick by which Zhang measures postmodernism. On this basis, Zhang is able to assert that "postmodernism has no way out at all in today's China" using the reason that China is among the "countries that have started late on the modernization process." The uncompromising nature of Zhang's assessment reflects the strength of his belief in modernization. Such belief can be argued, in Lacanian terms, as one that is fundamentally framed and sustained by fantasy. Fantasy is, as Žižek defines it, "the little piece of imagination by which we gain access to reality"; it thereby "constitutes the primordial form of narrative" (Žižek 1999b: 122; Žižek 1998: 196). Modernization functions as a fundamental fantasy for Zhang because in his vision only modernization provides a "way out" for today's China. When Zhang praises Rorty, he assigns him the positive role of a "modern" thinker (as opposed to a postmodern one). Thus, Zhang announces at the start of his book on Rorty that "This book is an attempt to elaborate the basic argument that Rorty is among the few *modern* thinkers who have attempted a fundamental transformation of *modern* Western philosophy, and to some extent, a transformation of Western culture in its entirety, in order to give it a brand-new appearance" (Zhang Guoqing 1999: 1, emphases added). In other words, Zhang is "sympathetic" towards Luo Di because he views the latter as a modern thinker instead of a postmodern one.

What also should be noted here is that even those post-Tiananmen Chinese intellectuals who styled themselves as "postmodernists" also defended many stated goals of China's modernization under the new "postmodernism" banner. In Zhang Fa, Zhang Yiwu and Wang Yichuan's well-debated 1994 article where they suggest a paradigm shift from modernity to "Chineseness," they elaborate a set of "normative and dominant elements of the original Chinese culture," including "the marketization of society," "consumerization," "secularization," the "pluralization of cultural values," etc. (Zhang Fa *et al.* 1994: 15–17) One can find, by comparing the official documents of the Four Modernizations campaign and the intellectual discussions in the 1980s New Enlightenment movement, that these normative elements of "Chineseness" in their account are the exact same stated goals of China's modernization, considered from both cultural and political aspects. In this sense, the paradigm of the allegedly postmodern "Chineseness" that those Chinese postmodernists call for is not for a return to classical Chinese culture, as they claim. Rather, this "Chineseness" is envisaged as a product of successful modernization. It is thus just as totalistic as the vision that proponents of modernization offer. In this regard, the opposing groups share the same dream (or fantasy) of a rich and modernized China.

Moreover, Zhang Fa, Zhang Yiwu and Wang Yichuan add a tone of nationalistic pride to their vision of Chineseness:

> The blueprint of the great circle of Chinese civilization (*Zhonghua wenhuaquan*) that we put forward is not, and could not be a suggestion that asks us

to retreat to the old imperial system of tribute (*chaogong*) established in China's classical times. Rather, it advances *the realization of modernization in the East Asia*, making it reach the internationally advanced level, and at the very same time excavating the deep cultural resources, and thus letting the East contribute to the world. (Zhang Fa *et al.* 1994: 18–19, emphasis added)

In this statement, the authors present the confused claim that they are attempting a paradigm shift from modernity to "Chineseness" in order to attain, paradoxically, "the realization of modernization" — whose death they have just announced in an earlier section of their article. The appeal to the postmodern "Chineseness" actually is, as the authors themselves avow in the last section of the paper, to make the "Chinese nation keep its Chinese characteristics when undertaking modernization" (Zhang Fa *et al.* 1994: 20). Hence, in the debate between postmodernists and advocates of the humanistic spirit in the early to mid-1990s, both camps — admitted or not — are sympathetic towards the New Enlightenment enterprise of cultural modernization, which was brutally halted by the 1989 purge of the Tiananmen student protest. Whilst some postmodernists attempted to develop "a new cultural strategy" to advance modernization, their discursive opponents claimed that the primary goal of the 1980s "cultural fever" is to resuscitate the "humanistic spirit," regarding the triumphal emergence of Chinese postmodernism is in fact a cynical denial of the traumatic event that put an end to the "new era." Thus, contemporary intellectual debate on "postmodernism" is very different from the Western debate on that subject in the 1980s and 1990s. Rather, it manifests in different ways via the attempts of post-Tiananmen Chinese intellectuals to promote a new path after that traumatic event. Though attacking each other, Chinese postmodernist discourse and the humanistic spirit discourse both attempted to resume China's modernization enterprise and eventually recover the lost essence of Chinese civilization (whether the postmodern "Chineseness" or the classical "humanistic spirit"). In other words, these two antagonistic discourses are both inherently loaded with the fantasmatic promise of the fullness once the perceived missing piece is retrieved.

In mainland China, the advocacy of postmodernism and other "post-isms" has gradually faded since the mid-1990s. As noted earlier, Chen

Xiaoming claimed in the preface of *Postmodernism* (a book he edited and published in 2004), that the debate that took place between Chinese postmodernists and their detractors in the 1990s was extremely unbalanced. While dozens of famous scholars and intellectuals condemned the arrival of postmodernism in China, only a handful of relatively young scholars firmly defended it (Chen 2004: 4). Even among those several self-styled Chinese postmodernists, a few have now given up this radical thesis, such as the Beijing-based philosophers Wang Zhihe and Ouyang Kang. They have turned instead to a kind of "constructive postmodernism," which they claim is more appropriate for China's current socio-historical context. In his essay entitled "Another Kind of Postmodernism," Wang Zhihe includes Rorty in the list of what he calls "constructive postmodernists," differentiated from the group of what he calls "radical postmodernists" such as Foucault and Derrida (Wang Zhihe 2004[1998]: 204, 212–213). Ouyang Kang also makes a discursive distinction between "constructive postmodernism" and "deconstructive postmodernism." The latter according to Ouyang is only meaningful in Western developed societies. Moreover, in Ouyang's view, "the modern spirit is not yet totally outdated." "In fact we can see that both from the spiritual aspect and material aspect, today's world is still heading in the direction of modernization." Ouyang ends his essay with a grand statement that "[T]he rational development and successful advance of socialist modernization construction with Chinese characteristics will make great and specific contributions to the development of the world-scale modernization in the twenty-first century" (Ouyang 2004[2002]: 93, 96).

The discourse of "constructive postmodernism" in the late 1990s and the early 2000s no longer poses a threat to the New Enlightenment enterprise of China's modernization. It has instead effectively merged with the Chinese discourse of modernization. Whereas Chinese postmodernists such as Zhang Yiwu, Chen Xiaoming, and others in the early and mid-1990s still oscillated between the thesis of the "end of modernity" and that of "the realization of modernization"; a group of postmodernists in the late 1990s started to establish "another kind of postmodernism" in order to posit postmodernism not as a threat to the realization of modernization. Furthermore, the rapid growth of China's economy in the 1990s has diluted and diverted the trauma of Tiananmen. Both Chinese postmodernists such as Zhang Yiwu, Chen Xiaoming and the advocates for the New Enlightenment project of modernization passionately acclaimed China's economic development. In the mid- to late 1990s, this "unbalanced" debate on postmodernism gradually faded and was replaced by the controversy over the discourse of the "New Left," which directly posed an intellectual challenge to the model of China's economic development. Compared with the Sinophone discourse of postmodernism, this "New Left" discourse indeed entails an "uncompromised" critique of modernization. Hence, it started to be identified by opponents of postmodernism like Xu Youyu in the mid-1990s as a growing but much bigger threat to the New Enlightenment enterprise of modernization.

Chapter 4

Liberals and New Leftists as "Discursive Enemies"

Liberalism and Its Critics

From 1997 onwards, the debate over postmodernism in China was replaced by the more heated and vehement debate between "liberalism" and the "New Left." This debate was, in terms of the number of scholars and intellectuals who participated and the scale of the issues discussed, arguably the biggest intellectual debate in the post-Maoist age. An important feature of this debate is that it started with serious intellectual conversations and discussions but ended with vicious personal attacks between the warring participants who themselves later referred to the debate as "a spitting war" (*koushui zhan*). At first, participants of the debate referred to their opponents as "friends" and even "brothers" (*xiong*),[1] but their exchanges soon became abusive. As Geremie Barmé and Gloria Davies observe in their essay "Have We Been Noticed Yet? Intellectual Contestation and the Chinese Web," "the mutual attacks among these intellectuals remind us of the writing style of the 'big-character poster' culture of the early Cultural Revolution era (1966–1967)" (Barmé and Davies 2004). In Chinese, the term most frequently employed to refer to opponents in a debate — *lundi* — literally means "discursive enemy." In the debate between "liberalism" and the "New Left," this term gained its literal accuracy: these writers became true enemies, both intellectually and socially, as a result of this debate.

What is interesting is that there is a meaningful connection between the postmodernism debate of the mid-1990s and the New Left versus

[1] It is a cultural custom for Chinese literati to frequently address each other by "*xiong*" instead of "Mister," irrespective of their actual age difference. Hence, though "*xiong*" sounds intimate, it does not necessarily indicate closeness.

liberalism debate that followed. For a period of time, especially between 1996 and 1997, "postmodernist" and "New Leftist" were treated as overlapping terms. Thus, intellectuals such as Wang Hui, Han Yuhai, Kuang Xinnian, Chen Yangu, etc. were labeled as both "postmodernists" and "New Leftists." This was done for the simple reason that these intellectuals employed terms from Michel Foucault, Fredric Jameson, and other "postmodern theorists." What is more important, however, is that at that time the defenders of the New Enlightenment enterprise tended to label all critiques of China's modernization as "postmodernist." It was not until the publication of Wang Hui's lengthy paper entitled "Contemporary Chinese Thought and the Question of Modernity" at the end of 1997 in which Wang criticized heavily the works of Chinese postmodernists that the term "New Left" came into use. This was because people who regarded themselves as New Enlightenment thinkers saw that the Enlightenment enterprise they defended was being challenged by a set of ideas which were not the same as the ones they had criticized as "postmodern." Later on, because Wang Hui was one of the two chief editors of *Reading*, intellectuals and scholars who frequently published in *Reading* became generally identified as "New Leftists." Similarly, the journal *Frontier* (*Tianya*), which published Wang Hui and other scholars who problematize the developmental model of "capitalist modernization," also became labeled as a "New Left" journal.

Coincidently, around 1997 the term "liberalism" started to appear publicly in scholarly and intellectual writings. What should be noted here is that after Deng Xiaoping's death in February 1997, there was a temporary relaxation of state censorship. Thus, in the late 1990s and early 2000s, intellectuals were able to publish more freely and this encouraged renewed debate on China's future.[2] Liberalism or *ziyouzhuyi* was formerly a politically sensitive term in mainland China because of its negative connotations in Sinophone discourse since the early 1950s. Mao denounced it in his famous essay "*Fandui ziyouzhuyi*" (Against Liberalism, written in 1937). According to the Shanghai-based historian Zhu Xueqin, 1998 was

---

[2]After Hu Jintao took total power from Jiang Zemin in 2004, this space has been severely narrowed. Many mainland Chinese intellectuals have difficulties to voice their concerns, even encounter indirect or direct political oppression.

the year when the discourse of liberalism flourished for the very first time in the intellectual world of post-1949 mainland China. By the end of the 1990s, liberalism had become a key term in Chinese intellectual discourse. As Xu Jilin notes, "There had been a thoroughgoing victory of liberalism in the realm of popular ideas. The word 'liberalism' itself had achieved a cultural cachet previously enjoyed by such terms as democracy and science, even a certain sacred inviolability." (Xu Jilin 2000[1999]: 184)

For intellectuals such as Li Shenzhi, Xu Youyu, and Zhu Xueqin, "liberalism" embodies the legacies of the May Fourth Enlightenment movement and the 1980s New Enlightenment movement. Since the late 1990s, these intellectuals have publicly identified themselves as "Chinese liberals," and made it their goal to resuscitate the "liberal tradition" of pre-1949 China. The two leading Chinese liberals of this time were Li Shenzhi, the former Vice President of the Chinese Academy of Social Sciences and later a leading exponent and advocate of liberalism in China, and the Beijing-based political theorist Liu Junning who was a research fellow in the Chinese Academy of Social Sciences until he was expelled in 2002 for spreading liberal ideas and criticizing CCP policies in his lectures. Both claimed that liberalism was the guiding concept of intellectual life at Beijing University (Peking University) in the 1910s and early 1920s (see Liu Junning ed. 1998: 4, 7). Thus, when the university celebrated its centennial in 1998, Liu Junning compiled a book entitled *The Tradition of Beijing University and Modern China: The Pioneering Voice of Liberalism*, and invited Li Shenzhi, to write the preface for the book. In the concluding passage of this essay, Li claims that "Liberalism represents the best and most universal human value." He claims that liberalism was the defining feature of a modernized society. Li also stresses that liberalism remained undeveloped in China and urges Chinese people to be confident about China's modernization. He contends that there were three positive reasons for such confidence: (1) China had already more than a century of modernization; (2) in recent years China had been undergoing a transformation towards the market economy; and (3) the age of globalization had arrived, and China had become part of this "big current." So, Li claims that, if the liberal tradition of Peking University was resuscitated, China would become a modernized nation that would be fully integrated with the developed world (Li Shenzhi 1998: iv–v).

In another influential essay entitled "Re-igniting the Torch of Enlightenment" written in 1999 to celebrate the eightieth anniversary of the May Fourth Enlightenment movement, Li Shenzhi defines liberalism as the overcoming of despotism and Maoist collectivism. Opposing the arguments of the "postmodernists" and "New Leftists" who proposed an end to Western-style Enlightenment, Li calls for the attainment of liberalism to strengthen Western-style Enlightenment. He writes:

> Though we are frustrated by the experiences of the past eighty years, we should not be depressed, for the goal of the May Fourth thinkers is the shared enterprise of all mankind. Its success might be postponed, but it will not be replaced by failure. (Li Shenzhi 2000b[1999]: 272)

Li makes the point that the effort to promote liberalism in the 1990s is also an effort to resume and advance the Enlightenment enterprise — the unfinished project of the 1920s Enlightenment movement and the 1980s New Enlightenment movement. Similarly, Xu Youyu also emphasizes in his 1999 essay entitled "Liberalism and Contemporary China" that "liberalism flourished in the 1990s as a development of the Enlightenment discourse that dominated the 1980s cultural fever" (Xu Youyu 2000[1999]: 414). Zhu Xueqin, an active participant in the 1990s debates over the humanistic spirit as well as liberalism, states that it was the 1980s New Enlightenment movement that paved the foundation for liberal discourse to emerge in the late 1990s. Zhu also identifies the year 1998 as marking the proper re-emergence of Chinese liberalism (Zhu Xueqin 1999: 388).

In the early 2000s, the central idea that the majority of Chinese liberal intellectuals endorsed was "globalization." These self-identified liberal writers understood "globalization" as the continuation of New Enlightenment thinking. Li Shenzhi quoted the famous words of Sun Yat-sen (1866–1925), the first president of the Republic of China that "the world's current is unstoppable; following it would lead to prosperity, and going against it would lead to death" (*shijie chaoliu, haohao dangdang, shunzhizhe chang, nizhizhe wang*) (Li Shenzhi 1998: iv). In Li's view, "globalization is synonymous with modernization." He claims that "Eventually, cultural particularities (national or local identities) would be replaced by the universal culture (of a global humanity)" and further adds that "This is what we call 'modernization'." By stressing the conception of cultural conflation and the creed that "there is only one earth; and one human family," Li defines modernization as the passage from cultural particularities to universality, from multiple local identities to a singular global identity (Li Shenzhi and He Jiadong 2000: 20, 75, 91). I have argued in Chapter 2 that one of the goals of the New Enlightenment discourse is to replace the old *spatial* dichotomy between "China" and "the West" with the new *temporal* dichotomy between "modern" and "traditional." I have sought to show how the term "Westernization" carries ambivalent connotations in the Chinese language. This ambivalence, psychoanalytically speaking, is reflected in the representations of "Westernization" as involving a historical tragedy and as a traumatic encounter with hostile foreigners or "barbarians" (*yi*). By contrast, the term "globalization" (*quanqiuhua*) is less complicated. This is one possible reason why many New Enlightenment intellectuals such as Li Shenzhi liked using the term (in place of "Westernization") and understood it as similar to "modernization."

This current of liberal discourse soon encountered its "discursive enemy" in the Chinese intellectual world, and an intense debate — in fact better described as fight or even war — ensued. Rising as opponents of Chinese liberals in the late 1990s, a group of intellectuals started to turn their attention to various contemporary leftist or Marxist discourses and suggested alternative paths instead of embracing and merging into today's capitalist-inflected globalization. A common view shared by many commentators[3] is that Wang Hui's article, "Contemporary Chinese Thought and the Question of Modernity" published in 1997 in *Frontier*, was the first substantial attack on the liberal position.[4]

---

[3]See, for example, Xu Jilin 1999: 276; Gao Like 2007: 199.

[4]Barmé and Davies have observed with regard to the English translation of Wang's paper: "[T]he title of Wang's original Chinese text, '*Dangdai Zhongguode sixiang zhuangkuang yu xiandaixing wenti*,' signals an intention to diagnose the 'state' (*zhuangkuang*) of contemporary China's intellectual health and carries within it a certain imperative tone. In the publication of this essay in English translation, that imperative tone has been erased through a slight but crucial modification of the title into the more benign 'Contemporary Chinese thought and the question of modernity'." Barmé and Davies also correctly point out that "The edited and fluent English version of the article elides a number of key rhetorical registers that in the original Chinese have powerful resonances of authorial assertion." See Barmé and Davies 2004.

Labeled as a leading representative of China's "New Left," Wang Hui has been at the center of intellectual debates since the late 1990s and begun to gain international reputation in the 2000s. Part of his work has already been translated into English and published by prominent academic publishers (for example, Wang Hui 2006, 2010, 2011). Wang started his intellectual project by criticizing the "New Enlightenment thinking."[5] In the following discussion, I will examine Wang Hui's texts as representative of the "New Leftist" criticism of the 1980s New Enlightenment discourse and its "liberal" successor in the 1990s. I have chosen Wang Hui for two reasons: (1) Wang Hui is seen by most commentators as the leader of the "New Left" camp and a key figure in the debate that followed the publication of his essay; (2) Wang's writings are among the most well-argued and systematic of intellectuals who have been labeled "New Leftists." In particular, his "Contemporary Chinese Thought and the Question of Modernity" has been widely discussed and studied. In this essay, Wang provides a substantial critique of what he calls "Enlightenment as an ideology of modernization" and examines its contemporary formation. There is a key section of this essay in which Wang argues that,

> The theoretical fountainhead of the Chinese New Enlightenment movement was not socialism but early French Enlightenment thinking and Anglo-American liberalism. Its critical stance toward Chinese socialism was subsumed under a critique of tradition and feudalism. Consciously or unconsciously, New Enlightenment thinking pursued Western capitalist modernity. In other words, the New Enlightenment critique of politics (and of the state) was couched in an allegorical critique of Chinese socialism as feudal tradition; it thus avoided discussing the modern content of this historical experience. The result of this allegorical strategy is that reflections on China's modernity (whose major characteristic is socialism) are subsumed under the tradition/modernity dichotomy, where modernity is

[5] What should be noted is that though Wang claims that he started his critical reflection on Western modernity in the 1980s, he nonetheless obviously shared the sentiments of most New Enlightenment thinkers at that time, and in fact was one of the protesters on Tiananmen Square who withdrew from the spot in the last minute (i.e. the early morning of June Fourth).

> completely reaffirmed. In the Thought Liberalization movement of the 1980s, intellectual reflections on socialism were undertaken under the slogan of anti-feudalism, thereby avoiding any discussion of how the difficulties of socialism were part of "crisis of modernity." In many respects, particularly in its desire to incorporate China into the global capitalist economic system, China's New Enlightenment has many points in common with the socialist reforms. Painting Mao's socialism as a relic of feudal tradition was not merely a tactic on the part of the New Enlightenment intellectuals, it was also a means of self-identification. It allowed them to identify themselves with the antichurch and anti-aristocratic European bourgeois social movement. However, such a self-understanding obscures the fact that both the New Enlightenment movement and Marxism, as ideologies of modernization, have many common values and common modes of historical understanding: belief in progress, belief in the promise of modernization, belief in nationalism as a historical teleology, and particularly, belief in the ideals of freedom, equality, and universal harmony. These latter ideals are linked to individual struggle and the existential significance of the individual — both hallmarks of the modern attitude that understands the present moment as the temporal transition to a better future. (Wang Hui 1998: 18–19)

In this critical analysis of the 1980s New Enlightenment, Wang Hui attempts to disclose the close connection (common values, common modes of historical understanding, etc.) between the New Enlightenment discourse and CCP official ideology (the socialist reforms). He writes of their shared agenda, despite the New Enlightenment's ostensible "critical stance toward Chinese socialism." Though Wang raises this point in the form of an academic criticism, his analysis nonetheless implies that the 1980s New Enlightenment movement was in alliance with the Party's agenda, and thus was a contributing factor to the state repression of 1989 Tiananmen protest. As Barmé and Davies have pointed out, "Wang Hui's article was, in this sense, a not-so-heavily coded indictment of the state of intellectual independence and participation" (Barmé and Davies 2004). Wang's point effectively angered many New Enlightenment intellectuals because he accused them of having produced an ideology that ran with rather than against the state ideology. This in turn makes him a main target of the intellectual camp of "Chinese liberals."

Wang's criticism of the New Enlightenment thinking indeed moves beyond this political accusation. Wang argues that as an influential ideology of modernization, the New Enlightenment has shifted from a passionate critical intellectual discourse to a cultural discourse that complemented the rise of contemporary Chinese capitalism.

> The discourse of the Chinese New Enlightenment movement is built upon the basic goal of the modernization of the nation-state, whose origins are in Europe and have by now become the global prescription of the capitalist process. New Enlightenment thinking has been unable to transcend these goals to formulate a critique of the problem of China's modernity in the era of global capitalism. In the wake of decline of New Enlightenment thinking, what we see are its remnants; upon these ruins sits the capitalist market that crosses all national boundaries. Even the very dictatorial state behavior that was the primary target of New Enlightenment thinking has been constrained by this huge market. (Wang Hui 1998: 34; see also Wang Hui 2000b: 60)

Wang acknowledges that in the 1980s the New Enlightenment movement was a critical discourse against Maoist ideology. However, with the rapid social change and the rise of Chinese capitalism in Deng's era, it started to lose its "critical potential" (*pipan qianneng*) and thus converged with the state ideology of the 1990s. Thus, it failed to function as a powerful critical voice in the post-Tiananmen context. Wang's diagnosis is that "[N]ew Enlightenment thinking has dominated and still dominates intellectual discourse in China. But in the rapidly changing historical context, what used to be China's most vigorous intellectual discourse has increasingly descended into equivocation; it has gradually lost not only its ability to critique but also its ability to diagnose problems in contemporary Chinese society." (Wang Hui 1998: 27) Hence, the historical limitation of the New Enlightenment, according to Wang, led to its failure to tackle "the rapidly changing historical context." Wang regards this as a "severe problem" of the New Enlightenment discourse.

Then, what does Wang mean by "the rapidly changing historical context"? Wang Hui's paper starts with the sentence that "The year 1989 was a historical watershed" (Wang Hui 1998: 9). According to Wang, China's socio-political condition changed significantly after the year 1989, and therefore the target of intellectual analysis and criticism also needs a corresponding shift. While Xu Youyu and his allies evoked frequently the argument of China's "social condition" (*guoqing*, literally meaning the "current state of the nation") in order to dismiss Chinese postmodernists' proposal, Wang Hui implies that this argument is not valid anymore because the "historical context" has rapidly changed after 1989 (for instance, the speedy and pervasive rise of market society). While Xu Youyu, Li Shenzhi and many other liberals uphold globalization as an unstoppable current that China must embrace, Wang Hui sees this same post-1989 trend toward globalization as marking the further rise of capitalism. He argues: "Some scholars regard globalization as a new world order, forgetting that this order has been long in the making; as a process set in motion by the rise of capitalism, it has already passed through several stages" (Wang Hui 1998: 36). By referring to the "problem of China's modernity in the era of global capitalism," Wang Hui implies that the New Enlightenment discourse was incapable of providing a persuasive critique of the inter-related forces of the global capitalist market system and "the dictatorial state."

More importantly, for Wang, another fundamental limitation of the New Enlightenment was its reliance on the tradition/modernity dichotomy. He claims that this dichotomy framework handicapped New Enlightenment thinkers and confined them to thinking about "modernity" from a falsely universal (but actually Eurocentric and capitalist) perspective. He contends that because they failed to tackle the "question of modernity," they could not see that the binary frame of tradition/modernity had already lost its "critical potential" by the late 1980s. In Wang's view, the post-Maoist language of New Enlightenment canceled out the uniqueness of China's approach to modernity, or "Chinese modernity." By emphasizing what he calls the "question of modernity," Wang attempts to challenge the liner narrative of modernization that liberal intellectuals have advocated since the 1980s New Enlightenment movement (Wang Hui 1998).

Hence, these theoretical and historical limitations of the New Enlightenment, according to Wang, led to its failure to tackle "the rapidly changing historical context." Wang regards this as a "severe problem" of the New Enlightenment discourse.

While claiming that New Enlightenment discourse, once vigorous in the 1980s, has lost its "critical potential" after 1989, Wang acknowledges that it did develop various new intellectual approaches in the 1990s. He regards these as the "remnants" of the New Enlightenment movement, and includes among them, "Confucian capitalism," the "rural industry mode" of modernization (proposed by Gan Yang), the humanistic spirit discourse, economic liberalism, the discourse of civil society and public sphere, and even "Chinese neo-Marxism" and "Chinese postmodernism." According to Wang, these "remnants" all failed to "face the twenty-first century," and in turn failed to transform themselves into "critical thoughts in the era of global capitalism" (Wang Hui 1998: 14). He is especially critical of "Chinese liberals" who regard themselves as the inheritors of the 1980s New Enlightenment movement yet chose to remain "totally silent" about the relation between the Chinese state and global capital. Wang Hui calls them "vulgar liberals" (*yongsu de ziyouzhuyizhe*) and writes that "they were fighters who held a critical stance in the past; however, even fighters in the past can turn into defenders of today's new order" (Wang Hui 2000b[1998]: 347).

Wang's magnum opus *The Rise of Modern Chinese Thought* (four volumes in total) appeared in 2004. Its primary object is the search for the "seeds" of an alternative modernity in intellectual legacies of the "premodern" Chinese past, a "native modernity" rooted in China's traditional culture before it was polluted and shaped by "modern institutions." The presupposition of Wang's intellectual project is that the rich intellectual dynamics embedded in China's premodern thought that Western-style modernity arrogantly refuses can in fact open up radical possibilities, and thus be able to serve as intellectual resources in overcoming the crisis of modernity. For Wang, many moments in China's history of thought can provide resources for us to transcend the present Western model of modernity. The aim of Wang's *Rise of Modern Chinese Thought* can be seen as an intellectual search for a new theoretical framework to present sociopolitical critique in an age in which global capitalism is generally regarded as the only path (Wang Hui 2004). Though Wang's work may not impress his worldwide readers as a striking alternative project,[6] his lengthy historical elaboration of "Chinese modernity" nonetheless has successfully earned him international reputation as a prominent leftist thinker from China.

An Intellectual Debate Turning into a Spitting War

Wang Hui's critical analysis of the New Enlightenment thinking, which was later criticized by the Guangzhou-based liberal philosopher Ren Jiantao as "an utter negation of the 1980s Chinese intellectual discourse and a total condemnation of the various discourses of the 1990s" (Ren Jiantao 2000[1999]: 195), together with his project of constructing Chinese modernity, provoked a strong response in two ways. On the one hand, Wang received the support of many young intellectuals (such as Beijing-based literary critics Han Yuhai, Kuang Xinnian, Chen Yangu, and a few Shanghai-based literary critics such as Wang Xiaoming, Luo Gang, etc.). On the other hand, Chinese liberal intellectuals such as Xu Youyu, Zhu Xueqin, Ren Jiantao turned him into a target of their verbal attacks. Heated criticism and equally passionate praise quickly made Wang Hui a leading figure of the "New Left" intellectual group.

What is worth noting in this intersection is the political connotations of the label of the "New Left" in mainland Chinese public discourse. Xu Jilin has noted in this regard that the term "New Left" is one that "because of obvious historical and ideological associations has, unfortunately, accrued a negative inflection in popular discourse in China; an odium that is not shared by the expression 'liberals'" (Xu Jilin 2000: 185). Barmé

---

[6]Wang Hui's theorization of "Chinese modernity" is rather ambiguous and, to some extent, still left "unfinished," since what he provides in *Rise* is nothing close to a clearly stated normative project, but instead, to borrow Zhang Yongle's phrasing, basically "an epistemological reconstruction of the successive systems of knowledge, or belief, that dominated China from the Song to the early Republic." As Zhang writes in his book review, "[T]he modernity or 'early modernity' [Wang] seeks in Chinese history is an open possibility rather than a structured project. The only thing we know about its meaning is that it involves the emergence of new pathways, not the replication of any version of modernity confected in the West." (Zhang Yongle 2010)

and Davies further point out that "the term the 'New Left' resonates unavoidably with entrenched namings of, as it were, the 'failed' left of the Cultural Revolution and the Maoist past within mainland Chinese discourse, not to mention the residual Maoism of stalwarts within the party old guard" (Barmé and Davies 2004). Thus, while the label "liberalism" gains "a certain sacred inviolability" in contemporary Chinese discourse, the term "New Left" on the other hand is deemed generally as a derogatory label.

Wang Hui's detractors are intellectuals who see themselves as committed to the project of Enlightenment. They write of embracing globalization and championing democratic reform, constitutional rule, and other primary liberal values such as free speech. In his essay "Liberalism and Contemporary China," Xu Youyu responds to Wang's paper by arguing that with regard to China's "social and historical context," there is no such significant or drastic change after 1989. He states this in order to claim that the unfinished task of Enlightenment must continue. According to Xu, the major disagreement between Chinese "liberals" and "New Leftists" is that whereas the former sees China in the 1990s basically as a continuation of the past four decades without fundamental change, i.e. a socialist totalitarian state, the latter sees post-1989 China as already a capitalist state. In Xu's view, Wang failed to see that capitalism relies on the idea of private property and claims that China has not yet become capitalist since it is a state where private property is still not protected by its constitution (Xu Youyu 2000: 427–429). In an essay written in the early 2000s reviewing his debate with Wang Hui and other "New Left" intellectuals, Xu argues that "There is no fundamental change with regard to China's reality. What has changed is the attitude and perspective of intellectuals. Many people, consciously or unconsciously, now regard China as different — this China is totally different from China in the 1980s, especially, in the year 1989." Xu implies here that Wang Hui saw a difference that was false or unreal, when China's basic problem (e.g. CCP's dictatorship) had not changed at all. He then accuses Wang of confusing the social problems of the United States for those of China. Xu concludes: "The fatal deficiency of 'New Left' thinking is *its disengagement from reality*. In order to get their ready-made conclusions and to apply to China the most updated theoretical analysis they have just learned from the West, these intellectuals *distort and mutilate China's history and reality, and force reality to fit into their theoretical framework*." (Xu Youyu 2003[2001]: 265–267, emphases added)

Xu insists that as a country still struggling to modernize itself, China's situation is totally different from the developed Western countries. He claims that although there were a few new phenomena emerging in the 1990s, they were still primarily generated by the old system — that is, the system of the CCP's totalitarian rule. Thus, "although the situations are new, the problems are old (*xin qingkuang, lao wenti*)." That means, for Xu, the solutions for China's problems are really nothing new — Chinese intellectuals have to advance the unfinished Enlightenment enterprise. Xu names, in particular, the introduction of effective political reform, the development of constitutional rule, restrictions on state power, and the normalizing of the market economy (Xu Youyu 2003[2001]: 266). For Xu, these must be installed in the post-Tiananmen China to prevent traumatic events from happening again such as the political oppression of the Cultural Revolution era and the brutal massacre of June Fourth 1989.

Based on this argument, Xu Youyu argues that Wang's promotion of a critique of "global capitalism" is an avoidance of the problems caused by the CCP's dictatorship. Xu writes that "This kind of 'critical spirit' seeks what is far and neglects what lies close at hand (*shejin qiuyuan*). He claims that it 'avoids the concrete problems to pursue an empty point' (*bishi jiuxu*)," and is "the result not only of silliness but an unstated agenda" (Xu Youyu 2000: 429–430). Xu also uses a joke to make his point: In the era of Cold War, an American citizen argues with a USSR citizen about whose country is more democratic. The American man says: "We can yell in public 'Reagan, go to hell!' Can you do the same in your country?" He gets his answer very quickly: "Who said we can't? Of course we can yell in public 'Reagan, go to hell!'" After telling the joke, Xu writes: "Is there any difference between condemning American imperialism in Beijing and yelling in public 'Reagan, go to hell!' in Moscow? Is this the so-called 'critical spirit of intellectuals'?" (Xu Youyu 2003[2001]: 277) Herein Xu offers not only a criticism of Wang Hui's analysis, but a moral evaluation of Wang as lacking real intellectual independence. He insinuates that Wang has an "unstated agenda" of favoring the ideological framework of Party-state rule. When Wang Hui accuses New Enlightenment intellectuals of assisting Party-state rule, he perceives the official ideology in terms of marketization and capitalist modernization. Conversely, Xu Youyu accuses "New Left" intellectuals such as Wang Hui of endorsing the CCP's authoritarian dictatorship.

As noted in previous chapters, the fantasmatic narrative that supports the subject's perception of reality is highly sensitive to alternative narratives that challenge its key assumptions. In fact, when Chinese intellectuals developed different perceptions of Chinese reality in the post-1989 era, they inevitably became involved in debates that exceeded academic concerns. These were debates about the "correct" way forward for China. Whilst Chinese liberals such as Li Shenzhi, Zhu Xueqin offer a narrative of resistance against an authoritarian state by investing hope in China's market development, "New Left" intellectuals such as Wang Hui, Cui Zhiyuan see the dominance of a global capitalist order that promotes itself as the "end of history" and that suppresses social progress and innovation. The debate between liberals and "New Leftists" quickly turned personal because *it involved how mainland intellectuals coped with post-1989 reality*. The debate was soon described as a "spitting war" by commentators and even participants themselves. This violent clash over "China's reality" also led the debatants themselves to regard the perceived "homogeneity of attitude" of the 1980s New Enlightenment as having come to a quick end.

The enormous gap between liberal and "New Left" ways of seeing China is even much more sharply reflected in Zhu Xueqin's texts. As one of the initiators of the humanistic spirit discussion in the mid-1990s and a famous self-avowed liberal in the late 1990s, Zhu states that "New Left" intellectuals use the phrase "critical spirit" to do nothing more than "to pick on a soft and easy target (*shizi jian ruan de nie*)" (Zhu Xueqin 1999: 402–403). He implies that the "New Left" is morally wanting in this regard. Zhu explains that the "global market" is one such "soft and easy target" because it can be safely attacked without posing a direct threat to its critics. Zhu also implies that because liberal intellectuals are critics of the CCP's authoritarian rule, they are true critics who put their own safety at risk. Zhu writes that although there are numerous social problems such as endemic corruption that has occurred together with China's economic reform, the expansion of the market system is nonetheless still the "correct direction" to take. The real problem, in Zhu's view, is a delayed political reform. He notes that since Deng Xiaoping launched the economic reforms, political reform has been on the CCP's agenda but appears to have been indefinitely postponed after June Fourth in 1989. Zhu thus warns his readers that the New Left discourse not only risks ignoring "long overdue" political reform as the cause of China's social problems but wrongly attacks economic reform and globalization as well (Zhu Xueqin 1999: 388–389, 397). The point Zhu emphasizes is that "market mechanisms" (both domestic and global) should not be blamed for the range of problems of social injustice and corruption that beset post-Maoist China. According to Zhu, it is authoritarian Party rule rather than market mechanisms that should be held responsible for China's social problems in the 1990s. Zhu uses the phrase "the struggle between the 'hand' and the 'foot'" (*shouzu zhi zheng*) to describe the difference between liberal and "New Left" views. Using the "hand" to refer to market mechanisms and the "foot" to refer to Party rule, he implies that the New Left attack the "hand" of market mechanisms while avoiding direct confrontation with the "arbitrary foot" of Party rule. Hence, according to Zhu, whilst New Left reflections of the limitations of 1980s discourse were useful, they rapidly became subjected to the unhealthy "influences of domestic politics and fashionable foreign discourse" (Zhu Xueqin 1999: 388, 398, also, 402–403).

In a similar style, Ren Jiantao, another influential liberal commentator who attacked the New Left, uses the phrase the "fallacy of misplaced concreteness" (*cuozhi jutigan de miuwu*) to describe what he perceives as the primary problem of the "New Leftist" discourse. This is a phrase borrowed from Alfred N. Whitehead. According to Ren, Western New Leftist discourse is simply unsuitable for China because it offers a critical attitude towards an advanced form of capitalism that China has not yet reached. Ren claims that as a country which "still expects modernization and is still in the course of modernization," China's market system should not be subjected to a fashionable Western-style discourse that wrongly "subjects the various complicated problems of contemporary China to the discursive framework of Western leftism" (Ren Jiantao 2000[1999]: 200–206, 213). Ren also questions the moral integrity of the Chinese New Left, noting that "'New left' intellectuals do not have the courage to reveal the truth about the cause of the problem, but blame liberalism which is consistently very weak in China, and cannot influence the development of Chinese society. It is as if these intellectuals seek to quench the dissatisfaction of common people by attacking liberalism and thus to evade the real problems brought by social changes in the last twenty years. Their "critique" in fact is an attempt to surrender to despotic power and to show arrogance (*shiwei*) to the poor. This is a disgusting display of the 'New Left' attempt to appear brave and wise." (Ren Jiantao 2000[1999]: 207) Hence, Zhu Xueqin and Ren Jiantao, just like Xu Youyu, also radically differ from their opponents regarding their perception of China's socio-political reality, and further offer the moral judgment that "New Left" discourse is cowardly.

Li Shenzhi's critical response towards Wang Hui is slightly different from Xu Youyu and others. In response to Wang's criticism of globalization as the latest form of capitalist imperialism, Li Shenzhi argues that Wang should approach the 1990s wave of globalization quite differently. Li claims that it is not the continuation of what happened after the great geographic discoveries in the fifteenth century:

> Why have people only started to say that the world is entering the age of globalization? This is because in the past five hundred years, what we see primarily is the expansion of the power of nation-states, the collision of national interests, the spread of religions, the infiltration of cultures… In brief, the clashes and conflations were caused by "local powers." But now, we can see clearly the motions and actions of transnational, global forces transcending national boundaries. We can also see the spread of global problems. […] The age of globalization has arrived. The process of [true] globalization has just begun. (Li Shenzhi 2000a [1994]: 4–5)

As this excerpt makes clear, Li disagrees with Wang Hui's negative appraisal of globalization and advocates globalization as a positive trend that would accelerate the completion of China's unfinished modernization. Both Wang and Li agree that the massive force of the global market is able to "constrain" the actions of the state. However, the difference between them is that whereas Wang sees the transnational force of globalization as dangerous for China, Li sees it as a necessary corrective to the

CCP's authoritarian rule. Thus, Li argues that Wang Hui's negative attitude toward globalization should not be regarded as critical reflection since, "In fact, this so-called 'reflection' is simply fear." In his view, most of the "critical reflections" of the New Enlightenment that occurred in the 1990s were the result of intellectuals' fear of punishment from the Party-state.

Hence, like other Chinese liberals, Li views "New Leftists" as people who sought to avoid making trouble for themselves. They claim to be critical intellectuals, he argues, but without drawing attention to increased censorship after 1989, in which the government was ready to use force to silence true dissent. Li claims that, contrary to what the "New Left" claims, China's situation in the 1990s is not much different from the 1980s because the nation remains under authoritarian rule (Li Shenzhi 2000b[1998]: 248–249). What Li also implies is that by criticizing the New Enlightenment enterprise, Wang Hui and other "New Left" intellectuals are promoting authoritarian rule.

What is noteworthy here is that when Li Shenzhi, Xu Youyu and others criticize Wang Hui from a liberal perspective they also claim that they are defending the interests of the majority and not the elite minority. In this regard, they imply that the "New Left" is an elite minority that lends support to the CCP's authoritarian rule. Similarly, Wang Hui's critique of the 1980's New Enlightenment project also denounces it as something that benefits only an elite minority and not the majority of the population. In this sense, both sides in fact share the same self-perception of intellectual independence defined in terms of defending the rights and well-beings of the people against an oppressive force, whether viewed as authoritarian Party-state or an authoritarian state supported by global capitalism.

This type of moral judgment, which is repeated in the writings of other Chinese liberals, indicates that there is a deeply personal dimension to the promotion of liberal values. Similarly, "New Left" intellectuals offer their own moral judgment of the liberal advocacy of market mechanisms as the promotion of social inequality. Wang Hui's claim that the New Enlightenment discourse is to a large extent consistent with the official ideology in China is one such instance. This type of mutual moral accusation between the liberals and the "New Left" in the 1990s was not common in the intellectual writings of the 1980s. For most mainland intellectuals in the 1990s, the June Fourth massacre was a traumatic event that they could not discuss because of state censorship. Thus, in the 1990s, intellectuals often reacted badly to the accusation of being compliant with the Party-state precisely because of the implication that they have contributed in some way to the tragedy of the Tiananmen protest in 1989. From this psychoanalytic perspective, one can also understand why the term "New Left" was seen by Wang Hui and other intellectuals whom this term was used upon as a vicious "curse" (*zhouyu*) (Wang Hui 2000b: viii) — the term "leftists" (*zuopai*) in post-1949 mainland China has been associated frequently with radical Maoists, "conservative" Marxists, and anti-reformists. Thus, those who are labeled by their opponents as the "New Left" become, by implication, associated with the authoritarian state that brutally suppressed the 1989 student protest movement. Wang explicitly wrote that "these people [liberal intellectuals] often imply that the agenda of so-called 'New Leftists' is to return to the old, extreme left route. Pardon me for knowing too little but I never found any tenable arguments provided by them in this regard." (Wang Hui 2000b: ix) This comment of Wang's reflects his anger towards his detractors' implicitly linking him to that "old, extreme left route."

In his rebuttal to the liberals' critique of his thesis on "the question of modernity," Wang Hui wrote: "I am surprised that those intellectuals who always talk about freedom are entirely intolerant of alternative views, that people who call themselves 'scholars' are full of hypocrisy and malice, and that so many celebrities and big names are inclined to listen to hearsay and rumors. All of these are, really and truly, nothing new. If one wishes to speak of the 'current state of the nation' (*guoqing*) and the "present reality" (*xianshi*), then this phenomenon is part of the reality of our nation at present." (Wang Hui 2000b: xxiv) Later, Xu Youyu responded to Wang in a similar style: "How can a scholar be so unreasonable as to adopt the following kind of ridiculous logic: You criticize me for not understanding the current state of the nation without understating what the current state of our nation is? Let me tell you: your willful attack on me is in itself an example of the current state of the nation!" (Xu Youyu 2000: 7–9)

My thesis here is, however, that what this style of debate demonstrates is not that contemporary Chinese intellectual inquiry is unprofessional or inferior; rather, it is symptomatic of the deep attachment of rival Chinese intellectuals to their competing solutions (as fantasmatic narratives) about China.

Lacanian psychoanalysis offers us a way of engaging with these heated debates about "liberalism" and the "New Left." As noted in previous chapters, if we take fantasy as a psychoanalytic term to mean the necessity of a given point of view that guarantees the subject's access to reality, we can see that the powerful fantasy of modernization that educated mainland Chinese perceived as their collective endeavor in the 1980s, eroded after 1989. When Žižek speaks of the "uncanny absolute proximity of trauma and fantasy," what he means is that traumatic experiences are that which emerge when one's "sense of reality" collapses[7]; meaning that the fundamental fantasy holding that "reality" in place has collapsed. A new way of seeing reality — in the form of a modified fantasy — thus becomes necessary (Žižek 2003: 283). If China's modernization functioned in the 1980s as the socially shared fantasmatic narrative that enabled Chinese intellectuals to distance themselves from the traumatic experience of the Cultural Revolution, then a bifurcation of that narrative occurred after 1989. In the post-Tiananmen era of the 1990s, Chinese intellectuals who were traumatized by the brutal violence on the streets of Beijing needed a new account of reality (or in the Lacanian sense a new fantasy) to show that a path to greater freedom in China can yet be found, in resistance to the official modernization construction of the CCP. Both the proponents of the liberal discourse and the "New Left" discourse can thus be described as offering competing fantasmatic narratives, in the attempt to show the best way forward. In this sense, they were competing not only for intellectual dominance, but also for *which fantasy that should be promoted in the name of "the correct way."*

The psychoanalytic concept of trauma further helps us to explore the personal dimension of the post-Tiananmen intellectual writings: after the New Enlightenment movement was violently cut short in 1989, how did intellectuals move forward to a post-Tiananmen reality? The liberal and

[7] In Lacanian theory, the Real is experienced as something akin to trauma or shock because it is "outside" language. Thus, the intrusions of the Real haunts "reality" in the guise of unexpected events about which we are fearful, that are beyond our control and for which we have no easy explanation.

the "New Left" discourses can be seen as conflicting ways to cope with the trauma caused by June Fourth 1989, in the context of state censorship. For Chinese liberals, the New Enlightenment failed because it focused too much on "cultural" modernization instead of political modernization. In other words, the New Enlightenment thinkers did not target CCP's authoritarian rule as the primary object of their critique. As two liberal representatives who emerged in the Chinese intellectual scene in the 1990s, Zhu Xueqin and the Beijing-based economic historian Qin Hui both engaged in criticizing what they call "cultural determinism" (*wenhua juedinglun*) and claimed what is more important for China is to launch a process of political institutional transformation (Zhu Xueqin 1997: 141–147; Qin Hui 1999: 285–349). The killings in Beijing also made Chinese intellectuals realize that intellectual voices lacked the force to help create political change in China. By praising globalization and endorsing China's entry into the WTO, the unspoken agenda of these liberal intellectuals was to subject China's Party-state rule to the regulative force of the global market. However, some intellectuals such as Wang Hui started to analyze the New Enlightenment discourse much more comprehensively after 1989. When Wang Hui criticized the New Enlightenment discourse for being too close to the official market reform ideology, he was also promoting a new role for critical intellectuals in the post-Tiananmen era. He argued that it was time to move beyond Enlightenment ideology to reconceptualize Chinese problems (*chongxin sikao Zhongguo wenti*) as a question of studying China's unique path to modernity. As the debate progressed, the differences between the two sides became more sharply defined. By the early 2000s, liberals were insisting on a Western model of liberal democracy for China whereas "New Left" intellectuals were equally convinced that China must develop its own cultural path to modernization through a process of what Cui Zhiyuan calls "institutional innovations" (*zhidu chuangxin*).

"The Question of Modernity": From Theoretical Critique to Linguistic Politics

Like the negative mainland Chinese reception of postmodernism examined in Chapter 3, Wang Hui's phrase "the question of modernity" was also subjected to much debate and regarded by his liberal critics as an unnecessary question. So, what does Wang mean by the "question of modernity"?

Wang used this phrase in several papers during the 1990s. In his essay entitled "Weber and the Question of Chinese Modernity" published in 1994, Wang Hui first raised what he has since called "the question of modernity." Wang's approach in that paper is to treat modernity as a divided concept. To support his argument, he uses Habermas's interpretation of Weber's concerns about modern society ("the crisis of rationalization") and Foucault's reading of Baudelaire. On this theoretical basis, he concludes that political and economic modernity is mostly defined in terms of a capitalist process while aesthetic modernity (or modernism) is mostly associated with ideas that are radically anti-capitalist. He thus refers to this divided concept of modernity as "a tradition against itself." Wang then argues that when Habermas writes of modernity, he fails to ask "whose modernity" he is referring to. By quoting Octavio Paz's work, Wang emphasizes that modernity is a concept that has been derived from Christian civilization. He argues that, for this reason, it should not be used as if it were universally relevant.

In Wang's view, Habermas' reading of Weber is actually inferior to Weber's because Wang regards Weber as having correctly identified the interdependence of the Protestant tradition and modernity. He further praises that Weber connected the concept of "rationalization" with Christian (Protestant) ethics and highlights the cultural or civilizational origins of modernity as a European concept. Wang also notes that in his study of China and its religions, Weber answered the question as to why modern capitalism originated in the West and addressed the issue of China's lack of capitalism. Most importantly, Wang reads Weber as arguing that "rationalization" is a concept unique to the West and one that should not be universally applied.

In this regard, when Wang uses the phrase "the question of modernity," it is to point out, with reference to Weber, that there is no such concept as "rationality" or "rationalization" in the Chinese language. He argues: "In the European context, these concepts and their signified objects have at least a historically established relationship, while in the Chinese context, this kind of conventional relationship does not exist. Rather, there is only the linguistic domination of a powerful [Western] culture over a weak [Chinese] culture." Based on this analysis, Wang further discusses what he calls "Chinese modernity," which he claims cannot follow the model of Western modernization, but must "search for [essentially Chinese] ways of using language and categories to properly describe Chinese society and culture. These uses of language and categories constitute the established norms of communicative practices within a given linguistic community." Only through this new methodological vision can one properly deal with "the question of Chinese modernity" (Wang Hui 1997[1994]: 4–35).

In his 1997 article "Contemporary Chinese Thought and the Question of Modernity," Wang further developed this issue of a "modernity" unique to China. He argues that Chinese intellectuals should shift their critical focus to reflect on modernity as a concept in crisis because of the contradictions between capitalist and socialist models of modernity. In this regard, Wang explains that if we view "Chinese Marxism" as "an ideology of modernization," then Maoism is a development out of Chinese Marxism that offers a "theory of modernity that contradicts [capitalist] modernity" (*fan xiandaixing de xiandaixing lilun*). He also states that "Mao's socialism is both an ideology of modernization and a critique of Euro-American capitalist modernization" (Wang Hui 1998[1997]: 13–14). In stark contrast to the language of modernization that was popular in the 1980s Chinese intellectual discourse and that continued to be used in the 1990s, Wang argues in favor of seeing "a huge paradox" in modern Chinese thought that "embodies a critique and a re-conceptualization of modernity." Using Chinese Marxism and Mao Zedong Thought as examples, he writes that "in China's historical context, modernization and the rejection of rationalization have proceeded together, and this has produced profound historical contradictions" (Wang Hui 1998[1997]: 14–15, translation slightly adjusted).

By this means, Wang implies that the 1980s' post-Maoist language of New Enlightenment undermined the uniqueness of China's approach to modernity, or "Chinese modernity." He thus makes it his goal to point out how the New Enlightenment discourse is an "ideology of modernization," built upon a European nation-state model that had become "the global prescription of the capitalist process." He then uses the term "Chinese modernity" to mean a socialist-inspired critique of Western modernity (Wang Hui 1998[1997]: 19, 34). In conclusion, Wang writes:

> The upshot is: The teleology of modernization that has dominated Chinese thinking for the past century must now be challenged. We must reconsider our old familiar patterns of thought. Even though there is no one theory that can explain the complex and often mutually contradictory problems that we now face, it nevertheless behooves Chinese intellectuals to break their dependence on time-honored binary paradigms, such as China/West and tradition/modernity, and to reconsider these questions in the context of globalization. This is an urgent theoretical problem. Socialist historical practice is part of the past; the future designs of global capitalism, by the same token, do not promise to overcome the crisis of modernity that Weber wrote about. The modern era, as a historical phase, continues. This the impetus for the continued existence and development of critical thought; it may prove for Chinese intellectuals to be a historic opportunity for theoretical and institutional innovation. (Wang Hui 1998[1997]: 37)

In a 1999 interview Wang Hui, having been loudly denounced by his liberal critics, described them as "arrogant New Enlightenment intellectuals" who "do not understand the internal tension of modernity, and therefore embrace modernity entirely. For this reason, they have totally lost their basic ability to reflect." Against the universalist model of modernization, he argues for attention to be given to new ways of studying the "interdependent relations" (*hudong de guanxi*) between China and the West (Wang Hui 2000b: 8–14, 18). Hence, by emphasizing the "question of modernity," Wang Hui attempts to challenge the liner narrative of modernization that Chinese liberals have advocated since the 1980s New Enlightenment movement.

The main purpose here in outlining Wang Hui's conceptualization of the "question of modernity" is to show that he raised a serious critique of the concept of modernity as widely understood among Chinese intellectuals in the 1990s. This is why the self-identified liberals who continued to promote the New Enlightenment project of modernization in the 1990s reacted so strongly to his argument. In the preface of his 2000 book *Dead Fire Rekindled*, Wang Hui wrote about the negative reception of his article

"Contemporary Chinese Thought and the Question of Modernity" in the mainland Chinese intellectual world. He mentioned that around 1994 when he finished the first draft of this article, a friend told him that "this article must never be published in mainland China!" (*fabiao shi wanwan-buke de, zuoyou shangxia jun buke*), and at that time he accepted this advice. Wang also mentioned that from 1989 to 1996, he devoted his time to pure academic research in order to prevent himself from saying something that would upset some "gentlemen" (*junzimen*). Then he said that later he did not heed his friend's warning and published this article in *Frontiers* magazine. After its publication, according to Wang, "this paper became an 'event' but without any real discussion, because they [his opponents] did not regard it as an article. Rather they saw it as some sort of a symbol [of the rise of a 'New Left']." He observed that the so-called debate over his article amounted to no more than "rumors upon rumors" traveling widely, "without any substance" (*wuwu zhi zhen*) (Wang Hui 2000b: i–iv). Wang then expressed regret about having published the article: "I really should have kept my focus on academic research and self-cultivation. Why did I have to disturb the beautiful dreams of others?" (Wang 2000b: iii) Here, Wang also views this part of his work that moves beyond "academic research" as a breaker of other intellectuals' fantasy (to use Lacan's jargon). Thus, though Wang Hui's description of what happened before and after the publication of his paper was perhaps biased by his personal perspective, his comments about disturbing "the beautiful dreams of others" are nonetheless psychoanalytically sound. This also indicates how both sides assumed that whereas they were seeing reality, their opponents were lost in their own "beautiful dreams."

The liberals' responded by accusing Wang Hui's defense of "Chinese modernity" as deluded. They focused primarily on two aspects of his argument to criticize: (1) his depiction of "Chinese modernity" as obscuring China's current reality (*xianshi*) or current state (*guoqing*) as an oppressed nation under authoritarian rule; (2) his use of language as overly theoretical. We have discussed the first aspect in the preceding sections of this chapter. Let us now take a look at how liberals criticize Wang Hui's style of argumentation. After the publication of Wang's 1997 paper, quite a few commentators directly stated that they did not understand Wang Hui's "awkward" expressions or what he meant by "the question of modernity." For example, the Shanghai-based philosopher Lu Xinghua characterizes Wang Hui's writing style as "confused, empty, meaningless, and self-destructive" (*cuoluan, kongdong, wuqu, ziqiang*), and avers that Wang does not have the basic skill to write a simple grammatically correct Chinese sentence (Lu Xinghua 2004[2000]).

As a leading figure of the liberal camp, Li Shenzhi refers to the "New Left" style of argumentation as "the complication of simple problems." He writes:

> Nowadays, a lot of new-style scholars in both Western and Chinese academia write their essays in a deliberately repetitive and unreadable style. I cannot understand these essays, and I am sure that normal readers also cannot understand them. In fact, I doubt whether these scholars actually understand each other. In this sense, their writings are a waste of mental effort. (Li Shenzhi 2000b[1998]: 258)

Li then compares the "New Leftists" of the 1990s to Mao Zedong (as the exemplary writer of the "old left") and states that they were far inferior to Mao as they could not simplify complex issues as effectively as he did. Li writes that "In his later years, Mao had a particular skill in simplifying difficult issues. His speeches were what common people liked, since they were very easy to understand. He was a real success in this respect." (Li 2000b[1998]: 258) Li's view is shared by other liberal intellectuals. For example, Zhu Xueqin accuses the "New Left" of writing in an "obscure and hidden (*huise yinbi*)" manner that requires special reading skills (Zhu Xueqin 1999: 391). Zhu was especially sarcastic about Wang Hui's use of "modernity." In this regard, Zhu writes that "[I]n the old days, literati used adjectives and adverbs to express their emotions but now they have suddenly changed to using foreign concepts and nouns" (Zhu Xueqin 1999: 386, 401).

Indeed, the New Leftists' increased use of theoretical language in the 1990s is an important departure from the 1980s language of modernization. To appreciate the depth of the rupture in the 1990s of the 1980s' shared "fantasy" of China's rapid modernization, we need to see that the theoretical language used by "New Left" intellectuals in the 1990s was understood by Chinese liberals not only as a display of arrogance but as a betrayal of the 1980s language of Enlightenment used in the 1980s: a language that the liberals continued to uphold. Barmé and Davies have explored the differences between reading Wang Hui in English and Chinese. In their discussion of Wang's controversial 1997 paper on modernity and Chinese thought, they point out that the English translation of this essay actually erased certain distinctive features of Wang's Chinese original:

> The edited and fluent English version of the article elides a number of key rhetorical registers that in the original Chinese have powerful resonances of authorial assertion. Transposed into English, Wang's language appears to echo well-rehearsed arguments that have convenient theoretical underpinnings laid out by a range of authoritative EuroAmerican authors and texts. In Chinese, however, Wang's discourse partakes of what one might call the politicized "translationese" of EuroAmerican scholarly idioms (an ungainly yet culturally authoritative vehicle for expression in that language since the time of the first appearance of cumbersome translations of Marx and others in the early Republic). As a mode of discourse, "translationese" developed complexly coded moral-evaluative vocabularies that changed and were extended over the course of the twentieth century, particularly during the Cultural Revolution, in which one passed judgement on one's discursive opponents from the moral high ground of one or another chosen set of Western-inspired theoretical arguments. That is to say, Wang Hui's text bears a narrative message in Chinese readily identifiable to Chinese readers, that had a far more significant and disturbing set of meanings than the genteel form of theoretical disquisition that the same text communicates in English. While it surveyed the scene from the kind of critically-informed moral high ground readily taken by the theoretically sensitive left-leaning academics in Anglophone scholarship, it also passed judgement on intellectuals and their activities in general with a series of prescriptive remarks and moral-evaluative statements that are "invisible" to the English reader. As a result the impact it had in the Chinese intellectual scene is read very differently by (Anglophone) outside observers and (Sinophone) insider-participants. (Barmé and Davies 2004).

It is because Wang was read in Chinese as passing judgment on his intellectual peers that people like Li Shenzhi felt the need to judge him in return. In Chinese intellectual circles, Li's cutting observation that Mao Zedong's language was far more effective than Wang Hui's writing constitutes a strident attack intended to hurt the reputation of the person accused (in this case Wang). But Wang Hui's engagement with modernity is clearly a serious undertaking. What Li's attack on Wang, repeated by others like Zhu Xueqin and Xu Youyu, demonstrates is that Chinese liberals are not interested in dealing with the type of language that the "New Left" intellectuals had begun to use.

The intolerance that liberals showed to Wang Hui's style of argumentation led them to accuse him of using the phrase "the question of modernity" purely as a rhetorical strategy to shift critical attention away from the issue of authoritarian rule. Xu Youyu further argues that by phrasing modernity as a paradox or a structure full of contradictions, Wang is concealing his thin formula which equates the enterprise of enlightenment to the introduction of the capitalist market. In other words, Xu accuses Wang of falsely using "capitalism" to criticize his opponents' promotion of modernization. This criticism is also personal insofar as Xu implies that Wang is pretending to be a Western leftist critic of liberalism, as if he was addressing people who live in a liberal democracy. Xu is particularly angry with Wang for not mentioning that in an authoritarian socialist state, liberalism is confined to an academic discourse and cannot be used to criticize socialism (Xu Youyu 2003[2001]: 273, 276). His point is valid to the extent that numerous self-identified liberal intellectuals are censored and prevented from publishing in China.

As a reaction to Wang Hui's argument in favor of "Chinese modernity," Zhu Xueqin and Ren Jiantao defend their liberal endorsement of further modernization as plain "common sense" (*changshi*) (Zhu Xueqin 1997: 134–140; Ren Jiantao 2000[1999]: 207–210). Similarly, in his debate with "New Leftists," Qin Hui employs the term "commonsensical rationality" (*changshi lixing*) (see Qin Hui 2000: 131). In the late 1990s and early 2000s, Jin Guantao and Liu Qingfeng, two historians and leading figures of the 1980s New Enlightenment, also write about what they call "the spirit of commonsensical rationality," and regard it as not only one of the defining features of traditional Chinese culture, but also what characterizes "Chinese-style liberalism" (*Zhongguo shi ziyouzhuyi*) (Jin Guantao 1997; Jin Guantao and Liu Qingfeng 2001). What these New Enlightenment thinkers and liberal intellectuals imply in calling for "common sense" is that they regard Wang Hui's argument as lacking "common sense." Specifically, they regard Wang Hui as failing to identify Party-state authoritarian rule as the real reason for the problems that China faced after the purge of the protest movement at Tiananmen in 1989. They are convinced that further marketization (understood as the positive forces of capitalism) would aid China's political reform rather than hinder it (as the "New Left" claims). In this way, liberals defend their language of New Enlightenment as realistic and relevant (as plain "common sense") and they criticize Wang Hui's language as obscure and awkward (and thus lacking "common sense"). Zhu Xueqin further argues in his essay entitled "Introducing Common Sense" that "New Left" intellectuals should be enlightened by the common people. Zhu writes:

> The common people (*laobaixing*) need the intellectual enlightenment from intellectuals. Also, intellectuals need the "common-sense enlightenment" from the common people. What those imported concepts do is to disturb our memory. When this kind of writing style prevails, common sense is the best antidote. Common sense can awaken memory, and our memory in turn can tell us exactly where we are right now and what age we're living in. Why do we have to use those imported concepts, ideas, and symbols to frighten people? (Zhu Xueqin 1997: 139–140)

For Zhu, Wang's style of argumentation is a strategic move the sole purpose of which is to frighten his readers. Also, in this passage Zhu directly links "common sense" to the category of "memory," which often functions in contemporary Chinese intellectual discourse as a coded way to refer to the crimes under the Maoist rule and the killings that occurred around Tiananmen Square on 4 June 1989. According to Zhu, when Wang Hui uses concepts like a "theory of modernity that contradicts modernity" to describe Mao Zedong Thought, he is actually justifying Mao's destructive authoritarianism. This is, for Zhu, unacceptable because it betrays the "collective memory" of the Chinese people and "common sense." Hence, Zhu claims that there is a "spiritual consanguinity" (*jingshen xueyuan*) between Maoist "Cultural Revolution" and contemporary "New Left critique" (Zhu Xueqin 1999: 404). In short, Wang and other "New Leftists" are viewed by their discursive enemies as theorists who use obscure imported concepts irresponsibly; who show that they have lost touch with history and reality; and who lack "common sense."

Because the necessary fiction that we call "reality" is dependent on language, it is not surprising to find that both sides attack the language of their opponents. I will now go on to discuss one of the most vehement criticisms of Wang Hui by Wu Jiaxiang, an influential figure in the 1980s who endured years of jail after 1989, and how Wang Hui then replied just as aggressively to such critics. When defending liberalism and condemning the discourse of the "New Left," Wu lambasts Wang Hui's account of modernity as "a reanimation of the corpse" (*jiangshi huanhun*). By "the corpse" Wu implies the corpse of Mao Zedong. "Compared to the old left, the new-ness of the New Left is nothing but phrases and quotations" (Wu Jiaxiang 2000). Wu avers that "reading the writings of New Leftists is a painful experience; especially, reading Wang Hui's essays is almost a torture." The major problem of Wang Hui's writing style is that "he cannot write without quoting some foreigners' words." Wu argues that quoting the critiques made by foreign masters does not prove the objects of those critiques are not suitable for China.[8] Especially with regard to liberalism, Wu argues that since there is still no freedom of the press nor freedom of association in present-day China, "New Leftist" critique of liberalism is much too hasty and ahead of its time:

> To hold forth on the challenge communitarianism poses to liberalism without according at least equal space to discussing the lack of the freedom of association in China is the same as debating the virtues of sexual abstinence and birth control with infants. Or one could also say that it is the equivalent of giving condoms and contraceptives to babies. (Wu Jiaxiang 2000)[9]

Wu Jiaxiang not only criticizes Wang Hui's style of argumentation, but also emphasizes the current situation of authoritarian rule in China. Wu's

---

[8]Coincidently (or not), liberals and their New Enlightenment predecessors are also blamed for — to quote Wang Hui's ally Pan Wei's phrase — being "fetishistic with Western dogmas" (*mixin xifang jiaotiao*). See Pan Wei 2009: 6.

[9]This translation is adopted from Barmé and Davies 2004.

references to Mao's corpse, and to giving condoms and contraceptives to babies, and his use of such "simple language," were denounced by his opponents as unacceptable and vicious.

In his rebuttal to such accusations made by his detractors, Wang Hui claims that when liberals suggest using "the question of liberalism" to replace "the question of modernity," they simply "turn this discussion into a frivolous game of concepts" (Wang Hui 2000b: 28, 41). In response to Zhu Xueqin's appeal to collective "memory," Wang replies that his liberal critics tended to "simplify history" and "turn the complexity of historical processes into the wholeness of memory (*jiyi de zhengti*)": "Their attitude seems 'correct,' but in fact is a rejection of any historical analysis of historical realities such as the 'Cultural Revolution' which had very complicated elements" (Wang Hui 2000b: ix). In the preface of his 2000 book *Dead Fire Rekindled*, Wang further accuses his critics of using the sordid title "New Left" to hinder critical thinking in China (Wang Hui 2000b: v, vii). Wang argues that those despicable acts of using gossips and rumors to attack their opponents and assigning bad names to them are attempts to cancel all kinds of serious critiques. He claims that his opponents were perpetuating an unequal world with their poorly conceived ideas. In this regard, Wang states:

> In the past couple of years, I have witnessed the growth and development of critical thinking, but have not seen any powerful explanation or analysis of the contemporary world from those liberal heroes. It seems to me that they have nothing to do except to make up some vicious titles and labels, or repeat some dogma. [...] To be frank, I reject all labels not because I hate titles like "New Left," "postmodernism," and so forth, but because I resent the use of such names to demonize intellectuals and to turn intellectual discourse into a kind of swearing. Moreover, I am sick of the closed minds of those who promote all kinds of fetishisms. I am surprised that those intellectuals who always talk about freedom are entirely intolerant of alternative views, that people who call themselves "scholars" are full of hypocrisy and malice, and that so many celebrities and big names are inclined to listen to hearsay and rumors. All of these are, really and truly, nothing new. If one wishes to speak of the "current state of the nation" and the "present reality," then this phenomenon is part of the reality of our nation at present. (Wang Hui 2000b: xxiv)

In accusing Chinese liberals of launching personal attacks and spreading rumors rather than engaging in serious "critical thinking," Wang Hui shows an aggressive attitude not unlike Wu Jiaxiang's. Wang also explains that the reason he wrote such strong criticisms of the liberals is because "those gentlemen possess a kind of unique skill — which is, to appear innocent while viciously attacking others." By stating that he on the contrary does not have "such skills," what Wang implies is that he wrote down such passages because he was viciously attacked by liberal intellectuals first, so that to fight back, he had to lower himself to their level (Wang Hui 2000b: xxv). One can see that although Wang strongly condemns his opponents' acts of assigning titles and labels, he nonetheless also customizes various derogatory titles for his critics, such as "hypocrites" (*weishi*), "liberal heroes" (*yingxiong*), "celebrities" (*mingren*), "big fellows" (*wenren*), etc.

Besides those obvious mocking or cursing labels, Wang also employs the term "neoliberalism" to refer to his discursive enemies in order to replace the inviolable, sanctified label "liberalism."[10] Wang states that this debate has been "inappropriately described by some as a dispute between 'liberalism and the New Left.' For me, the core of this debate is a debate over 'neoliberalism'" (Wang Hui 2008: 139). Wang defines "neoliberalism" as a dominant, antipolitical ideology in the contemporary world and claims that it was especially influential in China. In this way, he implies that neoliberalism was closely linked to the official policy on socio-economic reform and thus to the perpetuation of one-party rule.[11] "While neoliberalism takes every opportu-

[10] I owe this point — to read Wang's later employment of the term "neoliberalism" as a *discursive strategy* — to Liu Qing. He shares this insight of his during a conversation.

[11] In 2001, Wang Hui published in a Taiwan academic journal a lengthy essay entitled "The 1989 Social Movement and the Historical Origins of China's Neoliberalism: Revisiting the Issues of Contemporary Chinese Thought and the Question of Modernity." (In order for avoiding the censorship in mainland China, the title of this essay was changed to "The Historical Origins of China's Neoliberalism" when it was compiled in Wang's 2008 book *The De-Politicalization of the Political*, and several paragraphs were deleted.) In this sequel to his 1997 influential essay that initiated this vehement debate, Wang basically rearticulates his critical analysis of contemporary Chinese thought from the angle of the critique of "neoliberalism." Wang claims that contemporary Chinese "liberals" actually should be properly regarded as representatives of "neoliberalism," which in Wang's

nity to cast itself in the image of 'resistance,' this does not prove that this ideology of the market is in actual opposition to the practical operations of the state: on the contrary, the state and neoliberalism exist in a complex relationship of codependence" (Wang Hui 2006: 60). Hence, contemporary Chinese "neoliberalism" is, in Wang's account, not only filled with all the Thatcher-Reaganite connotations that the term implies, but also tightly connected with CCP's policy.[12] In his 1999 interview "An Interview on the Question of Modernity," Wang claims that those self-styled Chinese "liberals" in fact have very few serious discussion of liberalism; instead, what their writings reflect is a kind of "fetishism about liberalism" (*ziyouzhuyi baiwujiao*). They are only good at "cursing and defaming other people in order to cover up their own theoretical weakness" (Wang Hui 2000b[1999]: 27, 30). Not only substituting the label "neoliberalism" for "liberalism," Wang also employs the phrase "critical intellectuals" (*pipan de zhishifenzi*) to replace the term "New Left." According to Wang, "the group of critical intellectuals represents a broad social movement instead of a small factional circle." Wang claims that what his opponents attribute to "liberal" values are

---

definition "is a dominating discursive formation and ideology that has no capacity to describe actual social and economic relations, but neither is it unconnected to actual social and economic relations. As an ideology imbricated with national policy, the practical thought of the intellectuals, as well as the values of the media, it uses concepts concerned with 'transition' and 'development' to patch up its internal contradictions." When discussing "the specific nature of Chinese neoliberalism," Wang further argues that "Neoliberalism depends on the force of national and supranational policy and economic power; it has also relied on a theoretical discourse centered on formalist economics in order to establish its discursive hegemony. *Its apolitical or even antipolitical features (or its antihistorical method and antagonism to traditional socialist ideology) cannot in the slightest obscure the fact of its solid connection with state economic policy. The hegemonic status of Chinese neoliberalism took shape as part of the process by which the state used economic liberalization to overcome its crisis of legitimacy.*" (Wang Hui 2006: 43–44, emphases added)

[12] In the same paper, Wang Hui further challenges the popular perception of the link between the 1989 social movement and the 1990s discourse of liberalism. Opposite to the common depiction of the 1989 movement as a failed endeavor of democratization and liberalization of China, Wang defines it as "a spontaneous resistance to inequalities springing from the growth of markets" (Wang Hui 2006: 58). According to Wang, "neoliberalism" has improperly taken credit for heroically continuing the unfinished enterprise of the 1989 movement as well as the 1980s New Enlightenment movement.

actually an organic part of the endeavors of contemporary "critical intellectuals"; for example, Wang states that "Establishing individual political rights is an important task in contemporary Chinese society and critical intellectuals never, and should not, ignore or negate the importance of this matter" (Wang Hui 2000b: viii, vi). In this sense, whilst praising Wang's critical analysis of modernity, Barmé and Davies however comment that "Wang's piece itself is a fascinating source for the study of rhetorical moves in contemporary Chinese intellectual debate" (Barmé and Davies 2004).

What is interesting here is that Wang did not respond in "academic style" (i.e. employing jargons, etc.) to his critics' claim that China cannot be depicted as having achieved the status of "a market society or capitalist society" (Xu Youyu 2000: 8). Instead, Wang used plain and simple language (instead of academic "translationese" depicted by his opponents as obscure and awkward) to "fight back." Similarly, when Wang responded to Zhu Xueqin's claim that the year 1998 marked the (re)emergence of liberal discourse, he did not discuss Zhu's text in a scholarly fashion. Instead, he drew attention to the disastrous floods in the south-eastern provinces of China during the summer of 1998 to imply that Zhu's celebration of liberalism was misplaced. Just as his liberal critics accused him of misrecognizing China, he accused them in turn of celebrating the rise of liberalism in ignorance of the hardships faced by the poor in China. Wang writes in a sarcastic tone that "1998, a year of disasters and social crisis, demands our serious reflection. However, under the pen of some Shanghai celebrity, it becomes the year that so-called 'liberalism' rises to the surface. [...] How great 1998 was! Yet the terrible floods did not awaken our hero; instead it gave him the passion to surf the currents! This gentleman is really good at swimming!" (Wang Hui 2000b: v) This is an arbitrary moral judgment because Zhu's essay was merely his personal account of liberal intellectual discourse in 1998. It was not intended as social criticism and while Zhu did not discuss the floods in his essay, it does not mean that he was ignorant of and unsympathetic to the hardships people suffered as a result of the social problems and disasters that happened in 1998. Wang's intention was entirely polemical. He sought to reduce his liberal critics to a position of total moral bankruptcy.

When reading such passages of Wang Hui's, his liberal enemies were clearly "enraged" (*jinu*, a phrase used by Xu Youyu to describe his reaction to this essay by Wang). Xu Youyu claims that Wang chose not to tackle directly those issues raised in his published critical response to Wang's 1997 article but resorted instead to making "an arrogant and reckless rejoinder." Xu is especially unsatisfied with Wang's disregard to "the entire series of arguments I raised and the grounds upon which I made these arguments" (Xu Youyu 2000: 7–9). In another essay, Xu targets Wang Hui's attack on Zhu Xueqin and claims: "The reason Wang links Zhu's writing to the massive floods in 1998 is clear: to issue the death penalty to his discursive enemy in the court of moral justice (*daoyi*). Is this a smart move? I don't know. But at least I know it indicates that Wang lacks scholarly argument (*jiqiong*)." "In brief, what matters is to provide a justification for one's argument. [...] To claim that 'I have noble spiritual status' does not prove that your discursive enemies are despicable little people (*xiaoren*)." (Xu Youyu 2003: 287)

From Wang Hui's attack on Zhu Xueqin and Xu Youyu's dismissive comments about Wang Hui, one can see that as the debate progressed, the intellectual content of such phrases as "the question of modernity" and "marketization" were completely disregarded and replaced by abusive exchanges on both sides. Thus, the "New Left" and liberals proceeded from disagreements over whether China should adopt a socialist and communitarian or capitalist and liberal path to simply denouncing each other for lacking moral decency.

These increasingly personal attacks between liberals and the "New Left" peaked during the Cheung Kong-*Reading* Awards (*Changjiang Dushu jiang*) controversy that unfolded in the summer of 2000. Barmé and Davies (2004) provide a wonderful detailed analysis of this controversy. Most of the criticisms of the Cheung Kong-*Reading* Awards were about the selection process. The controversy became focused in particular on what many perceived to be the questionable nature of Wang Hui's nomination for and subsequent acceptance of one of the book awards. As Barmé and Davies have observed, "the accusations leveled at Wang were informed by more complex motivations than that of exposing procedural irregularities, although the latter provided a convenient excuse for many to engage in Wang Hui-bashing on the grounds of demanding 'accountability' (*fu zeren*) from a leading light in the Chinese intellectual scene" (Barmé and Davies 2004). This "Wang Hui-bashing" involved several prominent scholars and intellectuals including Chinese liberal representatives such as Xu Youyu, Zhu Xueqin, Qin Hui, and Qian Chendan. Many other prominent liberal and liberal-inclined intellectuals such as He Weifang, Lei Yi, Ding Dong, Ge Jianxiong, Mao Shoulong, Xie Yong and Zhang Shuguang also joined in the criticism. To defend himself and the journal *Reading*, Wang Hui employs phrases echoing the language frequently employed in the official discourse of the Maoist time, especially the big-character posters (*dazibao*) of the Cultural Revolution era. This is the point Barmé and Davies have made in their critical analysis of Wang's writing style — "his use of the communist-style rhetoric that features so significantly in official Chinese discourse." Barmé and Davies also point out that in these paragraphs, "Wang availed himself of the same diction of moral high dudgeon, the rich and ready-made vocabulary of categorical assertion, the colorful prose of denunciation as well as the biting satire of excoriation previously employed by Xu Youyu." They further comment that this style that is "heavily indebted to the mock-heroicism of party propaganda" is shared by both sides of the debate (Barmé and Davies 2004).[13]

At the end of an essay entitled "The Self-Destruction of the Enlightenment," the introductory chapter of a coauthored book on Chinese intellectual discourses since the 1990s (published under the same title), Xu Jilin writes:

> The debates among intellectuals subsided at the beginning of the twenty-first century. However, this does not mean the resolution of the problems [that were introduced], but indicates our incapacity to resolve these problems: a united civil intellectual sphere formed in the 1980s has become deeply fragmented and there are now opposing feudalist camps that each

[13]In 2010, Wang Hui was accused of plagiarism, and this further divided the Sinophone academic community: while over 100 prominent scholars including Lin Yü-sheng and Yu Ying-shih (most of them are liberal-minded) agreed that plagiarism charges are basically sustained and called for the Chinese Academy of Social Sciences and Tsinghua University (Wang's former and current employer) to launch serious investigation, also over 100 well-known scholars — including internationally renowned scholars such as Slavoj Žižek, Fredric Jameson, Michael Hardt, Arif Dirlik, Gloria Davies, etc. — publicly endorsed Wang Hui's scholarly integrity and viewed the plagiarism accusation as a new episode of the continuing "Wang Hui-bashing."

> hold its own set of knowledge claims, value stance, and ideological belief. This is a malignant further complication (*houyizheng*) of the debates of the 1990s. (Xu Jilin 2007: 41)

The phrase "self-destruction of the Enlightenment" that Xu employs as the title of his essay implies that the 1980s enterprise of New Enlightenment carried within it the seeds of its own destruction. Xu views such "self-destruction" as the "fate of Enlightenment" (Xu not only refers to the collapse of the "consensus" and "homogeneity" of the New Enlightenment of the 1980s, but also that of the May Fourth Enlightenment of the 1910s and 1920s). In this sense, Xu imagines the 1990s as a time of intellectual fragmentation after the trauma of 1989. Thus, though writing in a pessimistic tone, Xu Jilin still expects a "reconstruction of the basic consensus of modernity" (Xu 2007: 41–42). That is to say, while acknowledging the "incapacity" of post-Tiananmen Chinese intellectuals to realize the modernity they had promoted in the 1980s, Xu nonetheless still hopes that the future will bring about a less divided Chinese intellectual world whose participants will be united once again in a "homogeneous attitude" to resolve China's problems. From the perspective of Lacanian psychoanalysis, such wholeness or homogeneity is purely fantasmatic: It structurally requires a fantasy that offers the promise of fullness. Those violent acts of writing produced by post-Tiananmen Chinese intellectuals can be interpreted as acts aiming at (morally, socially) discrediting competing figures ("discursive enemies") and re-establishing a hegemonic fantasmatic scenario in the Chinese intellectual scene.

The 1980s New Enlightenment movement, as discussed in the preceding chapters, is based on a discourse and a vocabulary that revolves around seeing a national destiny for China. In the idea of New Enlightenment, the image of a collective enterprise has a particular symbolic importance — the envisaged ideal of a "homogeneity of attitude." Wang Hui's idea of "Chinese modernity" also attempts to produce such a homogeneity for it is predicated on the idealization of a collective practice. In this sense, Wang's writings are also fundamentally shaped by the fantasmatic scenario that shaped the New Enlightenment discourse of the 1980s, which I refer to as the "Great Dragon fantasy." For example, as a leading figure of the New Left camp, Wang Hui writes passionately that

"I rejoice that I was born in China since what could be more heartbreaking and also more exhilarating than the glorious revival of a decaying civilization of which so many generations of people have dreamed? And what could be more thrilling than to watch and experience the minutiae and process of this collective dream?" (Wang Hui 1994: 21–22) The aim of Wang's "modernity critique" is, as he clearly states, to advance "the glorious revival of the Chinese civilization." (Wang Hui 2000b: 473) That is to say, what drives Wang to critique the "New Enlightenment as an ideology of modernization" and in turn become a "traitor" of the New Enlightenment enterprise is that in his view, the glorious revival of Chinese civilization cannot be achieved through the project of modernization; thus, Chinese critical intellectuals have to explore alternative ways to achieve this goal. Wang's late works, especially *The Rise of Modern Chinese Thought*, are intellectual endeavors to explore "Chinese modernity" — a "native modernity" rooted in China's traditional culture before it was polluted and shaped by "modern institutions." In this regard, Wang avers that "I believe that the glorious revival of Chinese civilization relies on the rational efforts of several generations" (Wang Hui 2000b: 473).

Thus, Wang Hui offers his version of the fantasy of "homogeneity": instead of accepting the existing model of Western modernization, Wang suggests that the Chinese have to "search for the basic words and categories that properly describe Chinese society and culture. These basic words and categories are conventionally established in the communicative practices of each specific linguistic community." (Wang Hui 1997[1994]: 4–35) Therefore, Wang regards the task for contemporary Chinese intellectuals as one of constructing a different pattern of modernity through understanding China's "cultural homogeneity" (*wenhua tongyixing*) as a form of uniqueness that had prevailed before the late Qing era. In his view, the late Qing was an age that was already subjected to Western-influenced "modernization" (Wang Hui 1994: 21–2; 1999). In this sense, Wang attempts to re-establish a "homogeneity" which is based on traditional Chinese culture instead of Western modernization.

In Chapters 1 and 2, I referred to the post-Maoist fantasmatic narrative of reviving China's civilizational grandeur as the "Great Dragon fantasy" and the New Enlightenment discourse of modernization as a specific embodiment of this fantasy in the 1980s. Though Wang Hui's critics position him as an enemy to modernization, he nonetheless writes from within the same grounding fantasy of the New Enlightenment project of reawakening the "Great Dragon" that is China. His defense of a unique "Chinese modernity" seeks just as much as those who promote a universal model of modernization to restore "clear-sightedness" to the Dragon (to recall the lyrics of Hou Dejian's song). In this regard, those Chinese post-modernists who propose the paradigm shift from modernity to "Chineseness" discussed in Chapter 3 also write within the same fantasmatic frame.

Evaluated from the academic standards of contemporary Anglophone scholarship, the style of intellectual engagement in contemporary mainland China, as I illustrated in detailed textual analyses in this chapter, would be deemed unprofessional. However, what is unique about Chinese intellectual discourse is *its historical importance as a nation-building tool*. Thus, its producers (that is, people who regard themselves as intellectuals) regard their writings as a tool for shaping the future by showing others how they can establish a proper way of life for themselves, to recall again the Confucian axiom of *anshen liming* (to settle down properly one's own lives). This type of discourse is about the quest for true knowledge capable of guiding oneself and others forward. In this aspect, Chinese intellectual discourse cannot be evaluated from a narrow academic perspective. This is why the Lacanian notion of a fantasmatic narrative is particularly useful in exploring the conflicts and divisions that have arisen in post-Maoist intellectual discourse. Thus in the Chinese intellectual world, any academic critique of the hegemonic discourse that has acquired the "homogeneity of attitude" among intellectuals is no longer academic, but a violent attack on the "heart" of the Chinese (recall the title of the pop song "My Chinese heart" discussed in Chapter 1), an attack that obstructs China to achieve its national and/or civilizational perfection.

Besides the post-Tiananmen discourses of postmodernism and the "New Left," there was also another influential anti-modernization (and anti-liberalism) discourse in the 1990s, which attempts to "combine the whole nation into one heart" on another foundation. This is the discourse of nationalism that I will discuss in the next chapter.

Chapter 5

China's New Nationalism and Its Obscene Core

Nationalism at the Gates

From the mid-1990s onward, "nationalism" has grown in influence in the Chinese intellectual world. Different from other more scholarly-oriented intellectual discourses in contemporary China (such as postmodernism, the "New Left"), nationalism is a discourse that not only can be found in bestselling books, magazines and newspapers, but also becomes prevalent on the Chinese Internet where it has acquired a particularly virulent form as anonymous cyberchatter. During the debate between liberalism and the "New Left," especially after the year 1999 when NATO bombed the Chinese embassy during the Kosovo War, a group of intellectuals led by Wang Xiaodong, Song Qiang and Fang Ning, among others, called themselves "Chinese nationalists." They publicly sided with the "New Left" and targeted liberal intellectuals as their "discursive enemies." (However, most intellectuals in the "New Left" camp are in fact not willing to be regarded as "nationalists.") Despite the attempts of prominent intellectuals like Wang Hui to distance themselves from nationalists,[1] the nationalist discourse has nonetheless become one of the most distinctive characteristics of contemporary Chinese intellectuality. Owing to the rising role it plays in the Chinese intellectual life as well as daily life, this nationalist current in the post-Maoist era has already become the topic of a dozen of research monographs and numerous papers (see, for example, Unger ed.

---

[1]Wang Hui deliberately distanced himself from "Chinese nationalism." In numerous essays, he has insisted that "nationalism is double-edged: on the one hand, it could integrate the national spirit, on the other hand, it would engender a great deal of negative effects." "Facing today's globalization process, facing the power-relations between oppressor and the oppressed that exist explicitly in this process, there is no way out if we simply fight against today's globalization by engaging ourselves in nationalism" (Wang Hui 2000a: 400; 2000b: 397).

1996; Yongnian Zheng 1999; Li Shitao ed. 2000; Rebecca E. Karl 2002; Gries 2004; Le Shan ed. 2004; Xu Xun 2005; Pal Nyiri and Joana Breidenbach eds. 2005; Christopher Hughes 2006; Xu Wu 2007; Simon Shen and Shaun Breslin eds. 2010; Zheng Wang 2012; Wang Jun 2012).

There are also several works that are critical of Chinese nationalism. For instance, a widely discussed book published in 2000, *Intellectual Positions: Nationalism and the Fate of China in a Transitional Era* is mainly focused on what nationalism means. There are only a few essays in that book that actually adopt an explicitly nationalist stance. In 2004, another collection with the title *Undercurrents: Critiques and Reflections on Extreme Nationalism* was published. This volume's 27 essays are all critical of "Chinese nationalism." Wang Xiaodong's writings were a particular target of criticism (with two essays devoted entirely to a negative appraisal of Wang).[2] Most of the contributors to both these anthologies are influential scholars actively engaged in publishing social criticism, including many who are regarded (or who see themselves) as liberals. Many of the contributors were well-known intellectuals, including Li Shenzhi, Zhu Xueqin, Liu Junning, Qin Hui, Xu Jilin, Wang Yi, Qiu Feng, Yang Zhizhu, Xiao Xuehui, as well as Xiao Gongqin, Xu Ben, Sheng Hong, Gu Xin, Ge Hongbing, Xu Xun and Luo Houli. Le Shan, the editor of *Undercurrents*, states two points in the "introduction": (1) although the views of the Chinese nationalist intellectual discourse are quite superficial and extreme, the nationalistic sentiments they present should not be overlooked; (2) although nationalist discourse is not dominant and remains only an "undercurrent," it has never ceased to exist and has erupted from time to time in mainland Chinese public culture (Le Shan 2004: i). From these two anthologies, we can see that contemporary Chinese nationalism, even though it is subjected to a lot of criticism nonetheless has become a topic of concern in contemporary Chinese intellectual discourse.

It is worth noting that when speaking of China's so-called "new nationalism" or "contemporary Chinese nationalism," it is useful to differentiate three dimensions: state nationalism, intellectual nationalism, and popular nationalism. By "state nationalism" I refer to the specific

[2] This anthology partly overlaps with *Intellectual Positions*, because some of the essays in both books are the same.

ideology that the Party-state leadership has been actively advocating for nearly three decades. Nationalism and patriotism have been used to *produce political legitimacy and social solidarity* in post-Maoist China, especially in the post-Tiananmen era (1989–present).[3] Also, since the late 1990s, the CCP has nurtured some specific anti-foreign sentiments (especially anti-American sentiment) in order to tackle the increasing difficulties of "information-control" (*xinxi kongzhi*): in the age of the Internet it is almost impossible to totally block the information flow into China, and thus the focus has been turned to the task of *shaping* how Chinese citizens think about what they learn from abroad. Chinese citizens have been constantly told (and schoolchildren have even been directly taught) that China is re-emerging as a benevolent great power while Western powers — especially the U.S. — are determined to hold China back. The state-controlled media have been depicting American advocacy of democracy, press freedom and individual rights in China as a conspiratorial plot to destabilize the country.[4]

By "intellectual nationalism" I mean the nationalist trend in the intellectual circles, for which the following three books are representative: *China Can Say No, China's Path in the Shadow of Globalization*, and *China Is Unhappy*. The term "popular nationalism" is used to designate nationalistic sentiments expressed in everyday life, especially large-scale events such as the anti-foreign demonstrations of recent years (e.g. the 1999 anti-U.S. demonstrations, the 2005 and 2012 anti-Japanese demonstrations, and incidents of hostility expressed towards Japan during and after football matches between Japan and China). Also, as mentioned earlier, violent expressions of these nationalistic sentiments frequently appear on the Chinese web. These three dimensions of contemporary

[3]For a detailed empirical study on the post-Tiananmen CCP's advocating nationalist-patriotic ideology, please see Baogang He and Yingjie Guo's paper "State Nationalism in Post-Fourth June China" (He and Guo 2000: 25–52).

[4]These efforts are effective. A March 2006 opinion survey by the *Global Times*, a Chinese newspaper, showed that 59% of city-dwellers believe the U.S. seeks to contain China. The 2005 Pew Global Attitudes Project survey showed that only 42% of Chinese view the U.S. favorably. A 2003 survey by Duke University of hundreds of Chinese cities and rural counties indicated that the more educated people are, the more likely they are to hold negative views of the U.S. See McGregor 2006.

Chinese nationalism are inter-related but nonetheless remain quite distinctive. My analysis of contemporary Chinese nationalism here will be primarily focused on intellectual and popular nationalism.

The question that many Chinese intellectuals ask with regard to the emergence of these anti-foreign mass demonstrations is the following: where did this militant-flavored nationalism come from? "It would be unimaginable if it appeared in the 1980s," said Chen Shaoming, a Guangzhou-based philosopher in his essay entitled "Nationalism: A Way towards Renaissance?" (Chen Shaoming 2000: 389) Recently, the Sydney-based artist Kylie Wilkinson produced a documentary film in which she interviewed quite a few contemporary Chinese artists and intellectuals, centering the question on what they feel about contemporary Chinese nationalism ("What is 'nationalism'?" "Does everyone 'feel it'?" and "Who's asking anyway?" etc.).[5] What most interviewees expressed is that they personally do not really "feel it," though they have been well aware of the rise of a popular nationalist discourse and mass explosions of nationalistic sentiments since the late 1990s. Similarly, only a few contemporary Chinese intellectuals, notably the Beijing-based research fellow Wang Xiaodong, have sought to declare themselves as "nationalists." Although most intellectuals are aware that there has been a growing nationalist current after 1989, they choose to distance themselves from it, instead of embracing it.[6]

In his editorial "Introduction" to *Chinese Nationalism* published in 1996, Jonathan Unger noted the sudden shift from the "open-minded

[5] Some descriptions of this documentary film are available online.

[6] During the heated intellectual debates in the late 1990s which has been widely termed as the "debate between liberalism and the New Left," the self-styled nationalists regarded themselves as standing in the same trench as the "New Leftists." To people who followed these debates, the "New Leftists" and the nationalists appeared to be fighting the same foe, namely, people who regarded themselves as "liberals." Many commentators for this reason simply use the label "nationalist" to refer to all those intellectuals who engaged in debates with "liberals" (for example, Yingjie Guo 2004: 24; Mobo Changfan Gao 2004: 44). However, the representatives of the "New Left" were unwilling to be mixed with Chinese nationalists, though the two share the anti-globalization ("anti-Westernism") stance. The leading "New Leftist" figure Wang Hui's anti-nationalist attitude is a case in point.

optimism" of the 1980s to the "anti-foreign resentment" of the 1990s.[7] His prediction of this emerging nationalist trend is that

> So long as the economy continues to do well, so long as the future seems bright for China in the world economy, openness may well prevail, with perversely nationalistic sentiments emotionally satisfying within popular entertainment but muted in real-life appeal. If, contrarily, the current economic expansion sours, if Chinese aspirations come to nought, a repertoire of highly nationalist emotional sentiment is available for more serious consideration. (Unger 1996: xvii–xviii)

Unger's view has been accepted by quite a few Chinese intellectuals (see Li Yonggang 1999; Xu Xun 2005: 288). The 2005 mass demonstrations, however, contradicted Unger's prediction: it *is* still very "bright for China" in terms of its position "in the world economy" — China now is widely seen as "a rising world power" (see Ronald C. Keith ed. 2005); yet "nationalistic sentiments" have nonetheless exploded. Thus, the question that has troubled contemporary Chinese intellectuals should be seriously re-examined: Where did this militant-flavored nationalism come from? Why is it that the "open-minded optimism" of the 1980s (best expressed in the frequent calls made by intellectuals for the Chinese people to "open their eyes to see the world" or to "rub their eyes to see clearly") turned into "anti-foreign resentment" in post-1989 China?

Xu Jilin observed in his essay entitled "China's Anti-Westernism in the 1990s" that there have been three waves of "anti-Westernism" (*fan xifangzhuyi*) since 1989. The first wave is (semi-)official scholar He Xin's anti-Westernist writings in the early 1990s which had little lasting influence in the intellectual circles. The second wave consists of three parts: Chinese "post-colonial cultural criticism" represented by Zhang Yiwu and Chen Xiaoming, the call for "institutional innovation"

[7] In his book *China's New Nationalism* published in 2004, Peter Gries captured an ironic contrast of this shift: "During the 'May Eighth' nationalist protests of 1999, for instance, one group of students demonstrated with a painting of what might best be described as the 'Demon of Liberty.' During Beijing Spring a decade earlier, Chinese students became famous for their statue the 'Goddess of Democracy'." (Gries 2004: 5–7)

put forward by Cui Zhiyuan and Gan Yang, and the discourse of "civilizational comparison" represented by Sheng Hong. The third wave is marked by the publication of *China Can Say No*, a book which was published in 1996 and became extremely popular in the market. Xu argues that in spite of the "vulgarity of its content," this third wave should be given special attention, for it raised the issue of the "awakening of Chinese nationalism" (Xu Jilin 2011: 163–164). Now at least we should add a "fourth wave" — a huge one indeed in terms of intensity and impact — represented by Wang Xiaodong and his two books *China's Path in the Shadow of Globalization* and *China Is Unhappy* — both coauthored with Song Qiang (the main penner of *China Can Say No*) and other a few. The former book was published after the bombing of the Chinese embassy in Belgrade on 8 May 1999; and the latter one was published as a response to the 2008 global financial meltdown triggered by the U.S. subprime mortgage crisis.

The editors of *China's Path*, Ma Lijun and Cao Hongju, claimed that the book represents a further development of earlier books such as *China Can Say No* (which they evaluated as being "quite vulgar but which nonetheless provided readers with the opportunity to modify their thinking") and *The Plot to Demonize China* (which they praised as a book that "provided the real story of how the West has restrained China"). According to Ma and Cao, *China's Path* "would elevate readers' minds to a new level," and they thereby congratulate themselves for having achieved excellence in this process. Ma and Cao stressed that the authors of all these books were members of a close-knit group that had come to be labeled as the "Say-no Club" (*"shuobu" julebu*), and they also noted that these authors represent "the voice of nationalism" (*minzuzhuyi de shengyin*) in contemporary China (Ma Lijun and Cao Hongju 1999: i–v). This description is widely accepted. Besides being a further development, there are two other ostensible distinctions to be made between *China's Path* and earlier books: (1) unlike the authors of earlier books, Wang Xiaodong explicitly accepts the label "Chinese nationalists"; (2) in contrast to *China Can Say No* which primarily addressed the general reading public, especially undergraduate university students, Wang Xiaodong's writings have a much stronger intellectual flavor, employing many academic terms and expressions, and engaging in debates with other contemporary intellectuals, especially Chinese liberals.[8] Consequently, most scholarly critical responses of "Chinese nationalism" also targeted Wang Xiaodong's writings, because Wang, as a critic notes, "became the spokesman of Internet nationalists and young extreme nationalists in the intellectual circles" (Ren Bingqiang 2004).

Let us have a close look at Wang Xiaodong's nationalist arguments. Wang claims in *China's Path* that "so far Chinese 'nationalists' have not fully articulated their position. This is partly because they are unable to find a forum for expressing their views that would distinguish them from the dominant theories circulating in mainland intellectual circles, but also because 'nationalism' is condemned by the Western media and Chinese 'liberal' intellectuals." The task he sets for himself in that book is thus to "elucidate as clearly and as frequently as is required, the political ideas that a Chinese 'nationalist' should hold" (Wang Xiaodong *et al.* 1999: 99). In *China's Path* as well as *China Is Unhappy*, Wang focuses primarily on articulating what he considers as two key elements of "Chinese nationalism" — its foundation, and its basic proposition.

Wang determines the foundation of "Chinese nationalism" as ethnic and racial. Thus, in his view, "nationalism" (*minzuzhuyi*) is synonymous with "racism" (*zhongzuzhuyi*); these two terms are often used interchangeably by Wang (Wang's main accusation of 1980's intellectual movement is that it is a form of "reverse racism"). In response to Samuel Huntington's account of the "clash of civilizations," Wang argues that the "clashes in the future" are the ones among ethnic groups; "ethnic borders are still the firmest borders" because they are grounded in "biological foundations." "The so-called 'clash of civilizations' is actually ethnic conflict"; it is "just a euphemistic expression of racism" (Wang *et al.* 1999: 188–189, 222, 218). Wang further argues that the "fundamental cause" of this clash, and thus of the rise of Chinese nationalism, is still the "economic elements" (i.e. scarce resources, national interests) (Wang *et al.* 1999: 161–163, 225–226).

---

[8] In the preface of *China Is Unhappy*, the authors clearly state that it is " 'intellectual elites' such as Long Yongtu, Li Yining, Lin Yifu, Fan Gang, Ding Xueliang, Cui Weiping, Zhu Xueqin, Yu Shicun, Song Hongbing, Ma Licheng, Wang Meng, Wang Shuo, Li Yinhe, Zhou Xiaozheng" that constitute the main target of the book (Wang Xiaodong *et al.* 2009: 9).

The "political" proposition Wang suggests is that "to enrich the country, what must first be done is to strengthen the army": the only "way out" (*chulu*) for China is to "awaken the ancient cultural gene" — the "spirit of upholding militancy" (*shangwu jingshen*), i.e. to be inspired by the spirit of the Chinese knight errant (*xiake*) who is capable of "killing one person every ten paces" (*shibu sha yiren*).[9] "What we need is," writes Wang, "a group of true heroes who inherits spirit of upholding militancy to lead this nation." China must turn itself into a "heroic state," developing the "great goal" of offering the world "true management and leadership, and eradicate evils for the entire human race." In order to become a heroic state, China must be determined to "break itself from the West," and to "control resources which lie beyond national borders." Wang even explicitly claims that "the coverage of the force of the People's Liberation Army should reach every single corner of the world where lies China's core economic interest. [...] We must go to business with holding swords at hands (*chijian jingshang*)." (Wang *et al.* 1999: 12, 15, 380; Wang *et al.* 2009: 10, 15–16, 182–199) Lucian W. Pye claimed in his 1993 essay "How China's Nationalism Was Shanghaied" that the emerging nationalist trend in post-1989 mainland China is a "contentless nationalism." It is merely based on "the sentiments associated with Chinese ethnicity" and thus "a shallow version of nationalism" (Pye 1993: 130–131, 133). He was "achronologically" right in terms that apart from identifying the enemy and strengthening the army, there is little normative content in Wang Xiaodong's nationalist arguments.

For Wang Xiaodong, there are two main "targets" of this contemporary "spirit of upholding militancy": Japan and the U.S. (see Wang *et al.* 1999: 12, 15, 42, 380; Wang 2003). Wang writes,

> In fact, whether or not Japan is able to invade China again, and commit something like a "Beijing massacre" depends on whether or not China is able to strengthen itself. [...] When we are insulted, we should fight back

---

[9] *Shibu sha yiren* is a line Wang Xiaodong borrowed from a famous poem, *The Travels of Swordsmans* (*Xiakexing*), written by Li Bai, one of the most important great poets in Chinese history. However, Wang's employment of the phrase "cultural gene" here also manifests that for him, what makes "the Chinese nation" unique is fundamentally based on biological grounds (rather than cultural ones).

> with blade and sword because we are men. If we are not as strong as the enemy, then we should spend years on sharpening our swords. When the time is ready, we will seek revenge. (Wang *et al.* 1999: 42)

This statement is disturbing because it offers a highly paranoid account of the "international situation" *as if* it were fact. Wang *assumes* that the Chinese people are really facing a hostile foreign enemy and his use of the phrase "whether or not" is crucial in this context: the hidden implication of the phrase "whether or not Japan is able to invade China again, and commit something like a 'Beijing massacre'," is that the possibility of such an invasion is strong and that the safety of Chinese citizens will "depend on whether or not China is able to strengthen itself." Thus, Wang implies that Japan *is going to* "invade China again, and commit something like a 'Beijing massacre'." But it is also clear that if one were to refute Wang's paranoid view with a factual account of current Sino-Japan relations, he could easily respond that he was merely outlining a "possible" future event.

This is exactly the way in which ideology operates in China today: a particular set of beliefs or values (constitutive of a symbolic fiction) is widely disseminated and declared as the "reality" experienced by all Chinese citizens. This stands in sharp contrast to the advocacy of the "scientific" approach to improving Chinese "reality" that was popular in the 1980s. To put it in abstract and theoretical terms, (1) the "scientific" way to present the picture of "reality" is to *directly describe what it is* in the name of "(objective) knowledge"; in contrast to this "modern" approach of comprehending "reality," (2) today's "postmodern" ("reflexive") way of rendering fiction as "reality" disguises itself in the pretense of "uncertainty," "possibility," the "impenetrable other," and so on.

In the 1980s, Chinese thinkers were focused on producing a "modern" and "scientific" account of "reality" and this is a mode of writing that is constrained by the empirical evidence (data, statistics, social survey, opinion polls, etc.) on which it draws. The 1980s Chinese intellectual discourse of the New Enlightenment is characterized by the passionate call for "rubbing eyes to see the reality clearly" as if it is something that can be positively grasped and thus improved by adopting and using science. The "postmodern" account relies on rhetoric alone to make its case (this applies not only to Wang Xiaodong's "reasoning" of his "upholding-militancy" project, but — let us not forget — also to the Bush administration's justification for "preemptive strikes"). For Wang, *today* "we will seek revenge" and sharpen "our blade and sword," *not* because of *historical* atrocities committed by the Japanese army (such as to Nanjing massacre), but because there *might be the possibility* of a future massacre — a fantasmatic "Beijing massacre," an event that is at present still a fiction but that Wang implies is about to take place. It is this fictitious event that justifies Wang's demand that "we should fight *back*." But we should also acknowledge that the discourse of the 1980s, with its reliance on "science" and "modern reason," is also not transparent. In fact, it is a discourse that is contingent on the data it offers as historical or empirical fact.[10] What is interesting about Wang Xiaodong's argument is that he claims to be producing a factual analysis but the "facts" he offers are actually hypothetical (fantasmatic) scenarios of a frightening future.

The other main target of Wang's militant proposition is the U.S., with regard to which he writes:

> China must ensure itself the capability of killing a hundred thousand American soldiers in a war. This is the real safeguard of peace and security. Only this can really stop a war. (Wang 2003)

One can detect once again the same ideological operation at work: under the banner of "we-want-peace," there is the smell of gunpowder and blood; moreover, by saying "stop a war," Wang fabricates a "reality" that a "war" (between the U.S. and China) *is about to take place*, if we Chinese do not do what he suggests, which is, to "awaken our ancient cultural gene — the spirit of upholding militancy," to enhance our "capability to kill," then the U.S. will surely attack us. In such supposedly "theoretical" formulation, Wang Xiaodong's mode of reasoning provides us with useful clues about why militant slogans and calls for violence were so popular in the 1999 anti-American and 2005 anti-Japanese demonstrations.

---

[10] See my detailed analysis of Jin Guantao and Liu Qingfeng's account of "ultrastable structure" in Chapter 2.

When examining the violent slogans of the young activists participating in these nationalist mass demonstrations and Wang Xiaodong's intellectual arguments of nationalism, one must ask the question: Are these contemporary Chinese nationalists really nationalists *per se*?

This question actually originates in a dilemma inherent to modern nationalist thought, which is, as Ernest Gellner has already stated in his seminal work *Nations and Nationalism*, the ineffaceable contradiction between pure nationalism — what Gellner calls "nationalists-in-the-abstract" — and what is suitable to be described as "egotistic nationalism." "The national principle" of modern nationalism, as Gellner summarizes, "can be asserted in an ethical, 'universalistic' spirit," which implies that all nations should have their own "political roofs" (Gellner 1983: 1–2). However, in examining nationalism at the empirical level (contrary to the theoretical or normative level) — e.g. those recent nationalistic outbursts in China, one can see that the historical "concretizations" of this national principle often takes the form of advocating some specific, *anti-universalistic* "national spirit" that contradicts the supposedly "universalistic" character of modern nationalism. Thus, as Gellner observes, the "sweetly reasonable," "non-egoistic nationalism" always mutates to its opposite — unabashed egotistic nationalism. In this sense, the type of nationalism advocated by Wang Xiaodong and other "Say-no Club" members is clearly of the egotistic nationalistic type and is opposed to the very defining feature of modern nationalism, the universalistic idea that the political and the national unit should be congruent.

Here, a further crucial issue with regard to Chinese nationalism needs to be addressed: Since when, and how, did China become a nation? In today's China, the concept "nation" is widely accepted, though up to the late nineteenth century, it remained unknown in the Chinese language, and was thus completely alien to Chinese understandings of the world. Contemporary studies of nation and nationalism presented by theorists such as Benedict Anderson, Ernest Gellner, and Eric Hobsbawm remind us that the nation is a relatively recent human invention, a modern creation. Nation is not a pre-existing fact, but an "imagined community" (Anderson 1983), and "it is nationalism which engenders nations, and not the other way round" (Gellner 1983: 55; also see Hobsbawm 1992: 10). Anderson calls it an "imagined community" and this is because the idea of a nation is based to a large extent on what can be remembered and what must be forgotten (Homi Bhabha 1990). We could also put the same explanation in Lacanian terms: "Nation" as a (floating) signifier is always-already a *symbolic and/or fantasmatic fabrication*, a concept whose validity rests on the modern discourse of "nationalism" as a collective identity. As Slavoj Žižek asks, "What is 'national heritage' if not a kind of ideological fossil created retroactively by the ruling ideology in order to blur its *present* antagonism?" (Žižek 1993: 232) The word "antagonism" here refers to the structural necessity of an enemy that radically fails the promise of a harmonious order by the ruling ideology.

Let us go back to the question: Since when, and how, did China become a "nation"? This perhaps belongs to the kind of "enigmatic question" that, according to Žižek, guarantees the community's consistency: no one really knows about it, but each of them somehow presupposes that others know... Everyone nowadays refers to China as a nation, but no one really knows about how — and why — it became a nation. Žižek argues that it is this *shared ignorance* that ironically binds the group together and that makes them a "nation" (Žižek 2000: 115).[11] Why do members of a "national community" have to remain *ignorant* about what makes them a "nation" (in order for their idea of the "nation" to be meaningful)? Because, once they directly confront such question and actively seek an answer, the very "national community" will break down and dissolve in the process of interrogation. In our case, once everyone really knows about China's "nation-formation," "China" — which is, from the viewpoint of Lacanian psychoanalysis, nothing but an empty signifier — can no longer be simply equated with the concept of a "nation." How is so?

The term *Zhonghua minzu* (the Chinese nation) itself was in fact invented in the 1910s.[12] In 1912, the president of the Chinese Republic, Yuan Shikai first used this term in his letter to the leader of Outer

[11] As Bruce Fink points out from the Lacanian psychoanalytic view, "The essential feature of the subject is that *he does not know*." Hence, "Whereas philosophy — at least Hegel's philosophy — situates the subject on the basis of a relationship to knowledge, psychoanalysis situates the subject on the basis of her lack of knowledge, her inscience" (Fink 2004: 108).

[12] In what follows I primarily draw on Wang Ke-wen ed. 1998: 421.

Mongolia, arguing that the Mongols were in fact part of the greater nation of China. *Zhonghua* had been used in imperial times as one of several forms in reference to China. Both *min* and *zu* had appeared in ancient Chinese texts as well, meaning "commoners" and "tribes" respectively, but the combined term was borrowed from Japan at the turn of the twentieth century as a translation of the English word "nation." Concerned about the possible fragmentation of the Chinese state, though the revolutionary movement that toppled the Qing dynasty had been shaped, to a great extent, by anti-Manchuism, the government of the Chinese Republic established by the Revolution of 1911 abandoned the initial anti-Manchu agenda and proposed instead a commonwealth (*gonghe*) of the five major ethnic groups, i.e. Han, Manchus, Mongols, Muslims, and Tibetans, that it currently governed. The government declared that all the ethnic groups in *Zhonghua minzu* enjoyed equal status. Although the attempt failed to prevent Outer Mongolia and Tibet from pursuing political independence, since then, *Zhonghua minzu* has become part of the everyday language of Chinese people. It is here that one can see that China as a "nation" was once *a conscious fabrication*, a story invented to serve a specific ideological purpose and pragmatic political strategies. But finally story-tellers end up believing their own story, regarding it as an unquestionable "fact."

Also, there is another inherent problem of contemporary Chinese nationalism: though Wang Xiaodong claims that "ethnic borders are still the firmest borders" because they are grounded in "biological foundations," and "the so-called 'clash of civilizations' is actually ethnic conflict," and so on and so forth, he and other nationalists have ironically never ever addressed the issue of ongoing ethnic conflicts *within* the currently existing *Zhonghua minzu*. This also shows that the type of nationalism to which these "Chinese nationalists" attached themselves thwarts the universalistic principle of modern nationalism, which requires each nation to have its own political roof under which all the different groups that make up the "nation" could be sheltered. Otherwise, there will only be endless conflicts between different ethnic groups. It is interesting that for all their talk of nationalism, Wang and other nationalists do not pay any attention to the claims of ethnic minorities or the risk of separatist movements in China today.

The "Bio-Operations" of Nationalist Discourse

On the contrary, the new nationalist discourse in China is focused only on conflict and enmity between China and the U.S. or China and Japan. The nationalists draw on rhetoric such as "our compatriots' blood" and refer to foreign attempts to "humiliate" China, citing both contemporary events (e.g. the 1999 Belgrade bombing) and historical tragedies (e.g. the 1937–1938 Nanjing Massacre).

The point here is that what matters in terms of the structure of this nationalistic discourse is not merely the content of its public statements, but also its *generative mechanism.* The book *China's Path in the Shadow of Globalization* itself is a "product" of the 1999 Belgrade bombing, just as *China Can Say No* was triggered by the 1996 "defending Senkaku Islands" movement (*Baodiao yundong*). Apropos of the discursive structure of *China's Path*, the "blood debt" — three Chinese journalists were killed in Belgrade — functions as a *generative core*, and structurally molds the militant feature of Wang Xiaodong's "upholding-militancy" proposition. In that book, Wang uses many extremely violent expressions, such as "kill one person every ten paces," "if you are strong enough, you will undoubtedly kill Americans," "after spending ten years on sharpening the sword, then we are able to take revenge"... (Wang *et al.* 1999: 27, 42, 380). At this juncture, one can say that these "blood debts," both contemporary and historical, constitute the justification for violence. In other words, these "blood debts" function as a generative mechanism of the violent nature of nationalist discourses that facilitate, in turn, actual protests and demonstrations: when we read closely Chinese intellectual writings and socio-political events in the last two decade, we can see that whenever these "blood debts" are evoked (by international events, or the provocative writings of Chinese nationalists), a violent outburst will easily explode.

Now we might go one step further by positing a crucial "psychological" question onto the above analysis: Do these Chinese nationalists really care about their "compatriots' blood"? The authors of *China's Path* and the young protestors in the 1999 anti-U.S. demonstrations seem to care a great deal about the three Chinese journalists who died in the Belgrade embassy bombing. Before hastily jumping to this apparent conclusion, let us juxtapose a few more parallel events here.

In July and August 2005, just three months after the big anti-Japanese demonstrations, hundreds of mineworkers in Guangdong province died as victims of the corrupt dealings between capital and power (the local government officials themselves invested in this very business, so they tacitly approved the abusive treatment of the workers).[13] No demonstration took place at all, and there was no outcry over this shedding of "our compatriots' blood." Wang Xiaodong and other members of the "Say-no Club" were totally silent about the alarming death rate of Chinese mineworkers. At the other end of China, Heilongjiang province, in June 2005, two months after the anti-Japanese demonstrations, over one hundred people, most of whom were just children (elementary school students) died in a flood as a result of official negligence.[14] No protester took to the streets after the tragic event, no outcries such as "the blood debt must be repaid in blood" were circulated. Quite a few liberal intellectuals wrote essays to voice their strong criticisms, but no protest was made on behalf of the victims by those famous nationalist intellectuals. Another widely repeated tragedy happened in March 2003: a young rural migrant named Sun Zhigang was beaten to death in police custody in Guangzhou after he was illegally detained under the "custody and repatriation" (*shourong qiansong*) regulation applicable to people who held only a temporary residential permit.[15] Eight

---

[13] Official declarations and news reports are available at <http://news.sina.com.cn/z/mzmkts> (accessed on 23 June 2006).

[14] The official declaration is 117 victims, and 105 are pupils. See Sina News Centre, <http://news.sina.com.cn/c/2005-06-21/12076230866s.shtml> (accessed on 23 June 2006). The flood actually ran quite slowly. Before the tragedy occurred, the local police station got an emergency call in terms of the coming flood and the danger it presented to Shalan central elementary school owing to its location. But the officer in charge answered: "Even though a few kids die, what is the big deal? We don't know how to swim, so it will be useless for us to go there!" Even those official reports which concealed lots of details admitted the local government did not take calls and the local police station refused to offer help immediately and responded to the emergency calls by saying "We are busy." See Sina News Centre, <http://news.sina.com.cn/c/2005-06-14/03396931782.shtml> (accessed on 23 June 2006). Many reporters went to Shalan town after the incident; however, the reports they wrote were banned owing to the censorship and then only can be read in Internet.

[15] "Custody and repatriation" was an administrative procedure established in 1982 by which the police in the People's Republic of China could detain non-residents if they did not have a "*hukou*" and return them to their place of origin.

intellectuals including legal theorists He Weifang, Xu Zhiyong, Xiao Han, and economist Sheng Hong wrote public letters to the Standing Committee of the National People's Congress, calling for attention to Sun's death and questioning the constitutionality of this regulation. As a direct result of this public action, former Premier Wen Jiabao announced in June 2003 that the "custody and repatriation" regulation would be abolished to be replaced by "Measures for Assisting Vagrants and Beggars with No Means of Support in Cities" (*Chengshi shenghuo wuzhao de liulang qitao renyuan jiuzhu guanli banfa*). Once again, all those "Say-no Club" nationalists who all the time draw their arguments on "our compatriots' blood" maintained total silence, as if the deaths of migrant peasant workers (*nongmingong*) like Sun Zhigang could not be likened to the shedding of their "compatriots' blood."[16] Once we turn our observing focus from "presence" to "absence," the obscene character of this nationalist discourse is revealed: if the journalists who were killed in Belgrade were "our compatriots," then how about all those victims who were killed on Chinese soil? If these nationalist intellectuals and young nationalist activists do not care about horrible events — the tragic loss of their compatriots' blood — that are actually occurring *around* them, who will believe that they actually care about people who are not their contemporaries, who died over sixty years ago as victims of the Japanese army, in a war that these new Chinese nationalists never fought?

The only consistent answer to these questions is that these banner-holding nationalists do NOT care about their compatriots' blood, despite their voluble demands for "the blood debt to be repaid in blood." In his elaboration of the Lacanian "big Other," Žižek draws attention to what he calls the "public symbolic Law" and its "obscene supplement" (see, for example, Žižek 1994a: 54–85; 2000: 130–132; 2005a: 285–306; 2005b). With regard to the structure of discourse, these two phrases can be understood as follows. The public symbolic Law implies the focus on the positive content of discourse (i.e. the explicitly written claims, statements,

---

[16] One can find many more similar tragic events in contemporary China. Another now half-forgotten event, for example, also happened in Guangdong province on 6 December 2005. Several rural protestors in the town of Dongzhou were killed by local police. See Philip Pan 2005.

arguments and propositions) while its "obscene supplement" is similar to the hidden generative mechanism of any given discourse. It is this very "obscene core" of the discursive realm that Žižek pleads to pay critical attention. In light of this Žižekian analysis of the structure of discourse, it is not hard to locate the "obscene core" of contemporary Chinese nationalist discourse represented by the "Say-no Club": "compatriots' blood" should not be taken *literally* (i.e. at the level of the written content); rather, it functions precisely as a generative site of "China's new nationalism."

In his famous speech "Serve the People" (1944), Mao Zedong articulated his authoritative thesis on the "value" of death. By quoting Sima Qian's motto "though death befalls all men alike, it may be weightier than Mount Tai or lighter than a feather," Mao claims that to die for the People is of the "highest value" (*si de qi suo*) (Mao Zedong 1944). Today's nationalist discourse has turned this thesis around: instead of *whom* one dies for, what really matters is *where one dies* (the literally meaning of the Chinese character *suo* is "location"), which is to say, a death that is of "highest value" must happen in the "right" spot. If these 105 Chinese children who died in a small town of Heilongjiang province had died instead in Belgrade, just imagine the nationalist outrage that would have erupted! Hence, the *place* of death rather than the loss of Chinese lives functions as the hidden generative mechanism of contemporary Chinese nationalist discourse. It is so because the former matters exactly in terms of *who will be responsible for the loss of lives*: if Chinese lives are lost in domestic land (often ensuing to be acute evidences of domestic problems), such deaths simply *do not count* as our "compatriots' blood."

A perfect metaphor for this perverted function of "compatriots' blood" in contemporary nationalist discourse is the "blood-soaked breadroll" (*renxue mantou*), penned by Lu Xun, China's most influential writer, in his famous novel *Medicine* (*Yao*), in which the phrase is employed to refer to breadroll soaked in the blood of an executed revolutionary, which is believed to be some sort of powerful medicine. Through the perverted discursive mechanism of contemporary Chinese nationalism, "our compatriots' blood" turns into something similar to the "blood-soaked breadroll" that Lu Xun wrote about. This is because they attribute magical powers to nationalism and see bloodshed as inspiring. The nationalists see themselves as similar to powerful knights errant who have inherited the ancient "spirit of upholding militancy" and bravely fight "national enemies" to repay "blood debts." However, as noted earlier, like the magical "blood-soaked breadroll" that Lu Xun wrote about, which has to be taken from the blood of an executed criminal, the nationalist discourse also has its obscene "requirement": the "blood" that makes nationalistic discourse meaningful has to be from specific sources or "locations." The small town in Heilongjiang where 105 Chinese children died, for example, obviously does not meet this "requirement." The "blood debts" of these Chinese lives, for contemporary nationalist "knights errant" have no value — they are "lighter than a feather"... It is here that one can see the *violent character* of nationalist discourse, which does not even reside in its ostensibly violent "content" (such as violent slogans and militant propositions), but in its *generative mechanism*: the phrase "compatriots' blood" is used as justification for violence. It is perhaps meaningful and useful to coin a new term — the "bio-operation of discourse" — to denote this generative mechanism of contemporary Chinese nationalist discourse. And, the people whose deaths are used for this purpose can be described as *homo sucked*[17]: their deaths are violently (and *literally*) "sucked" by the hidden mechanism of nationalist discourse insofar as the discourse of contemporary nationalism in China (re)gain its "energy" through the deaths of *certain* Chinese lives...[18]

To extend this analysis of the "bio-operation of discourse" to another striking feature of the contemporary nationalist discourse in mainland China, one could say that what is "sucked" by the hidden mechanism of the nationalist discourse is not only "our compatriots' blood," but also "our women's bodies." To put it metaphorically, if the "compatriots' blood" is just conveniently used as the "bread" of nationalist discourse,

[17] This neologism is, derived from Žižek's phrase *homo sucker*, which he uses to develop Agamben's re-articulation of the ancient Roman notion *homo sacer* and refers to today's predominant liberal mode of subject, "when we are making fun of the ruling ideology we are merely strengthening its hold over us" (see Žižek 2002a: 71).

[18] We could also ask: do not today's prevailing "critical" discourses in Western scholarship, from "Holocaust studies" to "identity politics," also share the similar generative mechanism of discourse featured by "homo sucked," insofar as they all implicitly require — even solicit — "human victims"?

then the "women's bodies" are sumptuous, succulent feasts. Peter Gries notes in his recent book *China's New Nationalism* that

> [F]oreign men are the object of many Chinese nationalists' anxiety: the recurring figure of China as a raped woman has recently reemerged in nationalist discourse, and many of its young male exponents are enraged by the very idea of white men intimately involved with Chinese women (Gries 2004: 10).

Gries illustrates how the authors of *China Can Say No* wrote about many anecdotes which show this Chinese male anxiety about foreign men's intimate involvement with Chinese women. Among these the most famous rumor is about an American man named "Mark," who is said to have prowled Chinese streets and campuses with condoms in his wallet. The authors tell us that "his love is like spit, it flows so easily" (see Song Qiang *et al.* 1996: 60). In *China Is Unhappy*, Wang Xiaodong tells several similar stories, one of which is about a Caucasian man who was diagnosed with AIDS. He nonetheless kept having unprotected sexual intercourse with many young Chinese students before being reported and eventually deported from China. Wang claims that what this foreigner got should be the death penalty instead of deportation because "there is no difference between what this guy did to the Chinese people and the bacterial weaponry those Japanese devils developed in Heilongjiang in the 1930s and 40s." "How long," asks Wang, "would foreigners keep enjoying such privilege — fucking Chinese women — in the Chinese soil?" (Wang Xiaodong *et al.* 2009: 360–370). As Gries observes, many young male readers, especially college students, frequently generalize from such anecdotes to make racist remarks about all foreign males (Gries 2004: 153).

There are many examples of this racism on nationalist-flavored web-fora. In one such discussion, someone pasted a web-link of a porn film clip in which a Chinese male porn actor is having sexual intercourse with a white Caucasian young actress. The comments posted were approving ones, such as: he is "a good boy" (*haoyang de*); this guy is truly our "national hero," and so on and so forth.[19] Let us give another example. In

[19]This post can be found at <http://www.pen123.net/bbs/15800/messages/1163.html> (accessed on 20 March 2007).

the sixth season of *24*, the American TV drama series, the Chinese secret Agent Chen becomes one of the evil (terrorist) bosses. There is a scene in which several Chinese agents conquer the CTU headquarters and capture all the personnel. Of course, the hero (CTU former agent Jack Bauer) eventually kills all the intruders. In one of the Chinese web forums themed on *24*, many angry Chinese young men wrote that Zhou Yong (the commander of the Chinese assault team) should kill all the CTU personnel instead of just holding them in custody. Several men even suggest raping Nadia (the acting CTU director)... In another post, a man suggests an "effective way to quench the anger (caused by the 'unfortunate fact' that Chinese agents are killed and their secret operation eventually fails in the *24* TV show)": just keep imagining that these Chinese men in the TV scene are actually all played by Japanese actors.[20]

Here, perhaps we should raise such a question: Do these nationalist intellectuals themselves really believe what they wrote (since their younger followers — these emotional "Internet nationalists" — undoubtedly really believe these nationalist narratives)? The only consistent answer is: both yes and no.

It is evident that these authors consciously manipulate obscene anecdotes to provoke their readers into equating racist hatred with nationalism. However, these authors also indicate that they are deeply convinced of the truth of what they say and the personal stories they circulate among themselves are a good example. For instance, Song Qiang, the main author of *China Can Say No*, discussed his personal life three years after the publication of that book. He wrote that his wife had originally planned to go overseas to pursue further studies, and Song said "no" to her because he "knows" what would happen to their relationship (Song even noted that the fact that his wife is a good-looking woman made the situation worse...). Song claimed that by emphatically saying "no" to his wife, he saved their marriage (Song Qiang in Wang Xiaodong *et al.* 1999: 134). From the anxiety Song expresses one can see clearly that he believes what

[20] See "Why Zhou Yong withdraws? He should kill them all," <http://post.baidu.com/f?kz=204152203>; and "My wife teaches me an effective way to quench my anger," <http://post.baidu.com/f?kz=204656605>; another post that expresses the similar "solution" can be seen at <http://post.baidu.com/f?kz=204312188> (both accessed on 25 May 2007).

he wrote in *China Can Say No*. His anxiety ultimately serves as the justification for racial hatred.

Wang Xiaodong's writings reveal a similar attitude. He is supposed to be a sophisticated, theoretically-informed nationalist but is preoccupied instead with using nationalism as a protective shield against "Western sexual invasion." In his essay entitled "On the Spirit of Upholding Militancy" he writes:

> Without the spirit of upholding militancy, without nationalism, what would happen to us? What I intend to tell the young generation of China is that you would have no chance to even get a woman. (Wang Xiaodong 2005)

Wang uses as an example the recent heated discussions of *Shanghai Babe*, a novel written by the young "beautiful woman writer" Wei Hui. "Beautiful woman writer" (*meinu zuojia*) is a term coined by the popular media to refer to young female writers who become famous by "writing about their bodies" (*shenti xiezuo*), i.e. writing frankly about sexual intimacy. In *Shanghai Babe* Wei writes about young Chinese girls' "feel-good" experiences of having sexual intercourse with German men. Wang Xiaodong made the following comment on the recent wide-scale discussions of Wei's novel in his essay "On the Spirit of Upholding Militancy":

> Facing this kind of crisis that threatens the most fundamental interest of Chinese men (*Zhongguo nanren*), I believe that it is understandable that people should feel driven to accuse Wei Hui: when seeing that beautiful Chinese women are raped by those old foreigners, if Chinese men do not feel woeful and wrathful, but feel happy [for this to happen], then they are truly ill and no medicine can help them (*buke jiuyao*). Unfortunately, this kind of man does exist. A vivid description of them can be found in *China Can Say No*. What should we do? It won't do any good if we just condemn Wei Hui: what she did is no more than a true expression of the thought of many Chinese women. Nor should we blame Chinese women for not liking us — it would only make Chinese women dislike us even more. On the other hand, when we are feeling sorry for ourselves, we should also feel sorry for Chinese women: they left their homeland to a place where they cannot communicate owing to the language problem; they marry those old,

> ugly and stupid (sometimes also very poor) foreign men without feeling any love for them; they may even be ill-treated, but dare not say a word and have to pretend in front of their parents that they live a wonderful life. It's really not easy for them to do so. If we [Chinese men] have capability and spirit, we should recapture them. (Wang Xiaodong 2005)

No wonder that today there are so many young people who are emotionally driven to participate in these anti-American and anti-Japanese demonstrations. Wang's speech as quoted in the above leaks the "obscene secret" behind the grandiose rhetoric of those "blood-debt" bounty hunters: what "we"[21] actually want is Chinese women's bodies; "our true anxiety" is that "we" have "no chance to get a woman"...

Geremie R. Barmé wrote an essay in 1995 on the issue of the rise of Chinese nationalism, entitled "To Screw Foreigners Is Patriotic? China's Avant-Garde Nationalists" (Barmé 1996). Wang Xiaodong quickly penned a highly critical essay in which he claimed that Barmé totally misread contemporary Chinese nationalists including himself. Wang argues that "the vision of Chinese 'nationalists' is much broader than the imagination of those Western scholars who study 'Chinese nationalism'" (Wang Xiaodong *et al.* 1999: 125, 132). What this "vision" — as Wang himself declares — focuses on, is the alleged "most fundamental interest of Chinese men," which is, they have "no chance of getting a woman" because of competition with foreign men. Thus, women's bodies are actually at the center of the "big vision" of Chinese nationalists. (Of course, those bodies that motivate the nationalists to "action" belong only to "beautiful Chinese women"...) Probably, this "vision" *is* indeed beyond the "imagination of those Western scholars who study 'Chinese nationalism'."

In this "battle" for (re)capturing women's bodies, Wang Xiaodong was probably right in his reproach of Barmé's essay "To Screw Foreigners Is Patriotic?" that in terms of "screwing women," he is really not an

[21] In the texts written by Chinese nationalist writers, intellectuals or web-bloggers, such "we" is always a male we. By the same token, "Chinese nationalists" are (self)construed as always "male," and women are objects of their consumption. I thank Leigh Janco for bringing this self-image issue to me.

"aggressive" nationalist. What Wang preaches to the "younger Chinese generation" (actually, to younger Chinese men) is that they must not lose their "own Chinese women" to foreign men. This is indeed a rather defensive stance. He has not gone so far as to advocate the utterly aggressive and vulgar gesture that Barmé illustrated in his essay, that of "screwing-foreign-cunts" (*cao waiguo bi*): according to Barmé, this aggressive gesture of "screwing-foreign-cunts" is what exactly goes on in the mind of many young "avant-garde" nationalists, for whom "to screw foreign women" is a form of patriotism. Barmé's observation is truly backed up by numerous instances (just recall the compliments written about the pornographic film mentioned earlier where a Chinese man has sex with a white woman — "a good boy," "national hero"...).

Now we can see more clearly where this trend of nationalism comes from: it is this "most fundamental interest of Chinese men," plus the militant-violent "spirit of upholding militancy," that drives the anti-foreign sentiments among Chinese men today and that accords perfectly with what Žižek calls "the obscene supplement" of "public symbolic Law." In other words, what many young Chinese men receive as the hidden and undeniably obscene message of the grandiose public statements about having Chinese pride and demanding the repayment of blood debts is something along the lines of "we must ensure that Chinese women are ours in order to be full-blooded Chinese men" as well as "screwing foreign women to make us feel proud." These "hidden" messages are indeed actually not so hidden. They are evident in online chats as long as one knows where to look,[22] and this is also what gives young Chinese men who engage in such discussions a sense of belonging to a "meaningfully Chinese" community. So, the perfect *Western* response to the rise of Chinese "avant-garde" nationalism should be the title of Tom Tykwe's avant-garde film — "Run Lola, Run"!

Here, we do not even need to start a *feminist* analysis in order to point out the patriarchal ("phallocentric") logic of contemporary Chinese nationalist discourse, because everything is already on the surface:

[22] For instance, one can easily find many vivid examples at "Strengthening Nation Forum" (*Qiangguo luntan*).

"Chinese" is reduced to virile "Chinese men" ("the young generation of China" to the young, virile "Chinese men"), women are reduced to "property" (to be captured and recaptured by young Chinese knights errant) and so on and so forth. It is sufficient to focus on the symbolic function of women's bodies in the structure of nationalist discourse as *generative* in its discursive effects: "no chance of getting a woman" is not merely blatantly phallocentric but also an effective way to spur nationalist discourse and sentiments among young Chinese men who may be anxious about their own virility.

Furthermore, apropos of the generative mechanism of nationalist discourse, "our women's bodies" in fact serve as a crucial *supplement* to "our compatriots' blood": the latter is eruptive, a "tragic event," while the former is a part of "everyday experience," invisible but constantly there. The point is that the blood of "our compatriots" serves very well as an effective source of generating nationalist discourse, the only problem, however, is that this kind of "tragic event" does not happen very often. It is a rare occurrence for Chinese citizens to be killed by foreign military forces in the post-1989 era. But those who die on Chinese soil by Chinese hands, for a variety of political and personal reasons, simply *do not count*. One is thus tempted to say that public expressions of nationalistic outrage such as the 1999 anti-U.S. demonstrations were in fact "generated" by some specific "event" which *must* involve Chinese blood and happen in the "right" place (not on Chinese soil), while those such as the 2005 anti-Japanese demonstrations were, to some extent, "generated" by the "trivial," "invisible" settings in everyday reality that always somehow involves a narrative about how Chinese *men* are being humiliated by foreign *men*. As we shall see, the question of who should have access to the female sex again plays an important part in online discussions among young Chinese men.

Why Is Nationalism an Obscene Discourse?

Let us thus take a close look at the 2005 anti-Japanese demonstrations. April 2005 was a special month in the lives of many Chinese people. Within one short week, mass protests swept across mainland China. Tens of thousands of Chinese citizens took to the streets in Beijing and

Guangzhou on April 9, and hundreds of thousands of protestors followed in Shanghai one week after. There were also numerous protestors who organized demonstrations in other twenty major cities in late March and April 2005.[23] During the demonstrations, many Japanese restaurants and shops were attacked and smashed; cars produced by Japanese companies were burned and turned over. Even a few Japanese businessmen were assaulted on the street and seriously injured in the April Sixteenth Shanghai demonstration when someone started shouting "Look, they are Japanese, kill them!"

These mass demonstrations that emerged "all of a sudden" were evoked by two events: one, a new Japanese history textbook called *Atarashii Rekishi Kyokasho* (or New History Textbook) that fails to admit the extent of Japan's World War Two atrocities; two, Japan's bid to become a permanent U.N. Security Council member. However, one cannot help but notice that many of those young protestors who were offended by the Japanese history textbook that is said to have whitewashed Japan's World War Two atrocities, had not even actually seen or read it before they rushed on to the streets. (Interestingly enough, the citizens of the People's Republic of China had hitherto never protested so violently against Japan, and there have been numerous revisionist Japanese history textbooks published in the sixty years between the end of World War Two and the 2000s.) How do we account for this phenomenon? Despite the public claims that these demonstrations were held to protest against Japan's bid for a permanent seat in the U.N. Security Council and that the publication of that particular revised history textbook was evidence of Japanese duplicity, from the discussions that were conducted on the Internet and among groups of young men who were active organizers and participants of the demonstrations it is clear that there were several other more disturbing sources of resentment.

If we confine ourselves entirely to the public domain, that is, to the reasons that nationalists are prepared to publish in print, then there are two common ways to explain the rise of "new nationalism" in China: (1) it is

---

[23]The details of protests in these cities can be found in *Wikipedia*, an online encyclopedia <http://en.wikipedia.org/wiki/Main_Page>, under the entry of "Anti-Japanese demonstrations, 2005."

caused by acts of aggression committed against China since the nineteenth century (understood as historical events); (2) it is the result of current international relations in which Japan and the U.S. are perceived as having an unjustly greater importance (understood as contemporary events). These are also the two "commonsensical" ways to explain why Japan and the U.S. have become the main targets of contemporary Chinese nationalists. Peter Gries, for example, follows precisely these two approaches in his book *China's New Nationalism* to analyze the causes of this recent nationalist trend in post-Maoist China ("a century of humiliation," U.S.–China relations, and so on, see Gries 2004). Apropos of contemporary anti-Japanese sentiments that were expressed in the 2005 demonstrations, the two prevailing explanations of where such strong, intense, and even violent sentiments of resentment come from are that (1) historically speaking, the Japanese army committed so many atrocities during its invasion of China in the 1930s and 1940s, and (2) in terms of current events in the realm of international relations, Japan's state leaders still pay their respects to the war dead at the Yasukuni Shrine, which commemorates all those who fought and died for Japan during World War Two, including over one thousand convicted war criminals. In this regard, the Japanese are also accused of constantly seeking to whitewash the history of its World War Two atrocities, especially the Nanjing massacre.

I am not saying these are all platitudes, but they are *definitely* not the whole story, since an account of what is said in the public domain does not explore the statements exchanged among Chinese nationalists. There is thus a hidden disjuncture in the structure of contemporary nationalist discourse, which is, the gap between the nationalist-patriotic "content" that is publicly stated and declared on the one hand, and less public statements that constitute its secret underside on the other hand. The crucial problem with these two aforementioned explanations is that *they both only focus on what has been explicitly stated in contemporary Chinese nationalist discourse, i.e. the positive content of the discourse* ("the blood debt must be repaid in blood," etc.).

As I have sought to argue thus far, contemporary anti-Japanese sentiments feature much hatred and violence not so much because the Chinese protestors are outraged over the Japanese army's killing of Chinese people in World War Two but because these historical atrocities provide a respectable reason for expressing anxieties on the part of young Chinese men about their own manliness that *they know they cannot publicly state.* Žižek prefers to use the word "obscene" to describe the hidden perverse core of an ideologically structured public discourse. In my analysis of contemporary Chinese nationalist discourse here, the word "obscene" can be employed more properly than anywhere else. This is not merely with regard to the "women's bodies" deeply associated with the nationalist sentiment that I discussed in the preceding section. Rather, the "obscene" underside of Chinese nationalism has distinctive features worthy of a further analysis.

In contemporary studies of the paranoiac obsession with the Jewish plot within Western societies (or so-called "studies of anti-Semitism"), there is a term which I find very illuminating — the "conceptual Jew,"[24] which suggests that the key problem is not so much about actual Jewish people who live in the community or neighborhood, but the "concept" of the Jew, as Žižek puts it, "the mythical-invisible agent of Jewish conspiracy, who, hidden behind the curtain, pulls the strings of our lives." The "magical" symbolic power of this "concept" resides in the *secret, publicly disavowed belief* — "I know very well that Jews are people just like others, but still there is something strange about them" (Žižek 2005a: 287). I would like to use the term "conceptual Japanese" in my analysis of contemporary Chinese anti-Japanese sentiments, especially when such sentiments are expressed in abusive, violent language. The vision opened by the "conceptual Japanese" enables us to see the "obscene" underside of contemporary Chinese anti-Japanese sentiments quite vividly.

In the eyes of many contemporary Chinese people, especially young men who are in their twenties and thirties, the Japanese are viewed with resentment as people who have access to some form of secret enjoyment that is not available to "us Chinese." For example, the figure of the "conceptual Japanese" is that common image of the wealthy Japanese so often recalled in everyday private Chinese conversations, in which the Japanese are described with relish as a perverse people who indulge in excessive sexual pleasures (e.g. many Chinese people believe that Japanese people

---

[24] An insightful elaboration of the "conceptual Jew" can be found in Žižek 2005a: 257–259, 287–288, 304–305.

(both men and women) practice some obscene form of penis worship; or that there are restaurants in Japan where people can eat their dinner off the naked bodies of young girls; or that Japanese people are fond of freaky S/M sexual games…). This is what really irritates young Chinese (especially, young Chinese men) who consider themselves as "civilized" (Confucian) people who condemn such sexual perversions. However, alleged Japanese access to these sexual perversions functions as what Lacan calls "surplus-enjoyment": it enhances the identity of those young Chinese men who want to see themselves as superior "civilized" beings, and yet threatens their own sense of masculine virility. That is why, whenever there are some news reports about Japanese businessmen having sex with young Chinese girls (frequently described as "whores"), these can always become opportunities for an explosion of "national hatred."

Chinese nationalist narratives since the early twentieth century have effectively established a robust anti-Japanese fantasy scenario, in which the Japanese people are belittled — *literally* demonized — as *riben guizi* (Japanese devils).[25] Such fantasmatic figure of the "conceptual Japanese" evokes again the logic underlying any effective operation of fantasy: there is no such thing, yet it is true (such devilish figure does not really exist, yet …). Žižek thus writes apropos of the Jewish plot: "We must confront ourselves with how the ideological figure of the 'Jew' is invested with our unconscious desire, with how we have constructed this figure to escape a certain deadlock of our desire." In other words, "we must recognize in the properties attributed to 'Jew' the necessary product of our very social system; we must recognize in the 'excesses' attributed to 'Jews' the truth about ourselves" (Žižek 1989: 48; 128). With regard to our case, the question to be raised is: Why do these young Chinese who actually do not care at all about the loss of Chinese blood under Japanese occupation, nonetheless still need such fantasmatic scenario about the obscene, devilish Japanese to maintain their own psychic balance? The cause of this contemporary "national hatred" towards Japanese people can hardly be pinpointed to some clearly defined observable properties of theirs. The Lacanian lesson is: when failing to locate the cause of the symptom in the

[25] Correspondingly, in many Chinese narratives Americans and Europeans also have their fantasmatic name — *yang guizi* (alien devils).

symbolic level ("actual observable properties," etc.), one should immediately investigate the fantasmatic space. In psychoanalysis, fantasy is the very device that provides a "spectral" space where *such obscene gap between knowledge* (I know the Japanese are people just like others) *and belief* (I nonetheless still believe that they are "devils" who have illegitimate access to excessive enjoyments) is magically removed: the fantasmatic figure of the "Japanese devil" is both imaginary, and real (in terms that it reveals the truth about the subject).[26] What is truly "magical" about fantasy is it organizes and sustains "the way things 'truly seem to me,' although I never effectively experience them this way" (Žižek 2005a: 113). The Japanese may look and act like "us Chinese," but there is something excessively evil, something "in them more than themselves" that makes them "not quite human" (i.e. "devils"). Žižek is right to emphasize that "Our relationship to this unfathomable traumatic element that 'bothers us' in the other is structured in fantasies (about the other's political and/or sexual omnipotence, about 'their' strange sexual practices, about their secret hypnotic powers, etc.)" (Žižek 2005a: 256).

The function of the "national hatred" for those young nationalists is to produce a form of *self-satisfaction* that is aimed mainly at restoring Chinese male pride: only through violent hatreds — verbal as well as physical — towards "devils" they can "regain" their psychic balance in the fantasmatic space. Wang Xiaodong's above-cited speech on "recapturing our women" clearly illustrates this perverse function of contemporary Chinese nationalist discourse. The extremely violent slogans and acts during the 2005 anti-Japanese demonstrations were another case in point. This violent hatred is not limited to the "actual properties" of the Japanese, but targets their "surplus-enjoyment." For Chinese nationalists, social harmony can be achieved only by taking Japanese and Western "devils" out of the picture. This, is the nationalist fantasy *par excellence*, which

[26]Bruce Fink's observation from the angle of clinical practices regarding "the *belief* that some other group enjoys more than another group does" is pertinent here: "Is it true that we have less *jouissance* than other people or other animal species? Do we really see people around us who enjoy more than we do? Perhaps occasionally. [...] And yet that belief is usually based on next to nothing: racists have rarely if ever seen any such thing in the peoples they discriminate against. But that does not stop them from believing it." (Fink 2004: 156)

posits such fantasmatic figure as *the* obstacle hindering the final attainment of full *jouissance*. Thus, the perverse core of the discourse of China's new nationalism is, to paraphrase Žižek, that the figure of the "Japanese devil" does not exist (as part of our experience of social reality), yet for that reason we hate him even more! "At its most radical level, violence is precisely an endeavor to strike a blow at the unbearable surplus-enjoyment contained in the Other" (Žižek 2005a: 256–257). In this sense, the "national hatred" toward "the Japanese" is indeed "the necessary product of our very social system." Hence, we have to pay attention to the "fantasmatic background of the public written ideological text" (Žižek 2005a: 303). This psychoanalytic approach, in my view, is a much more productive way to analyze the causes of these intense, violent contemporary anti-Japanese sentiments and outbursts. Going through or traversing the fantasy, for Lacan and Žižek, means exactly to recognize that that which really "bothers us" (in the fantasmatic figure) do not exist, that it is "invented" in our fantasies to maintain our own psychic balance by covering up our very inability — an *a priori* impossibility indeed since we are castrated, barred subjects — to obtain full *jouissance*.

In March 2003, Donald Rumsfeld expressed his by now (in)famous formulation of the relationship between the known and the unknown with regard to the Iraq war: there are known knowns, known unknowns, unknown unknowns. Later, Žižek added the fourth variation that is absent in Rumsfeld's formulation: the unknown knowns (see Žižek 2004b: 9). What do these mean? Let me explain them here with regard to contemporary Chinese anti-Japanese sentiments. There are known knowns — things we know that we know. For example, we know that the Japanese army invaded China in the 1930s and 1940s. There are known unknowns — things that we know we don't know. There are some historical "files" which are still frozen by national governments, containing "secrets" that we know we don't know about. There are also unknown unknowns — things we even don't know we do not know. For example, the Japanese army may have committed some horrible atrocities during its occupation of China, but because there were no survivors, we simply don't know about it, and we don't even know that we don't know this. Žižek's fourth variation, however, is actually the most crucial one: the unknown knowns, the "knowledge which does not know itself," "the disavowed beliefs and suppositions we are not even aware of adhering to ourselves" (Žižek 2004a: 9–10). This is what we have in contemporary anti-Japanese sentiments. For example, a young Chinese man who is cynical, ruthlessly pragmatic, and does not care about historical atrocities and the shedding of his "compatriots' blood" finds himself still emotionally driven to participate in the anti-Japanese demonstrations. He himself does not know why, but he knows it *unconsciously*.

The way that ideology works in China today can also be illustrated through the device of the Freudian slip. For example, an ostensibly decent man invites a woman to a restaurant to have dinner. Instead of saying "a table for two," he says to a waitress "a bed for two please." This man who has not made a specific sex plan does not know why these horrible, embarrassing words suddenly came out of his mouth. But he knows it *unconsciously*. The point to be made is that this is not a *subjective matter*, but implied by the secret structure of social rituals: going out and having dinner with a member of the opposite sex (in the heterosexual case) is not only what is publicly claimed; there is *something more* — a chance to have sex afterwards.[27] This "obscene" knowledge which has to be disavowed beforehand is one of those secret suppositions that people themselves are not even aware of adhering to. What ideological analysis aims at is precisely this hidden gap between public claims (having dinner, or demanding a repayment of a "blood debt," etc.) and their secret, unstated or disavowed underside which is always, more or less, *obscene* (and that is why it has to be publicly disavowed, kept unwritten).

This type of secret "transgression" of the publicly written statements is referred to by Žižek as "inherent transgression": instead of being truly subversive to the ruling ideology, tearing apart the fabric of the ideological fabrication, "inherent transgressions" are themselves *inherent to ideology*, necessary for ideology to operate effectively. In other words, these "transgressions" of what is publicly written and established, are necessary means for sustaining an existing ideological edifice. As Žižek puts it, "the public Law is compelled to search for support in an *illegal* enjoyment"; therefore, "periodic transgressions of the public law are inherent to the

[27] This story is from one of Žižek's recent seminars, although he uses it to illustrate a different point.

social order; they function as a condition of the latter's stability" (Žižek 1994a: 54–55). With regard to contemporary Chinese nationalism, obscene elements like which "race" of men has the best access to women's bodies are necessary for the nationalist discourse and movement (including those violent outbursts) to thrive.

With regard to the types of discussions that the Chinese government permits, and that shape the everyday lives of mainland Chinese citizens, we can argue that contemporary Chinese nationalism, to the extent that it is allowed to circulate as a discourse in mainland public culture, far from endangering the ruling ideology functions effectively as its protective shield: *it displaces the socio-economic struggles with ethnic hatred; that is to say, it displaces a (political) transgression with an obscene "inherent transgression."* In this sense, what the 2005 anti-Japanese demonstrations really demonstrate is this *hidden displacement*, which effectively sustains the established socio-symbolic order of everyday life under Party-state rule. By such blind, violently charged outbursts, the repressed, unsatisfied sentiments are rapidly released, and people are able to go back to their "normal" lives again.

In this sense, what the post-1989 Chinese "new nationalism" effects is precisely the *hidden displacement* that sustains the existing symbolic order: by expressing violent and militant slogans of "national hatred" against foreigners (primarily Japanese and Americans) perceived as external enemies, the nationalist discourse thus provides a "shortcut" for people to go back to their "normal" daily lives to embrace their "reality" under authoritarian rule. This "new nationalism" is thus reminiscent of an old, well-known joke about a man who lost his key in the dark but began to search for it beneath the light. In response to suggestions that the search was futile as the key had not been lost at the spot where this man was searching, he replied "I know I lost it in the dark but it is easier to look for it in the light."[28] Isn't it much harder for these young Chinese to really face the domestic socio-political problems, like the "1989 generation" did, than to shout some violent anti-foreign slogans, beat up some Japanese businessmen, targeting "external enemies" (foreigners) as the sole cause of their anxieties and fears about their rapidly changing environments as well as their personal circumstances?

[28]This joke was mentioned in one of Žižek's recent seminars.

Let us here engage in a further comparison between the 1989 student demonstrations and the 2005 anti-Japanese demonstrations. Similar to the former event, the latter also erupted as a total shock to the government. Owing to the strict control of the Party-state, demonstrations are very rare in mainland China — among those rare cases of actual protests, most were actually sanctioned beforehand and in some cases, even organized by the government.[29] On the contrary, the April 2005 protest demonstrations that took place without government sanction (and eventually led to brutal suppression[30]) were unquestionably the largest "spontaneous" civic protest movements since the 1989 Tiananmen student protests.[31] In post-Tiananmen China, an era of growing political apathy and unabashed economic egotism, these urban mass demonstrations contradicted the official ideological theme that "maintaining stability is of top priority" (*wending yadao yiqie*) coined by Deng Xiaoping and pierced the ideological veil of "prosperity" (economic developments, new metropolitan fashions, novel lifestyles, and so on) fabricated by the (state-owned) media discourse, and thus marked, in psychoanalytic terms, a *symptomatic* moment in contemporary China's "social reality."

Symptoms (both psychic symptoms and social symptoms), for Žižek, are *returns of the repressed* in the form of "abnormal" exceptions to "normal" regularity, "enigmatic messages" that cannot be deciphered by everyday language and thus disrupt the smooth running of "reality" (see, for example, Žižek 1989: 21–23, 73–75). In this sense, "symptom" as a psychoanalytic concept acquires a *political* connotation: the intrusion of (social) symptoms indicates not just the absence of harmony but

---

[29]The May Eighth 1999 anti-NATO (anti-U.S.) student demonstrations, for example, were arguably organized by university authorities and formally sanctioned by the government.

[30]In the second half of April 2005, the *People's Daily* published several articles to calm down the protestors; the Ministry of Public Security declared that "unauthorized marches were illegal." A Shanghai local citizen Tang Ye was arrested on 26 April for his active engagements in organizing the April Sixteenth Shanghai demonstrations, and sentenced for five years. Besides Tang, other a few dozen of protestors in Shanghai and Beijing were arrested for vandalizing property.

[31]They were "spontaneous" in the sense that it was primarily through mobile-phone text messages (SMS), emails, websites, and online instant messaging (e.g. MSN, QQ, GTalk, etc.) that those large-scale social protests were "organized."

the impossibility of its achievement. The common assumption is that problems can be resolved to achieve harmony. In Žižek's view, however, the meaning of the political is that antagonism is inherent to the social field. It is antagonism that inspires visions of harmony. In other words, it is only *a fantasy* that the social can be rendered as harmonious and whole. Furthermore, it is only *through fantasies* that the social can be rendered as harmonious and whole (see Žižek, 1990; Laclau and Mouffe, 1985). Žižek makes the following remarks about Ernesto Laclau's thesis on the political:

> [P]olitics exists because "society doesn't exist": politics is the struggle for the content of the empty signifier which represents the impossibility of Society (Žižek 1999a: 177).

The domain of the political thus originates in the *irreducible gap* between the empty Universal (the universal impossibility of Society), and the currently hegemonized *particular* content ("reality" *qua* an ideological matrix, which is, the particular hegemonic content of an ideological universality). It is in the very intersection of the *universal* and the *particular* that comes the Lacanian conception of symptom: symptom represents the *exception* that disrupts "reality" (the ideologico-symbolic matrix). It is such "symptomatic excess which undermines the hegemonic content." In the domain of the political, the individual symptom "bears witness to the gap between the Universal and the Particular," because it is an individual event which takes place in the register of the Symbolic (the socio-ideological field), but nonetheless tears its very fabric apart (Žižek 1999a: 180–181). Owing to the "disruptive" feature of the 2005 anti-Japanese protests, one can say that it — as an "individual symptom" — evoked the political as the domain of antagonism: insofar as the matrix of China's present "social reality" (along with the CCP's official ideology of "maintaining stability is of top priority," "constructing a harmonious society," etc.) was drastically disrupted in March and April 2005, these mass demonstrations took place as a *political* event.[32]

---

[32]Yannis Stavrakakis also offers a clear elaboration on the thesis "politics versus the political," see Chapter 3 of his *Lacan and the political* (Stavrakakis 1999).

However, there is a twist, which lies — once again — in the obscene gap between the form and the content. During the demonstrations, protestors called for a radical boycott of Japanese products, burning flags and shouting anti-Japanese slogans, such as "Japanese are pigs," "Fuck Japanese devils," "Japanese go to hell," "Kick Japan out of Asia, and out of the Earth," "The blood debt must be repaid in blood," "Let us march to Tokyo and kill all Japanese devils," "Use nuclear bomb to eliminate Japan"... A popular poem, written anonymously and widely circulated in internet was printed on T-shirts, worn by many young protestors:

> We have the Great Wall, we have a billion soldiers
> Why still wait for our sons and grandsons to wipe out national humiliations
> I am willing to lead a hundred thousand hand-picked troops
> to conquer Tokyo by swords and guns.

Also, as mentioned earlier, during the demonstrations many Japanese-style restaurants were smashed, Japanese-branded cars burned, Japanese businessmen assaulted... The nationalistic sentiments, along with these strong militant-flavored outbursts of resentment, turned the protests into an emotional, violent *acting out*. This vulgar, carnivalesque character of the 2005 demonstrations is clearly in sharp contrast to the subversive-suicidal character of the political *act* proper of which the 1989 can serve as an example.[33] Here, I follow the Lacanian-Žižekian distinction between "act" and "acting-out": the former refers to a radical (suicidal) *ethico-political* action that breaks the foreclosure of the ideological matrix and brings about something totally *new*, while the latter refers to a kind of simple action that merely reproduces the ideological coordinates in which it takes place.

Furthermore, different from the 1989 demonstrations, the 2005 demonstrations were organized around an ethnic differentiation of "races." As these protests consisted of highly emotional and militant outbursts with no

---

[33]Recall the famous lines from *Manifesto of Hunger Strike* (*jueshixuanyan*) in the 1989 student protest: "It is with spirit of death that we fight for life. It is with the desperation of saving this dispirited and selfish nation. We are offering ourselves — if we are not willing to die, who will?" It is available online at <http://tieba.baidu.com/p/687007760> (accessed on 24 October 2012).

pretense to any kind of concrete political agenda, they were arguably *pre-political.* In contrast to the 1989 protest in which students and citizens organized themselves as political agents defending clear aims that were intended to break with the ideological coordinates of "social reality" at that time, there was almost no political program in the April 2005 protests. Whereas the 1989 Tiananmen student protest literally became "a bone in the throat" for those who eventually dispatched military force to "eliminate" it, in 2005 there was only resentment based on "nationalistic" sentiments. Hence, in terms of its *form*, the 2005 protests were quite symptomatic, disrupting the everyday running of reality; while in terms of its *content*, far from constituting a truly subversive political event, they were merely violent emotional outbursts. Žižek has argued that the operation of ideology structurally needs its obscene "exceptions" (in the appearance of symptoms), whereas true symptom is always *the universalized symptom.* It is in the latter sense that Žižek avers that "'going through' the social fantasy is likewise correlative to identification with a symptom"; and "[t]o 'identify with a symptom' means to recognize in the 'excesses,' in the disruptions of the 'normal' way of things, the key offering us access to its true functioning" (Žižek 1989: 127–128). On the other hand, those 2005 anti-Japanese demonstrations are, in Žižekian vocabulary, *inherent transgression* at its purest — an act of sustaining the existing order in the form of (pseudo)transgression. Such carnivalesque transgression — one breaks the rule a little bit, here and there, without touching the fundamental framework of the system, leaving it intact — is not just harmless to the operation of the system; it even strengthens its rule. The ideological profit of such nationalist outbursts is: by attributing all the problems to the plot of the West and their evil operation of demonizing China, the nationalist "resistance" effectively deters people (i.e. discontent angry protesters) from probing into the causes of their predicament — i.e. from politicizing their situation. In other words, the nationalist fantasy turns people into the stupid guy believing that he can find his lost key beneath the "ideological light." The fantasmatic narratives of the Japanese and Americans being "devils" (responsible for killing our compatriots, stealing our beautiful women, demonizing China...), close up the gap between nationalistic acting out and everyday normal life, making the two shift smoothly and consistently. This type of "resistance" ("saying-no") is *obscene* precisely because of its perverse character of not aiming at changing the big game, the way power operates itself. Differently put, the inherent transgression emerges when transgression itself comes with no big goal, political agenda, with no ultimate destination. What one gets or achieves from such "resistance" is effectively nothing other than secret, perverse enjoyments permitted only in the fantasmatic space.

On the question of what is truly political, Žižek has a very good elaboration in his critical analysis of Jacques Rancière's political theory,

> This identification of the non-part with the Whole, of the part of society with no properly defined place within it (or resisting the allocated subordinated place within it) with the Universal, is the elementary gesture of politicization (Žižek 1999a: 188).

In other words, the political agents are (to put it in Rancière's terms) the "part of no part," presenting themselves as the representatives, the "stand-ins," for the Universal (in contrast to some particular privileged interests). In contrast to *positive socio-symbolic groups* (e.g. "women," "gay," "working class," "Chinese," and so on) that emerge within the ideological coordinates of "reality," *political* agents *per se* break and change these very coordinates: the former are often deemed as a pre-existing fact (a set of pre-determined properties attributed to a group); while the latter is always a *subjective position*, an agent constituted only through his/her *politicization*. Žižek especially elaborated this idea of resistance to the *status quo* by distinguishing between the "proletariat" (as the embodiment of the "part of no part") and the "working class." He argues that the "working class" is a "positive" social group while the "proletariat" should be read as the subjectivization of the "part of no part," "elevating its injustice into the ultimate test of universality." Žižek also adds: "Once a worker 'considers himself to belong to the ranks of the proletariat', this changes his very reality: he acts differently" (Žižek 1999a: 188; 2006b: 15–16). This is to say, a rich man whose wealth "empirically" far exceeds the level of the "working class" can *choose* to be a proletarian (as a pure political agent) through his/her own radical *acts*, "I can participate in this universal dimension *directly*, irrespective of my special place within the global social order" (Žižek 2000: 120); also, because it is not inscribed "objectively" in the society, the emergence of the political agent (the revolutionary subjectivity) has no guarantees. The student protestors of 1989 did something similar when they demanded political reforms. They assumed the right to speak directly to the Party leadership, thereby elevating themselves to representative spokespersons for the nation.

As to this differentiation between the "positive" social groups and political agents *per se*, another crucial point is that these struggles initiated by the "positive" social groups are based on their *socio-symbolic identities* (from the "classical" class struggles, to all sorts of contemporary "postmodern" struggles, e.g. multiculturalist struggles, feminist struggles, etc.). These are struggles that can be easily compromised and turned into pragmatic reconciliation, strategic negotiations, while *political* agents, on the contrary, radically reject accepting at any degree the "necessary" gap between the "reality" situation and their political agenda, and by doing so, *reject reducing antagonism to "difference,"* and *stand for the universal dimension of the political*. A *political* agent thus is *an individual embodiment of the symptomatic excess*, a "bone in the throat" that poses a threat to existing norms of "reality." In the light of this distinction between socio-symbolic groups and political agents, what essentially turns the 2005 protests into an emotional, violent *acting out* is not only just some specific resentment (against Japanese); but the *way* the agents (protestors) engaged themselves in these demonstrations: they in the first place grounded their protests in their socio-symbolic identity, which is, their "national" identity. (And so did the student protestors at Tiananmen in 1989 — but they did it to bring about political change, not to accuse a foreign people as an enemy of the "nation.")

The fact that there was no *political* agenda attached to the post-Tiananmen demonstrations but merely explosions of nationalistic-militant sentiments manifests a key feature of the post-1989 Chinese politico-ideological constellation: the space of the political has been totally suspended and the *only choice* for Chinese people is the one between playing by the rules and exploding into blind violence, a violence that is claimed to be derived from "patriotism." The fact that the government eventually suppressed the April 2005 anti-Japanese demonstrations should not be interpreted that there is no room for this kind of "patriotic-nationalistic" demonstration in contemporary mainland China: if so, there would be no large demonstration at all in the first place; but as a matter of fact, the anti-Japanese demonstrations went on for several weeks and spread quickly from one city to another. This nationalist-patriotic ideology has been advocated by the government since the 1980s. In post-Maoist China, especially after 1989, the CCP has actively sought to find a new basis of legitimacy to sustain its rule. Nationalism/patriotism has thus played a significant role as a unifying ideology to maintain socio-political stability and produce so-called social "harmony." (Just as described above, "maintaining stability" has been designated as the top task of the CCP since the early 1990s. Also, "strengthening patriotism" has been specifically emphasized by top Party leaders for over two decades.) That helps explain why in early April 2005, the anti-Japanese demonstrations were not suppressed but in fact tolerated, and even encouraged. What the eventual suppression of the demonstrations indicates however, is that what substantially threatens the government is not the nationalist "content" of the protest, but rather its *formal structure*. That is to say, what the government is afraid of is that if these demonstrations were to continue, there might be the risk of *political programs* emerging out of this mass protest that would threaten its legitimacy. This might then turn the focus of the protest from anti-Japanese feeling to local socio-political problems (for example, the growing involvement of discontented workers during the course of the demonstrations can easily trigger a revolt against the government).

What the Facts Do Not Tell Us...

A report by Howard W. French on the April Sixteenth 2005 Shanghai anti-Japanese demonstration in *The New York Times* describes this event in the following way, "at its most basic level this was a festival of runaway nationalism, of a government-nurtured Chineseness" (French 2005). For (Western) media, April 2005 is reminiscent of May 1999, when crowds rallied outside the U.S. embassy in Beijing, shouting anti-American slogans, smashing embassy cars, throwing rocks at embassy buildings, and burning American flags, after the Chinese embassy in Belgrade was bombed by North Atlantic Treaty Organization (NATO) — three Chinese journalists died in this tragic event and twenty-three others were injured.[34] There is nonetheless an

[34]The bombing occurred on 7 May 1999, just before midnight of 8 May. News of the bombing became widely known to the Chinese public during the following afternoon. Therefore, the Belgrade embassy bombing has been often referred to as the "May Eighth incident" by commentators.

important difference between these two with regard to the Party-state's attitude: the 2005 protests ultimately met with state suppression, while in the case of the 1999 protests, as Jeffrey N. Wasserstrom notes, "[t]he regime reversed its nearly decade-long policy of discouraging all forms of student activism and allowed, even encouraged, students to take to the streets to express patriotic outrage" (Wasserstrom 2003: 257). The Belgrade bombing, as well as the mass protests in China afterwards the bombing, soon led to a large-scale intellectual debate on the issue of nationalism, turning the debate between the "New Left" and liberalism into one between nationalist "anti-Westernism" and liberal globalization.[35]

Many Chinese liberals wrote essays, expressing worries and anxieties about those explosions of nationalistic sentiments manifested in the 1999 anti-U.S. demonstrations. This demonstration was the first large emergence of this type of nationalistic outburst in the form of a massive social protest in post-Maoist China. Zhu Xueqin, for example, wrote after NATO's bombing of Chinese embassy: "In response to NATO's bombing, Chinese intellectuals and college students cursed the U.S. with much emotion. This tendency is one that allows people to condemn the acts of the U.S. government, but by throwing away the values of democracy and freedom as well" (Zhu Xueqin 1999: 456). Another Shanghai-based historian Xiao Gongqin, who has been labeled as a "neo-authoritarian" since the late 1980s,[36] was originally an active advocate and defender of Chinese nationalism: in the mid-1990s, he famously advocated the use of a nationalism derived from Confucianism to fill the ideological void opened by the collapse of communism (Xiao Gongqin 2000). After NATO's bombing, however, Xiao joined the camp of liberalism and wrote in an essay entitled "Be Cautious about Extreme Nationalism":

> These days my heart has been full of worries. Under the circumstance of the severe crisis in terms of credibility between Chinese and American

---

[35]Thus, some commentators simply use the label "nationalist" to refer to all those intellectuals who engaged in debates with "liberals."

[36]Xiao Gongqin's "neo-authoritarian" thesis is that authoritative leadership is highly required in the process of reform. Exactly for the purpose of boosting the pace of democratization in post-Maoist China, the "dictatorship" of the CCP still needs to be tolerated in the "transition period."

> nations, the only ones who can benefit are those who do not want these two nations to be on friendly terms. This confrontation [between Chinese and American nations] only benefits the conservatives of both nations, and harms the enlightened. For the last couple of years I have been holding a positive attitude about Chinese nationalism. Now facts push me to realize the immaturity of my own past view. Actually, all kinds of nationalism have a very dangerous quality.

According to Xiao, it is China's unfortunate experiences since the late Qing era that makes all kinds of nationalism potentially dangerous:

> Owing to the sufferings of Chinese people in history, and their oppression under long-term despotism, the lethal weakness of Chinese people is that once nationalism is evoked, it will easily become highly irrational. From the Boxer Uprising to slogans shouted on the campus of Beijing University today, what appears to me is that our nation is still far from being mature. What worries me most is perhaps that some shortsighted politicians are not able to resist the great temptation of manipulating this nationalist sentiment. What should we do if this Pandora's Box of nationalism is opened?

As to the bombing of the Chinese embassy in Belgrade which triggered the later nationalist demonstrations, Xiao continued to comment,

> The lethal weakness of American people is their overwhelming confidence: they believe too much in their messianic moral emotions. [...] I really cannot imagine that Clinton would actually order a bombing of the Chinese embassy, unless he suddenly went mad. However, the explanation that the bombing was a technical mistake is also really not convincing. If there is no convincing reason, it would be very hard to calm Chinese people down. It is here that the problem resides. Is there someone who did this horrible thing without getting permission from Clinton? At this crucial moment, there are actually very few people [in China] who can think and analyze the problem rationally. This really makes me very anxious. (Xiao 1999: 474–475)

Xiao Gongqin's arguments reflect the attitude of the liberal intellectual community towards the deluge of nationalist sentiments after the anti-U.S.

protest held on 8 May 1999. In his rebuttal to Xiao, Wang Xiaodong claims that Xiao's arguments — in particular, Xiao's claim that Clinton might be neither informed about this attack nor its perpetrator — "are very representative of the attitude of many Chinese intellectuals" (Wang Xiaodong *et al.* 1999: 76–77). Wang Xiaodong accuses Chinese intellectuals like Xiao Gongxin as "dumb ostriches":

> In my view, some Chinese intellectuals are really like "dumb ostriches": when someone is kicking their asses, they still comfort themselves that "he would not kick me; he is actually kicking other people or himself." Who can be dumber than these "ostriches"? (Wang Xiaodong *et al.* 1999: 77)

In his rebuttal, Wang focuses on Xiao's comments about the embassy bombing, claiming that "many Chinese intellectuals really cannot face the reality that the U.S. bombed the Chinese embassy." To support his arguments, Wang further offers many "hard facts" drawn from the realm of international relations (such as U.S. policy in relation to Taiwan, Western criticism of China's handling of Xinjiang and Tibet issues, and cooperation between Japan and the U.S. with regard to military defense) to illustrate his point that "the U.S. does not care its relationship with China." With regard to the embassy bombing, he claims that as a matter of fact, "the U.S. gains a great deal of strategic interests through this 'bombing-by-mistake'" (Wang Xiaodong *et al.* 1999: 3–6).

Wang's assertions about the "hard facts" of foreign exploitation clearly had greater appeal among Chinese readers than arguments that counter the nationalist discourse. In the 2000s, the critics of nationalism lost not only "moral battles" (they were attacked as "unpatriotic" and defamed as *yiye Meiguoren*, the literal translation of which is "overnight Americans"). They were also ridiculed as incapable of comprehending the current situations of international relations.

The point here is not that the "hard facts" offered by Wang Xiaodong and other nationalists are simply wrong: most of these are basically true (three Chinese journalists were killed in the NATO bombing of the Chinese embassy in Belgrade, etc.). The point, rather, is that Xiao Gongqin and other critics of strident nationalists fought what Žižek would have called the "false battle": the moment they accepted this debate as concerning facts — e.g. they were keen to claim that the NATO bombing was not necessarily the result of a conspiracy and that Clinton might not have known about the attack beforehand; there were "legitimate reasons" for the attack that were not made public and so on), they had already lost the "battle."

Let us once again go back to Žižek's analysis of the "conceptual Jew." What would be the result if one tries to fight Nazi's "anti-Semitic prejudices" on the basis of "hard facts"? In the Germany of the late 1930 it was really not a hard task for Nazi to provide factual evidences for their anti-Semitic claims (financially exploiting the rest of the population, seducing other people's young daughters, not washing regularly, and so on and so forth). Žižek's point is, facts "ha[ve] nothing to do with the real roots of our anti-Semitism":

> The proper answer to anti-Semitism is therefore not "Jews are really not like that" but "the anti-Semitic idea of Jew has nothing to do with Jews; the ideological figure of a Jew is a way to stitch up the inconsistency of our own ideological system" (Žižek 1989: 48).

Once we accept that the battle against anti-Semitism should take place on the empirical ground, we have already been deeply trapped by the ideology of anti-Semitism, remained victims of those anti-Semitic prejudices. The real question we should raise is: Why Nazi needs the Jews to form their entire ideological edifice? (In exactly the same way, Chinese nationalists need the Japanese to maintain their psychic balance.)

Psychoanalysis can provide insights on this matter. In one of his recent seminars, Žižek discussed the following Lacanian motto: even if jealousy has grounds, it is still one kind of pathology. Say, there is an old fashion, terribly jealous husband who is always obsessed with the idea that his wife is sleeping around with other men. The Lacanian point is that even if what he suspects turns out to be true, grounded in facts (his wife really did have an affair), his jealousy is still pathological. The psychoanalytic question is not whether his wife really slept around or not, but why he needs this obsessive jealousy to retain his own psychic stability.

The key question with regard to contemporary Chinese nationalism is thus not whether or not NATO had "legitimate reasons" to bomb the

Chinese embassy, or whether or not it was Bill Clinton himself who sanctioned this attack. The question is not on the factual level at all: even though what we have been informed about embassy-bombing are all true at the level of fact, it still conceals the cunning ideological manipulation. Xiao Gongqin, Zhu Xueqin, and many other critics of Chinese nationalism thus missed *the* crucial problematic of Chinese nationalism: What makes people attracted to expressing violent feelings towards foreigners (whether Japanese, Americans, or the vague category "Westerners") to sustain their own psychic balance in the guise of "national integrity"? Do these people really care about the tragic loss of the Chinese lives? What, instead, really triggers such mass demonstration of anti-foreign hatred? (We should remind ourselves that most of young protestors who passionately engaged in the 2005 anti-Japanese demonstrations had no interest to find out the actual contents of the new Japanese history textbooks which triggered these massive demonstrations.) That which these contemporary critics of nationalism missed is exactly its *generative mechanism*.

Lacanian psychoanalysis tackles this question in terms of the operation of fantasy. As we argued in previous chapters, what fantasy provides is an imaginary promise that the realm of social can and will be full (again) and antagonism (i.e. the realm of the political) can be removed. However, the trick is that the realization of such promise is forever deferred and postponed. The achievement of the fullness is thus necessarily conceived as hindered by some external barriers or obstacles — the West, the "Japanese devil," etc. Thus the problem does not reside on the factual level (whether or not NATO bombed the Chinese embassy intentionally becomes irrelevant), but on the fantasmatic level: the NATO bombing merely serves as the external enemy needed for people to maintain their own psychic stability. By means of violent anti-foreign sentiments or "national hatred," the concealed (obscene) jealousy that disturbs people's everyday psychic balance finds release, and they are able to go back to their "normal" routine lives again. No wonder that in the April Sixteenth 2005 Shanghai demonstration which involved at least one hundred thousand protestors, the majority of the demonstrators were young middle-class "white-collars" (some of them even directly work in the Shanghai branches of those

Japanese international corporations).[37] Since the basic middle-class attitude is to maintain a comfortable everyday life, the anti-Japanese demonstration therefore has — as discussed earlier — the *form* of an intrusive "political event," and a *depoliticized* fantasmatic kernel.

Therein also resides the crucial problematic of today's Anglophone Leftist intellectuals, notably Noam Chomsky, who are inclined to base the foundation of their critical analysis on "facts." The hidden assumption is that *the* task of critical intellectuals is to show correct "facts" which have been concealed or distorted by the mass media and government. By arguing over facts, these intellectuals fall into the trap of disputing over the "empirical proofs" each other provides (the credibility of "the source," etc.). According to Žižek such arguments are an obscene trap of today's ideology:

> An ideology is thus not necessarily "false": as to its positive content, it can be "true," quite accurate, since what really matters is not the asserted content as such, but *the way this content is related to the subjective position implied by its own process of enunciation* (Žižek 1994b: 8).

Terry Eagleton, another influential thinker on the left, in his 1991 book *Ideology: An Introduction* offered us a similar argument concerning the irrelevance of "facts":

> [A] racist who believes that Asians in Britain will outnumber whites by the year 1995 may well not be persuaded out of his racism if he can be shown that this assumption is empirically false, since the proposition is more likely to be a *support* for his racism than a *reason* for it. If the claim is disproved he may simply modify it, or replace it with another, true or false. (Terry Eagleton 1991: 23, emphases mine)

What truly needs to be tackled critically, as both thinkers suggested, is indeed not facts themselves, but *the very way facts are organized into*

[37] Before the demonstration, all university authorities in Shanghai strictly banned their students to go to street in advance. Those found participating the protest will be directly expelled. Thus, the student participation was minimal in the April Sixteenth Shanghai anti-Japanese demonstration.

ideological discourses: Why some "facts" (the deaths of certain Chinese lives) can quickly trigger large-scale demonstrations while other similar facts not? Why some "facts" about Jews ended up to serve as Nazi's rationalization for their holocaust programs?

In the case of contemporary Chinese nationalist discourse, its most "factual statements" are empirically "true" (there were three Chinese journalists killed by NATO bombs in Belgrade, there are some unacceptable "blood debts," etc.). However, the crucial point here is that even what these nationalists said is empirically right, *the way* they said it is structurally wrong. The "obscene" core of contemporary Chinese nationalist discourse is that these nationalists in fact do not even care about the "blood debt." They are merely interested in creating "national hatred" in order to regain a form of "psychic integrity" necessary for their own identity. Hence, what contemporary Chinese nationalist discourse demonstrates is the inherent transgression of ideology, which effectively sustains the established symbolic order by balancing the symbolic Law and its transgressive exceptions: by such blind, violently charged outbursts, the "obscene" hatred is rapidly released, and people are able to go back to their "normal" lives.

The discourse of China's new nationalism thus can be regarded as another fantasmatic narrative that attempts to maintain social stability by identifying certain foreign enemies as the primary cause of China's domestic problems. It offers a simple solution to all social problems in post-Tiananmen China — the "evil force" is the U.S. or Japan… Such operation of fantasy is called by Žižek "disturbing paranoiac fantasy which tells us why things went wrong (why we did not get the girl, why society is antagonistic)" (Žižek 1998: 210). Stavrakakis phrases it as the "horrific side of fantasy": "it reduces anxiety and creates a semblance of harmony but this harmony may depend on a picture of the Other as demanding something horrible and unpleasant." Fantasy (the horrific modality of fantasy) gets rid of the uncertainty of what causes the Other lacking by positively identifying external barriers or obstacles that damage the harmony and fullness of the Other. In his *China's Path in the Shadow of Globalization*, Wang Xiaodong has depicted a paranoiac, "horrific" picture in which China is surrounded and besieged by vicious enemies (the U.S., the E.U., Japan, even Russia is "unreliable"). "China should be prepared both psychologically and materially for being isolated." Wang calls this the thesis of "splendid isolation." Wang claims that such picture is drawn on facts (Wang Xiaodong *et al.* 1999: 54–7). Again, the point here is not whether or in what extent Wang's depiction accords to "reality"; rather, the question that should be raised is — Why nationalist narratives *structurally* entail such "horrific" picture? Stavrakakis, following Lacanian argument, provides the answer — "Even this horrifying picture of the Other is preferable from the state of uncertainty regarding the lack and the desire of the Other" (Stavrakakis 1999: 151). By blaming the cause of all the problems onto external enemies, nationalism as an influential post-Maoist fantasmatic narrative promises that once those enemies are removed, China can be whole and harmonious again. In this sense, contemporary "China's new nationalism" indeed shares the fantasmatic core of fascist ideology: in such fantasmatic narratives — to paraphrase Žižek's note apropos of fascism — antagonism is displaced onto the "enemy" in order that an imaginary wholeness can be presented as the result of the enemy's removal (see Žižek 2006a: 328).

There are two assumptions that govern the arguments of contemporary Chinese nationalists: (1) these nationalists always presuppose a "totalistic" character of the enemy ("the West is ever wary of China," Japanese and Americans always hate us Chinese people, and so on, see Wang Xiaodong *et al.* 1999: 168)[38]; (2) for Chinese nationalists, China's domestic problems are not caused by the inadequacy of its own socio-political system but by external enemies. The assumption here is that what Chinese people face is just the malfunctioning of the system, caused by all sorts of evil interventions on the part of external enemies; and by getting rid of these enemies, the system can properly function again. Therefore, in terms of its *formal structure* (not just its publicly written claims, but its unstated implications), what this nationalist discourse secretly endorses — namely, the presupposition that the system would be fully functioning once the external problems have been eliminated — is exactly what it explicitly fights against, which is, the 1980s modernization discourse that suggests a "wholesale" Westernization project: though it opposes itself to the 1980s

[38]A detailed survey of various, often conflicting, images of China in today's U.S., see Gries 2004: 1–4.

modernization discourse, contemporary nationalist discourse actually offers a similar *telos* — to recover China's lost glory. The shared assumption of both discourses is that China will be on the correct path towards *a bright future* once it sees the world clearly. (The only difference is that the nationalists have reversed the argument of the 1980s proponents of Westernization to claim that: we do not have "real" problems except those caused by the intrusions of the external enemies.) In psychoanalytic terms, both discourses are generated and sustained by the same *fundamental fantasy*, which I have called the "Great Dragon fantasy" in this study. No wonder that nationalists like Wang Xiaodong on the one hand fiercely attack the project of full-scale modernization (Westernization) proposed by the 1980s New Enlightenment discourse (termed by Wang as "reverse racism," "national self-abuse," and "national nihilism"), yet on the other hand also often suggest that "we still need to learn from the West," especially in relation to the modernization of national defense (Wang *et al.* 1999: 82–88).

China's "new nationalism" emerged in a time (i.e. the late 1990s) when the fantasy of "modernizing China" shared by the New Enlightenment intellectuals significantly waned. New intellectual trends such as "postmodernism" and the "New Left" became influential in narrating about China's future path. If we regard "modernization" as a dominant fantasmatic scenario of post-Maoist China (i.e. the status of a fundamental fantasy), then it would seem that even though it has been depreciated in the post-new era, no other powerful paradigm has so far come to replace the one of modernization. The rise of "new nationalism," in this sense, can also be seen as a reaction to the collapse of the fundamental fantasy: as Žižek already points out, *what comes after the collapse of the fundamental fantasy is none other than the blind acting out* (i.e. the discharge of conflicted mental content by means of willful action). We have discussed how these post-Tiananmen nationalist demonstrations can be likened to a pseudo-politics of acting out, when compared against the democracy movement of 1989. Let us now turn to a new trend of discourse that seems to have the potential to become the next hegemonic "paradigm" in the fantasmatic sphere of the Sinophone intellectual world.

Chapter 6

Narrating the Fantasmatic Past: Ancient and Recent

China's Civilizational Subjectivity: The Dragon Rises Again?

Since 2003, the discourse of China's "civilizational subjectivity" (*wenming de zhutixing*) has emerged in the Sinophone intellectual scene, with "Chinese values" (*Zhongguo jiazhi*), "the China way" (*Zhongguo daolu*), "the China model" (*Zhongguo moshi*) serving as its key words. It is generally regarded by commentators (e.g. Xu Jilin 2011; Lei Yi 2012) as an offshoot of the 1990s New Left discourse. The discourse is perceived as being driven by China's remarkable economic achievements and as shifting from the previous negation of New Enlightenment and capitalist modernization to the positive search for China's cultural or civilizational uniqueness. Mainland-based New Confucian scholars also contributed to this intellectual trend of establishing China's civilizational subjectivity.[1]

In 2003, Gan Yang published an essay entitled "From 'Nation-State' to 'Civilization-State'," in which he claims that China's "historical civilization" (*lishi wenming*) — by which he means China as a "historical civilizational community" whose people share a unique cultural tradition and a set of "customs, rites and laws" (*xisu lifa*) — is the most valuable resource for its modern-state building. This is so because China is in essence "a civilization pretending to be a nation-state."[2] He claims that it is only by (re)constructing its "civilizational subjectivity" that China would be able to create "great prospects" (*da geju*) in the twenty-first century (Gan Yang 2012a[2003]: 1–15; 2007: i). Also, in 2003 an

[1] In contrast to the rather vulgar trend of "new nationalism," China's "new Confucianism" (see Daniel A. Bell 2008) — an intellectual mixture of various attempts to resuscitate classical Confucian ideas — established itself as an "elite" discourse.

[2] Here, Gan is quoting Lucian W. Pye but without acknowledgement.

influential book was published, entitled *Political Confucianism.* Its author, Jiang Qing since then has become one of the representatives of contemporary mainland-based New Confucianism. The main argument of Jiang's book is that modernization is the wrong path for China, that there is already a highly developed political system which is truly suited for post-Maoist China — the "system of rites and laws" (*lifa zhidu*, a term referring to various specific institutions, regulations, and customs which were effective in imperial China since Han dynasty). By proposing a "tricameral" (instead of bicameral) representative system and a Chinese-style "Confucian constitutional system" as an alternative to Western models, Jiang believes that 'Confucianizing the contemporary Chinese political order" is the sole path to restoring China's civilizational glory (Jiang Qing 2003; 2005).[3] Wang Hui's *Rise of Modern Chinese Thought* was published one year later in 2004. Wang's is a substantial study of Chinese intellectual history from the Song dynasty to the early Republican era. The book's aim is to establish a "native modernity" rooted purely in China's own civilization, and this four-volume work is seen by mainland scholars as marking a significant turn of the New Left intellectual camp from radical leftism to cultural conservatism.[4]

Although New Left and New Confucian scholars seem to share much in common with Chinese nationalists who regard the exponents of

[3]In Jiang's view, Chinese intellectuals in the last 150 years have searched for modernization in the wrong place: they all believed that in order to achieve China's modernization, Chinese people had to implement social and political reforms in accordance with knowledge learned from the West. This is for Jiang a false belief shared by Chinese liberals and Chinese Marxists alike. He also accuses the representatives of Hong Kong- and Taiwan-based "Neo-Confucians" such as Tang Junyi (1909–1978), Xu Fuguan (1904–1982), Mou Zongsan (1909–1995), of having been equally mistaken in their insistence on liberal democracy as the only path of political modernization for China. Rejecting all such propositions, Jiang claims that the Chinese people already possessed a highly developed political system, i.e. the system of rites and laws.

[4]This change is called by Xu Jilin "radical leftists' collective act of turning-right." Xu argues that New Leftist intellectuals achieved such radical shift through a psychological "mechanism of selective recollecting and forgetting," implying that these intellectuals intentionally makes the 1989 Tiananmen event oblivious and irrelevant (Xu Jilin 2011: 238–239).

modernization and liberal globalization as enemies,[5] they have a different agenda. In fact, these promoters of China's "civilizational subjectivity" are critical of the recent rise of nationalism in mainland China. In the previous chapter, we have already noted Wang Hui's attitude toward nationalism. He sees it as a dead end ("there is no way out if we simply fight against today's globalization by engaging in nationalism"). Jiang Qing also distances himself from the nationalists and he criticizes their views as amounting to merely a "rootless nationalism." Jiang argues that his approach is the only "sustainable nationalism based on Confucian culture" (Jiang Qing 2003: 396–415). In Gan Yang's view, "Nationalism is an ambiguous noun. Both good and bad things have emerged under its name." The counter-nationalist argument Gan insists on is the following one: China has never truly been a modern "nation-state" and it should stop regarding itself as one. China's "subjectivity" should not be founded merely on "national sovereignty" for this is Western-derived concept. He argues that the only solid foundation for China's "subjectivity" is its millennia-old civilization. In order to sustain "Chinese identity" and resist the temptation of becoming "overnight Americans," the real quest for today's Chinese people should be to establish, instead of national sovereignty, China's civilizational subjectivity in the era of globalization (Gan 2012a: 168–169).

Owing to his prominent status in this new intellectual current, Gan Yang will be the main subject of critical analysis in this chapter. Though

---

[5] Gan Yang explicitly took over powerful rhetorical expressions from nationalists such as "overnight Americans" to attack liberals (Gan Yang 2012a: 168). In fighting against Chinese liberals, a few young (neo)Confucian scholars write even more viciously than "vulgar" nationalists: "Sometimes liberals seem young naïve girls in terms of their emotion towards the U.S.: they have watched again and again the U.S.'s shameless shows, and they do nothing but keeping telling themselves 'I don't believe this is real.' They don't believe their dream lover would trample upon their vulnerable feelings. But liberals are actually thick-skinned whores: they can quickly self-repair themselves after getting trampled, and keep pretending that they are young naïve girls." Evoking Confucian doctrine (indeed in a twisted way), these authors even go so far as to claim that "Those who endorse freedom and democracy are dogs, beasts. For thousands of years, we Chinese as human beings have never talked about such things [e.g. freedom, democracy, etc.]. This is why one of the crucial aspects of Confucian doctrine is the differentiation of humans from beasts." (Zeng Yi and Guo Xiaodong eds. 2013: 3, 11)

he was a leading proponent of the 1980s modernization project, Gan parted ways with his New Enlightenment friends in the 1990s. During the heated debate between the New Left and liberalism, Gan joined the New Left camp and was labeled as one of the four leading representatives of the camp (the other three being Wang Hui, Wang Shaoguang and Cui Zhiyuan). Like many other figures of the group, Gan Yang himself, though, resents the "New Left" label. He preferred instead the label "liberal left" (*ziyou zuopai*) (Gan 2003a[2000]: 110–120). However, several years later Gan quickly shifted his preference to the label "cultural conservative" (Gan Yang 2012a: 25, 487).

Since the late 1990s, China has achieved great economic growth. For Gan Yang, China's "rise" — in term of its position in world economy and geopolitical constellation — is an "unquestionable fact." However, in the economic aspect, China has nothing really unique or special enough to be called the "China model" or the "China way." In his influential essay entitled "Revisiting the China Way" Gan notes that "Many of today's promoters of the 'China model' have focused on the aspect of China's economic development. But I don't see anything special in terms of China's current economic development mode." Thus, for Gan, China's true rise cannot be merely founded on economic basis. He argues: "As a country of several-thousand-years civilization, China's rise necessarily entails the rise of Chinese culture, rather than a mere economic rise." In order for a "China model" to truly exist, the goal of China's development should be shifted "from wealth and might to civility and elegance." Hence, instead of more factual proof of its economic success, what China really needs at this stage is normative values and ideas, that which prescribe what China should be or become. Gan argues in this regard that "China has to establish an organic relationship with its several-thousand-years civilizational tradition in order to regain its civilizational confidence." Only by "consciously setting its feet in the continuous tradition of its historical civilization" China is able to ensure its civilizational subjectivity in the era of globalization. Gan praises the concept "harmonious society" (*hexie shehui*) and calls it "the most successful concept the CCP has put forward in the last thirty years," because as he sees it, "it is an ideal, a goal, which fits both China's original civilizational orientation and its modern pursuit." Gan urges the CCP to move further beyond Deng Xiaoping's pragmatic principle by (re)establishing its "core values" (*hexin jiazhi*) (Gan Yang 2012a: 35, 45–56, 111, 143, 293–294; 2007: vi).

Gan Yang disagrees with Jiang Qing in terms of how to establish China's civilizational subjectivity, rejecting his appeal for a thorough Confucianization of China's socio-political structure. Jiang regards his ideas as modeled on those of the famous Han scholar-official Dong Zhongshu (179–104 B.C.), who convinced Emperor Wudi to elevate Confucianism to the ruling doctrine. By claiming that his works represent a "modern form of Dong Zhongshu's reform through returning to the ancient (*fugu genghua*)," Jiang endeavors to convince the top leaders of the CCP to resuscitate the former status of Confucianism as the "learning of kings and officials" (*wangguan xue*) (Jiang Qing 2005). Although many of Gan Yang's suggestions are also made explicitly and exclusively to the CCP's top leaders,[6] he nonetheless deems that the Party would not accept a direct installment of a Confucianized political system in China. In an interview Gan says,

> I often joke with Jiang Qing: your intentions are good, but you don't have the means to actualize it. There are other ways to establish China's civilizational subjectivity. I have been concentrating on general education (*tongshi jiaoyu*). China's historical civilization has been fundamentally founded on education. It is useless to rebuild Confucianism if the educational system remains handicapped. (Gan 2012a: 168)

What Gan implies in this passage is that in the near future the CCP seems unlikely to adopt a Confucianized "constitutional system" organized around traditional rites and laws. He suggests instead a more preferable way to reestablish China's civilizational subjectivity: the goal could be achieved through the renewal of general education at mainland universities, based on China's classical tradition. (Hence, Gan called his 2012 book of collected essays *Civilization, State, University*.) As opposed to

---

[6]That's why these authors regard their discourse an "elite" one. Such elite approach can be traced back to the tradition of elite Confucian scholar-officials in dynastic time, who regarded their primary task as ensuring the present emperor to play the role of "a good emperor" (*hao huangdi*) by making suggestions and offering good counsels to him.

Jiang Qing's promotion of Confucianism as a form of religion or "political theology," Gan believes that the true core of Confucianism is its doctrine of education, and that through general education Chinese people would regain what he calls "civilizational consciousness" (*wenming yishi*) and "civilizational self-awareness" (*wenming zijue*). "China's biggest problem," writes Gan, "is that [its people] do not have the consciousness of civilizational subjectivity. They don't know they are Chinese. They want to become 'overnight Americans'." Hence, the prerequisite for Chinese civilization to revive and thrive again is the emergence of new generations of "educated Chinese who have absolute confidence in Chinese civilization." Civilizational confidence, argues Gan, is the "only yardstick" by which one can judge a country's rise. According to Gan, "A true Chinese elite first and foremost has cultural-civilizational confidence" (Gan 2012a: 29, 83, 158, 168, 175).

With the emphasis on the "consciousness of civilizational subjectivity," Gan believes that the revival of Chinese civilization depends on psychological instead of economic factors. He insists: "There is a gap between the external rise of Chinese civilization and the inner mentality of the Chinese people. This means that we don't have cultural-civilizational confidence." The most crucial task for the Chinese people is thus to "set [their] inner mentality right, and establish [their] selfhood." Such enhanced "inner mentality" — civilizational consciousness, confidence, etc. — would in turn significantly augment "China's soft power." The emergence of the Sinophone discourse on China's civilizational subjectivity in the 2000s, represents for Gan the true "maturing" of post-Maoist Chinese intellectuality. He claims, repeatedly: "The next thirty years will be the most critical moment for the revival of Chinese civilization. We have reason to believe, after one or two generations' endeavors, the goal can be achieved." "If [the rising generations] put three-thousand-years Chinese civilization in their hearts, then with no doubt Chinese civilization will revive in the next thirty years" (Gan 2012a: 26, 134, 138, 169; 2007: vi, 86).

Gan's formulation relies heavily on the presupposition of the *homogeneity of Chinese civilization*. Thus, he faces such a question: In what way can one refer to today's China under the CCP's leadership as "a three-thousand-year-old civilization"? In order to tackle this issue, Gan proposed his famous thesis — the "fusion of three traditions" (*tong santong*). In an essay entitled "The Fusion of Three Traditions and the Revival of Chinese Civilization" Gan writes,

> China has three traditions, inaugurated respectively by Confucius, Mao Zedong, and Deng Xiaoping. These three traditions belong to the same continuous tradition of Chinese historical civilization. The task of China's reform is to "produce the fusion of these three traditions" in the new era. (Gan 2007: vi, 5, 46; see also 2012a: 44)

Gan Yang further adds that the respective key words for these three traditions are: benevolence and communal affinity (Confucius' tradition); equality and political participation (Mao's tradition); the conviction of market economy and the pursuit of liberty (Deng's tradition) (Gan 2007: 3; 2012a: 27). Gan believes that with efforts, these three traditions can be turned into one great tradition, because they already "belong to the same continuous tradition of Chinese historical civilization." (Is not such "argument" itself a tautology — they can be turned into one tradition because they already belong to this continuous tradition?) To defend his fusion-of-three-traditions thesis, Gan boldly translates — an interpretive move which indeed surprised many commentators — the "true meaning" of the People's Republic of China into "the republic of Confucian socialism," implying that the "fusion of three traditions" has been already promised in the founding moment of the PRC (Gan 2012a: 26, 35–36).

Gan's theorization of China's civilizational subjectivity has become very influential since the mid-2000s. Huang Ping, another famous member of the New Left camp, also started to preach in the mid-2000s the secret to the success of the "China way" as lodged in China's old but still powerfully living civilization (Huang Ping 2012[2005]: 269). Later, Han Yuhai, Wang Shaoguang, Hu Angang, Huang Ping and Zhou Jianming — all leading figures of the New Left camp — coauthored a book entitled *The Correct Way in the Human World* in 2011. As the authors stated, this book was written in a spirit of celebrating the CCP's ninetieth birthday. The novelty of this book is that it does not attribute the success of the "China Way" merely to the CCP. Rather, the authors argue that "Our way is the correct way because China is the only civilization in human history that has continuously lasted over several thousand years. [...] If the economic development comes with the loss of cultural self-awareness and civilizational confidence, we would then lose the legitimacy of political and economical development. This thesis also works in reverse: if we cannot sufficiently articulate the legitimacy of China's socialist way, we fail in terms of cultural construction." (Han Yuhai *et al.* 2011: 224, 160–161) At the same year, another influential book entitled *The China Impact: the Rise of a Civilization-State* was published. It became very quickly one of the top bestsellers of 2011. Zhang Weiwei, the author of the book, was soon viewed as one of the principal promoters of the "China model." Echoing Gan Yang's thesis, Zhang contends that China's rise is crucial in that "instead of being the rise of an ordinary country, China's rise represents the revival of a five-thousand-years great civilization; such great 'civilization-state' is unheard of in human history." Its developmental model thus does not require "the approval of the West" (Zhang Weiwei 2011: 1–3).

While attracting many followers, Gan's thesis has also encountered serious criticisms, raised mainly by liberal intellectuals. The main counter-argument is as follows: China's rise is the result of its three-decades-long modernization rather than its several-thousand-years civilization; it is the result of following the "common path" shared by all countries seeking modern development. In essence, China's rise is the "success of modern civilization in China" and not the "success of Chinese civilization in the modern world" (Liu Qing 2012: 49, 47; He Huaihong 2012: 178; Zi Zhongyun 2012: 78; Chong Ming 2012: 16). This debate can be seen as a continuation of the debate between liberalism and the New Left, with the latter's focus shifting from the critique of modernity to an acclamation for the China way.

What I would like to focus on here is Gan's assumption of a *homogeneous* Chinese civilization, and the opposing argument. Gan's theorization of the "fusion of three traditions" relies heavily on Gadamer's hermeneutic framework. Let us recall what we have discussed in Chapter 2: from the late 1980s to the mid-1990s, Gadamer and Huntington had been turned in Sinophone intellectual discussions into two symbols respectively for the modernization/globalization thesis (the fusion of "blue" [i.e. Western] and "yellow" [i.e. Chinese] civilizations) and its antithesis (the clash of civilizations). Gan Yang, in particular, used Gadamer's "fusion of horizons" thesis as the theoretical framework for China's "cultural modernization" (Gan 2012b[1987]: 55–58). However, in his later formula of the "fusion of three traditions," Gan holds that "China is completely external to the West, and vice versa. There is no family relationship between the two, so they don't have to be nice to each other." "Both Chinese and Western civilizations are featured by their 'holistic character.' They are totally incompatible." "We should not go to the West to search for the solutions for China's problems" (Gan 2007: 17; 2012a: 48, 134). Thus while he continues to use Gadamer to argue for the homogenizing of China's diverse "traditions" into one grand "civilization," Gan at the same time strongly defends Huntington's clash-of-civilizations thesis and warns that the talk of the "fusion of civilizations" is nothing more than a euphemism for Westernization (see Gan 2012a: 4–15, 152–156). What Gan fails to address, however, is: Why is a "fusion of three traditions" (with conflicting vocabularies) possible but not a fusion of two "civilizations" (a term used interchangeably by Gan with "cultural traditions")?[7] Gan's style of argumentation reflects a *fantasmatic projection* of China as an imagined totality.

In the 2000s, Gan claimed that a key contribution of the 1980s cultural fever was that it highlighted the need for an active consciousness of Chinese civilization: "In the 1980s, economic reform was never a central topic in the Chinese intellectual world. Everyone back then was talking about cultural and intellectual issues." (Gan 2007: 6, 13) But he failed to mention that the consciousness promoted in the 1980s was understood as the need for getting rid of traditional Chinese culture. Gan writes in his 2003 essay "From 'Nation-State' to 'Civilization-State'" that

[7] Compare the following passage that Gan wrote in 1987: "Today there is a broad, deep, complex, and systematic clash between China's modernization and its traditional culture, which I would like to call 'the clash of cultures.' This is a clash between traditional Chinese culture that has several-thousand-years history and modern Chinese culture that has been emerging. [...] Therefore, the basic assignment for contemporary Chinese intellectuals is to use their imagination to explore and inaugurate modern Chinese culture. And in order to accomplish such task, the most crucial thing for them is to understand the difference and clash between traditional and modern Chinese cultures." (Gan Yang 1987a: 6–7)

> In many people's view, China's great "civilization" is a great burden for China to become a modern "state." [...] However, if China loses its own "Chineseness" in its modern transformation, then such process would not lead to a rebirth of the civilization, but its withering and death. (Gan 2012a: 1, 3)

However, the following passages by the same author in the 1980s suggested that it was he (not "many people") who viewed China's traditional culture as the obstacle to China's modernization:

> Chinese culture before "May Fourth" is a form of premodern culture. "May Fourth" marks the historical starting-point of the radical shift of Chinese culture from its premodern to its modern form. The fundamental task of the 1980s cultural discussions in China is to decisively complete this historical shift, and to truly establish the system of modern Chinese culture. That is to say, the task is to wholly realize the "modernization of Chinese culture." [...] There are qualitative differences between "premodern culture" and "modern culture": the two are contradictory and clashing. I call this relationship between the premodern and modern the "clash of cultures." Any country that endeavors to modernize must inevitably encounter this clash. (Gan Yang 2012b[1985]: 25–26)
>
> If we really care about Chinese culture, we should first of all not worry about the sustainability of Confucianism, but ask from time to time whether or not our cultural form is still *outside* today's universal modern culture. If we really have cultural confidence and national pride, then instead of fantasizing blindly that "the world's future culture must be the revival of Chinese culture," we should be pondering this issue: whether the *present* Chinese culture is actually capable of getting rid of its traditional form, of transforming itself into its modern form. (Gan Yang 1987a: 18, emphases in original)

From the second passage, one can see that Gan also appealed for "cultural confidence" back in the 1980s. But gaining "cultural confidence" meant for the author a radical elimination of China's civilization (traditional culture) instead of its revival. In fact, in the 1980s, Gan regarded the latter as a "blind fantasy"! Also let us not forget Gan's famous thesis proposed in the same essay that "the most powerful way of inheriting and glorifying the tradition is 'anti-tradition'" (Gan Yang 1987a: 35). Gan argued that discarding traditional culture will not affect people's cultural identity because "no matter how intense and deep this change is, it is still *a change of the Chinese culture itself, which is,* the *self-transformation of the Chinese people and the self-development of Chinese culture.*" Gan insisted from a Gadamerian viewpoint that "the modern form of Chinese culture itself would soon become *a 'traditional' part of the Chinese culture*" (Gan 1987a: 25, emphases in original), hence his (ostensibly self-contradictory) thesis: getting rid of China's traditional culture is the most powerful way of defending it.

Gan's recent phrasing of "three traditions" is in stark contradiction to his 1980s proposal to annul "China's great 'civilization' as the only way to achieve a modern "cultural confidence." It is also quite reminiscent of the New Enlightenment phrasing of the "old and new traditions" (see Jin Guantao and Liu Qingfeng 2000; Tang Yijie 2001b: 130–131), but in which he views Confucianism and Maoism positively and to which he added Deng Xiaoping's reform as a third "newer tradition." Gan adds a third one by simply phrasing Deng Xiaoping's reform as a "newer tradition."[8] As we have examined in Chapter 2, the "old and new traditions" thesis operated under the dichotomy of traditional/modern. Gan himself also wrote within such dichotomy framework, claiming that there is a radical chasm between premodern and modern cultures (i.e. his thesis of the "clash of cultures"). The stress Gan has recently placed on the "remarkable continuity of traditional and modern China" (Gan 2007: 39) allows us to see the projection of a totality as his aim. What has changed in Gan's China phantasm is the removal of "clashes," "conflicts" and "qualitative differences" and their replacement with a synthesis of traditional and modern China.

Precisely regarding the possibility of a successful fusion of China's three traditions into one homogeneous civilization, the Shanghai-based political theorist Liu Qing holds that such fusion is illusory by implicitly evoking Gan Yang's own (old) thesis. In his essay entitled "Reclaiming the Modernization thesis" Liu writes: "Late Qing and the Cultural Revolution mark two great ruptures. In my view, this is a more important

---

[8]This is consistent with Gan's "old" contention that "The modern form of Chinese culture itself would soon become *a 'traditional' part of the Chinese culture.*"

fact [than a fusion of three traditions that only stays on the paper]. It is via these very raptures that China cut down its umbilical cord to tradition and advanced into modernity, though such development still takes form of a handicapped mode of modernity." In Liu's view, China's rise is a result of China's modernization in the post-Maoist era; it has nothing to do with China being a unique "civilization-state." The "civilizational subjectivity" discourse for Liu is a dangerous "bewitchment" (*guhuo*) that distorted facts (Liu Qing 2012: 47, 49). Liu's essay is collected in a book published in 2012 with the title *Which Civilization? Rethinking on the Rise of China*. Another essay in the collection, written by the Shanghai-based political scientist Chong Ming, also challenges Gan Yang's thesis of the "fusion of three traditions." Chong argues that Gan failed to provide any solid argument for his thesis but making "assertions and announcements," that Gan's "magical conception of the republic of Confucian socialism" is nothing but "a voluntaristic discursive fabrication, completely ignorant of history." For Chong, the discourse of China's civilizational subjectivity is symptomatic of "intellectuals' political romanticism": "Such civilizational construction heavily distorted history and common-sense" (Chong Ming 2012: 14–16). Taking into account the various "argumentations" on the fusion of three traditions provided by Gan Yang — such as, the above quoted declaration about the "true meaning of the PRC," the statement that "If seeing the achievements of [Deng's] reform, Chairman Mao would definitely not reject it" (Gan 2007: 23) — one would indeed tend to agree with Chong's criticism of Gan for only making "assertions and announcements."

In fact, Gan Yang is aware of the difficulties of homogenizing Chinese civilization. In a recent interview Gan was asked about the positive content of "Chineseness" or Chinese civilization. He nonetheless replied in an elusive tone: "I prefer to keep it as an open question. I don't want to define it. My reason is simple: once defined, Chinese civilization would be inevitably narrowed, fixated." (Gan 2012a: 159–160) In his lengthy commentary to Wang Hui's *Rise of Modern Chinese Thought*, Gan further notes:

> China does not exist. It is neither a substantial nor natural existence. Rather, it is constructed by various social and ethnic forces.

> Indeed, we are facing such a problem: China does not exist. What is China? "China" is a noun, which means, it is not reality as such. It is something that has been constructed (Gan 2012a: 85, 87).

In these above quoted passages, Gan Yang not only leaves the *content* of "Chineseness" open (to recall the Lacanian thesis that the *objet petit a* is always elusive, and once the desired object is fully defined or described in positive terms, it starts to lose its magical appeal), but also acknowledge the *non-existence* of China — "China" is a discursive, symbolic construction (to recall the other Lacanian thesis that the big Other does not exist). Now the (psychoanalytic) questions are: What *drives* Gan still to speak *metaphysically* about Chinese civilization and its homogenized nature ("Chineseness," China's civilizational subjectivity) so extensively? And, what *enables* him to speak against his (conscious) knowledge? Gloria Davies has insightfully observed in her *Worrying about China* that "although Sinophone inquiry now abound with statements that directly disavow essentialism and metaphysics, the argumentation offered in the interest of promoting an antiessentialist, antimetaphysical mode of reasoning reflects nonetheless an optimism about discerning and establishing an incontrovertible truth" (Davies 2007: 29–30).[9] What mechanism, then, has generated and is still sustaining such a stubbornly metaphysical mode of writing? When Gan and others appeal for civilizational consciousness and confidence, they explicitly talk about "China's several-thousand-years civilization" *as if* it were a "reality as such." How does the thesis of the non-existence of China "magically" coincide with China as a metaphysical presence?

---

[9] In the passage that immediately follows the quoted Davies continues to write: "Read from within the kind of Anglophone purview described here, much of Sinophone critical discourse cannot help but appear reductionist, magisterial, and even somewhat arbitrarily prescriptive. But to reduce Chinese critical inquiry merely to this would be ignore its distinctive conception of scholarship as a form of moral responsibility, and the difficulty of working in such a domain without certitude in the use of language." (Davies 2007: 30) This is for me indeed a too sympathetic reading. With the aid of Lacanian psychoanalysis, we can not only deconstruct the metaphysics of presence embedded in Sinophone "linguistic certitude," but also further tackle critically the very role such "moral responsibility" plays in sustaining and perpetuating the metaphysical character of Sinophone critical inquiry.

That Which Fixes the Splitting Between Knowledge and Belief

Here, let us briefly recount the Lacanian thesis that because the big Other — the ultimate ground of the symbolic order — does not exist, the object of desire (e.g. "Chineseness" as the essence of China) is *ontologically* elusive, and the desire is *never* satisfied. In other words, the *objet petit a* has to be unattainable in order for it to function as the imaginary "filling-in" of the ontological abyss. As Bruce Fink notes, "[D]esire is not so much something you have as something you do not have. It springs from lack." (Fink 1997: 64) Desire is not a relation to an object, but a relation to lack. Fantasy creates a scenario in which the fundamental lack is magically turned into the loss of some specific object — ergo, the "desired object." Thus, in order to trace the movement of desire, we have to step into the fantasmatic space.

What drives Chinese intellectuals like Gan Yang to write stubbornly within a metaphysical structure, which is typical of Sinophone critical inquiry, is their shared *desire* to resuscitate China's lost essence. Gan's appeal for civilizational confidence draws on the (imagined) integrity and homogeneity of Chinese civilization: his desire is for a complete sense of civilizational confidence that represents the restoration of China's lost greatness (as quoted earlier, Gan even imagines that the task will be completed over the next generation or two). Gan also contends that the revival of Chinese civilization depends on the psychological instead of economic factors. He was right insofar as what endows him and others with such confidence is indeed the "psychological instead of economic factor": instead of China's economic rise, the deep factor, from the Lacanian psychoanalytical view, is of course — fantasy.

It is the operation of fantasy that obscures this perverse split between knowledge and belief (in the form of "civilizational confidence"), an obscuration which generates the desire by making ordinary, petty objects (*objet petit a*) magically desirable. The desired object, as noted earlier, is perpetually out of the reach (and external forces or obstacles must be imagined to maintain one's distance from it). The symbolic "reality" is never fully constituted. Fantasy masks this ontological lack of the Other by turning it into a lack of some specific things, *as if* by (re)acquiring such missing pieces — i.e. the desired objects — the Other will be full (again). With regard to Gan Yang's writing, it is thus the "magical operation" of fantasy that enables the thesis of the non-existence of China "coinciding" with its very antithesis (or rather, being constantly overwhelmed and overwritten by the latter): the recognition that "China does not exist" is "dissolved" in the fantasmatic space, where some "spectral object" takes over the place of the abyssal spot of China, generating the desire to endlessly pursue it.

Hence, intellectuals like Gan serve as another exemplary case of the famous Žižekian analysis of fetishist disavowal: "They know very well, but...": Gan speaks about the non-existence of China, but he can't afford to really "believe in" it. When deprived of the fetish object, the fetishist experiences subjective disintegration.[10] In other words, the "China" fantasy, however imagined, supplies the fetish object necessary for planning and proposing China's civilizational return.[11] In his writings published in the 2000s, Gan Yang claimed with full "confidence" that different from "four small dragons in East Asia," China is a great Dragon which has its "civilizational desire" (*wenming yuwang*) and "civilizational interests" (*wenming liyi*) (Gan 2012a: 14). He writes:

> The significance of China's rise is totally different from the rise of four small dragons in East Asia: the latter only has significance in the history of local economy, while the former, which represents the revival of Chinese civilization, is an event in the history of world civilization (Gan 2007: 84).

In this style of so-called comparative analysis, "China" is explicitly posited as a *metaphysical entity*, "qualitatively" different from other East Asian countries because of its mysterious "civilizational core" — "Chineseness."

---

[10]The fetish, for Žižek, is that which denies the lack in the Other, that which disavows the castrative dimension of the phallic signifier. It is the "nothing" that necessarily accompanies its "all."

[11]For Žižek, what sustains such fetishist belief is, of course, the fundamental fantasy. His further point is: even if the fetishist subject — and this time also a cynical subject — *personally* doesn't believe (that X serves actually his fetish object, that something really *matters* to him), the fetishist belief nonetheless operates "objectively." "They no longer believe, *but the things themselves believe for them*" (Žižek 1989: 34).

Xu Jilin was right to point out that in the texts of New Left intellectuals such as Gan, Chinese civilization is turned magically into something "divine and charismatic" (*Zhonghua wenming de shenmeihua*) (Xu Jilin 2011: 236). He, however, did not further pursue what mechanism enables this type of "magical operation." It is indeed legitimate to say that the "Great Dragon fantasy" we have discussed throughout this book still fundamentally frames and sustains the coordinates of Gan's recent writings. To paraphrase Žižek's argument (1989: 126), we could say that the function of the "Great Dragon fantasy" is to construct a vision of China (or Chinese civilization) as if it was waiting to be realized as long as one protects this "entity" from being threatened by "inner" antagonisms or contradictions. For the fantasy to work, China has to be imagined as homogeneous in the sense that the relation between all parts is organic, complementary, and thus fully harmonious. Through the operation of the "Great Dragon fantasy," "Chineseness" — an empty signifier lacking clear definition or articulation — nonetheless acquires a powerful metaphysical authority. Meanwhile, the Great Dragon narrative also offers the explanation of why things went wrong: "Chineseness" was deprived by the violent intrusions of the West. In other words, the "Great Dragon fantasy" provides both beatific and horrific narratives.

One can further explain Gan's drastic shift of positions in the last three decades in terms of the operation of fantasy. As Žižek notes, the job of fantasy "is not to offer us a point of escape from our reality but to offer us the social reality itself as an escape from some traumatic, real kernel" (Žižek 1989: 45). In the 1980s the discourse of China's modernization, as a specific embodiment of the "Great Dragon fantasy," functioned as the fundamental fantasy through which Chinese intellectuals perceived China's past, present, and future. The 1989 Tiananmen protest and its brutal suppression were not only a tragic event on the streets, but also a heavy blow on the fantasmatic scene. The modernization fantasy started to lose its hegemonic power afterwards. However, instead of getting direct access to reality, "when our fundamental fantasy is shattered, we experience the 'loss of reality'" (Žižek 1999b: 122). This is because fantasy is a defensive shield that covers up the inconsistencies of the symbolic order (that which we experience as "reality"): with the withering of the modernization fantasy, what people encounter is not China's true essence, but the horrifying *inexistence* of "China" — the big Other does not exist. There is no ultimate support/guarantee of *the meaning of the Chinese life*, including all those self-assigned missions (of making China great again)...[12] Such traumatic experience, which can lead to complete "subjective disintegration," can be only repressed or "remedied" by (renewed) fantasy, for fantasy as "the primordial form of narrative [...] serves to occult some original deadlock" (Žižek 1998: 196). Since the mid-1990s many competing discourses have emerged including postmodernism, the New Left, nationalism, etc., representing Chinese intellectuals' efforts to establish new fantasmatic visions (Chineseness, Chinese modernity, the Chinese nation, and so on). The discourse of China's civilizational subjectivity that emerged in the early 2000s can also be regarded as one of such efforts, a very influential one indeed. That is to say, Gan's writings on Chinese civilization reveal an implicit fear that "China does not exist; it is not reality as such," a fear of a direct encounter with — using Žižekian phrasing — the horrifying "raw reality."

"China" in this sense is an exemplary case of "the paradox of a being which can reproduce itself only in so far as it is misrecognized and overlooked: the moment we see it 'as it really is,' this being dissolves itself into nothingness or, more precisely, it changes into another kind of reality" (Žižek 1989: 28–29). Hence, it is easy to recognize that in modern and contemporary Sinophone texts the Great Dragon, the Great Wall, the Yellow River, etc. are used to *symbolize* Chinese civilization; what could be made explicit only through proper psychoanalytic examination is: "Chinese civilization" is itself already *a product of the operation of symbolization.* (Do not forget: symbolization is the very operation by means of which "reality" becomes "what it is," the process working towards an entire cancellation of the Real.) "China" or "Chinese civilization" has a *fictional* (instead of *ontological*) structure, and is fundamentally sustained by various *fantasmatic supplements*, from obviously mythical popular narratives (the Great Dragon, etc.) to sophisticated "elite" intellectual discourses. Gan Yang's recent narrative of the "fusion

[12]Cf. Zhang Xudong's famous essay entitled "How to Live as a Chinese Person Today" (Zhang 2005).

of three traditions" serves exactly as such a fantasmatic story in supporting an imaginary homogeneity of Chinese civilization.

The discourse of China's civilizational subjectivity is clearly a variation of the "Great Dragon fantasy" that was first played out in the 1980s modernization discourse. Indeed, in Gan's recent writings China is still depicted as having unfortunately been suffering from "poor-sightedness," and the author appeals passionately for "clear-sightedness" – i.e. for an act of rubbing one's eyes in order to see things clearly — except for this time the perceived obstacle blocking/distorting China's vision is no longer traditional Chinese culture, but the post-Maoist project of Western-styled modernization: "We have looked at China through the eyes of the West over one hundred years. We haven't used our own eyes." In other words, the Great Dragon truly gains its "enlightened" vision once it, to quote Gan's words, "turns its attention onto the unique features of Chinese civilization, and stops assuming the 'transcendental' superiority of modern social form" (Gan Yang 2012a: 157, 145; 2007: 46). The project of China's modernization was understood in the 1980s as the search for what has brought about the *loss* of China's essence ("Chineseness"). However, in Gan's recent view, it is identified as precisely what has been causing China's essence remaining *lost*, as *the* hindrance that has been deferring the restoration of Chinese civilization, postponing the final achievement of the *fullness* of China. A truly "enlightened" vision, for Gan, would see this.

However, as noted in the Introduction, the lost object — e.g. the essence and fullness of Chinese civilization — is always *retroactively constructed* through fantasmatic narratives. "Enlightened vision" itself is also nothing other than a product of fantasy, of an imaginary "promise of fullness." The empty promise is: once (re)gaining "clear-sightedness," one is be able to see the "non-castrated" China — China *with* its missing piece (*with* "Chineseness" as its essence/root/genital).[13] In Lacanian terms, such promise of a final restoration of China's lost essence can only be an empty

[13] Of course, the beatific side of fantasy is always accompanied by its horrific side. On the other side of the same fantasmatic narrative, this missing piece has to remain *structurally* missing, unattainable, always unfortunately deprived by some external evil forces, as recounted in various narratives of modern China.

one in that it promises *an imaginary mastery of the impossible Real.* Hence, fantasy is the magical device that creates an imaginary illusion of the attainability of the lost object. What defines the "Great Dragon fantasy" is, as noted earlier, precisely the (doomed-to-fail) promise of recuperating the fullness of China. What ensues then is the other defining feature of the "Great Dragon fantasy": in such narratives China is always depicted as *dysfunctional.* Although Gan Yang has confidence that the task of restoring the greatness of Chinese civilization can be possibly achieved in the next thirty years, he nonetheless yet posits China as being highly dysfunctional (and even on the edge of becoming "a torn country"). That which is responsible for China becoming "a torn country" is for Gan, of course, the modernization project launched in the 1980s.

Contrary to Chinese liberals who see China's economic rise as the result of its three-decades-long modernization, Gan argues that modernization is a path of "self-castration" which will turn a country into "a torn country": "If a country cuts off its genitals, then no matter how rich and mighty it becomes, it is already dead" (Gan 2012a: 4–8). This bizarre statement was Gan's variation on the observation that Pye had made with regard to China's modernization. While Pye had suggested that as an ancient civilization, China should not "pretend to be a nation-state" but should develop a civil society, and "blend what is distinctive in a nation's culture with what is internationally or universally appreciated" (Pye 1993: 130–133), Gan's point is: since China is really a great civilization, why should it bother to pretend to be anything else? For Gan, the biggest problem is not that China's civilizational "nature" handicapped China's modernization, but that contemporary Chinese people lack the "consciousness of civilizational subjectivity." Hence, contrary to the main point of Pye's article, which is, the Chinese people should endeavor to construct a modern kind of nationalism that does not conflict with modernization, and "to modernize a great civilization" (Pye 1993: 133), Gan urges his readers to see China as a civilization only and to reject any modernization that does not accord with its original character. This difference between Pye and Gan is one reason why the latter fails to acknowledge the former when quoting his famous line. For Gan, "[t]he most important problem for today's Chinese people is whether or not they are able to continue to live as the descendants of Chinese civilization" (Gan 2012a: 56). What is striking is Gan's use of the idea of the male genitalia to represent the root or essence of Chinese civilization, and his depiction of modernization as a path of "self-castration." The implication is that, once castrated, China will fail to be the real home of the "descendants of the Great Dragon." Such arguments entail clearly *a metaphysical structure* — Chineseness as essence (or root, "genital"), without which China will become a torn/castrated country.

However, the psychoanalytic lesson is that both the subject and the big Other are always already castrated. Lacan, following Freud, reads "symbolic castration" as the interpretive activity that allows us to know our bodies through the medium of language. To experience the world through language is to be deprived of any direct access to our bodies. The resulting gap (as "symbolic castration") is both what fantasy endeavors to mask and what generates the fantasy.[14] "Thrown" into the symbolic order, the barred/castrated subject is fatefully "poor-sighted," to see reality by "looking awry" (to recall Žižek's phrase). Thus, the belief that with enlightened eyes we can see reality as such, is itself a fantasy at its purest. The scenario offered by the "Great Dragon fantasy" is at work in Gan's imagining of a "non-castrated" China (the fullness of Chinese civilization, an almighty Dragon without deformity). What he implies is that once China (re)gains its missing organ, the fullness of "Chineseness" will return. Yet what he fails to see is that he must present China as "castrated" and handicapped in order to present this solution. Žižek reminds us that "we must avoid the simple metaphors of demasking" (Žižek 1989: 29) for they prevent us from heeding the desire that these metaphors feed. It is also not hard to see that the metaphor of "clear-sightedness" functions to turn the fantasmatic scene magically into "objective reality."

Yet such "demasking" is central to much of Chinese intellectual argumentation. As we have discussed in Chapter 1, the Enlightenment discourse (of both the 1910s and the 1980s) relies structurally on the metaphysical presupposition that there is a Chinese essence to which one can remain true: this presumed genuine Chinese nature is however posited as something lost or distorted, that needs to be recovered and set straight.

---

[14]For an excellent elaboration of Lacan's revision of Freud's notion of "castration," see Evans 1996: 20–23.

With China becoming a rising world power at the dawn of the new century, influential Chinese intellectuals such as Gan Yang, who were leading New Enlightenment figures in the 1980s, started to talk extensively about China's civilizational subjectivity. Isn't this new discourse that ostensibly contradicts and rejects the 1980s New Enlightenment discourse, in fact reflecting the same metaphysical structure? The only difference is that in the 2000s and since, Chinese thinkers have acquired a new confidence to *envisage fantasmatically a final restoration of China's lost essence* (by getting rid of the "self-castrated" path of modernization)? In the passionate calls for "civilizational confidence" *an imaginary fullness of China* serves "to remedy the fundamental deficiency (impossibility) of the big Other, to 'restore' the fullness of the Other" (Stavrakakis 1999: 47). Of course, the realization of such promise must always be deferred, perceived as being halted by some contingent removable hindrances or obstacles: the "fatuous emperor," China's "unenlightened" premodern tradition, the "self-castrated" project of China's modernization... The promise, however, will persist, and new reasons will be found to explain the hindrances or obstacles in the path to China's perfection.

In his essay published in 1987, Gan called the contention that "the world's future culture must be the revival of Chinese culture" a "blind fantasy." (At that time he extolled China's modernization through getting rid of its traditional culture as "enlightened vision.") Two decades later, the author has completely reversed his position to praise the revival of Chinese culture. This radical shift is actually a change of vocabulary in which the "Great Dragon fantasy" remains fully intact. Gan Yang, like many other Chinese intellectuals, still writes as if their purpose is to resuscitate China's wholeness (via the act of seeing clearly China's true nature). From a Lacanian psychoanalytic point of view, Gan's radical shift, far from being a shift from "blind fantasy" to "clear-sightedness" (or from fantasy to reality), only indicates a radical change or renewal within his own fantasmatic space.[15] Despite such radical shift, the fact that his recent

[15] In fact, Gan's no longer seeing the contention that "the world's future culture must be the revival of Chinese culture" a fantasy precisely indicates that *this contention is operating and functioning as Gan's fundamental fantasy*, which creates the delusion that the real fullness can be achieved, and through which he can once again relate himself to "reality" (China's past, present, and future).

writings still demonstrate that the longing for clear-sightedness suggests that Gan Yang, like many other Chinese intellectuals, still writes within the fundamental scenario of the "Great Dragon fantasy." The desire to resuscitate China's wholeness (via the act of seeing clearly China's true nature), still constitutes the very core of "being Chinese" today.

Wang Hui's writings can be seen as another exemplary case of the fetishistic mode of "knowing very well, but not able to fully assume what he rationally knows." Wang wrote in the mid-1990s that "I rejoice that I was born in China since what could be more heartbreaking and also more exhilarating than the glorious revival of a decaying civilization of which so many generations of people have dreamed? And what could be more thrilling than to watch and experience the minutiae and process of this collective dream?" (Wang Hui 1994: 21–22) Wang has on several occasions in the 1990s and 2000s defined his intellectual goal as assisting in "the glorious revival of the Chinese civilization" (Wang 2000b: 473).[16] Recently, in his commentary on Gan Yang's essay on the "fusion of three traditions," Wang interprets Lu Xun's employment of the term *mixin* (superstition, blind belief) in the following way: "*Mixin* in Lu's employment refers to the origins of imagination inherent in Chinese civilization. In order words, the preservation of *mixin* entails a process of regaining our confidence." (Wang 2007: 56–58) Here, Wang Hui defines "confidence" less metaphysically than Gan Yang, since what he searches for is not the essence of "Chinese civilization" but the "origins of imagination inherent in Chinese civilization."[17] As such he renders explicit the fantasmatic character of such appeals for cultural confidence: imagination is vital in order for Chinese civilization to be restored. By insisting on such "preservation of *mixin*," Wang's formula further renders crystal clear the fantasmatic operation that covers up the splitting between knowledge and belief: despite *knowing* very well that China does not exist, that there is

[16] Wang also wrote that "I believe that the glorious revival of Chinese civilization relies on the rational efforts of several generations" (Wang Hui 2000b: 473). Writing such passages in the 1990s, Wang's "confidence" seems a little bit lower than Gan Yang's, who contends in the 2000s that the task can be fulfilled with the efforts of one or two generations.

[17] Still, "origins of imagination inherent in Chinese civilization" is a typical metaphysical expression, for it presupposes something essential, "original" inherent in Chinese civilization.

no essence inherent in Chinese civilization, one could (and should) nonetheless still *believe blindly* (*mixin*) the opposite. In this sense, similar to Gan Yang, Wang seeks to locate native roots that would allow China to be presented as unique and whole, and by doing so, fetishistically cover up the Real (the non-existence of China). For Wang, "superstitions" can be used as an instrument in constructing new fantasmatic visions.

Gan Yang's and Wang Hui's recent texts demonstrate the persistence of the "Great Dragon fantasy." As discussed in previous chapters, just like many other fantasmatic formations, the "Great Dragon fantasy" entails a two-layer structure (beatific and horrific sides): (1) stories about a continuous and homogeneous Chinese civilization, about its greatness and fullness, and (2) stories about what went wrong. What distinguishes the discourse of China's civilizational subjectivity from that of China's new nationalism is while the latter is primarily focusing on telling the second type of stories, the former's focus is with the first type. In other words, it focuses on constructing retroactively a coherent fantasmatic past — China as a "several-thousand-years continuous civilization." Žižek points out that "The basic paradox of the psychoanalytic notion of fantasy consists in a kind of time loop — the 'original fantasy' is always the fantasy of the origins" (Žižek 1991a: 197). This time-loop structure explains why stories about the past are constituent of the fantasy-constellation. What Žižek calls the "fantasmatic history" (e.g. the greatness and homogeneity of Chinese civilization) has played — and is playing — a fundamental role in China's present "national building." Let us recall here the argument I have presented in Chapter 1: *what essentially holds and sustains "China" as a (modern) "nation" is the fantasy of its (premodern) greatness, retroactively formed.* What holds essentially and effectively today's Chinese people together as a nation is the *enjoyment* of fantasizing about China as a great (even the greatest) civilization.

Wang Hui also notes in his commentary on Gan Yang: "Today we all wear Western-style clothes. National-style clothing is disappearing. This demonstrates that our self-consciousness is extremely weak." (Wang 2007: 56–58) This clearly reminds us the lyrics of the 1980s pop song "My Chinese Heart": "Although I wear Western-style clothes, my heart remains a Chinese heart. Every inch of my body has been branded by my ancestors with the stamp of China." The striking discursive similarity between Wang Hui's recent writings and the representative discourse of the 1980s shows that in spite of the difference in content and vocabulary between the two, *the same deep structure* shapes and molds both Wang's discourse and that of the 1980s, *functioning as a hidden generative mechanism, directing them to insist fully on the task of "being Chinese," i.e. of regaining the self-consciousness of "my Chinese heart."* Such mechanism is referred to in this study as the "Great Dragon fantasy."

No wonder accompanying the discourse of China's civilizational subjectivity, there soon emerged a strong "fever" for the age of the 1980s (*bashi nianshi re*) in the Chinese intellectual landscape. If the civilizational subjectivity discourse tells the story about China's ancient root, then the "fever" for the eighties is clearly about China's recent past. Let us now turn to this interesting intellectual phenomenon.

The Fantasy of the Eighties: "Self-Castration" and Perversion

Around the mid-2000s, quite a few influential Chinese intellectuals, especially former participants of the "cultural fever" of the 1980s such as Gan Yang and Jin Guantao started to discuss intellectual activities of the eighties in a strongly nostalgic tone. Soon their personal reminiscences of 1980s' intellectual activities gained public attention and became a topic of heated discussion. In the meanwhile, questions like "Why do people now start to reminisce about the age of the 1980s? What is the value of this reminiscence?" have also been frequently raised.[18] These questions are what I would like to explore now. Since my studies of contemporary Chinese intellectuality starts with the examination of the intellectual discourse of the 1980s, it also seems proper to end it with an examination of the recent intellectual discussion about the 1980s, via a detailed textual analysis of how intellectuals project their retrospective ideas about the eighties.

The mid- to late 2000s' discussion about the intellectual activities of the 1980s has been called by many participants and commentators a

---

[18]These two exact questions are raised in one of Gan Yan's recent interviews on the subject of the fever for the eighties. See Gan Yang 2006a.

"fever for the eighties." The word "fever" (*re*) used here obviously echoes the "cultural fever" — a term that was used interchangeably with the "New Enlightenment movement" — of the 1980s. Let us first take a look at how this fever for the eighties emerged. In May 2006, a book entitled *Conversations about the Eighties* was published and, quite unexpectedly, became extremely popular. Centering on the topic of the cultural and intellectual activities of the 1980s,[19] this book includes eleven interviews conducted by the Beijing-based cultural critic Zha Jianying. All the interviewees are influential intellectuals (scholars, critics, writers, artists) who were active in the 1980s. Although Zha says in the preface that her book is not a "big project" (*hongda gongcheng*) but a simple collection of a few personal conversations about cultural activities in the 1980s (Zha Jianying 2006: 6–7), its publication soon led to a large-scale trend of discussing and reminiscing about the eighties. During the next few months after the publication of *Conversations about the Eighties*, many influential journals including *Panorama* (*Wanxiang*), *Book-city* (*Shucheng*), *Frontiers* (*Tianya*) published numerous essays on this subject. As a timely response to this growing intellectual fever for the eighties launched by Zha's book, a conference on this topic was held at the end of June 2006 in Shanghai. Several dozen Shanghai- and Beijing-based intellectuals — not only scholars, academicians, researchers, but also writers, artists, literary critics, and so on, including Zha and quite a few of her interviewees — attended the conference (see Ge Hongwei 2006). One month after the conference, another book on the same subject was published, adding to the growing fever. This second book is entitled *The Cultural Consciousness in the 1980s*. It was edited by Gan Yang, who was one of the interviewees of Zha's book. Gan's book was originally published in 1989 in Hong Kong and Taiwan under the title *The Cultural Consciousness of Contemporary China*. 2006 was the first time that it was published and distributed in mainland China.

In the following discussion, among the many who contributed to this fever for the eighties, I once again take Gan Yang's texts as the main object of my critical examination. This choice is not done merely for the

[19] As Zha Jianying, the editor of the book, puts it in her editorial preface, this book focuses on "*wenhua wenti*" (cultural problems). See Zha Jianying 2006: 7.

purpose of making our current discussion continuous with the previous sections of this chapter. It is made solely because Gan did occupy a central spot in this intellectual fever — besides his involvement in the two above-mentioned books he also published several essays and gave lengthy interviews on the subject of the eighties. Gan collected these essays and interviews with his old writings in the 1980s later into a book, published in 2007 under a book series edited by himself with the title "New Series of Culture: China and the World," indicating a continuity of his intellectual engagements from the 1980s to the present.[20] It is fair to say that Gan's essays and books about the eighties boosted the popular appeal of remembering the 1980s "cultural fever."

As mentioned in the Introduction, in the early 1990s Chinese intellectuals stopped discussing ways of solving China's socio-political problems; instead, they focused on scholastic topics that had no direct relation to contemporary Chinese social and political issues. To some extent, the intense debates between liberalism and the New Left in the late 1990s reflected engagement with social and political issues but many of the debate's participants such as Wang Hui chose to write in a highly obscure, theoretical language to avoid making direct political comments.[21] In the post-Tiananmen era, it became impossible to discuss the events of 1989 and any attempt to do so normally ended in censorship. Thus, at the first glance, the recent fever for the eighties seems to indicate that the "political atmosphere" in mainland China had changed: the government did not seem to mind publications about the 1980s, and people who were closely related to the 1989 student protest movement were even allowed to talk about publicly their activities and engagements in the late 1980s… Regarding the current status of the Party-state censorship *vis-à-vis* the discussion of the 1980s, perhaps my own experience can offer some insights. In August 2006, right in the middle of the heated discussion about the 1980s, the editor of *Chinese Book Review* (*Zhongguo tushu pinglun*, one of the "key national journals" in China), invited me to

[20]Gan Yang was in the 1980s the editor-in-chief of the influential journal and book series *Culture: China and the World*. See the discussion in Chapter 2.

[21]As I discussed in Chapter 4, one of central criticisms Wang Hui faces is his obscure writing style, which is seen as a cynical gesture.

contribute a critical response to the 1980s fever brought about by Zha's and Gan's books. What is worth noting is that the editor specifically mentioned in his letter that:

> The space for public discussion (*yanlun kongjian*) for journals and the media in general has recently become much narrower. This subject in fact is quite sensitive. If you agree to write an essay for us, please make sure that you consider the political climate (*bawo zhengzhi chidu*).

When the editor received my essay one month later, he told me that he felt what I had written was "politically safe" for publication and jokingly added: "We don't need to perform self-castration (*huidao zigong*) on your essay." The phrase "self-castration" is commonly used by mainland Chinese intellectuals as a metaphor for self-censorship in which one must judge what to delete from one's own work. Nonetheless, the editor sent me an edited version of my essay that was much shorter than the original and quite a lot of the wording had also been revised. This shows that despite the editor's assurance, my essay had already undergone "castration."

But the situation became more complicated after this. Two weeks later, I heard from the editor again. This time he told me that at the last minute, my essay was taken out due to a "direct order from above" (*shangmian*). *Shangmian* is a phrase that refers to the "unit in charge" (*zhuguan danwei*) or "the governing unit" (*lingdao danwei*) of any workplace in China. From the document the editor forwarded to me, two reasons were given for the removal of my essay: "(1) the top leaders [of the Party-state] have paid special attention (*hen guanzhu*) to the publication of the book *Conversations about the 1980s*. Thus great care must be taken with this topic. (2) Wu Guanjun made use of this subject to discuss his own interests (*jieti fahui*): using Gan Yang's text as a camouflage (*huangzi*), Wu preaches a radical critical practice against the present ideological situation in China which, according to Wu, is full of holes and cankers (*qianchuang baikong*)."

From this recent experience of mine, the unambiguous message is that state censorship remains very strict. The scale of censorship since the late 2000s is perhaps even stricter than in the late 1990s. When the editor of

Chinese Book Review asked me to write with caution he implied that I should undergo a process of "self-castration" while writing this essay. Through such clear requirements for self-censorship, Chinese publishing has developed in conformity with state policy. This brings us to the discursive dimension of the heated intellectual discussion in the 2000s about the 1980s. The crucial question is whether the people who discuss the eighties practice or resist this form of internalized censorship?[22]

As discussed in Chapter 2, the large-scale intellectual discussions in the mid- and late 1980s, whose central theme is (Western-styled) "modernization," have close associations to the 1989 student protest movement. However, in his recent essays on the eighties, Gan Yang surprisingly denies this theme and stresses that "The intellectual discourse in the 1980s is a 'poetic critique of modernity'," "its mainstream is criticism of capitalism and modernity" (Gan Yang 2006a; 2006c: 198–199, 226, 207).

"Modernity" as an academic term, along with the discourse of the "critique of modernity," however, emerged in Chinese intellectual landscape in the mid-1990s.[23] It was hardly discussed in the 1980s. The Beijing-based historian Lei Yi's following note can also shed some light on this issue,

> In 1988 I stared to translate Paul A. Cohen's *Between Tradition and Modernity*. I didn't know how to translate the word 'modernity.' According to the dictionary, it should be translated as "*xiandaixing*," which was however at that time indeed very rarely seen. Very few people were using it. There was no such a word in our vocabulary. [...] After careful consideration I decided to use "*xiandaixing*" in my translation. I discussed my decision with quite a few scholars. Most of them disapproved of it by pointing out that there is no such word in Chinese language, and suggested translating it as "the modern" or "modernization." (Lei Yi 2009: 34)

[22] Gloria Davies (2007) offers an excellent critical analysis of "the pervasive practice of self-censorship among Chinese intellectuals," of how it has been deeply embedded in post-1989 Chinese intellectual production.

[23] Moreover, the main contributors to the modernity discourse of the mid-1990s were the Beijing-based historian Wang Hui and the Guangzhou-based philosopher Liu Xiaofeng. Gan Yang, on the other hand, hardly played any role in it.

In this sense, what Gan wrote is a counter-factual description of the 1980s intellectual discourse.[24] In fact, such statements even contradict Gan's own claims in the 1980s, since his influential argument in the 1980s was not "a critique of modernity," but indeed a typical discourse that fully embraces "modernization." For example, Gan wrote in his editorial introduction to the first issue of *Culture: China and the World* journal published in 1987, "As China works to achieve modernization, it is a corollary that the 'modernization of Chinese culture' must also be achieved. This is the shared belied of all people of conscience in the 1980s. This is an inevitable and logical part of China's historic take-off." (Gan Yang 1987b: 1) If Gan is right about the mainstream of the 1980s intellectual discourse being the "critique of modernity," how would he explain then the obvious contradiction of his earlier claim about the need for the "modernization of Chinese culture" as a "shared belief of all people of conscience in the 1980s"? Hence, Gan's depiction of the mainstream of the 1980s intellectual discourse as a "poetic critique of modernity" indeed has nothing to do with the intellectual discourse of the 1980s *per se*. It is purely a retroactive fantasmatic construction. From our discussions of Gan's texts in Chapter 2, it is clear that Gan Yang's formula of cultural modernization is no doubt one of the most radical models of the "project of modernization" in the Sinophone intellectual world of the 1980s. However, as discussed in previous chapters, facts hold no force in the fantasmatic space; they simply do not matter.

Through these simple (inter)textual analyses, what is explicit is that Gan negates his original 1980s argument but without stating that he was doing so. This suggests that when he wrote about the eighties in the late 2000s, he was exercising a degree of self-censorship: the eighties that Gan presented two decades later — indeed a fantasmatic picture of the eighties — is a clear distortion of his own previous argument. The extent of Gan's distortion, including self-censorship, is such that it can be described as "perverse."

[24]Gan's main justification is as follows: "What we now call 'the problem of modernity' (*xiandaixing wenti*) today, we called [the problem of] 'the technical age' (*jishu shidai*) [in the 1980s]" (Gan Yang 2006c: 222). This account is itself, however, extremely weak and untenable, since 'the question/problem of modernity' discussed in the Sinophone intellectual world since the mid-1990s is totally different from the "problem of the technical age," a thesis Gan explicitly took from Heidegger.

Here, I draw on the psychoanalytic account of *perversion*. Despite its everyday associations with so-called sexual deviancy, perversion is also a clinical term that Lacanian psychoanalysis employs to designate a (pseudo-)certainty that the subject knows what the Other wants. The pervert is therefore defined by a lack of questioning. He (or she) is convinced of the meaning of the desire of the Other. "The whole problem of the perversions," for Lacan, "consists in conceiving how the child, in his relation to the mother [...] identifies himself with the imaginary object of [her] desire" (Lacan 1977: 197–198). In this theoretical sense, perversion is such a make-believing ideological operation that convinces a subject to be the object-instrument that satisfies the desire of the (M)Other. Whereas the operation of fantasy turns the Other's desire into the subject's very own (symbolic castration), enabling him/her to enjoy through endlessly chasing the desired missing piece (*objet petit a*), the operation of perversion organizes a different way (a "perverse" way) to enjoy through enabling the subject to directly regard himself/herself as the very object of the Other's desire. By so doing, such operation turns a barred subject further into a pervert, who instrumentalizes himself/herself to satisfy the Other's desire, and who enjoys through such radical self-reification: "The subject here makes himself the instrument of the Other's *jouissance*" (Lacan 1977: 320).[25] With regard to our case, the operation embodied in the self-censorship of intellectuals like Gan Yang results in a perverted account of "the eighties." That which serves as the big (M)Other in Gan's discourse is, of course, the existing authoritarian Party-rule in China. This account of "the eighties" conceived of in the 2000s is inherently perverse because it accords with a self-castrated nostalgia in the present, not with the historical experience of the 1980s.

In an interview conducted in 2005, Gan Yang targets the TV series *River Elegy* and claims: "*River Elegy* simply differentiates Chinese and Western civilizations into yellow civilization and blue civilization. This is nothing but an effective propaganda. It did not deepen the discussion, but simplified the problem." (Gan Yang 2005) Owing to *River Elegy*'s explicit

[25]This is why, as Dylan Evans notes, "it is extremely rare for a perverse subject to demand analysis, and in the rare cases when he does, it is not because he seeks to change his mode of *jouissance*" (Evans 1996: 140).

association with Zhao Ziyang's administration, Gan's recent criticism of *River Elegy* can be read as making a clear gesture towards the 1980s intellectual movement and the Tiananmen incident in particular. Again, what Gan missed to mention is that his criticism of *River Elegy* can also be applied to his own 1980s' thesis on the "antagonism between the ancient and the modern," a thesis based on a "simple differentiation" of culture into "premodern culture" and "modern culture" with the latter being viewed as superior.

Gan has not offered any explanation regarding the gaps between his own writings in the 1980s and his review of the 1980s in the 2000s. Instead, he wants his readers to believe that he has held the same view all along. (This is why, as mentioned earlier, he named the book series he has been editing since 2006 "New Series of Culture: China and the World.") In a recent interview entitled "The Critique of Modernity in the 1980s and the Transformation in the 1990s," Gan states:

> *Many people* think the reason for China not being modernized yet is that "Chinese cultural tradition" has problems. Thus critiquing Chinese cultural tradition through a comparison with Western culture became the mainstream of the "cultural fever" of the mid-1980s. But on the other hand, *we* gradually found the problems of the West itself through reading thinkers such as Heidegger. Therefore, though still strongly opposing tradition, we became more focused on trying to understand the problems of Western modernity itself. (Gan Yang 2006a, emphases added)

It is basically true that the *Culture: China and the World* group published a series of translated works in the 1980s, including Heidegger's *Being and Time* translated by Chen Jiaying, Sartre's *Being and Nothingness* translated by Du Xiaozhen *et al.*, Nietzsche's *The Birth of Tragedy* translated by Zhou Guoping, Max Weber's *Protestant Ethic and the Spirit of Capitalism* translated by Yu Xiao *et al.* The crucial point is, however, not just which books have been *translated and published* in China in the 1980s, but how these books have been *interpreted and understood* by Chinese intellectuals in the 1980s. The very title of this particular book series focusing on translating "thinkers such as Heidegger" is "Modern Western Scholarly Works" (*xiandai xifang xueshu wenku*), which has already rendered us the crucial information: these Western thinkers and intellectual trends were sorted into the "modern/traditional" dichotomy. That is to say, all these Western trends have been understood by Chinese intellectuals in the 1980s as diverse *modern* trends. By reading them, intellectuals like Gan were not "trying to understand the problems of western modernity itself," but exactly the opposite, trying to use them to construct a "modern form" for Chinese culture. Hence, even though Gan Yang did "read the works of thinkers such as Heidegger" in the 1980s, this does not simultaneously mean that he had already in the 1980s engaged in the "critique of modernity." Every serious scholar should be clear that "reading somebody's work" is not tantamount to "following somebody." The question raised from the psychoanalytic angle would be: through what fantasmatic frame did these New Enlightenment thinkers understand and interpret the works of Heidegger and others?

The problem is therefore not whether Gan "read thinkers such as Heidegger" in the 1980s, but his confidence in asserting a Heideggerian nature to the claim that "Chinese culture must get rid of its traditional forms and run towards its modern forms." The statement has nothing Heideggerian about it, but in Chinese intellectual discourse, it became identified as such. One can argue psychoanalytically that the modernization discourse, as a distorting screen of fantasy, enabled Gan and other New Enlightenment intellectuals to make use of the names of major European thinkers like Heidegger to invest their own pro-modernization writings with the authority of twentieth-century European thought. During this heated discussion over the eighties, the Beijing-based philosopher Xu Youyu, one of the core members of the editorial committee of the *Culture: China and the World*, explained why they translated and introduced these Western intellectual trends at that time:

> The committee's works were undertaken very efficiently. Its goals and directions were in line with the social demand at that time. It became a cultural pioneer. Only one year later, it became very well-known in both mainland China and overseas, and has been regarded as a group strongly advocating "wholesale Westernization." We are quite satisfied with our position and the appraisals. (Xu Youyu 2006)

Xu's account is consistent with those of Gan's texts published in the 1980s. Thus, those Western intellectual trends including Heidegger's thought were translated and published in the 1980s precisely because they were overall marked as "modern Western thought": to import these "modern Western" humanistic "new knowledge" was regarded by New Enlightenment intellectuals as the key part of the self-assigned task of advancing China's "cultural modernization." When speaking of those imported Western thinkers such as Heidegger in his study of the 1980s New Enlightenment movement, Xu Jilin also commented:

> At the time, however, their powerful deconstructive impact on theories of modernity were little appreciated or understood... All these various Western humanistic trends were absorbed and understood under the totalistic goal of "advancing cultural modernization." (Xu Jilin 2000: 180)

In retrospect, what Gan devoted his intellectual endeavors and passions in the 1980s to was not a critique of Western modernity, but rather the modernization of Chinese culture. Bearing this in mind, let us turn again to Gan Yang's interview "The Critique of Modernity in the 1980s and the Transformation in the 1990s" quoted above. By stating — which is fabricating — this distinction between "many people" and "we," Gan conceals his own famous argument of the "struggle between the ancient and the modern" that calls for the modernization of Chinese culture. (Such early published statements, however, show that Gan himself was highly representative of the very assumptions he now negates, and attributes to "many people.") In doing so, Gan creates an imaginary "we" as a group of heroic pioneers who since the mid-1980s had begun to "try to understand the problems of Western modernity itself." In this sense, in Gan's (counter-factual) account of the 1980s intellectual movement, the anonymous "many people," to whom he attributes those wrong assumptions, become the scapegoat for the 1980s modernization discourse in which he participated. What is perverse about Gan's claims is that he intentionally "misreads" his own argument of the 1980s. The only conclusion that one can draw is that censorship, both external and self-imposed, has affected his retrospective account of the "heroic" 1980s.

To write of 1980s intellectual discourse while avoiding its highly political content has resulted in an oddly theoretical approach. This is the only way to read Gan's 2006 view of the 1980s as defined by the critique of Western modernity. Viewing "the eighties" in this abstract manner enabled it to become a hot topic in the mid- to late 2000s because the Chinese government allows this type of academic discussion: "modernity" does not threaten the political status quo. Hence, what this fever for the eighties in the 2000s reveals is the erasure of the political content of the 1980s through its greatly altered representation. This situation accords with Žižek's insight that "The threat today is not passivity but pseudo-activity, the urge to be active, to 'participate,' to mask the Nothingness of what goes on" (Žižek 2006c: 334). Contemporary Chinese intellectual discourse presents another perfect example of Žižek's point: intellectuals like Gan Yang praise "the eighties" so as to avoid discussing *what really happened in 1989*, as if the protest movement never happened.

Cynicism qua Pseudo-Activity

The recent nostalgia for the eighties includes the representation of this decade as a unique "golden age." According to Gan Yang, whose "Preface to the Second Edition" of *The Cultural Consciousness in the 1980s* was widely read on the Internet,

> The 1980s is not only an age full of primitive passions (*qingchun jiqing*), but also an age of purity, sincerity, and simplicity (*chunzhen supu*), with no strategic consideration (Gan Yang 2006b: iii; this statement also appears on the book cover).

Later, in his interview "The Critique of Modernity in the 1980s and the Transformation in the 1990s," Gan further claims that

> Comparatively speaking, in the 1980s, because the whole society was at the stage of groping for new ideas (*mosuo jieduan*), the ideas produced were very lively and the values they represent were truly plural. In comparison with the present, there was much more tolerance of different value-stances and much less parochialism (*xiaai*) and utilitarianism in the 1980s. (Gan Yang 2006a)

In another recent interview Gan asserts that "The 1980s perhaps marks the last shred of light of the tradition of Chinese scholar-officials" (Gan 2012a: 483). In those statements, Gan Yang draws his depiction upon a comparative framework between the 1980s and the present, which attributes a set of positive qualities (purity, sincerity, simplicity, primitive passions, and the absence of strategic consideration, parochialism, utilitarianism, etc.) to the former. According to the Shanghai-based critic Xiao Wu, among the present-day commentators about the eighties, Gan Yang's account is "the least rose-tinted" (Xiao Wu 2006). However, this is hardly the case: this is not only because there are other participants whose views are much less rose-tinted than Gan's; it is first and foremost because Gan's account departs so much from what he actually wrote in the 1980s.

In the heated discussion of the eighties, Gan Yang has not so much been criticized for the inherent (inter)textual contradictions embedded in his retrospective accounts of the 1980s,[26] but nonetheless has attracted a great deal of objections accusing him for distortions. Several veterans who participated in the 1980s intellectual activities have voiced their disagreements with Gan Yang's depiction: in their view, the eighties was far from being an age of simplicity, sincerity, etc.; quite on the contrary, it was full of strategic consideration and parochialism… Some directly accused Gan himself as one of the sources of these problems. For instance, the Beijing-based philosopher Li Youzheng wrote of his unpleasant interactions in the late 1980s with Gan Yang and other members of the *Culture: China and the World* group. Li illustrates a list of trivial incidents to demonstrate that the activities of the group could hardly qualify as pure, simple, and, sincere in their intellectual ambitions (Li Youzheng 2006).[27] Another similar account even comes from inside the group. Zhou Guoping, one of the "key members" (*hexin quanzi*) of the *Culture: China and the World* group, wrote in detail about the editorial committee of the *Culture: China and the*

---

[26]The arguably only exception is my invited essay on the subject mentioned earlier. Though it did not make to the *Chinese Book Review* owing to the censorship, it appeared in full length in my book published two years later. See Wu Guanjun 2008: 307–369.

[27]Li further offers his analysis: "Most intellectuals of Gan Yang's generation had experienced mass social migrations [in the Cultural Revolution era] and were thus very experienced in their social dealings." By that Li means that intellectuals like Gan "were very good at 'handling' people [to his own advantage]."

World — from its founding moment to its final "disbandment" — in his biography published in 2004. Zhou presented Gan as scheming, anti-democratic, and ruthlessly dictatorial and accused him of causing the breakup of the group (Zhou Guoping 2004).[28]

In presenting these objections to Gan, I am not interested in determining which account is closer to the 1980s' "true image." I seek only to show the antagonistic nature of recent Chinese discussion about the 1980s. During one of his interviews on the fever for the eighties, Gan offers the following comment when asked why the eighties was being discussed so heatedly:

> Probably people all feel that the present day is becoming less and less interesting; in contrast, the age of the eighties was really interesting (Gan Yang 2006a).

Surely, this is just Gan's subjective opinion and we have seen how he twisted the arguments he presented in the 1980s. What interests me is the *comparative* framework Gan adopts: Gan is using the eighties to criticize the present-day. However, the age of the eighties seems to be "really interesting" *precisely because commentators like Gan present it as having what the present-day lacks*. Thus, this picture of the eighties is itself a pure *contemporary* fantasmatic construction. It is a story about *the present* instead of the eighties: in order to criticize the present day as "becoming less and less interesting" the eighties is presented as an ideal age. (The antagonistic character of this discussion on the eighties demonstrated earlier, at least indicates that it was not so much of a "golden age.")

One could argue that the continuous debates among various intellectual fractions make the intellectual scene of the 2000s impossible for any one group to dominate. Hence, commentators who were once involved in the intellectual activities of the 1980s are nostalgic for a time when they

[28]What is worth noting is that during his interview with Zha Jianying, Gan dismissed the question "Why [the editorial committee of the *Culture: China and the World*] eventually ended on bad terms" by saying that "No one is willing to talk about why" (Gan Yang 2006c: 221). In fact, Zhou Guoping's biography has by then already become a bestseller. Other members such as Xu Youyu also talked about it.

aspired to achieve intellectual unity. It is this fiction of intellectual unity that makes the eighties a fond memory for its commentators in the 2000s. In Lacanian terms, the function of such fiction of intellectual unity is to *fantasmatically fill in what reality lacks*; in other words, the current discourse of the eighties functions as *a fulfilling and satisfying object-instrument of the desire of the Other.*

I have derived my analysis from what Žižek calls the fictional "construction of the Leninist age": Žižek pointed out in one of his recent seminars that when people in the post-Stalinist Soviet Union repeatedly stated that "Let us return to the true Leninism from the Stalinist deviation," this "Leninism" itself in fact had nothing to do with what Lenin did before the Stalinist age, but was a retroactively constructed invention in the context of a post-Stalinist socio-political constellation. As to the "age of the eighties" that has recently become topical in the contemporary Sinophone intellectual scene, what suddenly made it "really interesting" is indeed not the eighties *itself*, but a set of *fantasmatic images* to represent what the present-day lacks.

From the psychoanalytic perspective of fantasy, we can probably understand better the present nostalgic obsession with the age of eighties. Fantasy is, in our common everyday understanding, a hallucinatory "realization" of desire. However, as Žižek points out, its "twist" resides in the following operation: this "realization" is not a realization in the sense of fulfilling the desire as such; rather it generates the framework necessary for perceiving the desire as being fulfilled (Žižek 2005a: 304). Thus in Lacanian psychoanalysis, fantasy is in no way the opposite of one's sense of "reality"; on the contrary, it is a necessary window, through which a desired object is projected as the element that will complete one's life. What is actually missing or lacking is thus obscured. In this sense, one can say that *what people fantasize about* (e.g. having sex with famous models, having a beach house with luxury decoration, becoming a MTV star...) conceals the anxieties that are actually relevant to their lives. This also works for the "fantasy of the eighties" we discuss here: the function of those qualities presented as primitive passions, sincerity, purity, and so on that commentators like Gan Yang associate with the eighties is to conceal the problems that are pertinent to the present-day intellectual situation in China. In other words, what the current intellectual fever for the eighties generates is a fantasmatic framework to project the eighties as a model for present-day intellectual activities, even though the commentators themselves are aware that the model is impossible to emulate because the conditions now are very different.

Just like the post-Stalinist intellectuals in Žižek's account who avoided the problems of the present by revering an idealized "Leninist age," these contemporary Chinese intellectuals who have been reminiscing about the "age of the eighties" also sidestep the problems of the present by *generating highly positive images of the eighties in which these engagements have already been fulfilled*. These imaginary "critical engagements," far from posing a serious threat to the ruling ideology, designate *a supreme form of conformism*, since they saturate and "fill in" what is lacking today. For instance, the total absence of the discussion about the year 1989 in the "fever for the eighties" is a clear illustration of conformism with the state's banning of "June Fourth" as a topic of open discussion.

The "golden picture" of the eighties as a fantasmatic construction thus designates a *cynical gesture*. This cynical gesture is, however, not direct. If an honest cynicism takes the form of statements like "I don't care about social problems" or "They can do whatever they want to do, it's none of my business," then the cynicism of present-day Chinese intellectual discourse is clearly dishonest. This is because it is a cynicism expressed as its very opposite — a cynicism which takes the form of "pseudo-activity," to recall Žižek's term. Intellectuals like Gan Yang discuss the "golden eighties" as if this is equivalent to critical activity. Yet, this can only be pseudo-activity because no effective action is being taken. Thus *talking about "the eighties" serves only to turn the activism of the era into nothing more than a pleasant memory* — which is, of course, in psychoanalytic terms *an obscene enjoyment*.

We can find this pseudo-activity in many of the texts that contributed to this heated discussion of the eighties. Besides those claims already quoted above, I would like to add one more statement made by Gan Yang regarding the intellectual activities of the eighties. According to Gan, what made the eighties special was that intellectuals at that time spoke boldly and without constraint:

> The 1980s is so different from the present: at that time, everybody spoke passionately and directly (*fangsi wuqing*), and there was absolutely no problem [with the way that people spoke] (Gan Yang 2006c: 210).

In this statement Gan perceives that one of today's major "problems" is that people no longer speak the way they did in the eighties. But he merely states this without going further to explain that censorship (as well as "self-censorship") had made it impossible for people to speak their minds after the 1989 Tiananmen protest movement. He also does not discuss the rifts among post-Tiananmen intellectuals and the development of mutually hostile intellectual factions. In fact, as shown in the earlier discussion, Gan Yang's own intellectual stance and writing style changed significantly after 1989. Thus the question that Gan should not excuse himself from is: what makes intellectuals including himself not to speak "passionately and directly" anymore?

Hence, Gan Yang's gesture is that of cynicism *qua* pseudo-activity: he dismisses the present-day problems by actively praising the eighties as a (fantasmatic) golden age, and conceals his own cynical gesture by actively criticizing other people for being cynical. When talking about today's cynicism, Žižek points out insightfully that

> [T]he formula of cynicism is no longer the classic Marxian "they do not know it, but they are doing it"; it is "they know very well what they are doing, yet they are doing it" (Žižek 1994b: 8).

In other words, "The cynical subject is quite aware of the distance between the ideological mask and the social reality, but he nonetheless still insists upon the mask" (Žižek 1989: 29). This exactly describes the cynical core of the recent discourse of the eighties. For Gan Yang "not speaking and writing passionately" is a big problem of contemporary Chinese intellectual discourse, yet he does not tackle the issue in the passionate and direct style he praises but turns instead to reminisce about the eighties. In other words, *Gan recognizes the perceived problem, yet he does not address it.* The perverse phenomenon thus emerges: these intellectuals *speak about* "speaking passionately and directly" but show little of this attitude in their own speech.

This "golden picture" of the 1980s is therefore not only a *fantasmatic construction*, but also manifests a *cynical gesture* implicitly adopted by many contemporary Chinese intellectuals: instead of practicing those qualities they now attribute to the age of the eighties *right here and now*, and by doing that, bluntly stating what is lacking (what makes the present "less and less interesting") in an attempt to change reality, leading contemporary intellectuals such as Gan Yang choose to be nostalgic. The cynical message is: at least we "had" it all (in the eighties), although "the present is becoming less and less interesting." Isn't this precisely one of fantasy's perverse operations aiming at: to provide us an access to a harmonious and consistent reality by presenting what we should strive for as already accomplished?

This is a type of cynicism shared by different factions of contemporary Chinese intellectuals and its main purpose seems to be to enable these intellectuals to present themselves as cultural heroes. As an example, Gan Yang repeatedly refers to himself in his recent interviews as a "talented man" (*caizi*) and claims that he was among the most "influential" figures of the 1980, and the intellectual group led by him was dominant in producing intellectual ideas. In short, Gan depicts the *Culture: China and the World* group as a group of famous heroes by proudly mentioning lots of trivial facts to show the extent of the social influence and popularity of himself and his group (Gan Yang 2006c: 203, 208–209, 215, 219). The logic implied in such cynicism which poses itself as heroism is: what is wrong is not us, but the *present* external reality (see, we were able to realize our talents in the 1980s)... In terms of the perverse operation of evading engaging critically with the present by generating fantasmatic scenarios in which such engagement has already been "made," aren't these contemporary intellectuals repeating the typical practice of Confucian scholar-officials, as analyzed in the Introduction: instead of actualizing the Confucian ideals *here and now*, they provide fantasmatic narratives about the "three ancient epochs" (*sandai*, i.e. the dynasties of Xia, Shang, Zhou) and the "golden ages" of Han, Tang, Song, ages in which those ideals have been already "achieved"?

For these intellectuals the present is thus not a time for action but merely for reminiscence — ironically, such a cynical attitude is precisely what turns the present into a "less and less interesting time." Hence contrary to Gan's claim that "people all feel that the present is becoming less and less interesting," what we should note is that because of these very (cynical) *people*, "the present is becoming less and less interesting." Apropos of the style of intellectual discussions, the key problem is not that people today generally no longer speak *straightforwardly* but that *the people* making this claim are themselves the ones who are not straightforward.

Now, through the above analysis we are able to once again reach the perverse core of this intellectual fever for the eighties: *let us talk more about "the 1980s" in order to distance ourselves from the activism that characterized "the 1980s."* By discussing it in very vague terms and by simply upholding it as an abstract ideal against which "the present day" can be judged as inferior, Gan Yang's accounts of the eighties effectively covered his cynical cancellation of the pursuit of democracy that had characterized the intellectual endeavors of the late 1980s. The image of the eighties depicted in this recent fever is thus a fantasmatic scene retroactively constructed. It does not at all encourage people to contemplate the reasons for the absence of (truly subversive) intellectual activism in the post-1989 era. In this recent intellectual fever, there is little beyond nostalgia.

Before I conclude this part of the study, I must ask: why the eighties? In my view, the age of the 1980s — a recent past indeed — possesses two "unique" qualities, which enabled it to provide a *fantasmatic space* for contemporary Chinese intellectuals to fulfill the "hallucinatory realizations" of their critical engagements: (1) the distance between the 1980s and the present-day is great enough for contemporary intellectuals to exercise their "poetic" (*shiyi*, a phrase Gan Yang employed to describe intellectual activities of the 1980s) reconstruction of the era; and (2) this distance between the 1980s and the present-day is near enough so that most contemporary Chinese intellectuals would have no trouble in recalling that decade — those who speak of the "golden" age of the eighties are still able to present their fantasmatic versions based on selective use of well-known facts about the eighties. This is an ideological operation that can be likened to computer-programmed "Virtual Reality" games (electronic games, PC games, online games, etc.). These VR games are able to provide a similar fantasmatic space precisely because (1) they are "virtual" enough for game players to do things they are not allowed to do in "reality" (such as killing); and (2) they also provide "reality"-alike scenarios in which players are allowed to do all sorts of "role-playing."

In Place of a Conclusion Traversing the Fantasy

Hegel's Two Faces

To date, English and Chinese studies of contemporary Chinese thought (e.g. Zhang Xudong 2008; Xu Jilin 2011) have focused mainly on the *positive content* (various claims, statements, propositions, slogans, etc.) of the texts produced by contemporary mainland thinkers. They are not concerned with the *underlying forces* that have driven the changing contour of post-Maoist intellectuality — from the "homogeneity of attitude" toward modernization in the 1980s to recent Chinese knowledge production toward identifying China's civilizational uniqueness. Throughout this book, I have sought to respond to the question: Is there a hidden mechanism at work in the writings of contemporary Chinese thinkers, shaping their way of thinking and feeding their passions and disagreements? As we have discussed, Chinese intellectuality in the post-Maoist time has shifted its central theme from Western-style modernization in the 1980s to the discourse of China's civilizational subjectivity in the late 2000s. However, is this shift really as drastic as it appears? Is there any hidden logic or common denominator that underlies the post-Maoist Chinese intellectuality from the modernization discourse of the 1980s down to today's "China model" discourse?

Such "invisible framework" that implicitly confines and frames the coordinates of contemporary Chinese thought, perhaps can be properly described as "Hegel's two faces." As Frederick Beiser insightfully notes,

> [I]t is necessary to recognize that Hegel's philosophy of history operates on two levels, one horizontal and the other vertical. The horizontal level comprises the specific circumstances of a nation, its economic, geographic,

> climactic, and demographic conditions. Since each nation must adapt to these circumstances, and since these circumstances are unique, each nation will have unique and incommensurable values. Its constitution and ethos will be appropriate to, and therefore justifiable in the light of, its circumstances. The vertical level consists in world-history as a whole and the contribution each nation has made toward the realization of its end. It is clear that, from this perspective, different cultures will have different degrees of good and evil according to how they promote progress toward the self-consciousness of freedom. (Beiser 1993: 279–280)

Interestingly enough, contemporary Chinese intellectuality is "trapped" to oscillate between these two Hegelian propositions. On the one hand, the various discourses in the Chinese intellectual scene — the orthodox Marxist doctrine that is still powerfully present in Chinese intellectuality, "China's modernization project" initiated in the 1980s, and the "globalization (of liberal democracy)" discourse that has blossomed since the mid-1990s — all accord with the vertical level of Hegel's thought. Thus, despite sharp oppositions, these discourses nonetheless all share one of Hegel's two faces — a teleological "face" of Universal History. That is to say, they all metaphysically posit, to employ Alexandre Kojève's term, an End-State that signals the end of History, and in turn, the Way to that End-State (be it socialist construction, modernization with Chinese characteristics, or the "joining-rails" into globalization concept). On the other hand, there have been, especially since the mid-1990s, various nationalistic discourses in mainland China, with demands for "recognition" of China's cultural-civilizational uniqueness, socio-historical distinctiveness, as well as its specific economic, geographic, climactic, demographic conditions, etc. Such discourses accord with the horizontal level of Hegel's thought. Or to put differently, they adopt Hegel's particularistic "face" of historically unique "characteristics."

The rise of the "China model" discourse in recent years, with its insistence on a geo-political naming of thought, seems to demonstrate an "eventual" prevalence of the second "face." But the unique feature of contemporary Chinese intellectuality is that it always has the structural possibility to "face metamorphosis" (*bianlian*): are we not witnessing that some advocates of the "China model" have, with (inflated) confidence, started to argue that this model is the "correct way in the human world" which *chaoyue* (transcends, goes beyond) ideological disputes, the "most successful way" to achieve social control and elimination of socio-economic crises, i.e. the Way to ultimate Social Harmony? For China-model advocates such as Pan Wei, this model is "a theoretical explanation of the way to success (*chenggong zhi lu*) that the People's Republic of China has taken in the last sixty years." Pan wrote in the editorial introduction of the influential book entitled *The China Model: Reading the Sixty Years of the People's Republic of China* published in 2009 that "The greatest nation in the world has successfully advanced [along that way] for sixty years. This fact assures its capacity to contribute fresh knowledge to the entire human race. Only those who lack self-esteem and self-confidence would think otherwise." (Pan 2009: 3)

According to Gan Yang, Chinese civilization will dominate the world in the twenty-first century and form a "new cosmopolitanism" (*xin shijiezhuyi*). Founded on Confucian concept of *Tianxia*, this "new cosmopolitanism" will eventually replace the "old cosmopolitanism" based on Western centrism and hegemony (Gan Yang 2012a: 189). Also, together with the Beijing-based philosopher Liu Xiaofeng (who was in the 1980s a key member of the *Culture: China and the World* group), Gan called for a thorough re-evaluation and re-interpretation of the Chinese classics by introducing Leo Strauss's obscure technique of "esoteric" reading, with the belief that ancient Chinese wisdom contains intellectual recourses to overcome the crisis of modernity (see, for example, Gan Yang 2003b; Liu Xiaofeng 2002). Gan Yang's view on Chinese civilization has been resonated by many recent intellectual and scholarly works. For example, the Beijing-based literary critic Mo Luo claims in his influential book *China Standing Up* published in 2010 that "The Chinese people will unify the whole human race politically in the near future by establishing a world government" (Mo Luo 2010: 255). The Shanghai-based philosopher Chen Yun, a specialist on classic Chinese thought, interprets the "China Way" as a "universal way discovered in China" rather than merely a "particular way featured by Chinese characteristics" (quoted from Xu Jilin 2011: 206). A group of young (neo)Confucian scholars recently published a book praised by commentators as a Confucian manifesto for universal values, in which the authors claim that universal values are necessarily supported and secured by wealth and might; hence "lacking wealth and might, small countries have no need to talk about universal values. On the contrary, China *qua* a great country with rising economic power and long-standing historical civilization, must have its own universal values." (Zeng Yi and Guo Xiaodong eds. 2013: 25) What is clear in such formulations is that the "China way" or the "China model," just like the now half-forgotten modernization discourse, is expansive in conception. The economic rise of the People's Republic in the last decade has brought a rapid resurgence of national pride and "civilizational confidence" to such a level that those Chinese thinkers start to publicly preach the "China model" as an advanced Way or even a new universal or at least universalizable Way.

The following argument offered by Chong Ming apropos of the discourse of China's civilizational subjectivity, is pertinent to my analysis of contemporary Chinese intellectual production: Chong points out that such discourse relies on the double connotations of the word "civilization." As an important Western conceptual invention, "civilization" has been raised first and foremost in contrast to barbarianism.[1] However, in the last several decades, with the rise of multiculturalism and relativism in the intellectual landscape, the dichotomy of civilization/barbarianism has been significantly blurred, and the concept is now widely used to denote various long-lasting historico-cultural traditions. "Barbarian tradition" in this new sense can also be seen as a civilization. Whilst the expression "modern civilization" evokes the term in its first connotation (i.e. its opposition to barbarianism), the expression "Chinese civilization" seems to appropriate its second sense (civilization as historico-cultural tradition). Chong nonetheless urges us to ponder on the very way "Chinese civilization" is employed by Gan Yang and his followers: according to Chong, these promoters of China's civilizational subjectivity use illegitimately the term in both senses. He writes:

---

[1] Chong argues that the concept was invented in eighteenth-century Europe. Voltaire and other Enlightenment thinkers invented the narrative of civilization in order to strengthen the historical legitimacy of Enlightenment values.

> If referring to a civilization in its multiculturalist sense, then Chinese civilization is merely one among many existing or vanished civilizations in the world. However, what today's proponents of the revival of Chinese civilization long for is apparently a civilization in the sense of value-superiority (*jiazhi youyuelun*). What, then, is Chinese civilization superior to? Here, Western modernity undoubtedly plays the role of its referential counterpart. (Chong 2012: 17)

Chong's argument is, in other words, that the discourse of China's civilizational subjectivity implies a new dichotomy of civilization/barbarianism, with Western modernity (Western civilization) being this time the barbarian "other." However, instead of providing substantive, solid arguments to illustrate in what way Chinese civilization is superior to its Western counterpart, Gan and his followers simply resort to the double connotations of the term "civilization." There is nothing other than a play of word. For Chong, such illegitimate use of the term "civilization" proves that the discourse of China's civilizational subjectivity is nothing but a "new ideological myth" (Chong 2012: 14–15). We can nonetheless go one step further: since the fantasmatic revival of Chinese civilization (i.e. the "Great Dragon fantasy") functions as a *generative mechanism* of contemporary Chinese intellectual production, is not such "illegitimate use of 'civilization'" precisely that which has been framing the *fundamental coordinates* of contemporary Chinese thought — taking into account all those vehement debates between intellectual camps, as well as those radical shifting-sides of some thinkers such as Gan Yang over the last two decades? In short, *it is the fundamental fantasy of reviving Chinese civilization, entangled with these two meanings of "civilization," that sets in motion the "face metamorphosis" of contemporary Chinese intellectuality.*

In this precise sense, one can say that contemporary Chinese intellectuality is fundamentally framed and supported by the "Great Dragon fantasy," that all the intellectual trends discussed in this book are mutations, or partial embodiments, of the same fundamental fantasmatic narrative, with the radically shifting accents.[2] This book is essentially a study

[2]Bruce Fink points out from the angle of clinical practices that the analysand can have many "permutations of the fundamental fantasy, usually presenting one facet

on — to paraphrase Žižek (2005a: 113) — "many variations of some underlying 'fundamental' fantasy." Within the fantasmatic scenario of the "Great Dragon fantasy," China's civilizational core (i.e. Chineseness) is staged as lost, deprived, thus in turn effectively functions as the object-cause of desire, the object of fantasy. Lacan is indeed right to link castration to desire: "Castration means that *jouissance* must be refused, so that it can be reached on the inverted ladder of the Law of desire" (Lacan 1977: 324; see also Fink 1997: 193). Fantasy performs the very act of the cut of symbolic castration by staging "the very narrative of this primordial loss." Through such story the subject is allowed to enter the symbolic order (Žižek 1998: 202–203, 209). Fantasy is a primordial lie, covering up the impossible Real. Hence, as I have discussed in Chapter 1, the magic of fantasy resides in that it operates via the logic of "there is no such thing, yet it is true": regardless the actual existence of the almighty "Great Dragon," resuscitating its lost glory is taken as *a shared mission* of contemporary Chinese intellectuals. The desire to restore the fullness of Chinese civilization does not need the support of facts, because it is staged in the fantasmatic space. Attempts to clarify what China's civilizational core is, instead of strengthening the desire to (re)gain it, can only lead to the awkward — ultimately traumatic — experience of the evaporation of enjoyment (phallic *jouissance*). Such preference for ignorance is phrased by Lacan as "a will not to know" (Lacan sometimes even calls it "a passion not to know," see Fink 1997: 7).[3] What is really worthy of my desire cannot be positively specified, fully articulated. "It is never possible for the subject fully to assume (in the sense of symbolic integration) the fantasmatic kernel of his or her being. When one approaches it too often, or

---

of that fundamental fantasy." And the goal of analytic works is to pin down "a 'single' fundamental fantasy, a fantasy that plays an important role in structuring the analysand's relationships with significant others in her life," and further "to bring her to modify that fundamental fantasy, to reconfigure or 'traverse' it" (Fink 2007: 124).

[3]The will not to know, as Fink interprets, is a will "refusing to know about the why and wherefore of *jouissance*." Hence, as Fink further notes, "Whereas philosophy — at least Hegel's philosophy — situates the subject on the basis of a relationship to knowledge, psychoanalysis situates the subject on the basis of her lack of knowledge, her inscience. This, in its own way, seems to be a relationship to knowledge via negation." (Fink 2004: 108)

when one comes to close to it, what occurs is the *aphanisis* of the subject: the subject loses his or her symbolic consistency, the subject disintegrates" (Žižek 1998: 209). To clarify the positive content of the object of one's desire, thus can be the worst, most humiliating kind of violence, "a violence that undermines the very basis of one's identity (of the 'self-image')" (Žižek 1998: 209), for such act intrudes the fantasmatic space that fundamentally sustains one's life, and dissolves the magical operation of fantasy (i.e. sublimation): once the content of the fantasmatic object is positively specified, its limitations will be revealed, and hence, its "magical appeal" will vanish: since it's just A (and/or, B, C, [...]), what is so fascinating about it (them)? Or, more radically, since there is no such Thing (except mere stories and myths), why is it still "true" for you? This is why, as discussed in Chapter 1, there is a "characteristic lack" of clear definition or articulation of "Chinese" or "Chinese characteristics" in post-Maoist Sinophone discourse. What the "Great Dragon fantasy" provides is precisely a powerful fundamental scenario that organically and primordially connects a contemporary "Chinese" person (a will not to know) with "China" (the nation-Thing). Through his/her fruitless pursuit of the elusive *objet petit a* (forever chasing but never attaining it), the subject nonetheless "achieves a fantasmatic sense of wholeness, completeness, fulfillment, and well-being" (Fink 1995: 60). Thus, the recognition that there is no such Thing, that the *objet petit a* merely functions as a formal frame embedded in the fantasmatic scenario, a frame "confer[ring] consistency on our desire" (Žižek 1998: 214), would mark the very moment of such fantasy being traversed.

The "Great Dragon fantasy," like all other fantasmatic formation, has two modes: the blissful, beatific mode (the narrative of a state without disturbances, the state of things "before the Fall") and the disturbing, horrific mode (the story explaining why things went wrong). The former is embodied in the call for the Dragon (China) to rub its eyes to regain clear-sightedness, the latter in the vision of the West's ongoing intrusions. The 1980s New Enlightenment discourse of China's modernization belongs apparently to the former mode, offering a fantasmatic picture of China on the correct path towards its perfection. In the post-1989 era, dominant intellectual discourses such as the New Left, nationalism, etc. moved to the other side of the fantasmatic realm. China is depicted in those narratives as suffering from external intrusion, be it the invasion of global capitalism, or the "total isolation" created by "Western" enemies. As Stavrakakis tells us, "Even this horrifying picture of the Other is preferable from the state of uncertainty regarding the lack and the desire of the Other" (Stavrakakis 1999: 151). In the 2000s, with China's economic rise, the fantasmatic field has changed once again — this time, of course, shifting back to the beatific mode. In the discourse of the China model, China is imagined as having regained its clear-sightedness, and advancing on the correct road to its civilizational perfection. Note that the CCP's recent official discourse has heavily echoed the discourse of China's civilizational subjectivity. At the Eighteenth National Congress of the Communist Party of China held in November 2012, Hu Jintao asked all Party members and all Chinese citizens to acquire "three confidences" — "confidence on path, confidence on theory, and confidence on institutions" (*daolu zixin, lilun zixin, zhidu zixin*), which reminds us of the appeal for "civilizational confidence" made by Gan Yang, Wang Hui, and other proponents of the China way. Two weeks after the Congress, the new General Party Secretary Xi Jinping proposed that the Chinese people should pursue "the Chinese Dream," explicitly referencing and contrasting "the American Dream." Xi defines "the Chinese Dream" as a dream about "the great renaissance of the Chinese nation."[4] What is psychoanalytically interesting is, of course, the fantasy-frame at work in the recent official slogans: is not "the Chinese Dream," replacing the "communist dream" in Mao's era, exactly another name for the "Great Dragon fantasy"? While the 1980s intellectual discourse of China's modernization was backed up by the CCP's ideological campaign (four modernizations, etc.), this recent China model discourse also seems to have been adopted by the Party's official discourse. Let us not forget: these two discourses also share another feature in common — i.e., both generate "beatific effects" in the fantasmatic space. Hence, opposing each other at the symbolic level (the level of positive content, i.e. propositions, claims, arguments, statements,

[4]See *Zhongguo tese shehuizhuyi lilun tixi xuexi duben* (A Learning Reader of the Theoretical System of Socialism with Chinese Characteristics), *shibada xiuding ben* (the 18th National Congress version), Beijing: The Central Party School Publishing House, 2012: 167–174.

slogans, etc.), these two discourses — two representatives of the distinctive feature of post-Maoist intellectuality that can be characterized as "Hegel's two faces" — nonetheless share at the fantasmatic level the same mode. That, too, explains why "face metamorphosis" is structurally possible in contemporary Sinophone discursive production.

Hence, once focusing our attention onto the "spectral" space of fantasy, we are able to detect in a very productive way the "invisible" *generative mechanisms* of contemporary Chinese thought. A further Lacanian point is: the beatific and horrific modes of fantasy are exactly the front and back of the same coin. "[T]he price you must pay for sticking, clinging to the first fantasy is the second, dirty fantasy" (Žižek 2005a: 63). Are not both the 1980s China's modernization discourse and the 2000s China's civilizational subjectivity discourse (two representatives of the beatific mode of fantasy) also entailing fundamentally the element of some identified disturbing obstacles or barriers — in the first case, the traditional form of culture, and in the second case, the post-Maoist project of modernization/Westernization — preventing us from achieving the fullness? Fantasy is never simply the fantasy of a harmonious state of things, but fundamentally a narrative of why it went wrong. "Fantasy provides a *rationale* for the inherent deadlock of desire" (Žižek 1998: 209–210). The effectiveness of the horrific mode of fantasy is the condition for the beatific fantasy to maintain its hold: the latter has to have recourse to the former in order to explain what has been responsible for hindering its full realization (i.e. the final acquisition of the object of desire). The "Great Dragon fantasy" is exactly such a fantasmatic formation, entailing structurally both beatific and horrific modes. All post-Maoist intellectual discourses discussed in this study, discourses "trapped" within the two Hegelian terrains, can thus be regarded as partial embodiments or permutations of the "Great Dragon fantasy."

Fantasy teaches us how to desire by letting us know what the Other wants from us, i.e., what the Other's desire is. As Fink observes, "The unknown nature of the Other's desire is unbearable here; you prefer to assign it an attribute, any attribute, rather than let it remain an enigma" (Fink 1997: 61). Fantasy creates a scenario in which the mystery of the Other's desire is unwrapped, the object of its desire identified. In turn, fantasy effectively offers us the object of "*our* desire": that which makes the Other full (e.g. the fullness of Chinese civilization, an almighty Dragon without deformity), can magically also make us full (being a Chinese, a descendant of the Dragon). In this very sense, "The Other's desire provides the minimum of fantasmatic identity to the subject" (Žižek 1998: 196). The missing piece that can "fill up" the Other's lack, is also magically transformed in the fantasmatic space into the *agalma* (hidden treasure) of our lives. Hence, although the contour of post-Maoist Chinese intellectuality has changed significantly, the fundamental fantasmatic scene functioning as its structuring mechanism — i.e. restoring China's fullness, living as a proper Chinese — has nonetheless remained rather unchanged. This fundamental scene is what I call the "Great Dragon fantasy" throughout this study. Adrian Johnston is right to argue that "the obsession with origins is the defining feature of fundamental fantasies" (Johnston 2008: 34). We were born — or as Heidegger would say, "thrown" — into a world not of our own making, and the fundamental fantasy offers us the story about our "origin" (e.g. descendants of the Great Dragon), which in turn bestows on us the underlying meaning of our lives. Thus with the decaying of the fundamental fantasy, we literally lose the coordinates of our lives, and the traumatic experience of the "loss of reality" ensues. The primary function of this "Great Dragon fantasy," is to manufacture the desire for an imaginary fullness of China (whether China as a civilization or as a nation) and to keep it alive, always running. Once produced in the fantasmatic space, desire seeks nothing other than its own continuation. Fink is right to stress that "Desire does not seek satisfaction; rather, it pursues its own continuation and furtherance — it merely seeks to go on desiring" (Fink 1997: 51). How, then, does fantasy keep the movement of desire forever going on? The answer is: fantasy provides not only narratives about "origins," but also stories about the primordial "loss" or "deprivation." Through such horrific narratives, fantasy explains why the satisfaction has been delayed, why the desired object is still out of our reach.

Moreover, according to Lacanian psychoanalysis, the agency of the superego also plays an important role in keeping desire constantly alive. Desire is always accompanied by superego injunctions: "the superego pressure demonstrates that we effectively are guilty of betraying our desire" (Žižek 2006b: 81). In the context of Chinese cultural tradition, the embodiment of such superego agency is precisely intellectuals' moral responsibility discussed in the Introduction. The personal responsibility for *Tianxia* (all under Heaven), which was traditionally assigned to scholars within the Confucian tradition of premodern China, has been carried through into the twentieth century and since in the adjusted form of moral obligation for China's (national or civilizational) perfection. The Lacanian point is: nothing forces anyone to enjoy except the superego. The superego is the imperative of *jouissance* — Enjoy! The Freudian superego, argues Žižek, is "the cruel and sadistic ethical agency which bombards us with impossible demands and then gleefully observes our failure to meet them. No wonder, then, that Lacan posited an equation between *jouissance* and superego: to enjoy is not a matter of following one's spontaneous tendencies; it is rather something we do as a kind of weird and twisted ethical duty." (Žižek 2006b: 79) Superego as the ethical agency, performs itself in the form of an impossible *gaze*,[5] for which — the point of view from which — I, in my activity depicted in the fantasmatic narrative, appear not only in a likeable way, but also truly enjoying the activity. Such enjoyment commanded and supervised by the superego agency is, of course, what Lacan calls phallic *jouissance*, or more vividly, "the *jouissance* of the idiot," for it becomes attainable only through the subject taking the Other's desire as his/her own.[6]

Žižek's favorite example of this relationship between the (fantasizing) subject and the superego agency, is — as always — distasteful, but nonetheless powerful: the pornographic scene. Say, during the shooting, a female porn star does her best to appear enjoying the anal penetration. Who is commanding her to "enjoy"? Rather than the repulsive director or the male star who is doing the act to her, the Lacanian answer is: the imaginary future spectator. It is his fantasmatic gaze functioning as the obscene superego agency, that constantly examines whether she fully

[5]As discussed briefly in the Introduction, rather than the symbolic Law which relies on a set of socio-institutional apparatuses (prison, court, police, etc.) to exercise its regulative power, the superego performs its regulation — exerting repression, passing judgment, establishing taboo, internalizing guilt, etc. — through an invisible (imagined) gaze.

[6]Hence, in terms of real/sacrificed *jouissance*, the superego injunction actually is — "Enjoy as little as possible!"

enjoys herself. The same agency commands her to present herself in the scene as much likable as she can (Žižek 1999b: 92). Are not contemporary Chinese intellectuals playing the same role as the female porn star, in their fantasmatic scene — instead of anal penetration, this time, the scene of restoring the greatness of Chinese civilization? The imaginary embodiment of the superego gaze is, needless to say, the gaze of the future Chinese, who might come across their books. When Chinese intellectuals wrote down such passages "I rejoice that I was born in China since what could be more heartbreaking and also more exhilarating than the glorious revival of a decaying civilization of which so many generations of people have dreamed? And what could be more thrilling than to watch and experience the minutiae and process of this collective dream?" (Wang Hui 1994: 21–22), are they not pathetically repeating exactly what the porn star does — try their best to demonstrate that they are indeed enjoying their activity?[7] The superego injunction "Enjoy!" is obscene precisely because it allows the introduction of our "dirty" fantasy, which provides the very setting for our enjoyment: corresponding to the relationship between desire and lack, enjoyment only derives from a deprived status (e.g. "a decaying civilization").

This Lacanian analysis of superego and enjoyment also shows that the selfless task of restoring China's lost greatness and finding a better future for the Chinese people is itself an utterly *selfish* act of enjoying oneself in the fantasmatic space. "Desire, the element that keeps everything going, is animated by the quest for a lacking/impossible fullness, around the promise of encountering *jouissance*" (Stavrakakis 1999: 45). In the form of fulfilling a moral responsibility to their nation or their culture (under the superego gaze), Chinese intellectuals are nonetheless commanded to pursue in their fantasmatic space an obscene enjoyment. Chinese intellectual inquiry thus can be indeed characterized as *altruistic and selfish at the same time*.[8] The "Great Dragon fantasy" provides the very

[7] *Qingshi liuming* (leaving good reputations in history), one of the powerful intellectual legacies of Confucian scholar-officials, is in this sense a pornographic act at its purest.

[8] Cf. Davies' observation: "They [Chinese intellectuals] write as if they are representing the collective interests of the Chinese people rather than defending their own informed preferences" (Davies 2007: 20).

space for the extremes — Chinese intellectuals' most selfless moral responsibility and their (inner)most selfish interest — magically coinciding with each other. In this sense, the "Great Dragon fantasy" also enables another kind (indeed, an obscene kind) of structural "face metamorphosis" of contemporary Chinese intellectuality, which is rooted this time not in Hegel's philosophy of history, but in its own intellectual heritage — the ethical-laden Confucian thought.

The End of Analysis

In the early 2000s when the "debate between liberals and the New Left" reached its zenith, Xu Jilin, Tong Shijun, and quite a few other scholars appealed for reestablishing "basic consensus" (*jiben gongshi*) in the Sinophone intellectual world through rational dialogues *qua* "communicative actions." Following Jürgen Habermas' theory, these Chinese thinkers argue that the only force that could prevent "these diverse intellectual trends, camps, and ideologies emerging since the 1990s from moving towards radical extremes" is the "force of better argument." In their view, the faculty of reason — in the form of "communicative reason" — would soothe and eventually remove the distinctively vitriolic and ferocious style of exchanges among contemporary Chinese intellectuals (Xu Jilin 2011: 63–64; see also Tong Shijun 2007: 223–241). However, such endeavor waned in the late 2000s, along with the Sinophone appetite for Habermas' communicative theory.[9] As we have already seen, in today's China, intellectuals drastically disagree with each other over, and thus are deeply divided by, "the problem of China" (*Zhongguo wenti*, a frequently employed phrase referring not only to China's current socio-political problems, but also to the visions about its future path, and evaluations about its dynastic and Maoist past).

[9] A critical discussion of Chinese intellectuals' effort of reestablishing consensus can be found in Gloria Davies' essay "Anticipating Community, Producing Dissent: The Politics of Recent Chinese Intellectual Praxis." Her another essay, entitled "Habermas in China: Theory as Catalyst," provides a very good critical analysis of the Sinophone reception and appropriation of Habermas' theory of communicative action (see Davies 2002: 1–35; 2007b: 61–85).

During those heated debates examined in this book (even during vehement "spitting wars"), what was going on is that besides resorting to sentiments (nationalistic or other kinds), moral accusation, etc.,[10] participants very often did demonstrate "reasons" for their respective propositions; however, the "reasons" from opposing camps are, also very often, fundamentally incompatible. There is no common frame or ground determining which one is "the better argument." The arguments proffered by one intellectual camp would not be recognized by its rival camp as "rational" or "reasonable" unless the latter is willing to shift its fundamental perspective, to see things through the former's "lenses."[11] Such fundamental perspective is called in psychoanalysis *fantasy*.[12]

[10]One of psychoanalysis's anti-Habermasian points is that during the intersubjective communication there is never only "reason" in play; other "irrational" psychological elements – e.g. emotions (love, hate, envy, nationalistic sentiments, etc.), and more fundamentally, the unconscious — are also there, playing certain roles, even the dominant role in leading the exchanges. Hence the "public sphere" would never be purely a "sphere of reasons." In terms of public deliberation, there are much easier ways to manipulate the "public opinion" than persuasion through reasons (for instance, resorting to nationalistic sentiments).

[11]Indeed such phenomenon happens frequently in our everyday life. For example, within the sphere of family, the husband and wife inevitably quarrel over some big or small issues. Very often the husband has his "reasons" and the wife has hers. No one can persuade the other party by relying on the "force of better argument" because there is no common ground or "denominator" between those "reasons," which can determine which side has the "better argument." Another example would be today's global capitalist order: from the angle of neo-liberal ideology, this whole system is perfectly rational. Theorists of rational choice theory, game theory and other schools have developed various quasi-scientific models to demonstrate that. But if viewed from an "external" angle, it is entirely crazy. The 2008 global financial meltdown explicitly demonstrated that today's globalized casino capitalism is most likely creating a new Titanic — only this time everyone will sink with it.

[12]Let us extent this argument to politics, which is essentially *asymmetry*: "rational dialogues" between the powerful and the powerless, very often, do not have expected results. If the powerless accept the perspective of the people in power, accept their "reasons," they have already lost the battle — the realm of the political is foreclosed. In Marxian terminology, the proletariat would be doomed to be forever enslaved if accepting the bourgeois ideology and "reasoning" on its ground (for example, seeing "surplus value" as legitimate "profit"). The Habermasian model of communication is only possible when all the participants share the same fundamental perspective. (I partly owe this point to Jacques Rancière, who shared with me his insights on Habermas during a private conversation.)

Let us now sketch once again the basic line of Lacan's theorization on fantasy, and our Lacanian analysis of contemporary Chinese intellectuality. According to Lacanian psychoanalysis, fantasy obscures our lack of access to the Real by presenting an effect of fullness that we experience as reality. Through fantasy, we experience the illusion of a coherent world. "When our fundamental fantasy is shattered, we experience the 'loss of reality'" (Žižek 1999b: 122). Thus, we gain access to reality through fantasy in the form of "looking awry." One of fantasy's most crucial functions is to stage the setting of our desire, to teach us how to desire; another major function is to sustain the neurotic illusion that *jouissance* would be attainable if it were not deprived or prohibited. These two functions are inherently correlated: the very deprivation/prohibition spurs the desire to attain full *jouissance*. While promising the attainability of *jouissance* (beatific mode of fantasy), fantasy at the same time identifies enemies or obstacles "responsible" for the constant failure of realizing such promise (horrific mode of fantasy). Through the operation of fantasy, the ontological impossibility (of encountering full *jouissance*, of mastering the Real) is covered up, and reduced into a series of contingent failures.

To apply this concept of fantasy to contemporary Chinese intellectual discourse, it is clear that China's "essence" (which entails its fullness and greatness) is fantasmatically presented as essential yet lost. The fantasmatic formation that I refer to in this study as the "Great Dragon fantasy" — with all its variations or partial embodiments discussed in each chapter — always contains the following two key parts (beatific and horrific modes): (1) the metaphysical presupposition that there is a Chinese essence to which one can remain true; (2) the deprived status of such essence (by the West, feudalist "ultrastable" structure, Maoist practices, the post-Maoist modernization project, or global capitalism, etc.) It is this missing object (the elusive Lacanian *objet petit a* as the object-cause of desire) that "stands-in" for and "positivizes" the fundamental lack in the Other in the form of a traumatic loss/deprivation preventing China from achieving its true fullness and greatness. As Stavrakakis notes, "Fantasy creates this illusion by offering us the *objet petit a* as embodying, in its absence, this fullness" (Stavrakakis 1999: 53). The trick of the operation of fantasy is that the attainment of such object is always *deferred*. The *objet petit a* is structurally elusive. "The object can only function as object of desire when it is absent." "Whenever we reach the object of our desire, any *jouissance* we get is nothing compared to what we were expecting" (Stavrakakis 1999: 45, 49).

In the 1980s, this fantasy of resuscitating China's greatness is embodied in the New Enlightenment enterprise of China's modernization. Various intellectual groups appeared united in what Xu Jilin calls the "homogeneity of attitude": they shared a common belief that Western-style modernization was the only path forward for China. This modernization narrative enabled them to imagine a coherent post-Maoist reality. "[F]or humans, reality needs to be coherent, and since it does not seem to be by itself it has to be constructed as a coherent harmonious whole (at least *a harmonious whole in the making*)" (Stavrakakis 1999: 63, emphasis mine). The modernization discourse of the 1980s precisely creates a fantasmatic vision of China advancing towards its perfection. It was this shared modernization fantasy that allowed the "homogeneity of attitude" to be formed.

After the 1989 Tiananmen incident, this fantasmatic promise of China's modernization was broken: the government-led modernization project lost its credibility in the intellectual circles; the optimistic 1980s imaginings of the imminent arrival of democracy collapsed. There was relative silence in the Chinese intellectual world from 1989 to 1992. This period of "aphasia" (*shiyu*), as it was subsequently called, is an indication that the passion with which intellectuals desired modernization in the 1980s was vaporized by their traumatic encounter with the violence of the Party-state. Since then the phrase "Tiananmen" (or "June Fourth") has become discussed by many Chinese intellectuals as the moment that modernization toward democracy turned out to be an illusion.

After 1989, Chinese intellectuals had trouble claiming the collective identity and subjecthood that they frequently used in the 1980s. Rather they now regard themselves as divided into different camps. In the post-Tiananmen era, many intellectuals perceived themselves as facing the question of "whither China."[13] They became highly conscious of the antagonisms among them. As illustrated in previous chapters, intellectuals engaged in fierce struggles for discursive hegemony. A few influential

[13] Cf. Zhang Xudong ed. 2001.

intellectuals' effort of reestablishing consensus through rational dialogues was eventually fruitless because there is no common "rational ground" upon which competing visions and proposals can be judged by the "force of better argument." A number of discourses prevailing in the post-Tiananmen Chinese intellectual scene including postmodernism, liberalism, the "New Left," nationalism, the "China model," etc., altogether have produced continuous vehement debates — very often, in the form of "spitting wars" — among intellectuals and intellectual camps. From the Lacanian psychoanalytic point of view, such debates can be explained as caused by a "clash of fantasies": after the withering of the fantasmatic narrative of China's modernization, Chinese intellectuality in the post-Tiananmen era became characterized by antagonistic fantasies. These fantasmatic projections about China's reality and its future path are not only incompatible but are used by rival groups to exert influence over others. As argued from the Lacanian vantage point, by defending their different narratives about China, contemporary Chinese intellectuals are actually defending their own sense of reality. This characteristic of post-Tiananmen thought has produced highly unusual hospitality among intellectuals, and turned the Sinophone intellectual world into a nasty battle-zone, for fantasies are extremely sensitive to the intrusion of others.

Thus, the post-Tiananmen Chinese intellectuality is not any more characterized by and represented as a homogeneous and unitary intellectual movement. Rather, it became represented by intellectual clashes over different propositions. These propositions, quite contrary to the optimistic scenarios of future success produced in the 1980s, can be understood as offering highly incompatible — and thus highly competing — visions of China's future path. They are, as we have seen throughout this study, frequently likened to a list of competing "choices," ranging from liberal proposals of globalization, marketization, democratization, "New Leftist" constructions of Chinese modernity, to postmodern, nationalistic, or "civilizationalistic" versions of "Chineseness." In other words, through those vehement debates in the post-Tiananmen intellectual arena, China as a collective Subject seems to have a few options at hands: moving back to China's civilizational tradition, merging into the liberal global community, re-inventing socialist values and learning from the Maoist legacy, or reconstructing Chinese modernity in other ways.

In 2003, a book on contemporary Chinese thought was published by Verso. This is a collection of post-Tiananmen intellectual views including essays by Wang Hui, Gan Yang, Zhu Xueqin, Qin Hui, and many others. The title of this edited volume indeed embodies the intellectual mood of the late 1990s and 2000s: *One China, Many Paths*.[14] The question here, however, is: Is it sufficient to simply *choose* one or several of these "many paths"?

What is at stake here, representing itself as an *intellectual dilemma*, is that what is being presented as a series of "choices" are really optional stories aimed at making something positive out of the tragedy of 1989 Tiananmen. Yet, the antagonism among these many different paths reflects not so much a variety of paths within the "one China" but indeed a discursive struggle for hegemony within a set of pre-given symbolic coordinates (China's cultural tradition, Maoist practice, Western ideologies and so on and so forth).[15] From a Lacanian psychoanalytic perspective, these can be properly described as a set of fantasmatic constructions that seek to resolve the anxiety of "worrying about China" (to quote again Gloria Davies' phrase). They are reactions to the indecidability of China's future, in a society where it is no longer possible for intellectuals to imagine themselves as united in their approach to the future. Thus, the recent intellectual fever about the eighties offers a retroactive fantasm of intellectual unity (a fantasmatic picture of "one China, *one* path"). This idealization of the recent past suggests clearly that the situation of "many paths" competing against each other is disastrous for repairing the fantasmatic space

---

[14]Cf. Wang Chaohua ed. 2003.

[15]That's why Žižek differentiates the "pure antagonism" from "the antagonistic fight in reality": the latter takes place totally within the symbolic field as the antagonism among different (personal/social) *fantasies*, whereas the former marks the *ultimate limit* of the symbolic itself, the *constitutive impossibility* around which the entire socio-symbolic field is structured (Žižek 1990: 252–253). It is the pure antagonism between the symbolic reality and the Real that opens an "impossible" space for an authentic pre-ideological choice, a radical choice that transcends the pre-given symbolic coordinates and requires a suicidal-heroic act of beginning something ultimately NEW.

in a "fundamental" level (i.e. reinventing a powerful fantasmatic scenario that the discourse of China's modernization once forcefully provided).

As I have shown in previous chapters, what the different varieties of Chinese intellectual discourse ("many paths") share in common is the importance they accord to "China" (the "Great Dragon"). What needs to be examined is: What is the relationship between this "many paths" and "one China"? With regard to this "one-China-many-paths" complex, Laclau's famous example of people who live in the neighborhood of a waterfall is quite illuminating:

> They live hearing all their lives the noise of the water falling — that is, the sound is the permanent background of which they are normally unaware. So they do not *actually* hear the noise. But if for any reason the fall of the water suddenly stops one day, they will start hearing that which, strictly speaking, cannot be heard: silence. It is the lack of something that has thus acquired full presence. Now, let us suppose that this silence is intermittently interrupted by noises of different origin that the fall of water had made inaudible before. All these sounds will have a split identity: on the one hand they are specific noises; on the other, they have the equivalent identity of *breaking* the silence. The noises are only equivalent because there is silence; but the silence is only audible as the lack of a former fullness. (Laclau 1996: 93–94)

With the destruction of the modernization discourse which formerly delivered a promise of fullness there emerged various "specific noises" ("many paths") in the post-Tiananmen era. "(One) China," on the other hand, is the empty site of the "silence." All these "specific noises" that appear in what Laclau calls "a chain of equivalences" compete against each other in order to occupy fully the site of silence, that is, to become *the* replacement of "the noise of the water falling," "a former fullness" which disappeared or collapsed. The fierce antagonism among "many paths" over the empty space of "one China" is exactly what Laclau calls "hegemonic struggles."

As Laclau points out himself, this example "however, misses one dimension of the communitarian lack": the silence "is experienced as deprivation." In the case of waterfall, one can be "perfectly indifferent to the presence or absence of the noise of the fall" (Laclau 1996: 94), while in the case of the communitarian lack, the silence itself signifies a *loss*, which triggers searches to retrieve the lost object, or attempts to fill in the emptiness (lack) with other replacements ("a chain of equivalences"). In this sense, the empty site of the silence ("one China") is what structurally generates fierce struggles for hegemony ("many paths"). Laclau notes that "the presence of the lack must itself be signified." He calls it the "empty signifier." In our case, "China" (or the "Chinese people"), of course, is the name for "the absent fullness within the structure." (Similarly, Laclau uses the "unity of the British people" as an example to illustrate the empty signifier that stands for the "name of an absent fullness.") "China," just like the signifier "the British people," cannot be fully exhausted by any concrete content. Such empty signifiers representing the general form of fullness — in Lacanese, phallic master-signifiers — are crucial because without them, as Laclau argues, "political argument would be impossible and political life would be a dialogue between the deaf." Thus, "the totality is essentially required," though it always remains an empty site, structurally impossible for any specific concrete content to fully fill in, for "there is no permanent attachment between the signifier of fullness and the various objects incarnating it" (Laclau 1996: 37, 94–95; Laclau 2004: 300). Laclau's perspective is helpful in terms of tackling the "one China, many paths" complex: the site of "one China" must be posited as an essential idea, though it remains structurally empty and cannot be fully exhausted by any of those "many paths."

In their criticism of Laclau's work, Jason Glynos and Yannis Stavrakakis see the "non-encounter" between Laclau and Lacan at the level of *jouissance*, fantasy, and *objet petit a* as an unfortunate deficiency in Laclau's theory of hegemony (Glynos and Stavrakakis 2004: 209–213). From the Lacanian perspective, we can go one step further from Laclau's "empty signifier," and regard "China" (with its imagined fullness and essence) as the *objet petit a*, which is, the object of fantasy. That is to say, through the critical lens of *psycho*analysis, "China" functions in contemporary Sinophone discourse not only as the master-signifier, but also as the *objet petit a*: as the constituting element of the narrative of the "Great Dragon fantasy," "China" plays the role of both the "phallic" signifier that guarantees the subject's identity and the "sublime" object that causes his/her desire. It is a fantastic signifier and a fantastic nation-Thing. Although "China" as a master-signifier itself has no signified (i.e. an "empty signifier"), it nonetheless symbolizes effectively the structural place of the *void*, onto which the subject attempts to fasten his/her efforts to come to terms with — or, avoid realization of — the trauma of the fundamental lack.[16] The "Thing" in Lacanian psychoanalysis refers to *the spectral element* occupying, filling out the very abyssal place. Hence, through the magical operation of fantasy, "China" not only symbolizes the primordial empty place (as the master-signifier), but also at the same time makes itself the object-cause of desire (as the nation-Thing).[17]

Understood as the Lacanian *objet petit a*, "China" is a conceptual edifice that *generates desire*: "China" is experienced as a loss/deprivation, and hence as a goal to be achieved. As shown in previous chapters, post-Maoist Chinese intellectuality first presents the problem — "the problem of China" — in terms of a fundamental *loss* (the loss of China's essence, its civilizational greatness), and then stages the spectacle of the passionate search for it. Through this Lacanian reading, various competing narratives about China and its future paths in the post-Maoist era can be seen as the very product of the unfulfilled desire to recover the primordial loss. Yet, as Lacan has repeatedly pointed out, the gap between the *jouissance* expected and the *jouissance* obtained is irreducible. Thus, to extend this argument, "China" or "Chineseness" as the *objet petit a* is structurally elusive. It must remain unrealizable. It is the site of the *void* (e.g. the ontological *non-existence* of "China") that inspires the desire to fill it with meaning. What magically turns this empty place into a homogeneous national and/or civilizational place of "China" is, of course, the operation of fantasy. Through powerful stories it narrates (e.g. one regarding the descendants of a blurry-eyed Dragon endeavoring to restore its former eyesight), fantasy serves also as the

[16]This can be rephrased in terms of Laclau's thesis that "the presence of the lack must itself be signified": "China" signifies nothing but the presence of the lack.

[17]Yannis Stavrakakis once theorized *objet petit a* in the following way: it "designates the effects of a signified or a transcendental signifier binding together signification, a lacking entity whose presence is always deferred" (Stavrakakis 1999: 50). However, in such theorization *objet petit a* becomes almost another name for master-signifier.

very device connecting "China" as a master-signifier/nation-Thing to each individual "Chinese" person.

Thus, those post-Maoist antagonistic narratives ("many paths") are all merely fantasmatic substitutes "standing in" for this fundamental void ("one China"), producing what is best described as a "clash of fantasies." Those "many paths" can be regarded as fantasies precisely because fantasy is that which offers the promise of encountering *jouissance*, and in turn, "constitutes the primordial form of narrative, which serves to occult some original deadlock" (Žižek 1998: 196). What fantasy conceals is, as Žižek notes, "the fact that the Other, the symbolic order, is structured around some traumatic impossibility" (Žižek 1989: 123). In this sense, when these contemporary Chinese intellectuals keep themselves busy at tackling the question of "whither China" (the question that logically follows the perceived situation of "many paths"), what they actually achieve is a covering up of *the constitutive nullity of "China."*

Though providing seemingly a menu of choices, what the idea of "one China, many paths" fails to address is the absence of a choice beyond the stated paths. I draw here on Žižek's statement that "the true free choice is a choice in which I do not merely choose between two or more options WITHIN a pre-given set of coordinates, but I choose to change this set of coordinates itself" (Žižek 2001: 121, 148, emphasis in original). The "many paths" presented by contemporary Chinese intellectuals are from an existing matrix of scenarios of future growth. What remains continuous from the Chinese modernization fantasy of the 1980s to those antagonistic narratives of the 1990s and 2000s is the fundamental fantasy of recovering China's lost fullness and greatness (i.e. the "Great Dragon fantasy"). So far, there is no "path" resembling what Žižek calls "the impossible": that is, *to choose to break with the seductive power of fantasizing China's fullness and greatness.*[18]

---

[18]Žižek himself provides us an example to support his argument that "conferring the formal freedom of choices does not make any difference" by analyzing a French TV talk show called *It Is My Choice*. Guests invited to this show are ordinary people who make a peculiar choice which determines his or her entire life-style. All kinds of choices are allowed except those which may disturb the public: for example, a person whose choice is to be a racist, is *a priori* excluded. The truly radical thing for this TV show, according to Žižek, is to focus precisely on those choices which seriously disturb the social and

As argued repeatedly, one of the main arguments of Lacanian psychoanalysis is that it is the fundamental fantasy that constitutes and guarantees the core of one's being. Lacan's further point is, according to Žižek, that the psychoanalyst is the one who can take away such a fundamental fantasy from the subject: "The analyst's ultimate aim is to deprive the subject of the very fundamental fantasy that regulates the universe of his (self)experience" (Žižek 2000: 43). Living in and through the operation of fantasy is for Žižek a "tragic mode of existence": the subject endeavors to sustain his fidelity to the mission which gives meaning and consistency to his life; nonetheless, his attempt is bound to fail because it is a fantasy that works only if all inconsistencies, antagonisms, dislocations, intrusions, etc. are blocked out. Hence, the fantasmatic kernel of the subject's being is never possible for him to fully assume (in the sense of symbolic integration) — when the subject comes too close to it, what occurs is what Lacan calls *aphanisis* (the self-obliteration) of the subject.

In opposition to living a life sustained by fantasy, Lacanian psychoanalysis suggests the act of traversing or going through the fantasy.[19] As Bruce Fink remarks, "the sense of being that is provided by fantasy is 'false being'" (Fink 1995: xii). In order to avoid such "tragic mode of existence," one has to traverse the fantasy, which is an act of disturbing the very fundamental scenario serving as the ultimate framework of our world-experience. The goal of psychoanalysis is to restore the barred subject in its emptiness, to enable his/her separation from the Other in such a way as to expose the fundamental lack in both the subject and the Other, which has been covered up by fantasy. Hence, the goal of the psychoanalyst is to *deprive the analysand of his/her very fantasmatic kernel* in order to free him/her — to quote Fink — "from the death grip of the Other's desire" (Fink 1997: 205). In this sense, Žižek puts the Lacanian

---

ideological balance and are able to do *make difference*. In short, "true freedom is not the freedom of choice but the accurate insight into the necessities that determine us" (Žižek 2001: 117, 122; 2004a: 39–40).

[19] As Evans writes, "In the course of psychoanalytic treatment, the analyst reconstructs the analysand's fantasy in all its details. However, the treatment does not stop there; the analysand must go on to 'traverse the fundamental fantasy.' In other words, the treatment must produce some modification of the subject's fundamental mode of defense, some alteration in his mode of *jouissance*." (Evans 1996: 60–61)

analyst in line with Hannibal Lecter, the notorious cannibal serial killer from Thomas Harris' novels:

> [B]y bringing-about going-through [the] fundamental fantasy, he [the analyst] literally "steals the kernel of our being," the *objet petit a*, the secret treasure, *agalma*, what we consider most precious in ourselves, denouncing it as a mere semblance. Lacan defines the *objet petit a* as the fantasmatic "stuff of the I"; [...] and it is precisely this "stuff" which the analyst "swallows," pulverizes. This is the rationale of the unexpected "eucharistic" element at work in Lacan's definition of the analyst, namely his repeated ironic allusion to Heidegger: "Mange ton *Dasein*!" — "Eat your being-there!" [...] So, in *The Silence of the Lambs*, Lecter is truly cannibalistic, not in relation to his victims but in relation to Clarice Starling: their relation is a mocking imitation of the analytic situation, since in exchange for his helping her to capture "Buffalo Bill," he wants her to confide — what? Precisely what the analysand confides to the analyst, the kernel of her being, her fundamental fantasy (the crying of the lambs). The *quid pro quo* proposed by Lecter to Clarice is therefore: "I'll help you if you let me eat your *Dasein*!" The inversion of the proper analytic relation consists in the fact that in compensation Lecter helps her track down "Buffalo Bill." Lecter is not cruel enough to be a Lacanian analyst: in psychoanalysis we must *pay* the analyst to allow us to offer our *Dasein* on a plate... (Žižek 1992: 262–263)

What if, then, there is no such a cannibalistic figure available there to "eat" the fantasmatic core of our being for us? What should one do — more precisely, *act* — to get rid of his/her fantasmatic kernel all by him/herself? The self-practice of traversing the fantasy, in Žižek's interpretation of Lacanian psychoanalysis, involves (1) the acknowledgement that fantasy merely functions to cover up the abyss or inconsistency of the Other, and (2) the creation of ruptures that break through this ideological closure and open up the *empty space* for the NEW to emerge. Žižek writes regarding the traversing of the fantasy,

> Fantasy is basically a scenario filling out the empty space of a fundamental impossibility, a screen masking a void. [...] As such, fantasy is not to be interpreted, only "traversed": all we have to do is experience how there is

nothing 'behind' it, and how fantasy masks precisely this "nothing." (Žižek 1989: 126; also 1999a: 307)

Hence, in order to traverse the fundamental fantasmatic formation shared so deeply by contemporary Chinese intellectuals — the "Great Dragon fantasy," one thus needs to recognize the constitutive nullity of "China": ontologically, there is really nothing behind "China," it is only an empty site, a void. It is the operation of fantasy that turns "China" into a meaningful and desirable "entity," into a nation-Thing, endowing it with specific stories, a set of symbolic properties, etc. The "Great Dragon fantasy" further fundamentally links contemporary Chinese people to the master-signifier "China": through this operation, they not only gain access to a meaningful symbolic world (experienced as "reality"), but also acquire their very identity or "self-image" ("the Chinese," "descendants of the Dragon"). In this sense, to traverse this fundamental "Great Dragon fantasy" (i.e. to recognize the non-existence of China), indeed is a *suicidal act*. Since "the sense of being that is provided by fantasy is 'false being'" (Fink 1995: xii), then, how do we free ourselves from this miserable status of living in "false being," how do we "empty" the innermost "fantasmatic stuff" that constitutes the very core of "our being"? The Lacanian–Žižekian answer is: by an act of suicidal "self-beating."

Žižek finds the exemplary embodiment of such act in the famous scene from David Fincher's film *Fight Club*: the hero (played by Edward Norton), whilst arguing with his boss over his salary, suddenly starts to beat himself up violently in his office. The critical lesson of *Fight Club* for Žižek is that "we cannot go *directly* from capitalist to revolutionary subjectivity." One has to go through the passage of this radical self-beating: "It is only through first beating up (hitting) *oneself* that one becomes free: the true goal of this beating is to beat out that in me which attaches me to the master" (Žižek 2002b: 252, emphases in original). By such suicidal act, I am emptied of all substantial content, of all symbolic identities as well as their fantasmatic supplements — hence I am, literally, beating the *shit* out of me. Hence, the Žižekian response to today's nihilistic slogan "I don't give a shit" is, of course: "You *should* give a shit!" For Žižek, we are ashamed of and disguised by our shit not because it smells, but "because, in it, we expose/externalize our innermost intimacy" (Žižek 2001: 59). The small child who gives his or her shit away as a gift is giving away the equivalent of the innermost self. In contrast to humans, animals do not have a problem with the disposal of shit, because *they do not live upon the support of fantasy*. Fantasy's operation of sublimation is precisely an operation on shit, "that which remains the same in all possible symbolic universes, within which it can assume different guises of a precious object" (Žižek 2001: 61). Sublimation is the very fantasy-operation magically turning shit into *agalma*, elevating it to the dignity of the Thing. Traversing the fantasy refers exactly to the act of reversing this operation, of turning the precious object back to shit. This is why the *objet petit a*, the object of fantasy, has to be elusive and/or metonymic: once one approaches it too closely, it turns into the excremental object. Herein resides Žižek's politico-psychoanalytic point: "when our innermost self is directly externalized, the result is disgusting" (Žižek 2001: 60).

So the best slogan for the traversing of the fantasy would be the following lines: If you cannot get some Lecter-like figure to eat your *agalma* (the fantasmatic kernel which is "in you more than yourself"), then why not shit it out by yourself? If you are also suffering from constipation, having trouble with shitting, then try harder, much harder — try self-beating. Violence, as Žižek often stresses, can be put into good use, when one is fighting the impossible fight, i.e. fighting against his/her "imposter" (his/her innermost self as "false being"). Carmela Levy-Stokes even describes the psychoanalytic act as "a cut":

> The analytic act is a cut, a break with a certain mode of *jouissance* fixed in the fantasy. The consequent [traversing] of the fantasy leaves the subject having to endure being alone with his/her own *jouissance* and to encounter its operation in the drive, a unique, singular way of being alone with one's own *jouissance*. The cut of analytic act leaves the subject having to make his/her own something that was formerly alien. (Levy-Stokes 2001: 107)

After such act of "cutting" oneself open, one encounters the truly disgusting form of his/her *agalma*. This encounter constitutes *the* moment of emancipation: the fantasmatic "self-image" is broken down. After traversing the fantasy (the sublime object-cause of desire turning back into shit), one can freely assume his/her *non-existence vis-à-vis* the Other.[20] Only in this way, one truly *subjectivizes* him/herself: instead of subjecting to the Law, (s)he is his/her own law, taking over *the place of the cause* occupied formerly by the Other. Only by assuming his/her own non-existence, one is able to recognize the non-existence of the Other. "[I]n accepting my non-existence as subject, I have to renounce the fetish of the hidden treasure responsible for my unique worth" (Žižek 2005a: 61). This emancipatory moment of "subjectification" and "desublimation" — even just a fleeting moment — is the moment when one can glimpse the Real in his/her everyday mundanity.[21]

Within the psychoanalytic terrain, what this suicidal act of self-beating/self-cutting embodies is, of course, the Freudian death drive.[22] After traversing the anamorphic screen of fantasy, the subject does not (re)gain the clear-sightedness, seeing everything "as it is." Rather, what is left in the subject is the *blind insistence* of the drive.[23] The subject of drive, is in Lacanese the "acephalous" (headless) subject. Žižek notes in this regard,

> In vain do we try to break out of the ideological dream by "opening our eyes and trying to see reality as it is," by throwing away the ideological spectacles. [...] The only way to break the power of our ideological dream

[20] See Fink's note: "There is nothing substantial about [the Freudian] subject: it has no *being*, no substratum or permanence in time" (Fink 1995: 42).

[21] The thesis that "fantasy is not to be interpreted, only 'traversed'," in this light, means that one can always glimpse, even for a brief moment, the fundamental lack of the Other as the inherent limitation of any symbolic order, "the inconsistency and/or non-existence of the big Other" (Žižek 1994a: 200), through everyday mundane contingent failures or personal traumatic encounters that cause the temporary breakdown of the horizon of meaning.

[22] See Leonardo S. Rodriguez's remark on desire *vis-á-vis* the (death) drive as the true cause of jouissance, "desire appears to be on the side of life preservation, as it opposes the lethal dimension of *jouissance* (the partiality of the drive, which disregards the requirements of the living organism)" (Rodriguez 2001: 59).

[23] For Žižek, modern science is one of the best examples of this "blindness" — it follows its own path regardless of "ethical constraints." It does not "see" things within the confines of human goals. "The notion of reinscribing scientific drive into the constraints of the life-world is fantasy at its purest — perhaps even the fundamental *fascist* fantasy" (Žižek 1998: 212–213).

> is to confront the Real of our desire which announces itself in this dream. (Žižek 1989: 48)

Such confrontation of one's *own desire* (i.e. the drive as the "Real of our desire") would bring about what Lacanian theorists call the "real knowledge." The end of analysis demands not only that the analysand *knows* his/her own desire, but also *acts ethically* in consonance with that knowledge. The psychoanalytic ethics as formulated by Lacan, is precisely to *insist on one's own desire*, which entails a radical renunciation of all the richness of desires based upon and framed by fantasmatic scenarios. Žižek further remarks: "Once we move beyond desire — that is to say, beyond the fantasy which sustains desire — we enter the strange domain of drive." In other words, "*fantasy is the very screen that separates desire from drive*: it tells the story which allows the subject to (mis) perceive the void around which drive circulates as the primordial loss constitutive of desire" (Žižek 2008a[1997]: 40, 43, emphases in original).[24] After traversing the fantasy, we encounter our own drive — the desire that is truly ours, not that of the Other's. At such truly emancipatory moment(s), we become *our own cause*; as Fink puts it, the subject "assumes the place of the cause, [...] coming to be in that place where the Other's desire — a foreign, alien desire — had been" (Fink 1995: 62). Fink continues to write,

> [T]raversing fantasy entails a separation from language itself, a separation of the subject — who will have become the cause — from his or her own discourse about his or her problem with the Other's desire, inability to deal with the lack detected in the Other (Fink 1995: 66).

That is to say, through this act of self-beating/self-cutting, the subject is temporarily separated from the "foreign" force of the Other's desire, and "is able to act (as cause, as desirousness), and is at least momentarily out of discourse, split off from discourse: free from the weight of the Other." After traversing the fantasy, "[t]here where it — the Other's

[24]Drive can, in the negative sense, be understood as the repeated folding back of the blind insistence of exposing the void which underlies reality.

discourse, ridden with the Other's desire — was, the subject is able to say 'I.' Not 'It happened to me,' or 'They did this to me,' but 'I was,' 'I did,' 'I saw,' 'I cried out'." In this sense, the traversing of the fantasy "consists in the temporally paradoxical move by the alienated subject to become his or her own cause, to come to be as subject in the place of the cause" (Fink 1995: 62, 66).

Thus, as Žižek points out repeatedly, the pre-symbolic drive is not a purely negative category; it is the active "driving force" of one's *own* desire, the ontological cause of real desirousness (see for example, Žižek 2005a: 208). Since fantasy is the very device that "castrates" our own drive and its satisfaction (*jouissance*), and organizes us to access only a specific kind of enjoyment (called by Lacan phallic *jouissance*, the *jouissance* of the idiot) through the "inverted ladder of the Law of desire,"

> "traversing the fantasy" equals to the passage from desire to drive. Desire is, at its most fundamental, "a defence against drive." Its emergence signals that the subject has renounced the excess of drive. (Žižek 1998: 209)

Contrary to desire which does not seek satisfaction, but its own perpetuation, the drive, as Jacques-Alain Miller notes in his "Commentary on Lacan's text," "follows its own bent and always obtains satisfaction" (quoted from Fink 1997: 208).[25] The drive could not care less about the Other, about the enjoyment deriving from fulfilling — arduously but futilely — the superego's injunction, which commands us not to betray the Other's desire. Hence, the drive can be phrased as "the kind of desire that no longer cares what the Other wants or says," and thus "appeals to no one, to no Other for guidance or permission" (Fink 1997: 206, 209). The subject of drive, as Finks further remarks, "is, prior to analysis, hemmed in, kept down, and silenced as much as possible by the ego and superego, by desire as it forms in language on the basis of the Other's discourse, which transmits the Other's desires, values, and ideals." To put it differently, prior to proper psychoanalytic process, "in his or her

---

[25] Thus, Carmela Levy-Stokes is right to argue that desire "aims at dissatisfaction," and "What lies beyond it is *jouissance*, and the drive of which *jouissance* is the satisfaction" (Levy-Stokes 2001: 102).

confrontation with the Other, the subject immediately *drops out* of the picture. While alienation is the necessary 'first step' in acceding to subjectivity, this step involves choosing 'one's own' disappearance." (Fink 1997: 208; 1995: 51) The force of the drive exists ("ex-sists") all along, but *has never been able to be in the place of the cause* after this "necessary step" of alienation (i.e. symbolic castration). The goal of the Lacanian psychoanalysis is precisely to rescue the subject from the grip of the Other, to let him/her encounter his/her *own* desire (drive), to turn him/her from the subject of desire (ultimately the Other's desire) to the subject of drive. "[W]ith the subject viewed as drive, the aim of analysis in clinic work with neurotics (not psychotics or perverts) is to transform the analysand's fantasy that props up his or her desire, for this desire impedes his or her pursuit of satisfaction." Fink often calls the subject of drive "the subject of *jouissance*," "a subject in the Real," in the sense that it entails a radical dislocation with the Other (its desire, and its discourse) and seeks satisfaction (i.e. the encounter of real *jouissance*) (Fink 1997: 209–210; see also Fink 1995; 2004).[26] Also, very crucially, this subject of drive is *not* amount to "the freedom of the psychotic Lacan mentions in his early paper 'Aggressivity in Psychoanalysis'; it is not a freedom 'before' the letter but 'after' it" (Fink 1995: 66).

Different from the fantasmatic *objet petit a*, the blind force of the drive does not fix or "fill in" the lack in the Other; rather, it circulates around the abyssal site of this fundamental lack, tearing apart fantasmatic scenarios which attempt to tame the blind force of the drive. Žižek sees the drive as the ontological force that constitutes the very core of the revolutionary subject. By pursuing his/her *own* desire (drive), the subject effectively creates the NEW into the symbolic order, radically changing its coordinates. In this sense, what the drive as the blind insistence on one's own *jouissance* generates is a circular movement that opens new spaces in the existing symbolic universe, and creates emancipatory moments of radical rupture and absolute freedom. Thus, entailing the act of traversing the fantasy and holding the empty/abyssal place in the symbolic order, the death drive is ironically the "possibility of all possibilities." In this precise

[26]Cf. Sarah Key's remark: "Drive is not the same as the Real, but it is the closest the psyche gets to it" (Key 2003: 162).

sense, Žižek stresses that "one has to 'subjectivize one's own death,' to recognize in it the only master [i.e. the death drive] to be obeyed, and thereby to get rid of all other master figures" (Žižek 2012: 511). The drive is that which endows us with the capacity of the truly *wild imagination* of the NEW. In other words, only after traversing the fantasy, one is truly opened to free imagination. For Žižek, traversing the fantasy

> involves our *over-identification* with the domain of imagination: in it, through it, we break the constrains of the fantasy and enter the terrifying, violent domain of pre-synthetic imagination, the domain in which *disjecta membra* float around, not yet unified and "domesticated" by the intervention of a homogenizing fantasmatic frame (Žižek 1999b: 122).

This is what Žižek has for today's revolutionary politics: if we *externalize* the blind force of the drive in the form of fragmental pre-synthetic imagination, the totalizing ideological system that makes everyone potentially a *homo sacer* can be undermined. Thus every drive for Žižek is death drive since its blind movement would bring about not only the suicidal act of self-beating on the individual level (i.e. the "death" of the desiring/fantasizing subject), but also on the social level the collapse of the symbolic universe (i.e. the "death" of the Other).[27] The subject of drive assumes both his/her own non-existence and the non-existence of the Other, and indeed "Realizes" both.

In clinical practices, patients (neurotics) often come to psychoanalysis when they get stuck in figuring out the Other's desire (what the Other wants from me). They want the analyst to tell them what to do. That is to say, they posit the analyst as the (temporary) embodiment of the Other, asking for his demands.[28] And what the Lacanian analysts do is the exact opposite. "By refusing to do so, the analyst seeks to open up a space of

---

[27] Cf. Evans' note: "The death drive is the name given to that constant desire in the subject to break through the pleasure principle towards the Thing and a certain excess *jouissance*; thus, *jouissance* is 'the path towards death' (S17, 17). Insofar as the drives are attempts to break through the pleasure principle in search of *jouissance*, every drive is a death drive." (Evans 1996: 92)

[28] As Fink remarks, "the patient does not to want to change, know, or give up anything" (Fink 1997: 8). This is called by Lacan "a will not to know" or "a passion not to know."

desire in which the analysand's desire comes to the fore in its subservience to the Other's desire. [...] The analyst seeks to throw into question the analysand's interpretation of the Other's desire in the fundamental fantasy and bring about its transformation, such that it no longer inhabits the pursuit of satisfaction." (Fink 1997: 210) Although contemporary Chinese intellectuals seem to be certain of what the Other wants from them, however, they still can be treated as the analysand who needs the psychoanalysis. In the Introduction we discussed the case of the Beijing-based literary critic Yu Hong, who committed suicide in the winter of 2007. Judging from those last pieces he posted on his personal blog, Yu was really troubled with the relationship between "China and me." This tragic case can be seen as resulting from the failed struggle of his to repair the fantasmatic relationship between the subject and the Other. Does not Yu's suicide mark a symptomatic moment within the symbolic universe of contemporary Chinese intellectuals? One encounters grave trauma — in the worst scenario, *aphanisis* (subjective disintegration) — once failing to defend his/her fundamental fantasy. This is exactly what Žižek calls a "tragic mode of existence." All these violent style, nasty attacks embedded in contemporary Chinese intellectual texts, show us that the authors *have to* attack violently their intellectual rivals to protect their fantasmatic narratives. All these are strong indication of the relevance of the psychoanalytic domain: the authors can indeed use a psychoanalytic intervention. Instead of beating other people in the fantasmatic battle-zone, what one should do is to traverse his own fundamental fantasy by beating himself up — beating the *crap* (the internalized Other) out of him. In opposition to the suicidal case of Yu Hong, the "suicidal act" of self-beating leads only to the subject's "symbolic death," which *paradoxically enables him/her to live in the full extent*, to live in the form of "I was," "I did," "I saw," "I cried out" (to quote Fink again). Far from being merely a negative category, the death drive — as Žižek stresses — is a positive, revolutionary force that has the ontological potential to open up the NEW in the existing symbolic order.[29] This is indeed *the* politico-psychoanalytic solution to break the "tragic mode of existence."

---

[29]This also corresponds to Žižek's following point: "it is the very trauma of the Real which again and again sets in motion the movement of history, propelling it to ever new historizations/symbolizations" (Žižek 1996: 218).

Lacanian psychoanalysis finishes at the point which the analysand traverses the fundamental fantasy by moving from desire to drive, and in turn establishes NEW relationship with the Other.[30] The analyst would definitely not go beyond this end point. Lacan's own note on this is very precise: "How can a subject who has traversed his most basic fantasy live out the drive? This is the beyond of analysis and has never been touched upon." (quoted from Fink 1997: 210 and Žižek 2005a: 49) In other words: no way should the analyst further posture himself as a man of clear-sightedness, as a "subject supposed to know"! Thus, the sole task for the analyst is to unwrap the mysteries of the analysand's desire. This is the aim of this study on contemporary Chinese intellectual inquiry.

To thoroughly dislocate oneself from the desire of the Other, one has to reach the traumatic recognition that the Other does not exist, and the acceptance that there is no "secret treasure" at all, that the support of the consistency and meanings of one's life is purely fantasmatic. This means, as Žižek writes, "that [the object of desire] *was lost from the beginning*, and that any given object is simply an attempt to fill in the empty place of this loss." At the end of analytic process, the analysand recognizes "the priority of the loss over the object" (Žižek 2005a: 52).[31] Žižek quotes Jacques-Alain Miller: "The end of analysis as such assumes an encounter with absence through the traversing of the fantasy and the separation from the object" (Žižek 2005a: 53). With regard to contemporary Chinese intellectuals' desire to restore Chiba's fullness and greatness, such recognition would be the following radical thesis: China does not exist. "China" is not naked Reality, but a symbolic "reality." That which resides beneath the symbolic world of "China," is *an ontological void.* No object can ultimately fill in this abyssal hole. Fantasy is thus crucial in framing and

[30]It is helpful here to quote Fink's following argument: "The analyst's intervention, including the scansion of the session, can lead to a new configuration of the analysand's fundamental fantasy, and thus to a new relation (stance or position adopted with respect) to the Other — the Other's desire and the Other's *jouissance*. The initial fixation of the analysand's desire no longer serves as a substitute for or hindrance to the pursuit of satisfaction." (Fink 1997: 70)

[31]In another place Žižek writes: "As soon as the symbolic order emerges, we are dealing with the minimal difference between a structural place and the element that occupies, fills out, this place: an element is always logically preceded by the place in the structure it fills out" (Žižek 2005a: 192–193).

sustaining reality in terms that it stages an imaginary scenario in which the ontological hole can be filled in by some (contingent) missing object, and the Fullness can be achieved. The fantasmatic formation that I have called the "Great Dragon fantasy," effectively covers up this ontological void of China, rendering it as a metaphysical Entity with some perceived missing piece. This fundamental fantasy of the post-Maoist Sinophone world has organized powerful stories — not necessarily mutually consistent — about China's fantasmatic past ("several-thousand-years great civilization"), present (deprivation of its fullness owning to external intrusions), and future (the promise of the fullness with "several generations' hard work"). In other words, through the very vista of this fantasy shared deeply by contemporary Chinese intellectuals, "China" magically becomes — more precisely, is experienced as — the ultimate support of the meaning of their lives, of that which makes them unique. Via the operation of the "Great Dragon fantasy," the missing piece that can make China full (the object of the Other's desire) is turned into the object of intellectuals' personal desire. It is their endless and fruitless pursuit of this elusive object that enables them to regard themselves as the glorious "descendant of the Dragon," as the Confucian "exemplary person" (*junzi*) who assumes personal responsibility for all under Heaven, etc., and in doing so, "patches up" the gap between their "actual ego" (self-image) and "ego-ideal."

The traversing of the fantasy, i.e. the traumatic recognition of the Other's non-existence, is thus the "experience of the priority of place in relation to the fantasmatic object, in the moment when, recalling the formula of Mallarmé, 'nothing takes place but the place" (Žižek 2005a: 47–48). To put it differently, place is more *primordial* than the signifier (the symbolic world) and the object (the fantasmatic kernel): the latter two do not have the ontological dignity. Hence, Žižek's slogans for revolutionary politics are "holding the place" that is ontologically prior to any symbolic texture and its fantasmatic support, and "burning the bridges" (see Butler, Laclau and Žižek 2000: 308–329; Žižek 1999b: vii–x). If "[f]antasy is basically a scenario filling out the empty space of a fundamental impossibility, a screen masking a void" (Žižek 1989: 126), the traversing of the fantasy, then, is exactly to take over and hold on this void place (the place of cause, the place of the fundamental lack), by emptying all the fantasmatic stuff filling it, and by recognizing the ontological non-existence of the Other. For Žižek, "Our very physical survival hinges on our ability to consummate the act of assuming fully the 'non-existence of the Other'." The ethics is "to make the 'collapse of the big Other' part of our everyday experience" (Žižek 1993: 237).

Hence, at the end of the analytic process, one reaches the recognition that China is precisely such a void place, an empty site, which can be radically opened up for the NEW. Only then one can have a post-fantasmatic relation with China. How, then, can one arrive at this empty place, occupy and hold onto it, and burn the fantasmatic bridges? Even Allen Chun, who is famous for his radical "anti-sinocentric" stance, nonetheless still admits in his influential article "Fuck Chineseness: On the Ambiguities of Ethnicity as Culture as Identity" that "Something called 'China' unquestionably exists" (Chun 1996: 111). How does one come to the traumatic recognition that China does not exist?

Here, Lacan's discussion of Shakespeare's *Hamlet* is of pertinence. According to Lacan, Hamlet's duel with Laertes is the most crucial moment of the play: it is only during the duel at the end of the play Hamlet is able to realize that the king is but a stand-in for the empty signifier (or in Lacanese, the "phallic signifier," the signifier of desire), and can be struck without throwing everything into question. "Until Hamlet could finally dissociate the king and the phallus ('the king is a thing of nothing'), action was impossible, for to take revenge on the king would have threatened to make Hamlet's whole world collapse" (see Fink 1995: 65). Similar to "the king" as the privileged phallic signifier, "China" is also such an empty signifier. Such master-signifier (privileged but empty signifier) is the fantasmatic signifier, the signifier of desire, the very supplement/excess that, by standing in and covering up the empty ground of the Other, holds all other signifiers into a differential system. "As it appears concretely in the analytic situation, a master signifier presents itself as a dead end, a stopping point, a term, word, or phrase that puts an end to association, that grinds the patient's discourse to a halt" (Fink 1995: 135). The traversing of the fantasy thus entails an act of "desublimating" this privileged signifier, which means, to turn it from the status of the master-signifier functioning as a dead end or a stopping point in the analytic process, back to an "ordinary" signifier in the signifier chain by cutting off all the fantasmatic attachments from the signifier itself. As Fink puts it, "The task of analysis is to bring such master signifiers into relation with other signifiers" (Fink 1995: 135). After the analytic process, one can traverse, go beyond "China" without experiencing the "loss of reality" (the collapse of the symbolic universe).

Although as Fink argues, "the symbolic order kills the living being or organism in us, rewriting it or overwriting it with signifiers, such that being dies ('the letter kills') and only the signifier lives on" (Fink 1995: 101), as speaking beings we cannot entirely live outside the symbolic world. We cannot afford to have the collapse of the entire symbolic universe, if we do not want to end up like Wang Guowei, Yu Hong, and others who tragically ended their lives. As argued, what the drive embodies is not a freedom "before" the letter but "after" it. The subject of drive does not move totally outside the symbolic world; rather, (s)he finds — even momentarily — in the very empty place occupied or "filled in" formerly by the phallic signifier the *residue* of real *jouissance* (termed by late Lacan as "feminine *jouissance*," i.e. that which *survives* the symbolic castration, in contrast to "phallic *jouissance*" which has to pass through speech).[32] This *jouissance* that is left over from the operation of symbolization, "a *jouissance* beyond the phallus" (Lacan 1999: 74), is not organized by fantasy and thus does not require its support.[33] In contrast, for the phallic *jouissance* is organized and sustained by fantasy, hence when we enjoy in the phallic form, "we never do it 'spontaneously'" (Žižek 1991a: 9). The agency that ensures us to enjoy through its injunction is of

[32] Lacan writes: "There is a *jouissance* that is hers, that belongs to that 'she' that doesn't exist and doesn't signify anything. There is a *jouissance* that is hers about which she herself perhaps knows nothing." (Lacan 1999: 74)

[33] Some Lacanian theorists interpret such *jouissance* beyond the phallus as the *jouissance* of God (the Real Other). See Levy-Stokes 2001: 108. As Fink comments, "There seem to be two faces of the Other: the locus of the signifier (which Lacan associates here with the father function) and 'the God face [...] based on feminine *jouissance*" (Fink 2004: 165). Thus, in contrast to phallic *jouissance* that is "fallible," this Other *jouissance* is characterized by "infallibility." Another way to phrase this contrast is: while phallic *jouissance* is a *jouissance* of desire, feminine *jouissance* is that of love. Fink calls the encountering of the Other *jouissance*, i.e. the satisfaction of the drives, "a *real* satisfaction" (Fink 2004: x; 1995: 115, 120).

course the superego. Therefore, Lacan stresses that what feminine *jouissance* manifests is the logic of "non-all" — which means, the *jouissance* available within the symbolic world, within the Law of desire, i.e. the phallic *jouissance*, is *a priori* "not all": feminine *jouissance* "shows up the paucity of phallic *jouissance*, which is the mere pittance of pleasure left after the drives have been thoroughly subjected [...] to the symbolic" (Fink 1995: 120). Lacan's point is: one *can* experience real *jouissance* (as the *jouissance* beyond the phallus, the "full satisfaction of the drives"), though one cannot say anything about it because it is ineffable. It does not "exist" in terms of being unarticulable in speech.[34] Lacan and his followers discerned a place for it within the symbolic universe by giving it a name (i.e. "feminine *jouissance*"), but this was itself an act of naming the unnamable.[35] It is around such little pieces of *jouissance* that the repetitive movements of drives are constantly circling. The simple massage of the Lacanian psychoanalytic ethics of "not compromising one's own desire (drive)" is, hence: there is a *possibility* to encounter *jouissance* (the satisfaction of one's own desire), do *not* give it up!

In the light of the above discussion opened up by the example of Shakespeare's *Hamlet*, a proper unmasking gesture of psychoanalysis is thus indeed close to Alphonse Allais' well-known joke, utilized by Lacan and repeated by Žižek: somebody points at a woman and utters a horrified cry, "Look at her, what a shame, under her clothes, she is totally naked" (Žižek 1989: 29). That's no longer exactly a big traumatic news! Using the same spirit, let us now look at "China": under its symbolic and imaginary "clothes," it is nothing but a void. The function of fantasy is to — to put it figuratively — stitch and patch up holes and fissures on the "clothes," and in doing so, turn magically "worn clothes" into "fancy clothes." This is what truly lies beneath the "one-China-many-paths" complex: no matter

[34] In contrast, China's non-existence resides at the ontological level; i.e. it does not (Really) exist precisely in terms of being fully articulated in speech.

[35] See Fink's argument: "All the *jouissances* that do exist are phallic (in order to exist, according to Lacan, something must be articulable within our signifying system determined by the phallic signifier); but that does not mean there cannot be some *jouissances* that are not phallic. It is just that they do not exist; instead, they ex-sist. The Other *jouissance* can only ex-sist, it cannot exist, for to exist it would have to be spoken, articulated, symbolized." (Fink 2004: 161, 163; 1995: 122)

how drastically Chinese authors fight against each other in the intellectual arena, they write nonetheless all under the presupposition that China is a metaphysically given Entity, and that they all have "a Chinese heart." The drastic disagreement lies only in the level of "clothes" — e.g. whether Western-style, national-style, or other "mixed-styles."[36] The psychoanalytic act of traversing the fantasy, in this sense, is precisely not to choose between these offered "clothes" (i.e. various symbolic narratives about China's past, present reality, and future-paths), but to radically recognize (1) that no "clothes" can fully cover up the empty core of "China" (Allais' joke shows us that even an idiot knows this "sham"), and (2) that "I do not have a Chinese heart" — in the very spot where one "feels" his/her "Chinese heart," (s)he can only find after the proper psychoanalytic process some "fantasmatic stuff" that magically transforms the Other's "foreign" desire into his/her "own" desire. Traversing the fantasy — i.e. beating the "fantasmatic stuff" out of me — therefore means that "where the Other pulls the strings (acting as my cause), I must come into being as my own cause" (Fink 1995: xiii).

Hence, instead of choosing among a pre-given set of options within the "realm of clothes" (such act of choosing has been functioning as the generative motor of Sinophone intellectual discourses), the psychoanalytic act is to choose to change this realm itself. It is not until the moment when one can finally traverse the "Great Dragon fantasy" that this radical choice of breaking his/her "tragic mode of existence" becomes possible: one can reach the recognition of the non-existence of China without encountering subjective disintegration (i.e. without experiencing the "loss of reality"). In order to traverse the "Great Dragon fantasy," one must signifierize and further desublimate "China," recognize that beneath its "clothes" there is only a void, and further take over this empty place based on which one can come into being as his/her own cause. After traversing the fantasy and recognizing the truth about his/her desire, one gains his/her *authentic*

[36]Wang Hui's following line is worth quoting here again, for it not only represents quite a few Chinese scholars view on "national/civilizational consciousness," but also touches the key dimension of contemporary Chinese intellectuality: "Today we all wear Western-style clothes. National-style clothing is disappearing. This demonstrates that our self-consciousness is extremely weak." (Wang 2007: 56–58)

ways of — to keep using the metaphors — dealing with the "clothes": only after traversing his/her fundamental fantasy one is able to create "clothes" that is truly NEW. Instead of moving within "one-China-many-clothes(paths)" coordinates, such new "clothes" is not at all "attached" to "China" as a metaphysical "body," nor to any "Chinese heart."

As discussed in Chapter 1, the "magical" operation of the fantasy enables the subject to (1) experience losing something that he never possessed, and at the same time (2) continue to succumb to the necessary illusion that he would otherwise possess it. In contrast to China's essence as such "lost object," the void of China can be interpreted in terms of the Hegelian–Žižekian "loss of the loss," which refers precisely to "the moment in which loss ceases to be the loss *of* 'something' and becomes the opening of the empty place that the object ('something') can occupy, the moment in which the empty place is conceived as prior to that which fills it" (Žižek 2005a: 47–48).[37] The drive, as noted earlier, always already "ex-sists," but the goal of the psychoanalytic practice is to make it — even momentarily — appear *there*, the place within the symbolic order occupied once by the fantasmatic (empty, phallic) master-signifier. Only in this way may psychoanalysis become the instrument of the analysand's access to his/her *own* desire.

Only when based on such radical recognition of China's non-existence would one be able to acquire the *authentic freedom of choice*, that is, freedom as the capacity to "transcend" all kinds of pre-given symbolic and fantasmatic coordinates that are vital for sustaining the significance of "worrying about China." Hence, in post-Maoist China, the issue of freedom of choice is far from being merely related to and circumscribed by the CCP's authoritarian control and censorship; rather, it is, in a much more fundamental basis, related to the possibility of a radical (suicidal) act which involves, as Hannah Arendt puts it, "the abyss of nothingness that opens up before any deed that cannot be accounted for by a reliable chain of cause and effect and is inexplicable in Aristotelian categories of potentiality and actuality" (Arendt 1968: 151). The freedom of choice is

[37] In parallel to this logic, for Žižek, castration is characterized by the Hegelian "negation of negation": (1) the traumatic imposition of the signifier (the negation of the presymbolic Real); (2) the ensuing repression of this fundamental trauma by the operation of fantasy.

thus displayed in a capacity "to begin something new and [...] not being able to control or even foretell its consequences" (Arendt 1968: 165).[38] In short, the point regarding freedom as an inaugurating capacity here is not pretty much to limit or cancel the formal freedom of choice organized structurally by the existing power relations, but to maintain the authentic *choice* — the point is to choose to break the "one-China-many-paths" matrix. To put more specifically, the authentic *choice* is not to choose within the symbolic realm of "many paths" (various symbolic "clothes"), but to freely choose to break through the fantasmatic framework of "(one) China" (the fantasmatic "heart").

Such freedom of "beginning something new" structurally requires violent (revolutionary) acts. Žižek's (in)famous thesis that Hitler was not violent enough (Žižek 2009) can be reformulated with regard to the operation of fantasy: in contrast to the Holocaust violence which is one exemplary case of *the kind of violence (castrated "phallic violence") exercised through and sustained by fantasy* (by getting rid of Jews the society can be organic and harmonious again), the act of traversing the fundamental fantasy (i.e. the act of cutting off all the fantasmatic attachments from the master-signifier) is the embodiment of real violence, the violence that aims at nothing but shattering the very fantasy-frame that structures the existing symbolic order and sustains its running. In this precise sense, Žižek is indeed right to claim that "Hitler did not 'have the balls' to really change things; he did not really act, all his actions were fundamentally reactions, i.e., he acted so that nothing would really change." (Žižek 2008b: 209-210; also 2009) The question for contemporary Chinese intellectuals is, hence: Do you really "have the balls" to *act* (beating the shit out of oneself, self-cutting) in order to traverse the "Great Dragon fantasy," to move beyond the whole matrix of "one-China-many-paths" and inaugurate something radically NEW?

The psychoanalytic act of traversing the fantasy, in terms of its "suicidal" character, is indeed to *do the impossible*. After the proper psychoanalytic process, nothing is changed (in terms of the Real), and everything is changed (in terms of the "sense of reality"): to quote once again Žižek, "what changes is only the 'perspective,' the position of the subject" (Žižek 2005a: 54).

[38] Arendt's passages were also quoted by Žižek (2001: 112–113).

Fantasy, embodying our everyday practices of "looking awry," is such a fundamental "anamorphic window" through which we see reality. The aim of the analyst is precisely to "deprive the subject of the very fundamental fantasy that regulates the universe of the subject's (self)experience" (Žižek 2005a: 114). By analyzing intellectual discourses of the post-Maoist era, what we can see is that what contemporary Chinese intellectuals deeply share is the desire to restore China's fullness and greatness. In endlessly pursuing this elusive object of desire, and during the course (re)producing a master-signifier (China as "the Great Dragon") they are able to maintain their identity as spokespersons for China (descendants of the Dragon). This is how the "Great Dragon fantasy" turns the Other's desire (the Dragon's desire to regain its eyesight) into the subject's own desire. What has been obscured in the writings of contemporary Chinese authors is precisely the Otherness of their desire, framed and sustained in the fantasmatic space. The only way for the Great Dragon to *enlighten* its vision — to use the metaphors from Hou Dejian's pop song, for the one last time — is paradoxically for its "descendants" to commit the "suicidal" act of recognizing the non-existence of the "Great Dragon," of recognizing its fantasmatic nature, and hence, the "fantasmatic stuff" constituting their own self-image. This recognition is a necessary condition for radically opening up the space for the truly NEW emerging in the Sinophone intellectual world.

Glossary

anshen liming 安身立命
bainian da keti 百年大课题
Bao diao yundong 保钓运动
Bao Zunxin 包遵信
bashi niandai 八十年代
bashi niandai re 八十年代热
bawo zhengzhi chidu 把握政治尺度
Bei Dao 北岛
biangou 变构
bianlian 变脸
bishi jiuxu 避实就虚
buhui decheng 不会得逞
bukejiuyao 不可救药
caizi 才子
Cao Hongju 曹宏举
cao waiguo bi 操外国逼
Changjiang 长江
Changjiang Dushu jiang 长江读书奖
changshi 常识
changshi lixing 常识理性
chao wending 超稳定
Chen Fong-ching 陈方正
Chen Jiaying 陈嘉映
Chen Shaoming 陈少明
Chen Xiaoming 陈晓明
Chen Yangu 陈燕谷
Chen Yinque 陈寅恪
Chen Yun 陈赟

Cheng Long 成龙
chenggong zhi lu 成功之路
Chong Ming 崇明
chongxin sikao Zhongguo wenti 重新思考中国问题
chou laojiu 臭老九
chulu 出路
chunzhen supu 纯真素朴
Cui Weiping 崔卫平
Cui Zhiyuan 崔之元
cuoluan, kongdong, wuqu, ziqiang 错乱, 空洞, 无趣, 自戕
cuozhi jutigan de miuwu 错置具体感的谬误
da geju 大格局
da wo 大我
Da xue 大学
Dao 道
daolu zixin, lilun zixin, zhidu zixin 道路自信, 理论自信, 制度自信
daoyi 道义
datong 大同
dazibao 大字报
Deng Xiaoping 邓小平
Ding Dong 丁东
Ding Xueliang 丁学良
disanzhong zunyan 第三种尊严
diulian 丢脸
Dongfang zaobao 东方早报
Dong Zhongshu 董仲舒
Du Xiaozhen 杜小真
Duan Baolin 段宝林
Dushu 读书
Ershiyi shiji 二十一世纪
fabiao shi wanwanbuke de, zuoyou shangxia jun buke 发表是万万不可的, 左右上下均不可
Fan Gang 樊纲
fan xiandaixing de xiandaixing lilun 反现代性的现代性理论
fan xifangzhuyi 反西方主义
Fang Ning 房宁

fangsi wuqing 放肆无情
fangyan kan shijie 放眼看世界
fayang guangda 发扬光大
Feng Youlan 冯友兰
fenhua 分化
fenzi 分子
fu zeren 负责任
fugu genghua 复古更化
gaige kaifang 改革开放
Gan Yang 甘阳
gao 搞
Gao Yuanbao 郜元宝
Ge Hongbing 葛红兵
Ge Jianxiong 葛剑雄
gebie 个别
gen 根
gong 工
gongfu 功夫
gonghe 共和
Gu Xin 顾昕
guhuo 蛊惑
gujin zhi zheng 古今之争
guojia hexin qikan 国家核心期刊
guoqing 国情
guoxue 国学
guoxue re 国学热
Han Yuhai 韩毓海
hanfu 汉服
hao huangdi 好皇帝
haoyang de 好样的
He Qinglian 何清涟
He Shang 河殇
He Weifang 贺卫方
He Xin 何新
He Xinquan 何信全
hen guanzhu 很关注

hexie 和谐
hexie shehui 和谐社会
hexin jiazhi 核心价值
hexin quanzi 核心圈子
hongda gongcheng 宏大工程
Hou Dejian 侯德健
hou xin shiqi 后新时期
houyizheng 后遗症
Hu Angang 胡鞍钢
Hu Jintao 胡锦涛
Hua Guofeng 华国锋
Huang Ping 黄平
Huang Renyu 黄仁宇
Huangdi 黄帝
Huanghe 黄河
huanglong qi 黄龙旗
huangzi 幌子
huanglao zhi xue 黄老之学
huanjue 幻觉
huaxia 华夏
hudong de guanxi 互动的关系
huidao zigong 挥刀自宫
huise yinbi 晦涩隐蔽
hukou 户口
hunjun 昏君
hunxiao shiting 混淆视听
huxiang canzhao, huxiang jiejian 互相参照, 互相借鉴
Ji Guibao 季桂保
Jiang Jingsong 蒋劲松
Jiang Qing 蒋庆
Jiang Zemin 江泽民
jiangshi huanhun 僵尸还魂
jiaohui dian 交汇点
jiazhi youyuelun 价值优越论
jiben gongshi 基本共识
jie 界

jiegui 接轨
jieti fahui 借题发挥
Jin Guantao 金观涛
jingshen neishang 精神内伤
jingshen xueyuan 精神血缘
jinu 激怒
jiqiong 技穷
jiyi de zhengti 记忆的整体
ju long 巨龙
jueshi xuanyan 绝食宣言
junzi 君子
junzimen 君子们
Kang Youwei 康有为
keai zhe bu kexin, kexin zhe bu keai 可爱者不可信, 可信者不可爱
kongshu 空疏
koushui zhan 口水战
Kuang Xinnian 旷新年
Lao Zi 老子
laobaixing 老百姓
Le Shan 乐山
Lei Yi 雷颐
Li Bai 李白
Li Hongzhang 李鸿章
Li Ka-shing (Li Jiacheng) 李嘉诚
Li Shenzh 李慎之
Li Xiaolong 李小龙
Li Yinhe 李银河
Li Yining 厉以宁
Li Youzheng 李幼蒸
Li Zehou 李泽厚
Liang Qichao 梁启超
Liang Shuming 梁漱溟
Liaowang 瞭望
lifa zhidu 礼法制度
lilun 理论
Lin Yifu 林毅夫

Lin Yü-sheng 林毓生
lingdao danwei 领导单位
linghun 灵魂
lishi wenming 历史文明
Liu Dachun 刘大椿
Liu Dong 刘东
Liu Junning 刘军宁
Liu Qing 刘擎
Liu Qingfeng 刘青峰
Liu Xiaobo 刘晓波
Liu Xiaofeng 刘小枫
Liu Xinwu 刘心武
Liu Zaifu 刘再复
Long de chuanren 龙的传人
Long Yongtu 龙永图
longzi longsun 龙子龙孙
Lu Xinghua 陆兴华
Lu Xun 鲁迅
lundi 论敌
Luo Di 罗蒂
Luo Gang 罗岗
Luo Houli 罗厚立
Luo Rongqu 罗荣渠
luowu tuibu 落伍退步
Ma Licheng 马立诚
Ma Lijun 马利军
Mao Shoulong 毛寿龙
Mao Zedong 毛泽东
meinu zuojia 美女作家
min 民
mingbai ren 明白人
mingren 名人
minzuzhuyi 民族主义
minzuzhuyi de shengyin 民族主义的声音
mixin 迷信
Mo Luo 摩罗

mosuo jieduan 摸索阶段
Mou Zongsan 牟宗三
nalaizhuyi 拿来主义
nanxun 南巡
naoju 闹剧
nong 农
nongmingong 农民工
Ouyang Kang 欧阳康
Pan Wei 潘维
pianju 骗局
ping Tianxia 平天下
pingfan 平反
pipan de zhishifenzi 批判的知识分子
pipan qianneng 批判潜能
pipanxing de sixiang 批判性的思想
qi jia 齐家
Qian Chengdan 钱乘旦
qianchuang baikong 千疮百孔
qianhou jiaji 前后夹击
qiannu 迁怒
qianzhi 牵制
qimeng 启蒙
Qin 秦
Qin Hui 秦晖
Qing 清
qingchun jiqing 青春激情
qingshi liuming 青史留名
qiongtu molu, cilu butong 穷途末路, 此路不通
Qiu Feng 秋风
quanqiuhua 全球化
qushe 取舍
re 热
Ren Bingqiang 任丙强
Ren Jiantao 任剑涛
renwen jingshen de shiluo 人文精神的失落
renxue mantou 人血馒头

riben guizi 日本鬼子
ruoshi jituan 弱势集团
sandai 三代
sanqian nian weiyou zhi bianju 三千年未有之变局
shang 商
Shanghai baobei 上海宝贝
shangmian 上面
shangwu jingshen 尚武精神
shehuizhuyi xinren 社会主义新人
shejin qiuyuan 舍近求远
Sheng Hong 盛洪
shenti xiezuo 身体写作
Shenzhen fazhi bao 深圳法制报
shi 士
shi dafu 士大夫
shibu sha yiren 十步杀一人
shiji 史记
shijian shi jianyan zhenli de weiyi biaozhun 实践是检验真理的唯一标准
shijie chaoliu, haohao dangdang, shunzhizhe chang, nizhizhe wang 世界潮流, 浩浩荡荡, 顺之者昌, 逆之者亡
shiwei 示威
shiyu 失语
shizi jian ruan de nie 柿子拣软的捏
shourong qiansong 收容遣送
shouzu zhi zheng 手足之争
Shucheng 书城
Shun 舜
"shuo bu" julebu "说不"俱乐部
si de qi suo 死得其所
Sihuo chongwen 死火重温
Sima Qian 司马迁
sixiang 思想
sixiangjia danchu, xuewenjia tuchu 思想家淡出, 学问家凸出
Song Hongbing 宋鸿兵
Song Qiang 宋强

Su Xiaokang 苏晓康
Sun Wukong 孙悟空
Sun Yat-sen 孙中山
Sun Zhigang 孙志刚
taidude tongyixing 态度的同一性
Taizong 太宗
Tan Yonglin 谭咏麟
Tang Junyi 唐君毅
Tang Yijie 汤一介
tangzhuang 唐装
tazhe 他者
Tiananmen 天安门
Tian-Dao 天道
Tianxia 天下
Tianxia xingwang, pifu youze 天下兴亡, 匹夫有责
Tianya 天涯
tianzi 天子
tiaochulai duojiao 跳出来跺脚
tong santong 通三统
Tong Shijun 童世骏
tongshi jiaoyu 通识教育
tongyixing 同一性
Tu Wei-ming (Du Weiming) 杜维明
waiqu shishi 歪曲事实
Wang Guowei 王国维
Wang Hui 汪晖
Wang Jisi 王缉思
Wang Lihong 王力宏
Wang Luxiang 王鲁湘
Wang Meng 王蒙
Wang Ning 王宁
Wang Shaoguang 王绍光
Wang Shuo 王朔
Wang Xiaodong 王小东
Wang Xiaoming 王晓明
Wang Xiaoyu 王晓渔

Wang Yi 王怡
Wang Yichuan 王一川
Wang Zhihe 王治河
wangguan xue 王官学
Wanli Changcheng yong budao 万里长城永不倒
Wanxiang 万象
Wei Hui 卫慧
wei shengmin li ming 为生民立命
wei tiandi li xin 为天地立心
wei wangsheng ji juexue 为往圣继绝学
wei wanshi kai taiping 为万世开太平
Wei Yuan 魏源
weiqi 围棋
weishi 伪士
Wen Jiabao 温家宝
wenbao wenti 温饱问题
wending yadao yiqie 稳定压倒一切
wenhua da geming 文化大革命
wenhua de xiandaihua 文化的现代化
wenhua juedinglun 文化决定论
wenhua paomo 文化泡沫
wenhua re 文化热
wenhua taidu de tongyixing 文化态度的同一性
wenhua tongyixing 文化同一性
wenhua wenti 文化问题
wenhua yingxiong 文化英雄
Wenhua: Zhongguo yu shijie 文化：中国与世界
wenming de zhutixing 文明的主体性
wenming liyi 文明利益
wenming yishi 文明意识
wenming yuwang 文明欲望
wenming zijue 文明自觉
wenren 闻人
Wo de Zhongguo xin 我的中国心
women 我们
women jintian zenyang zuo Zhongguoren 我们今天怎样做中国人

Wu Guanjun 吴冠军
Wu Jiaxiang 吴稼祥
wu zhong sheng you 无中生有
wuli de 无理的
wushi zhinian, zhiqian yisi, jingci shibian, yi wu zairu 五十之年, 只欠一死, 经此世变, 义无再辱
wushu 武术
wusi 五四
wuwu zhi zhen 无物之阵
wuxian 诬陷
wuyong gong 无用功
Xi Jinping 习近平
xia 夏
xiaai 狭隘
xiake 侠客
xiandaihua jianshe 现代化建设
xianshi 现实
xianzhuang 现状
Xiao Gongqin 萧功秦
Xiao Han 萧瀚
Xiao Xuehui 萧雪慧
xiaoren 小人
Xie Xuanjun 谢选骏
Xie Yong 谢泳
xifang fada guojia de zhidu 西方发达国家的制度
xin qimeng yundong 新启蒙运动
xin qingkuang, lao wenti 新情况, 老问题
xin shijiezhuyi 新世界主义
xin shiqi 新时期
Xinhuashe 新华社
xinsheng 心声
xinxi kongzhi 信息控制
xiong 兄
xisu lifa 习俗礼法
xiu shen 修身
Xu Ben 徐贲
Xu Fuguan 徐复观

Xu Jilin 许纪霖
Xu Xun 徐迅
Xu Youyu 徐友渔
Xu Zhiyong 许志永
xue 学
Xueren 学人
xueshu 学术
xueshu guifan 学术规范
Xueshu jilin 学术集林
xueshuo 学说
xuyi de 蓄意的
Yan Huang zisun 炎黄子孙
Yang Fan 杨帆
yang guizi 洋鬼子
Yang Zhizhu 杨支柱
yanlun kongjian 言论空间
Yao 尧
Yao 药
yi 义
yi 夷
yi tianxia wei jiren 以天下为己任
yifen tianying 义愤填膺
yingxiong 英雄
yiye Meiguoren 一夜美国人
Yiyongjun jinxingqu 义勇军进行曲
yong xin zhi shen 用心之深
yongsu de ziyouzhuyizhe 庸俗的自由主义者
youhuan 忧患
youhuoli 诱惑力
youji jiehe 有机结合
youshi zhi shi 有识之士
Yu 禹
Yu Hong 余虹
Yu Jie 余杰
Yu Shicun 余世存
Yu Ying-shih 余英时

yuan 元
Yuan Shikai 袁世凯
Yuan Weishi 袁伟时
Yuanxue 原学
Yue Daiyun 乐黛云
Yue Fei 岳飞
Zha Jianying 查建英
Zhang Dainian 张岱年
Zhang Fa 张法
Zhang Guoqing 张国清
Zhang Rulun 张汝伦
Zhang Shuguang 张曙光
Zhang Weiwei 张维为
Zhang Xudong 张旭东
Zhang Yiwu 张颐武
Zhang Yongle 章永乐
Zhang Zai 张载
Zhang Zhizhong 张志忠
Zhao Ziyang 赵紫阳
zhe 者
zhenjiu 针灸
zheng 政
zheng 正
Zheng He 郑和
Zheng He xia xiyang 郑和下西洋
Zheng Min 郑敏
zhenlong tianzi 真龙天子
zhi guo 治国
zhidu chuangxin 制度创新
zhishifenzi 知识分子
zhishifenzi re 知识分子热
zhizhe de zunyan 智者的尊严
Zhongguo 中国
Zhongguo daolu 中国道路
Zhongguo jiazhi 中国价值
Zhongguo moshi 中国模式

Zhongguo nanren 中国男人
Zhongguo qingnian bao 中国青年报
Zhongguo renmin zhanqilaile 中国人民站起来了
Zhongguo shehui kexue jikan 中国社会科学季刊
Zhongguo shi ziyouzhuyi 中国式自由主义
Zhongguo tushu pinglun 中国图书评论
Zhongguo wenhua shuyuan 中国文化书院
Zhongguo wenti 中国问题
Zhongguohua 中国化
Zhonghua 中华
Zhonghua minzu 中华民族
Zhonghua wenhuaquan 中华文化圈
Zhonghua wenming de shenmeihua 中华文明的神魅化
zhongshang 中伤
zhongzu zhuyi 种族主义
Zhou Enlai 周恩来
Zhou Guoping 周国平
Zhou Jianming 周建明
Zhou Xiaozheng 周孝正
zhouyu 咒语
Zhu Xueqin 朱学勤
Zhu Yong 祝勇
Zhuang Zi 庄子
zhuguan danwei 主管单位
zhuyi zhi zheng 主义之争
zisha buyi, huozhe gengnan 自杀不易，活着更难
ziyou zhishifenzi 自由知识分子
ziyou zuopai 自由左派
ziyouzhuyi baiwujiao 自由主义拜物教
ziyouzhuyizhe 自由主义者
zizhu de zhuti 自主的主体
Zouxiang weilai 走向未来
zouxiang zhongjie 走向终结
zu 族
Zun Long 尊龙
zuopai 左派
zuoyou weinan 左右为难

References

Ames, Roger and David Hall
2003. *A Philosophical Translation of Dao De Jing*, New York: Ballantine Books.
Anderson, Benedict
1983. *Imagined Communities: Reflections on the Origin and Spread of Nationalism*, London; New York: Verso.
Arendt, Hannah
1968. "What Is Freedom?" in her *Between Past and Future: Eight Exercises in Political Thought*, New York: Penguin Books.
Barmé, Geremie R.
1996. "To Screw Foreigners Is Patriotic? China's Avant-Garde Nationalists," in Jonathan Unger (ed.), *Chinese Nationalism*, Armonk, N.Y.: M.E. Sharpe.
Barmé, Geremie R. and Gloria Davies
2004. "Have We Been Noticed Yet? Intellectual Contestation and the Chinese Web," in Edward Gu and Merle Goldman (eds.), *Chinese Intellectuals Between State and Market*, London; New York: Routledge Curzon.
Bates, Roy
2002. *Chinese Dragons*, Oxford; New York: Oxford University Press.
Beiser, Frederick C.
1993. "Hegel's Historicism," in Beiser (ed.), *The Cambridge Companion to Hegel*, Cambridge: Cambridge University Press.
Bell, Daniel A.
2008. *China's New Confucianism: Politics and Everyday Life in a Changing Society*, Princeton, New Jersey: Princeton University Press.
Bhabha, Homi (ed.)
1990. *Nation and narration*, London; New York: Routledge.
Butler, Judith, Ernesto Laclau and Slavoj Žižek
2000. *Contingency, Hegemony, Universality: Contemporary Dialogues on the Left*, London; New York: Verso.

Chang Shiyan

2001. *Zhengzhi xiandaixing de jiegou: houxiandai duoyuanzhuyi zhengzhi sixiang fenxi* (The Deconstruction of Political Modernity: An Analysis on The Political Thought of Postmodern Pluralism), Tianjin: Tianjin People's Publishing House.

Chen Fong-ching

2001. "Popular Cultural Movement of the 1980a," in Gloria Davies (ed.), *Voicing Concerns: Contemporary Chinese Critical Inquiry*, Lanham: Rowman & Littlefield.

Chen Huaxing

1997. "Cong Luodi zhexue kan houxiandaizhuyi de jiji yiyi" (On the Positive Significances of Postmodernism through Rorty's Philosophy), in *Fudan xuebao* (*Fudan Academic Journal*), no. 3, 1997.

Chen Shaoming

2000. "Minzuzhuyi: fuxing zhi dao?" ("Nationalism: A Way towards Renaissance?" in Li Shitao (ed.), *Zhishifenzi lichang: Minzuzhuyi yu zhuanxingqi Zhongguo de mingyun* (Intellectual Positions: Nationalism and the Fate of China in a Transitional Era), Changchun: Contemporary Literature and Art Publishing House.

Chen Xiaoming

1996[1994]. "Renwen guanhuai: yizhong zhishi yu xushi" (Humanistic Concern: a Kind of Knowledge and Narative), in Wang Xiaoming (ed.), *Renwen jingshen xunsi lu* (In Search for the Humanistic Spirit), Shanghai: The Book Collection Publishing House.

2000[1994]. "Houxiandai: jingying yu dazhong de hunzhan" (Postmodernism: the War between Elites and the Mass), in Luo Gang and Ni Wenjian (eds.), *Jiushi niandai sixiang wenxuan* (The Intellectual Anthology of the 1990s), vol. 1. Nanning: Guangxi People's Publishing House.

2004. "Xuyan" (Preface), in Chen (ed.), *Houxiandaizhuyi* (Postmodernism), Kaifeng: Henan University Publishing House.

Chen Yinque

2005. "Wang Guantang xiansheng wanci bing xu" (Eulogy for Wang Guowei).

Chong Ming

2012. "Xiandai wenming jiangou zhong de guojia he minzhu" (State and Democracy in the Modern Civilization), in Xu Jilin and Liu Qing (eds.),

Hezhong wenming? Zhongguo jueqi de zaisikao (Which Civilization? Rethinking on the Rise of China), Nanjing: Jiangsu People's Publishing House.

Chun, Allen

1996. "Fuck Chineseness: On the Ambiguities of Ethnicity as Culture as Identity," *Boundary 2*, vol. 23, no. 2.

Cui Zhiyuan

1994. "Zhidu chuangxin yu dierci sixiang jiefang" (Institutional Innovation and the Second Liberation of Thinking), in *Ershiyi shiji* (*Twenty-First Century*), vol. 4.

Davies, Gloria

2001. "Introduction," in Davies (ed.), *Voicing Concerns: Contemporary Chinese Critical Inquiry*, Lanham: Rowman & Littlefield.

2007. *Worrying About China: the Language of Chinese Critical Inquiry*, Cambridge, Mass.: Harvard University Press.

Deng Yong and Wang Fei-Ling (eds.)

1999. *In The Eyes of The Dragon: China Views the World*, Lanham: Rowman & Littlefield Publishers.

Deng Zhenglai (ed.)

2010. *Zhongguo xueshu guifanhua taolun wenxuan* (A Collection of Essays in Debating the Standardization of Academic Researches in China), Beijing: The Press of China University of Political Science and Law.

Deng Zhenglai and Hao Yufan (eds.)

2008. *Zhongguo renwen shehuikexue sanshi nian* (Chinese Humanities and Social Sciences in the Last Three Decades), Shanghai: Fudan University Press.

Duan Baolin

2002. "Long de chuanren zhishuo wuyongzhiyi" (There is no doubt that we are decedents of the Dragon), in *Zhongguo wenhua yanjiu* (Chinese Culture Research), no. 1.

Eagleton, Terry

1991. *Ideology: An Introduction*, London; New York: Verso.

Evans, Dylan

1996. *An Introductory Dictionary of Lacanian Psychoanalysis*, London; New York: Routledge.

Fang Ning, Wang Bingquan and Ma Lijun

2002. *Chengzhang de Zhongguo* (China in Growth), Beijing: People's Publishing House.

Fink, Bruce

1995. *The Lacanian Subject: Between Language and Jouissance*, Princeton, New Jersey: Princeton University Press.

1997. *A Clinical Introduction to Lacanian Psychoanalysis: Theory and Technique*, Cambridge, Mass.: Harvard University Press.

2004. *Lacan to the Letter: Reading Écrits Closely*, Minneapolis: University of Minnesota Press.

2007. *Fundamentals of Psychoanalytic Technique: A Lacanian Approach for Practitioners*, New York; London: W. W. Norton & Company.

French, Howard W.

2005. "In China, Protests Recall a Manipulative Era," in *The New York Times*, 21 April 2005.

Gan Yang

1987a. "Bashi niandai wenhua taolun de jige wenti" (A Few Issues Concerning the 1980s Cultural Discussions), in *Wenhua: Zhongguo yu shijie* (*Culture: China and the World*), no. 1, Beijing: Joint Publishing House.

1987b. "Xuyan" (Preface), in *Wenhua: Zhongguo yu shijie* (*Culture: China and the World*), no. 1, Beijing: Joint Publishing House.

2003a. "Zhongguo ziyou zuopai de youlai" (The Origins of Chinese Liberal Left), in Gong Yang (ed.), *Sichao: Zhongguo "xin zuopai" jiqi yingxiang* (Intellectual Currents: Chinese "New Left" and Its Influences), Beijing: Chinese Social Science Publishing House.

2003b. *Zhengzhi zheren shitelaosi* (Leo Strauss as a Political Philosopher), Hong Kong: Oxford University Press.

2005. "Zhongguo: ruhe bimian 'zigongshi' de diandaihua?" (China: How to Avoid "Self-Castrated" Style Modernization?).

2006a. "Bashiniandai de xiandaixing pipan yu jiushiniandai de zhuanxing" (The Critique of Modernity in the 1980s and the Transformation in the 1990s).

2006b. "Zaiban xuyan" (Preface to the Second Edition), in Gan Yang (ed.), *Bashiniandai wenhuayishi* (The Cultural Consciousness in the 1980s), Shanghai: Shanghai People's Publishing House.

2006c. "Gan Yang," in Zha Jianying (ed.), *Bashiniandai fangtanlu* (*Conversations about the 1980s*), Beijing: Joint Publishing House.

2007. *Tong santong* (The Fusion of the Three Traditions), Beijing: Joint Publishing House.
2012a. *Wenming, guojia, daxue* (Civilization, Nation, University), Beijing: Joint Publishing House.
2012b. *Gujin Zhongxi zhizheng* (The Struggle Between the Ancient and the Modern, and the Struggle Between China and the West), Beijing: Joint Publishing House.
Gao Like
2007. "Ruhe renshi zhuanxing Zhongguo: guanyu ziyouzhuyi yu xinzuopai de lunzheng" (How to Understand Transitional China: A debate on Liberalism and the New Left), in Xu Jilin (ed.), *Qimeng de ziwowajie: 1990 niandai yilai Zhongguo sixiang wenhua jie zhongda lunzheng yanjiu* (The Self-Destruction of Enlightenment: Studies on the Important Debates in the Chinese Intellectual World Since the 1990s), Changchun: Jilin Publishing Company.
Gao, Mobo Changfan
2004. "The Rise of Neo-Nationalism and the New Left: A Postcolonial and Postmodern Perspective," in Leong H. Liew and Shaoguang Wang (eds.), *Nationalism, Democracy and National Integration in China*, New York: Routledge Curzon.
Ge Hongwei
2006. "Shanghai xueren guanyu bashiniandai de wenhuare de taolun" (A discussion on the 1980s Cultural Fever among Shanghai scholars).
Gellner, Ernest
1983. *Nations and Nationalism*, London: Basil Blackwell.
Glynos, Jason and Yannis Stavrakakis
2004. "Encounters of the Real Kind: Sussing Out the Limits of Laclau's Embrace of Lacan," in Simon Critchley and Oliver Marchart (eds.), *Laclau: A Critical Reader*, New York: Routledge.
Goldman, Merle, Perry Link, and Su Wei
1993. "China's Intellectuals in the Deng Era: Loss of Identity with the State," in L. Dittmer and S.S. Kim (eds.), *China's Quest for National Identity*, Ithaca: Cornell University Press.
Gries, Peter Hays
2004. *China's New Nationalism: Pride, Politics, and Diplomacy*, Berkeley: University of California Press.

Guo Guichun
1994. "Niwenxue zhexue de benzhi tezheng: Luodi 'houxiandai' zhexue sixiang fenxi" (The Intrinsic Features of Quasi-Literary Philosophy: An Intellectual Analysis of Rorty's "Postmodern' Philosophy"), in *Zhexue yanjiu* (*Philosophical Inquiry*), no. 7.
1998. *Houxiandai kexue zhexue* (*Postmodern Philosophy of Science*), Changsha: Human Education Publishing House.
Guo Guichun and Li Hong
1997. "Luodi houxiandai zhexue sixiang yanbian de tezheng" (The Features of the Evolvement of Rorty's Postmodern Philosophy), in *Waiguo zhexue* (*Foreign Philosophy*), no. 3.
Guo Yingjie
2004. "Barking Up the Wrong Tree: The Liberal-Nationalist Debate on Democracy and Identity," in Leong H. Liew and Shaoguang Wang (eds.), *Nationalism, Democracy and National Integration in China*, New York: Routledge Curzon.
Hall, David L.
1991. "Modern China and Postmodern West", in Eliot Deutsch (ed.), *Culture and Modernity: East-west Philosophic Perspectives*, Honolulu: University of Hawaii Press.
Hall, Stuart
1988. "The Toad in the Garden: Thatcherism among the Theorists." In G. Nelson and L. Grossberg (eds.), *Marxism and the Interpretation of Culture*, London: Macmillan.
Han Yuhai
2002. *Zhishi de zhanshu yanjiu: dangdai shehui guanjianci* (The Strategic Studies of Knowledge: Contemporary Social Keywords), Beijing: Central Translation Publishing House.
Han Yuhai, Wang Shaoguang, *et al.*
2011. *Renjian zhengdao* (The Correct Way in the Human World), Beijing: Chinese People University Press.
He Baogang and Guo Yingjie
2000. *Nationalism, National Identity and Democratization in China*, Aldershot: Ashgate.
He Huaihong
2012. "Gaige kaifang shi baituo 'Zhongguo moshi' de lishi guocheng" (The Opening and Reform Is the Historical Process of Getting Rid of the "China

Model"), in He Di and Lu Liling (eds.), *Fansi "Zhongguo moshi"* (Reflecting the China model), Beijing: Chinese Social Sciences Publishing House.

He Xin

1989. *Long: Shenhua yu zhenxiang* (Dragon: Myths and Truths), Shanghai: Shanghai People's Publishing House.

He Xinquan

1993. "Wenhua: shijie chongtu de laiyuan yihuo ronghe de qidian?" (Culture: The Origin of World-Clashes, or, the Starting-Point of Fusion?), in *Ershiyi shiji* (*Twenty-First Century*), no. 12.

He Yi

2004[1995]. "Quntixing jingshen taowang: Zhongguo zhishifenzi de shiji bing" (The Collective Spiritual Decampment: the Century Disease of Chinese Intellectuals), in Chen Xiaoming (ed.), *Houxiandaizhuyi* (Postmodernism), Kaifeng: Henan University Publishing House.

Heqc, Dominique

2001. "Foreclosure," in H. Glowinski, Z. Marks and S. Murphy (eds.), *A Compendium of Lacanian Terms*, London; New York: Free Association Books.

Hobsbawm, Eric J.

1992. *Nations and Nationalism since 1780: Programme, Myth, Reality*, Cambridge: Cambridge University Press.

Homer, Sean

2005. *Jacques Lacan*, London; New York: Routledge.

Hong Xiaonan

1999. "Lun Luodi de houxiandai kexue zhexue" (On Rorty's Postmodern Philosophy of Science), in *Luoyang shifan xueyuan xuebao* (*Academic Journal of Luoyang Normal College*), no. 6.

Huang Ping

2012. "*'Beijing gongshi' or 'Zhongguo jingyan'*" ("Beijing Consensus" or "Chinese Experiences"), in Zhao Jianying and Wu Bo (eds.), *Lun Zhongguo moshi* (On the China Model), Beijing: Chinese Social Sciences Publishing House.

Huang, Ray

1981. *1587, a Year of No Significance: the Ming Dynasty in Decline*, New Haven: Yale University Press.

1988. *China, a Macro History*, Armonk, N.Y.: M.E. Sharpe.

Hughes, Christopher
2006. *Chinese Nationalism in the Global Era*, New York: Routledge.
Jiang Jinsong
1998. *Cong ziran zhi jing dao xinnian zhi wang: Rortyzhexue shuping* (*From the Mirror of Nature to the Web of Beliefs: A Commentary on Rorty's Philosophy*), Changsha: Hunan Education Publishing House.
Jiang Qing
2003. *Zhengzhi ruxue: dangdai ruxue de zhuanxiang, tezhi, yu fazhan* (Political Confucianism: the Turn, Characteristics, and Development in Contemporary Confucianism), Beijing: Joint Publishing House.
2005. "*Guanyu chongjian Zhongguo rujiao de gouxiang*" (Thoughts on the Reconstruction of Chinese Confucianism), available at <http://culture.people.com.cn/GB/27296/3969429.html> (accessed on 18 June 2010).
Jin Guantao
1997. "Zhongguo wenhua de changshi heli jingshen" (The spirit of commonsensical rationality in Chinese Culture), in *Zhongguo wenhua yanjiusuo xuebao* (Academic Journal of Chinese Culture Research Institute), no. 6.
Jin Guantao and Liu Qingfeng
1992[1984]. *Xingsheng yu weiji: Lun Zhongguo shehui chaowending jiegou* (The Cycle of Growth and Decline: On the Ultrastable Structure of Chinese Society), Hong Kong: The Chinese University Press.
2000. *Zhongguo xiandai sixiang de qiyuan: chaowending jiegou yu Zhongguo zhengzhi wenhua de yanbian* (The Origins of Modern Chinese Thought: The Ultrastable Structure and the Evolution of Chinese Political Culture), Hong Kong: The Chinese University Press.
2001. "Shilun Zhongguo shi ziyouzhuyi" (On Chinese-Style Liberalism), in *Twenty-First Century*, no. 10.
Johnston, Adrian
2008. *Žižek's Ontology: A Transcendental Materialist Theory of Subjectivity*, Evanston, Illinois: Northwestern University Press.
Jullien, François
1995. *The Propensity of Things: Toward a History of Efficacy in China*, transl. Janet Lloyd, New York: Zone Books; Cambridge, Mass.: Distributed by MIT Press.
Karl, Rebecca E.
2002. *Staging the World: Chinese Nationalism at the Turn of the Twentieth Century*, Durham, N.C.: Duke University Press.

Keith, Ronald C. (ed.)
2005. *China as a Rising World Power and Its Response to "Globalization,"* London: Routledge.
Key, Sarah
2003. *Žižek: A Critical Introduction*, Cambridge: Polity Press.
Lacan, Jacques
1977. *Écrits: A Selection*, trans. Alan Sheridan, London: Tavistock Publications.
1979. *The Four Fundamental Concepts of Psychoanalysis*, transl. Alan Sheridan, London: Hogarth Press and Institute of Psycho-Analysis.
1988. *The Ego in Freud's Theory and in the Technique of Psychoanalysis*, transl. Sylvana Tomaselli, New York: Norton; Cambridge: Cambridge University Press.
1992. *The Ethics of Psychoanalysis*, transl. Dennis Porter, London: Routledge.
1993. *The Psychoses*, transl. Russell Grigg, London: Routledge.
1999. *On Feminine Sexuality: the Limits of Love and Knowledge*, transl. Bruce Fink, New York: Norton.
Laclau, Ernesto
1996. *Emancipation(s)*, London; New York: Verso.
2004. "Glimpsing the Future," in Simon Critchley and Oliver Marchart (eds.), *Laclau: A Critical Reader*, New York: Routledge.
Laclau, Ernesto and Chantal Mouffe
1985. *Hegemony and Socialist Strategy: Towards a Radical Democratic Politics*, London; New York: Verso.
Le Shan (ed.)
2004. *Qianliu: dui xiaai minzuzhuyi de pipan yu fansi* (Undercurrents: Critiques and Reflections on Extreme Nationalism), Shanghai: East China Normal University Publishing House.
Lei Yi
2009. "Wo fandui cong wenben dao wenben jiegou qimeng" (I Disagree Textual Deconstruction of Enlightenment), in Qin Xiao, *Dangdai Zhongguo wenti: xiandaihua haishi xiandaixing* (Contemporary Chinese Problems: Modernization or Modernity), Beijing: Social Science Text Publishing House.
2012. "Jintie dangdai Zhongguo shehui mailuo" (Being Close to Contemporary Chinese Social Context), in Ma Licheng (ed.), *Dangdai Zhongguo bazhong shehui sichao* (Eight Social Discourses in Contemporary China), Beijing: Social Science Text Publishing House.

Levy-Stokes, Carmela

2001. "Jouissance," in H. Glowinski, Z. Marks and S. Murphy (eds.), *A Compendium of Lacanian Terms*, London; New York: Free Association Books.

Li Shenzhi

1998. "Hongyang beida de ziyouzhuyi chuantong" (Carrying Forward the Liberal Tradition of Beijing University), in Liu Junning (ed.), *Beida chuantong yu jindai Zhongguo: ziyouzhuyi de xiansheng* (The Tradition of Beijing University and Modern China: The Pioneering Voice of Liberalism), Beijing: Chinese Human Affairs Publishing House.

1999. "Fengyu canghuang wushi nian" (Fifty years in Wild Wind).

2000a. "Bianyitong, hedongxi" ("The Differentiation of the Likenesses and Differences, the Unity of the East and the West"), in Luo Gang and Ni Wenjian (eds.), *Jiushiniandai sixiang wenxuan* (The Intellectual Anthology of the 1990s), vol. 2, Nanning: Guangxi People's Publishing House.

2000b. "Chongxin dianran qimeng de huoju" (Re-igniting the Torch of Enlightenment), in Li Shenzhi and He Jiadong, *Zhongguo de daolu* (China's Path), Guangzhou: South Daily Publishing House.

Li Shenzhi and He Jiadong

2000. *Zhongguo de daolu* (China's Path), Guangzhou: Southern Daily Publishing House.

Li Shitao (ed.)

2000. *Zhishifenzi lichang: Minzuzhuyi yu zhuanxingqi Zhongguo de mingyun* (Intellectual Positions: Nationalism and the Fate of China in a Transitional Era), Changchun: Contemporary Literature and Art Publishing House.

Li Yonggang

1999. "*Dangdai fazhanzhong guojia de minzuzhuyi*" (Nationalism in Contemporary Developing Countries), *Shehui kexue* (*Social Sciences*), December.

Li Youzheng

2006. "Bashiniandai wo yu Gan Yang tan jieshixue" (Debating with Gan Yang on Hermeneutics in the 1980s).

Lin Yü-sheng

1979. *The Crisis of Chinese Consciousness: Radical Antitraditionalism in the May Fourth Era*, Madison: The University of Wisconsin Press.

1988. *Zhongguo chuantong de chuangzaoxing zhuanhua* (The Creative Transformation of Chinese Tradition), Beijing: Joint Publishing House.

Liu Dachun

1998. "Xuyan" (Preface), in Jiang Jinsong, *Cong ziran zhi jing dao xinnian zhi wang: Rortyzhexue shuping* (From the Mirror of Nature to the Web of Beliefs: A Commentary on Rorty's Philosophy), Changsha: Hunan Education Publishing House.

Liu Dong

2001. "Revisiting the Perils of 'Designer Pidgin Scholarship'," transl. Gloria Davies and Li Kaiyu, in Davies (ed.), *Voicing Concerns: Contemporary Chinese Critical Inquiry*, Lanham: Rowman & Littlefield.

Liu Junning (ed.)

1998. *Beida chuantong yu jindai Zhongguo: ziyouzhuyi de xiansheng* (The Tradition of Beijing University and Modern China: The Pioneering Voice of Liberalism), Beijing: Chinese Human Affairs Publishing House.

Liu Kui

1995. "Dangdai kexue zhexue de kunjing yu Rortyhouxiandai zhexue de qishi" (The Predicaments of Contemporary Philosophy of Science and the Inspirations Brought by Rorty's Postmodern Philosophy), in *Jianghai xuekan* (*Academic Journal of Ocean*), no. 1.

Liu Qing

2012. "*Xiandaihua lunti de chongshen*" (Reclaiming the Modernization thesis), in Xu Jilin and Liu Qing (eds.), *Hezhong wenming? Zhongguo jueqi de zaisikao* (Which Civilization? Rethinking on the Rise of China), Nanjing: Jiangsu People's Publishing House.

Liu Qingfeng

2001. "The Topography of Intellectual Culture in 1990s," transl. Gloria Davies, in Davies (ed.), *Voicing Concerns: Contemporary Chinese Critical Inquiry*, Lanham: Rowman & Littlefield.

Liu Xiaofeng

2002. "Bianzhe qianyan" (Editorial Preface), in Liu (ed.), *Shitelaosi yu gudian zhengzhi zhexue* (Leo Strauss and Classical Political Philosophy), Shanghai: Shanghai Joint Publishing House.

Liu Zaifu

2006. "Liu Zaifu tan 1980 niandai" (Talking about 1980s), in *Shiji Zhongguo* (*Century China*).

Lu Xinghua

2004. *Lu Xinghua wenji* (The Collective Works of Lu Xinghua), available at <http://ishare.iask.sina.com.cn/f/13960570.html> (accessed on 2 February 2013).

Luo Rongqu

2004[1993]. *Xiandaihua xinlun* (A New Discussion on Modernization), Beijing: Beijing University Press.

Ma Lijun and Cao Hongju

1999. "Bianzhe de hua" (Introduction), in Wang Xiaodong, *et al.*, *Quanqiuhua yinying xia de Zhongguo zhi lu* (China's Path in the Shadow of Globalization), Beijing: Chinese Social Sciences Publishing House.

Mao Zedong

1944. "Serve the People," in *Selected Works of Mao Tse-tung*, available at <http://www.marxists.org/reference/archive/mao/selected-works/volume-3/mswv3_19.htm> (accessed on 6 June 2006).

McGregor, James

2006. "No More Chinese Whispers," *Wall Street Journal*, 12 September 2006, page A20.

Mo Luo

2010. *Zhongguo zhanqilai* (China Standing Up), Wuhan: Yangtze Literature and Art Publishing House.

Myers, Tony

2003. *Slavoj Žižek*, London; New York: Routledge.

Nyiri, Pal and Joana Breidenbach (eds.)

2005. *China Inside Out: Contemporary Chinese Nationalism and Transnationalism*, Budapest: Central European University Press.

Ouyang Kang

2004[2002]. "Xiandaihua de weicheng jiqi chaoyue" (The Limits of Modernization and Its Break), in Wang Yuechuan (ed.), *Zhongguo houxiandaizhuyi huayu* (The Postmodernist Discourse in China), Guangzhou: Zhongshan University Press.

Pan, Philip

2005. "Chinese Evade Censors to Discuss Police Assault," *Washington Post*, 17 December 2005.

Pan Wei

2009. "Dangdai Zhonghua tizhi: Zhongguo moshi de jingji, zhengzhi, shehui jiexi" (Contemporary Chinese Institutions: The Economic, Political and Social

Dimensions of the China Model), in Pan (ed.), *Zhongguo moshi: jiedu renmin-gongheguo liushi nian* (The China Model: Reading the Sixty Years of the People's Republic of China), Beijing: Central Translation Publishing House.

Parker, Ian

2004. *Slavoj Žižek: A Critical Introduction*, London: Pluto Press.

Pye, Lucian W.

1993. "How China's Nationalism Was Shanghaied," *The Australian Journal of Chinese Affairs*, no. 29, January.

Qian Chendan

1995. "'Wenming de chongtu?': yu Hentingdon xiansheng duihua" (Clash of Civilizations? In conversation with Huntington), in Wang Jisi (ed.), *Wenming yu guojizhengzhi: Zhongguo xuezhe ping Hengtingdon de wenming chongtu lun* (Civilization and International Politics: Chinese Scholars Remarks on Huntington's Account of "Clash of Civilizations"), Shanghai: Shanghai People's Publishing House.

Qin Hui

1999. *Wenti yu zhuyi: Qin Hui wenxuan* (Problems and Isms: An Anthology of Qin Hui), Changchun: Changchun Publishing House.

2000. "Dangdai sixiangshi shang de 'dushu jiang' shijian" (The Event of the "Cheung Kong-*Reading* Awards" in Contemporary Intellectual History), in *Xueshu quanli yu minzhu: "Changjiang dushu jiang" lunzheng beiwang* (Academic Power and Democracy: the Debate over the "Cheung Kong-*Reading* Awards"), Xiamen: Lujiang Publishing House.

Ren Bingqiang

2004. "Jiushiniandai yilai Zhongguo de minzuzhuyi sichao: jianping Wang Xiaodong de minzuzhuyi guan" (Chinese Nationalist Current Since the 1990s: Critical Comments on Wang Xiaodong's Nationalist View), in Le Shui (ed.), *Qianliu: dui xiaai minzuzhuyi de pipan yu fansi* (Undercurrents: Critiques and Reflections on Extreme Nationalism), Shanghai: East China Normal University Publishing House.

Ren Jiantao

2000. "Jiedu xin zuopai" (Interpreting the New Left), in Li Shitao (ed.), *Zhishifenzi lichang: Ziyouzhuyi zhi zheng yu zhongguo sixiangjie de fenhua* (Intellectual Positions: Debates over Liberalism and the Disconnection of Chinese Intellectual World), Changchun: Contemporary Literature and Art Publishing House.

Richards, Thomas

1993. *The Imperial Archive: Knowledge and the Fantasy of Empire*, London; New York: Verso.

Rodriguez, Leonardo S.

2001. "Desire," in H. Glowinski, Z. Marks and S. Murphy (eds.), *A Compendium of Lacanian Terms*, London; New York: Free Association Books.

Rorty, Richard

1991. "Solidarity or Objectivity?" in his *Objectivity, Relativism, and Truth*, Cambridge: Cambridge University Press.

Shao Jian

1995. "Shijimo de wenhua pianhang: yige guanyu Xiandaixing, Zhonghuaxing de taolun" (Cultural Yawings in the End of Century: A Discussion on Modernity and Chineseness), in *Wenyi zhengming (Debates in Literature and Art)*, no.1.

She Biping

2000. *Xiandaixing de yiyi yu juxian* (The Meanings and Constraints of Modernity), Shanghai: Shanghai Joint Publishing House.

Shen, Simon and Shaun Breslin (eds.)

2010. *Online Chinese Nationalism and China's Bilateral Relations*, Lanham, MD: Lexington Books.

Sheng Ning

1997. *Renwen kunhuo yu fansi: xifang houxiandaizhuyi sichao pipan* (Humanistic Perplexities and Reflections: A Critique to the Western Postmodernist Thought), Beijing: Joint Publishing House.

Song Qiang, Zhang Xiaobo, *et al.*

1996. *Zhongguo keyi shuo bu* (China Can Say No), Beijing: Beijing Chinese Workers and Businessmen's Union Press.

Stavrakakis, Yannis

1999. *Lacan and the Political*, London; New York: Routledge.

Tan Zhongyi

1998. "Lun Luodi houxiandai zhexue de renwen jingshen yiyun" (On the Humanistic Spirit of Rorty's Postmodern Philosophy), in *Huazhong ligong daxue xuebao (Academical Journal of Central China Technology University)*, no. 3.

Tang Hua and Chen Lian

1983. "Yi wei 'long de chuanren' huidao long de guxiang" (A "Descendant of the Dragon" Returns to the Homeland of the Dragon), in *Liaowang* (*Outlook Weekly*), no. 5.

Tang Yijie

2001a. *He er butong* (Harmony with Difference), Shenyang: Liaoning People's Publishing House.

2001b. "New Confucianism in 1990s Mainland Chinese Culture," transl. Gloria Davies, in Davies (ed.), *Voicing Concerns: Contemporary Chinese Critical Inquiry*, Maryland: Rowman & Littlefield.

Tong Shijun

2007. *Pipan yu shijian: lun Habeimasi de pipan lilun* (Critique and Praxis: On Habermas' Critical Theory), Beijing: Joint Publishing House.

Tu Wei-ming

1993. *Way, Learning, and Politics: Essays on the Confucian Intellectuals*, New York: State University of New York Press.

Unger, Jonathan (ed.)

1996. *Chinese Nationalism*, Armonk, N.Y.: M.E. Sharpe.

Waldron, Arthur

1989. "The Great Wall Myth: Its Origins and Role in Modern China," *Yale Journal of Criticism*, vol. 2, no. 1.

Wang Chaohua (ed.)

2003. *One China, Many Paths*, London; New York: Verso.

Wang Hui

1994. *Wu di panghuang*: *'Wusi' jiqi huisheng* (No Place to Hesitate: "May Fourth" and Its Echo), Zhejiang: Zhejiang Literature and Art Publishing House.

1997. *Wang Hui zixuan ji* (The Collected Works of Wang Hui), Guilin: Guangxi Normal University Publishing House.

1998. "Contemporary Chinese Thought and the Question of Modernity," translated by Rebecca Karl, in Xudong Zhang (ed.), *Intellectual Politics in Post-Tiananmen China*, Durham, N.C.: Duke University Press.

1999. "Gongli shijiguan jiqi ziwo wajie" (The World View of the Universal Principle and Its Self-Destruction), in *Strategy and Management*, no. 3.

2000a. "Wenhua pipan lilun yu dangdai Zhongguo minzuzhuyi wenti" (Cultural Critical Theories and the Question of Contemporary Chinese Nationalism), in Li Shitao (ed.), *Zhishifenzi lichang: Minzuzhuyi yu zhuanxingqi Zhongguo de mingyun* (Intellectual Positions: Nationalism and the Fate of China in a Transitional Era), Changchun: Contemporary Literature and Art Publishing House.

2000b. *Sihuo chongwen* (Reviewing the Quenched Fire), Beijing: People Literature Publishing House.

2000c. "Wo dui muqian zhengyi de liangdian shuoming" (Two Points of Clarification in relation to the Current Controversy), in *Xueshu quanli yu minzhu: "Changjiang dushu jiang" lunzheng beiwang* (Academic Power and Democracy: the Debate over the "Cheung Kong-*Reading* Awards"), Xiamen: Lu River Publishing House.

2004. *Xiandai Zhongguo sixiang de xingqi* (The Rise of Modern Chinese Thought), four volumes, Beijing: Joint Publishing House.

2005. "Xianshi de huanxiang he huangxiang de xianshi" (The Fantasy of Reality and the Reality of Fantasy), available at <http://talk.163.com/05/1118/08/22R03M6P00301IJQ.html> (accessed on 6 June 2009).

2006. *China's New Order: Society, Politics, and Economy in Transition*, transl. Theodore Huters, Cambridge, Mass.: Harvard University Press.

2007. "Pinglun" (A Commentary), in Gan Yang, *Tong santong* (The Fusion of the Three Traditions), Beijing: Joint Publishing House.

2008. *Qu zhengzhihua de zhengzhi: duan ershi shiji de zhongjie yu jiushi niandai* (The Depoliticalization of the Political: the End of the Short Twentieth Century and the 1990s), Beijing: Joint Publishing House.

2010. *The End of the Revolution: China and the Limits of Modernity*, London; New York: Verso.

2011. *The Politics of Imagining Asia*, Theodore Huters (ed.), Cambridge, Mass.: Harvard University Press.

Wang Jing

1996. *High Culture Fever: Politics, Aesthetics, and Ideology in Deng's China*, Berkeley: University of California Press.

Wang Jisi (ed.)

1995. *Wenming yu guojizhengzhi: Zhongguo xuezhe ping Hengtingdon de wenming chongtu lun* (Civilization and International Politics: Chinese Scholars Remarks on Huntington's Account of "Clash of Civilizations"), Shanghai: Shanghai People's Publishing House.

Wang Jun

2012. *Lengzhan jieshu yilai Zhongguo de minzuzhuyi* (Chinese Nationalism Since the End of the Cold War), Beijing: Social Science Documents Publishing House.

Wang Ke-wen (ed.)
1998. *Modern China: An Encyclopedia of History, Culture, and Nationalism*, New York: Garland Pub.
Wang Xiaodong
2003. "An Interview by Frederic Bobin."
2005. "Lun shangwu jingshen" (On the Spirit of Upholding Militancy), available at <http://www.aisixiang.com/data/6431.html> (accessed on 6 June 2012).
Wang Xiaodong, Fang Ning, Song Qiang, *et al.*
1999. *Quanqiuhua yinying xia de Zhongguo zhi lu* (China's Path in the Shadow of Globalization), Beijing: Chinese Social Science Publishing House.
Wang Xiaodong, Song Xiaojun, Song Qiang, *et al.*
2009. *Zhongguo bugaoxing* (China Is Unhappy), Nanjing: Jiangsu Renmin's Publishing House.
Wang Xiaoyu
2005. "'Pipan zhishifenzi' de chaoji huangxiang" (The Super Fantasy of "Critical Intellectuals").
Wang Yuechuan
1992. *Houxiandaizhuyi wenhua yanjiu* (A Study on Postmodernist Culture), Beijing: Beijing University Press.
Wang Zhihe
1993. *Pushumili de youxi: houxiandai zhexue sichao yanjiu* (Complicated and Confusing Games: A Study on Postmodern Philosophical Thought), Beijing: Social Science Documents Publishing House.
2004[1998]. "Bie yizhong houxiandai zhuyi" (Another Kind of Postmodernism), in Chen Xiaoming (ed.), *Houxiandaizhuyi* (Postmodernism), Kaifeng: Henan University Publishing House.
Wasserstrom, Jeffrey N.
2003. "The Year of Living Anxiously: China's 1999," in Wasserstrom (ed.), *Twentieth-Century China: New Approaches*, London: Routledge.
Wu Guanjun
2006. *Richang xianshi de biantai hexin* (The Perverse Core of Reality), Beijing: New Star Press.
2008. *Ai yu si de youlingxue* (The Hauntology of Love and Death), Changchun: Jilin Publishing Company.

Wu Jiaxiang

2000. "Xin Zuopai: Jiangshi huanhun" (The New Left: A Reanimation of the Corpse"), available at <http://www.aisixiang.com/data/detail.php?id=10471> (accessed on 1 June 2012).

Xiao Feng

2000. "Luodi de houxiandai kexueguan shuping" (A Commentary on Rorty's View of Postmodern Science), in *Waiguo zhexue* (*Foreign Philosophy*), no. 12.

Xiao Gongqin

1999. "Jingti jiduan minzuzhuyi" (Be Cautious about Extreme Nationalism), in Zhu Xueqin, *Shuzhaili de geming: Zhu Xueqin wenxuan* (Revolutions inside Liberty: An Anthology of Zhu Xueqin), Changchun: Changchun Publishing House.

2000. "Minzuzhuyi yu Zhongguo zhuanxing shiqi de yishixingtai" (Nationalism and Ideology in Transitional Era of China), in Li Shitao (ed.), *Zhishifenzi lichang: Minzuzhuyi yu zhuanxingqi Zhongguo de mingyun* (Intellectual Positions: Nationalism and the Fate of China in a Transitional Era), Changchun: Contemporary Literature and Art Publishing House.

Xiao Wu

2006. "Gan Yang de bashiniandai" (Gan Yang's 1980s), available at <http://xian-ren9000.bokee.com/5290549.html> (accessed on 20 September 2006).

Xu Jilin

1991. *Zhizhe de zunyan: zhishifenzi yu jindai wenhua* (The Dignity of Thought: Intellectuals and Modern Culture), Shanghai: Scholarly Collection Publishing House.

1996. *Disanzhong zunyan* (The Third Kind of Dignity), Beijing: The People's Literature Publishing House.

1999. *Lingyizhong qimeng* (Another Kind of Enlightenment), Guangzhou: Flower-City Publishing House.

2000. "The Fate of an Enlightenment: Twenty Years in the Chinese Intellectual Sphere (1978–98)," transl. Geremie R. Barme and Gloria Davies, in *East Asian History*, no. 20.

2007. "Qimeng de ziwowajie" (The Self-Destruction of Enlightenment), in Xu Jilin, Wu Guanjun, *et al.*, *Qimeng de ziwowajie: 1990 niandai yilai Zhongguo sixiang wenhua jie zhongda lunzheng yanjiu* (The Self-Destruction of Enlightenment: Studies on the Important Debates in the Chinese Intellectual World Since the 1990s), Changchun: Jilin Publishing Company.

2011. *Dangdai Zhongguo de qimeng yu fanqimeng* (Enlightenment and Counter-Enlightenment in Contemporary China), Beijing: Social Science Text Publishing House.

Xu Jilin and Chen Dakai (eds.)

1995. *Zhongguo xiandaihua shi* (The History of China's Modernization), Shanghai: Shanghai Joint Publishing House.

Xu Jilin, Wu Guanjun, *et al.*

2007. *Qimeng de ziwowajie: 1990 niandai yilai Zhongguo sixiang wenhua jie zhongda lunzheng yanjiu* (The Self-Destruction of Enlightenment: Studies on the Important Debates in the Chinese Intellectual World since the 1990s), Changchun: Jilin Publishing Company.

Xu Wu

2007. *Chinese Cyber Nationalism: Evolution, Characteristics, and Implications*, Lanham, MD: Lexington Books.

Xu Xun

2005. *Minxuzhuyi* (Nationalism), Beijing: Chinese Social Science Publishing House.

Xu Youyu

1997. *Jingshen shengcheng yuyan* (The Production of Language by Spirit), Chengdu: Sichuan People's Publishing House.

1999. *Ziyou de yanshuo* (Speech of Freedom), Changchun: Changchun Publishing House.

2000. "Ziyou zhuyi yu dangdai Zhongguo" (Liberalism and Contemporary China), in Li Shitao (ed.), *Zhishifenzi lichang: Ziyouzhuyi zhi zheng yu zhongguo sixiangjie de fenhua* (Intellectual Positions: Debates over Liberalism and the Disconnection of Chinese Intellectual World), Changchun: Contemporary Literature and Art Publishing House.

2003. "Ping 90 niandai xinzuopai" (Comments on the "New Left" of the 1990s), in Gong Yang (ed.), *Sichao: Zhongguo "xin zuopai" jiqi yingxiang* (Intellectual Currents: Chinese "New Left" and Its Influences), Beijing: Chinese Social Science Publishing House.

2004. "Houxiandaizhuyi jiqi dui dangdai Zhongguo wenhua de tiaozhan" (Postmodernism and Its Challenges to Contemporary Chinese Culture), in Chen Xiaoming (ed.), *Houxiandaizhuyi* (Postmodernism), Kaifeng: Henan University Publishing House.

2006. "Xu Youyu, Li Gongming tan 1980 niandai" (Talking about the 1980s: In Conversation with Li Gongming), in *Century China* (*Shiji Zhongguo*).

Yao Dazhi

2000. *Xiandai zhihou: 20 shiji wanqi xifang zhexue* (After Modernity: Western Philosophy in the Late Twentieth Century), Beijing: Oriental Publishing House.

Yu Hong

2006. "Wo yu Zhongguo" (China and Me), available at <http://blog.voc.com.cn/blog_showone_type_blog_id_375903_p_1.html> (accessed on 12 September 2011).

2007. "Yigeren de bainian" (A Century for a Person), available at <http://blog.voc.com.cn/blog_showone_type_blog_id_375907_p_1.html> (accessed on 12 September 2011).

Yu Ying-shih

1987. "Zhongguo jinshi zongjiao lunli yu shangren jingshen" (China's Modern Religious Ethics and the Spirit of Merchants), in his *Shi yu Zhongguo wenhua* (*Intellectuals and Chinese Culture*), Shanghai: Shanghai People's Publishing House.

Zeng Yi and Guo Xiaodong (eds.)

2013. *Hewei pushi? Shui zhi jiazhi? Dangdai rujia lun pushijiazhi* (What is Universalism? Whose Values? Contemporary Confucians on Universal Values), Shanghai: East China Normal University Publishing House.

Zha Jianying

2006. "Xie zai qianmian" (Editorial Preface), in Zha (ed.), *Bashiniandai fangtanlu* (Conversations about the 1980s), Beijing: Joint Publishing House.

Zhang Dexiang

2004[1994]. "'Houxiandai' lun: shijimo de lilun moshu yu wenhua yiyu" (Postmodernism: Theoretical Magic Show and Cultural Crazy-Talk in the End of Twentieth Century), in Chen Xiaoming (ed.), *Houxiandaizhuyi* (Postmodernism), Kaifeng: Henan University Publishing House.

Zhang Fa, Zhang Yiwu and Wang Yichuan

2000[1994]. "Cong 'xiandaxing' dao 'zhonghuaxing'" ("From 'modernity' to 'Chineseness'"), in Luo Gang and Ni Wenjian (eds.), *Jiushi niandai sixiang wenxuan* (The Intellectual Anthology of the 1990s), vol.1, Nanning: Guangxi

People's Publishing House (originally published in *Wenyi zhengming* (*Debates in Literature and Art*), no. 2, 1994).

Zhang Guoqing

1998. *Zhongxin yu bianyuan: houxiandai zhuyi sichao gailun* (Centres and Margins: the Introduction of Postmodernist Trend), Beijing: Chinese Social Science Publishing House.

1999. *Wugenji shidai de jingshen zhuangkuang: Rortyzhexue sixiang yanjiu* (The Spiritual Condition in the Non-Foundational Era: An Intellectual Study of Rorty's Philosophy), Shanghai: Shanghai Joint Publishing House.

Zhang Rulun, *et al.*

1996[1994]. "Wenhua shijie: jiegou haishi jiangou" (The World of the Cultural: Deconstruction or Construction), in Wang Xiaoming (ed.), *Renwen jingshen xunsi lu* (In Search for Humanistic Spirit), Shanghai: The Book Collection Publishing House.

Zhang Weiwei

2011. *Zhongguo zhenhan: yige "wenmingxing guojia" de jueqi* (The China Impact: the Rise of a Civilization-State), Shanghai: Shanghai People's Publishing House.

Zhang Xudong

1997. *Chinese Modernism in the Era of Reforms*, Durham, N.C.: Duke University Press.

2003. *Piping de zongji* (The Traces of Criticism), Beijing: Joint Publishing House.

2005. *Quanqiuhua shidai de wenhua rentong: xifang pubianzhuyi huayu de lishi pipan* (The Cultural Identity in the Age of Globalization: the Historical Critique of Western Universalism), Beijing: The Press of Peking University.

2008. *Postsocialism and Cultural Politics: China in the Last Decade of the Twentieth Century*, Durham, N.C.: Duke University Press.

Zhang Xudong (ed.)

2001. *Whither China: Intellectual Politics in Contemporary China*, Durham, N.C.: Duke University Press.

Zhang Yiwu

1996[1995]. "Renwen jingshen: zuihou de shenhua" (Humanism: the Last Myth), in Wang Xiaoming (ed.), *Renwen jingshen xunsi lu* (In Search for Humanistic Spirit), Shanghai: The Book Collection Publishing House.

2000[1994]. "'Xiandaixing' de zhongjie: yige wufa huibi de keti" (The End of "Modernity": An Unavoidable Topic), in Luo Gang and Ni Wenjian (eds.), *Jiushi niandai sixiang wenxuan* (The Intellectual Anthology of the 1990s), vol. 1, Nanning: Guangxi People's Publishing House.

Zhang Yongle

2010. "The Future of the Past: On Wang Hui's Rise of Modern Chinese Thought," *New Left Review* 62, 2010 (March–April).

Zhang Zhizhong

1996. "Renwen jingshen er bian" (Two Defences of Humanistic Spirit), in Wang Xiaoming (ed.), *Renwen jingshen xunsi lu* (In Search for Humanistic Spirit), Shanghai: The Book Collection Publishing House.

Zheng Wang

2012. *Never Forget National Humiliation: Historical Memory in Chinese Politics and Foreign Relations*, New York: Columbia University Press.

Zheng Yongnian

1999. *Discovering Chinese Nationalism in China: Modernization, Identity, and International Relations*, Cambridge: Cambridge University Press.

Zhou Guoping

1986. *Ni Cai, zai shiji de zhuanzhe dian shang* (Nietzsche, in the Intersection of the Centuries), Shanghai: Shanghai People's Publishing House.

2004. "Qimeng huo caodong" (Enlightenment or Rashness), available at <http://www.51ks.com/htm/book/454/96.html> (accessed on 12 September 2006).

Zhou Tiejun and Wang Chuanxi

1995. "Cong Luodi de 'houzhexuewenhua' kan dangdai xiwang zhexue de zhuti zhuanghuan" (An Examination on the Theme Shift of Contemporary Western Philosophy through Rorty's "Postphilosophical Culture"), in *Hebei xuekan* (*Hebei Academic Journal*), no. 2.

Zhu Xueqin

1997. *Bei yiwang yu bei piping de* (The Forgotten and the Criticized), Hangzhou: Zhejiang People's Publishing House.

1999. *Shuzhaili de geming: Zhu Xueqin wenxuan* (Revolutions inside Liberty: An Anthology of Zhu Xueqin), Changchun: Changchun Publishing House.

Zhu Yong

2009. *Diguo chuangshang* (The Trauma of the Empire), Beijing: Chinese Literary Publishing House.

Zi Zhongyun

2012. "Yetan 'Zhongguo moshi'" (On the China Model"), in He Di and Lu Liling (eds.), *Fansi "Zhongguo moshi"* (Reflecting the "China Model"), Beijing: Chinese Social Sciences Publishing House.

Žižek, Slavoj

1989. *The Sublime Object of Ideology*, London; New York: Verso.

1990. "Beyond Discourse-Analysis," in Ernesto Laclau, *New Reflections on the Revolution of Our Time*, London; New York: Verso.

1991a. *For They Know Not What They Do: Enjoyment as a Political Factor*, London; New York: Verso.

1991b. *Looking Awry: An Introduction to Jacques Lacan through Popular Culture*, Cambridge, Mass.; London: MIT Press.

1992. "In His Bold Gaze My Ruin Is Writ Large," in Žižek (ed.), *Everything You Always Wanted to Know About Lacan (But Were Afraid to Ask Hitchcock)*, London; New York: Verso.

1993. *Tarrying with the Negative: Kant, Hegel, and the Critique of Ideology*, Durham, N.C.: Duke University Press.

1994a. *The Metastases of Enjoyment: On Women and Causality*. London; New York: Verso.

1994b. "The Spectre of Ideology," in Žižek (ed.), *Mapping Ideology*, London; New York: Verso.

1996. *The Indivisible Remainder: An Essay on Schelling and related Matters*, London; New York: Verso.

1998. "The Seven Veils of Fantasy," in Dany Nobus (ed.), *Key Concepts of Lacanian Psychoanalysis*, London: Rebus Press.

1999a. *The Ticklish Subject: The Absent Centre of Political Ontology*, London; New York: Verso.

1999b. *The Žižek Reader*, eds. Elizabeth Wright and Edmond Wright, Oxford, Mass.: Blackwell Publishers.

2000. *The Fragile Absolute, or, Why Is the Christian Legacy Worth Fighting For?* London; New York: Verso.

2001. *On Belief*, London; New York: Routledge.

2002a. *Welcome to the Desert of the Real!: Five Essays on 11 September and Related Dates*, London; New York: Verso.

2002b. *Revolution at the Gates*, London; New York: Verso.

2003. "The Violence of the Fantasy," *The Communication Review*, vol. 6.

2004a. *Organs Without Bodies: On Deleuze and Consequences*, London; New York: Routledge.

2004b. *Iraq: The Borrowed Kettle*, London; New York: Verso.

2005a. *Interrogating the Real*, Rex Butler and Scott Stephens (eds.), London; New York: Continuum.

2005b. "The Obscenity of Human Rights: Violence as Symptom," available at <http://www.lacan.com/zizviol.htm> (accessed on 1 October 2006).

2006a. *The Universal Exception*, eds. Rex Butler and Scott Stephens, London; New York: Continuum.

2006b. *How to Read Lacan*, London: Granta.

2006c. *The Parallax View*, Cambridge, Mass.: MIT Press.

2008a[1997]. *The Plague of Fantasies*, London; New York: Verso.

2008b. *Violence: Six Sideways Reflections*, New York: Picador.

2009. "Who Are You Calling Anti-Semitic?" *The New Republic*, 7 January 2009.

2012. *Less Than Nothing: Hegel and the Shadow of Dialectical Materialism*, London; New York: Verso.

Acknowledgments

Part of this research, on the Lacanian theoretical framework introduced and developed by the works of Slavoj Žižek and its relevance to contemporary Chinese thought, was funded by the following three grants: the National Social Science Foundation of China (13CZX059), Shanghai Pujiang Program (12PJC036) and ECNU Elite Scholar Program. Preliminary versions of some of the material have appeared in "Contemporary Chinese Social and Political Thought," *Routledge International Handbook of Contemporary Social and Political Theory* (2011); "China's New Nationalism and Its Obscene Core," *History Research*, vol. 2, no. 8 (August 2012); "What Makes Contemporary Chinese Thought Unique," *Fudan Journal of the Humanities and Social Sciences*, vol. 5, no. 2 (September 2012); "Hegel's Two Faces: Chinese Thought Since the 'New Era'," *ECNU Review*, vol. 1 (December 2012); A Lacanian Analysis of the Post-Maoist Structuration of Chineseness," *Theoretical Studies in Literature and Art*, vol. 34, no. 1 (Januray 2014).

I owe an immerse debt to Ingrid Wang, my partner and soulmate, whose intelligence and passion has in a unique way shaped significantly my understanding of Lacanian psychoanalysis. At the final stage of revising this book (five months before the submission), she gave me the most wonderful gift of my life — our son, Sean, and thus is responsible for my ensuing more intimate ("extimate") understanding of the Lacanian interpretations of the drive, *jouissance*, the (M)Other, alienation, the paternal function, etc. I am also grateful to my family for their loving encouragement, moral support, and technical assistance, most especially my dear mother, Xu Lihua.

I have discussed the ideas in this book with many friends and colleagues. Some of them have also read earlier versions of some of the chapters. In this respect, I would like to thank Michael Janover, Timothy

Cheek, Natalie J. Doyle, Josef G. Mahoney, Johann P. Arnason, Richard Rorty, Tong Shijun, Geremie Barmé, Warren Sun, Leigh Janco, Xu Jilin, Liu Qing, Jin Guantao, Liu Qingfeng, Hong Lijian, Huang Hui, Chen Yan, Alexander Lugg, Damien Kinney, Robert Irving, Yuan Zaijun, Chen Zhiqun, Bi Lijun, Mark Harrison, Luo Gang, Zhu Guohua, Liu Qingping, Yan Bofei, Qin Hui, Lan Jiang, Lilac Liao, Sun Guodong, Steven J. Myers, Jordan Kane, Richard Wolin, and Slavoj Žižek.

In a good Žižekian fashion, since it is needless to add that Gloria Davies was present from the very conception of this study, that her work served as a crucial point of reference, or that she spent considerable time improving the manuscript, I will not do so! I now dedicate this book to her.

Index

www.ingramcontent.com/pod-product-compliance
Ingram Content Group UK Ltd.
Pitfield, Milton Keynes, MK11 3LW, UK
UKHW020645281026
9566IPUK00018B/3

9 789814 417914